AF560366

RIGHT TO HEALTH UNDER INDIAN LAW

RIGHT TO HEALTH UNDER INDIAN LAW

DR. SUNITA KASHYAP
Assistant Professor
Indian Institute of Legal Studies,
Hari Devi, Ganahatti , Shimla

REGAL PUBLICATIONS
New Delhi - 110 027

RIGHT TO HEALTH UNDER INDIAN LAW

ISBN 978-81-8484-527-3

Typeset by
THE LASER PRINTERS
8/15, 3rd Floor, Subhash Nagar, New Delhi-110027

Printed in India at
NEW ELEGANT PRINTERS
A-49/1, Mayapuri Phase-I, New Delhi-110064

Published by
REGAL PUBLICATIONS
F-159, Rajouri Garden, New Delhi-110027
Phones : 45546396, 25435369
E-mail : regalbookspub@yahoo.com, regaldeepbooks@yahoo.com

Contents

Acknowledgements

To write a book numerous activities and association of many people and the amount of contribution made by each cannot be measured, however, the absence of which the project would not have been possible. I take this opportunity to thank all those who have helped me in completion of this manuscript.

At the very outset I express my deep gratitude and thankfulness to my guide and teacher Dr. Sunil Deshta, Professor, Department of Laws, Himachal Pradesh University, Shimla, under whose scholarly guidance, unflinching commitment to academic values, his precious time, ideas and constructive criticism despite his busy schedule and other onerous responsibilities has helped me to take up this task.

I owe my thanks to Professor O.P. Chauhan, Professor Kailash Thakur, Professor H.R. Jhingta and Professor S.N. Sharma (all faculty members) for their co-operation and valuable guidelines. I am also thankful to Dr. Kiran Deshta and Dr. S.S. Jaswal for their valuable help and guidelines.

I also feel obliged and thankful to the Law Faculty, Himachal Pradesh University for making available to me sufficient study materials for writing this book. Thanks are also due to Shri Parmod Singh (Chief Librarian, Retd.), Indian Law Institute, New Delhi, Librarian of University of Delhi (Law Faculty), Librarians of Indian Institute of Advanced Studies, Librarians of State Library and Librarians of Secretariat, Health Department and Planning Department, Government of Himachal Pradesh, Shimla who have been generous enough in extending all possible material pertaining to the preparation of the manuscript.

I also express my immense gratitude to learned authors whose work I have consulted and who have also been listed in Bibliography. I am also thankful to world wide web, for providing access to rich material on health.

Over and above all, I owe, more than I could express my immense debt of gratitude to my parents for giving their love and understanding.

I express my profound thanks to my husband Mr. Dinesh Kashyap who was with me always on each step in completing this book. I have no words to express my love and deep sense of gratitude to him. During this period I kept busy in writing, I missed the sweet company of my sweet little daughters Shatakshi Kashyap and Samiksha Kashyap.

I must acknowledge my heart felt thanks to Regal Publications, New Delhi for publishing this book, I am sure this book will be extremely useful to law students, research scholars and those who are associated with health departments.

Shimla DR. SUNITA KASHYAP

List of Abbreviations

ACHR	:	American Convention on Human Rights
AERB	:	Atomic Energy Regulation Board
AHCs	:	Ayurvedic Health Centres
AID	:	Artificial Insemination by a Donar Sperm
AIDS	:	Acquired Immuno Deficiency Syndrome
AIIMS	:	All India Institute of Medical Sciences
AIMS	:	All India Medical Sciences
AIR	:	All India Reporter
ARI	:	Acute Respiratory Infection
ART	:	Anti Retroviral Therapy
ASEAN	:	Association of South-East Asian Nations
BMI	:	Body Mass Index
BMS	:	Basic Minimum Services
BMSs	:	Block Medical Officers
CDL	:	Construction of Dry Latrines
CDR	:	Crude Death Rate
CDs	:	Civil Dispensaries
CE	:	Council of Europe
CERC	:	Consumer Education and Research Centre
CHCs	:	Community Health Centres
CMOs	:	Chief Medical Officers
COTPA	:	Cigarettes and Other Tobacco Products Act
CSSMP	:	Child Survival and Safe Motherhood Programme
DLR	:	Delhi Law Reporter
DNA	:	Deoxyribo Nucleic Acid
DOT	:	Directly Observed Treatment
DPCO	:	Drug Price Control Order
ECHR	:	European Conviction for the Protection of Human
ECHS	:	Education Commission for Health Sciences

EMS	:	Employment of Manual Scavengers
EPI	:	Expanded Programme on Immunization
FAO	:	Food and Agricultural Organization
FDI	:	Foreign Direct Investment
FICCI	:	Federation of Indian Chambers of Commerce and Industry
GH	:	Government Hospital
GOHP	:	Government of Himachal Pradesh
GOM	:	Group of Ministers
GOs	:	Government Organization
HR	:	Human Rights
HFA	:	Health For All
HIV	:	Human Immuno Deficiency Virus
HMIS	:	Health Management Information System
ICCPR	:	International Covenant on Civil and Political Rights
ICESCR	:	International Covenant on Economic, Social and Cultural Rights
ICMR	:	Indian Council for Medical Research
ICSSR	:	Indian Council of Social Sciences Research
IDP	:	Iudine Deficiency Disorders
IEC	:	Information, Education and Communication
ILC	:	International Labour Conference
ILO	:	International Labour Organization
IMR	:	Infant Mortality Rate
IPC	:	Indian Penal Code
ISM&H	:	Indian System of Medicines and Homeopathy
IVF	:	In Vitro Fertilization
JE	:	Japanese Encephalitis
JAMA	:	Journal of American Medical Association
JETCO	:	Joint Economic Trade Committee
MCW	:	Maternal and Child Welfare
MDGs	:	Millennium Development Goals
MNP	:	Minimum Need Programme
MP	:	Madhya Pradesh
MT	:	Meteric Tonnes
MTPA	:	Medical Termination of Pregnancy Act
NACO	:	National Aids Control Organization
NFCP	:	National Filaria Control Programme
NFHs	:	National Family Health Survey
NGO	:	Non Government Organization

NHP	:	National Health Policy
NHRC	:	National Human Rights Commission
NHRM	:	National Health Rural Mission
NLCP	:	National Leprosy Control Programme
NMCP	:	National Malaria Control Programme
NMEP	:	National Malaria Eradication Programme
NREGA	:	National Rural Development Guarantee Act
NRHM	:	National Rural Health Mission
NURM	:	National Urban Renewal Mission
NVBDCD	:	National Vector Borne Disease Control Programme
PARIKAS	:	Parivar Kalyan Salahakar Samiti
PG	:	Post Graduation
PGIMER	:	Post-graduate Institute of Medical Education and Research
PHC	:	Primary Health Centre
PIL	:	Public Interest Litigation
PMGY	:	Pradhan Mantri Gramodya Yojana
PPP	:	Public Private Partnership
PRIs	:	Panchayati Raj Institutions
RCH	:	Reproductive and Child Health
RKS	:	Rogi Kalyan Samiti
RNTCP	:	Revised National Tuberculosis Control Programme
RTI	:	Right to Information
RWS	:	Rural Water Supply
SAARC	:	South Asia Association for Regional Cooperation
SC	:	Sub Centres
SCC	:	Supreme Court Cases
SGSY	:	Swaran Jayanti Gram Swarozgar Yojana
SHCs	:	Sub-Health Centres
SITA	:	Suppression of Immoral Traffic in Women and Girls
SSA	:	Sarva Shiksha Abhiyaan
STDs	:	Sexually Transmitted Diseases
TB	:	Tuberculosis
TCDC	:	Technical Cooperation in Developing Countries
TFR	:	Total Fertility Rate
U.K.	:	United Kingdom
UDHR	:	Universal Declaration of Human Rights
UGC	:	University Grants Commission

UNESCO	:	United Nations Educational Scientific and Cultural Organisation
UNICEF	:	United Nations International Children Emergency Fund
UPSC	:	Union Public Service Commission
USA	:	United States of America
VCTC	:	Voluntary Counseling and Testing Centres
WHO	:	World Health Organization

CHAPTER 1

Introduction

I. PRELUDE

Health is a precondition for life while life is the precondition for the existence of the society. Society cannot be conceived of without life. Therefore, life acquires the first and the foremost place among the social values. The acquisition of this place has, however, been a slow realization. Life must have always been an important value. But its first legal asset, appears in *Magna Carta* in the year 1215.[1] Though, the discourse on legal heights in terms of social values has been a long and continuous process, it slowly acquired the status of an inalienable right of the individual and has been incorporated in various legal documents including State Constitutions[2] and international instruments.[3]

Health is a common theme in most cultures. In fact, all communities have their concepts of health, as part of their culture.[4] Truly admitting, health is not perceived in the same way by bio-medical scientists, social science specialists, health administrators and ecologists and this gives rise to confusion about the concept of health. In the world

1. M.P. Singh, *Introduction to Souvenir of International Conference on Global Health Law*, December 1997.
2. *Ibid.*
3. Universal Declaration of Human Rights, 1948; International Covenant on Civil and Political Rights, 1966; UN Declaration on Elimination of Discrimination of Women, 1967; Convention on the Elimination of All Forms of Discrimination Against Women, 1979; Convention Against Torture and Other Cruel, Inhuman and Degrading Treatment or Punishment, 1984; Convention on the Rights of the Children, 1989; Convention for the Protection of Human Rights and Dignity of Human Being with regard to the Application of Biology and Medicine; Convention on Human Rights and Bio-Medicine, 1997, etc.
4. Avanish Kumar, *Human Right to Health*, 15 (2007).

of continuous change, new concepts based on new patterns of thoughts are bound to emerge. However, health has evolved over the centuries as a concept from an individual concern to a worldwide social goal and encompasses the whole quality of life.[5] Different perceptions about health need serious consideration. The concept of biomedical health based on "germ theory of disease" which dominated medical thought at the turn of the 20th century.[6] The concept of cause, embodied in the germ theory of disease, is generally referred to as one to one relationship between casual agent and disease. It is true that health care has benefited a great deal through research and development. The scientific and technological achievements of the twentieth century have helped in unfolding the hitherto unknown aspects of human life and provided a deeper insight into the human physiology, diseases and death. Researchers burned their midnight oil in producing new drugs, successful against oil in producing new drugs, successful against diseases hitherto incurable. The fatal consequences of diseases like cancer have been mitigated and epidemics tamed. Public health has received great attention at global level, impelling State governments to evolve effective strategies for prevention and control of epidemics.

Health, in this narrow view became the ultimate goal of medicine and it has minimized the role of the environmental, social, psychological and cultural determinants of health. So the deficiencies in the biomedical concept gave rise to other concepts. The ecological concept viewed health as a dynamic equilibrium between man and his environment, and disease a maladjustment of the human organism to environment. Dubos defined health as "the relative absence of pain and discomfort and continuous adaptation and adjustment to the environment to ensure optimal function". The ecological concept raises two issues, viz. imperfect man and imperfect environment. History argues strongly that improvement in human adaptation to natural environments can lead to longer life expectancies and a better quality of life even in the absence of modern health delivery services.[7] Contemporary developments in social sciences revealed that health is not only a biomedical phenomenon but one which is influenced by social, psychological, cultural, economic and political factors of the

---

5. *Id.*, at 15-16.
6. *Id.*, at 16. Also see, D.D. Kulpati, "The Basic Concepts of Health", C-9, C-13 at C-9 in P.C. Bhatla (ed.), International Conference on Health Policy, Ethics as Human Values (New Delhi: ICMR Secretariat, 1986).
7. R. Dubos, *Man Adopting, New Heaven* (1965) quoted in K. Park, Park's Textbook of Preventive and Social Medicine, 11 (2002). Also see World Health Organization (1986), Concept of Health Behaviour Research, Reg. Health Paper No. 13, (SEARO), New Delhi.

people concerned. Above all the holistic approach implies that all sectors of society have an effect on health, in particular agriculture, animal husbandry, food, industry, education, housing, public works, communications and other sectors. The main emphasis of all concepts are the promotion and protection of health.[8]

The question of right to health has emerged as one of the most significant issues for discussion in this new millennium. Health care involves ever-changing challenges. The national and local decisions regarding health are affected by global forces and policies. The effect of globalization on health has resulted in substantial gains for some groups and severe marginalization of others. India bears 21 percent of global disease burden on its shoulders. This is coupled with spiraling health costs, high financial burden on the poor and erosion in their incomes. Around 24 percent of all people hospitalized in India in a single year fall below the poverty line.[9]

In 1947, when the country gained independence, half the population was dying before the age of 10 years, the life expectancy was less than 30 years and the major cause of death was communicable diseases, with "fevers" accounting for more than half of the deaths.[10] As part of its welfare policy, the Indian government adopted the central guiding principle of the Sir Joseph Bhore Committee, 1946 that no individual should be denied medical care because of his/her inability to pay for it. Similarly, the Report of the Sub-Committee on National Health appeared in 1948.[11] In 1959, the government appointed a Committee under Dr. A.L. Mudaliar to review the health services and make recommendations. The Committee (1962) observed that rural services were not popular among the doctors. They wanted their services/posting in city hospital or in the health department. The report was criticized on the count of being urban-oriented public health policy. The main recommendations of the report were enhancement of reach of the delivery system, streamline of organization, development of training facilities for multipurpose para-medical personnel and expand sum of educational base for modern medicine. Another Committee under the Chairmanship of Dr. J.B. Srivastava was set-up in 1974 and it recommended an alternative strategy for the development more suited to

8. K. Park, *op. cit.*, p. 12; see also WHO (1978), Health for All, Sr. No. 1.
9. Peeyush Gaurav Soni, "Health Insurance—An Indian Perspective," *Kare Law Journal* at 101 (August 2006).
10. C. Sathayamala, "Reflections on Alma-Ata," *Economic and Political Weekly* at 32 (November 22, 2008).
11. This Sub-Committee of the National Planning Committee had submitted an interim report earlier in which it adopted a positive approach to primary heath care. The Sir Joseph Bhore Committee Report has a pioneering impact on all subsequent policy.

our conditions, limitations and potentialities based on the criteria of development of an integrated service covering promotive, preventive, and curative aspects of health services and family planning. It envisaged for universal coverage and equal accessibility to all citizens and full utilization of paramedical resources and supplementation by well structured system of referral services. Promotion of traditional knowledge and in modern medicines for the indigenous research in tune with latest scientific developments. Practical implementation was emphasized. The report led to the community health worker scheme in consonance with 1978 International Conference on Primary Health Care and Alma Ata Declaration India set before the world the target of health for all by 2000 A.D. The *Alma Ata* Conference of 1978 convened by WHO and UNICEF is considered as a historical turning point in health care provisioning for the developed world. The declaration adopted, with its rallying cry of "Health for All by 2000", captured the imagination of the public health community is no uncertain way. Though the promises made by the political leadership of the 134 countries to the people of the world remain largely unrealized, yet it continues to resonate even 31 years after the event. WHO's report of the year 2008, entitled as "Primary Health Care: Now More Than Ever", hoped to affirm that the concept is still valid. Under the backdrop of *Alma Ata* Declaration Indian Council of Social Sciences Research (ICSSR) and the Indian Council for Medical Research (ICMR) submitted report in 1980 which necessitated to develop a comprehensive national policy on health.[12] The report reiterates that health is function not merely of medical care, but overall development of society cultural, economic, educational, social and political development.[13]

Health is a State subject and health of all human beings is precious asset of the nation. It is nation's moral, legal and constitutional responsibility to promote, restore and maintain the health status of its population through meticulously designed policy, plans and programmes, effectively implementing monitoring and evaluating them to yield targeted result in respect of health care infrastructure, manpower support, provision of clean drinking water, sanitation and hygiene, besides a host of other inter-related activities. Health care is one of the thrust areas under the mandate of National Common Minimum Programme. The National Rural Health Mission was launched on 12th April 2005 for a period of 7 years (2005-12), that is two years of Tenth Plan and the full period of Eleventh Plan. The goals

12. Indian Council of Medical Research: A Report on Epidemic of Infectious Hepatitis in India (1956).
13. 'Paper on Health Policy', 31, *The Administrator*, 227 (1986).

of NHRM are to provide accessible, affordable, accountable, equitable, effective and reliable health care, especially to poor and vulnerable sections of the population in rural areas.

The NRHM provides an overarching umbrella, subsuming the existing programmes of the Ministry. It is operational over the entire country with special focus in 18 states viz. 8 Empowered Action Group States (Bihar, Jharkhand, Madhya Pradesh, Chhattisgarh, Uttar Pradesh, Uttaranchal, Orissa and Rajasthan), 8 North-East States (Assam, Arunachal Pradesh, Manipur, Meghalaya, Mizoram, Nagaland, Sikkim and Tripura) Himachal Pradesh and Jammu and Kashmir. The mission is an articulation of the commitment of the Government to achieve the goals and objectives of National Health Policy, 2002 and National Population Policy, 2000. Despite all the evidence that has accumulated to underline the interdependence of population growth and health, the dichotomy in approach has persisted. Since 2001, there has been a barrage of commissions, committees, campaigns, and advisory bodies in addition to the Planning Commission. They have produced drafts, discussion, papers, and policy guidelines for public, and not so public debates. Some amongst these are the population Commission, the Indian Commission on Macro Economics and Health, the Rural Health Mission, and the National Advisory Council. As early as 1992 the World Bank produced a document on 'Financing for India's Health Sector'[14] and another in 2001 on, 'Better Health Systems for India's Poor'.

In September 2000, 189 member-states of the United Nations adopted UN Millennium Declaration incorporating eight millennium goals of which three sharply focused on 'health', viz. (i) reduce child mortality; (ii) improve maternal health; and (iii) combat HIV/AIDS, malaria and other diseases. Indian government is committed to the objective of providing health for all. The health scenario of the country has undergone significant changes during the past few years. In a way the Sixth Plan can be called the last and the weakest milestone in India's experiment of establishing itself as an independent architect of its health sector services. It diverted resources into controlling communicable diseases, put restraints on pumping more resources into family planning but the upgraded infrastructure continue to serve the latter as it enjoyed the highest priority at the central level. The Seventh Plan under increasing pressure of neo-liberal policies scaled up investment in Family Planning and opened up to NGO and private sector partnerships.

14. World Bank Document, 1992 as quoted by Imrana Qadeer, Health Planning in India: Some Lessons from the Past, *Social Scientist*, May-June, 2008, Vol. 36, Nos. 5-6, pp. 51-52.

The Eighth Plan talked of privatization of medical care and of targeting the underprivileged for providing primary health care and national health programmes. The Ninth Plan envisaged the development of a well structured network of urban health care institutions providing health and family welfare services to the population within one to three km. of their dwellings by re-organizing the existing institutions. During the Tenth Plan every effort was made to implement the recommendations of the Seventh, Eighth, and Ninth Plan, that is, all hospitals and dispensaries below the district level were mainstreamed, recognized, restructured and integrated into the three-tier rural primary health care system in order to serve the population. The National Rural Health Mission was launched on 12 April 2005 for a period of seven years, that is the balance two years of Tenth Plan and the full period of Eleventh Plan.

At present in India there are 1,46,206 Sub-Health Centres (SHCs), 23,236 Primary Health Centres (PHCs) and 3,346 Community Health Centres (CHCs). To meet 2001 population norm, additional 19,269[15] SHCs, 4337 PHCs and 3206 CHCs are needed. External assistance in India has been channelled through centrally-sponsored programmes for communicable diseases and family welfare. In initial years, the funding was from USA and European countries. The World Bank funding for health was generally given as grants. Even then, the change in the context of health, though visible, is certainly not impressive as reflected by India's 127th position in the world in its human development index, poverty level of 31 percent, and literacy rates among women as low as 47. There are disparities between rural and urban areas to access to health care services. Most of the rural health centres had inadequate specialists, medical equipment and drugs. Since April 2009, the HINI influenza virus has killed over 12,500 people in 210 countries. India reported 28,251 cases with 1135 deaths till January 18, 2010.

II. PROBLEMS OF DEFINING HEALTH

'Health' is one of such terms which most people find it difficult to define though they understand what does it mean. Health is universally recognized as essential to human condition. A healthy physique and mind, apart from being the concern of the individual, is also the concern of the entire community, because without a healthy population no sustainable economic, scientific and technological development is possible. Truly speaking, defining health does not merely serve a nominal need of health analysis but has operational relevance for health

15. World Bank Document, 2001, *Ibid.*

practice. Keeping this in view, various efforts have been made to define health from time to time.

Health was defined, not negatively or narrowly as the absence of disease or infirmity, but positively and broadly as "a state of complete physical, mental and social well-being", the enjoyment of which should be part of the rightful heritage of "every human being without distinction of race, religion, political belief, economic or social condition".[16] In the same spirit as the UN Charter the Preamble of the WHO asserted that the principles it state were basic to the happiness, harmonious relations and security of all people, thus, expressing a modern set of universal aspirations. Health, it says, was an essential condition for their attainment, and the highest possible attainment of health was a fundamental right of every human being without distinction of any kind.[17] In the recent years, this definition has been amplified to include the ability to lead a 'socially and economically productive life'. Through this definition, WHO has helped to move health thinking beyond a limited, biomedical and pathology-based perspective to the more positive domain of "well-being". Further, by explicitly including the mental and social dimensions of well-being, WHO has radically expanded the scope of health, and by extension, the roles and responsibilities of health professionals and their relationship to the larger society.[18]

It is also revealed from different studies that from time to time many definitions of health have been offered, viz., (a) "the condition of being sound body, mind or spirit, especially freedom from physical disease or pain"[19]; (b) "soundness of body or mind; that conditions in which its functions are duly and efficiently discharged",[20] (c) "a condition or quality of human organism expressing the adequate functioning of the organism in given conditions, genetic and environmental"[21]; (d) "a *modus vivendi* enabling imperfect men to achieve a rewarding and not too painful existence while they cope with an imperfect world"[22]; "a state of relative equilibrium of body form and

16. WHO OR No. 2, Summary Report on Proceedings Minutes and Final Acts of the International Health Conference (New York: UN-WHO Interim Commission, 1948), at 16.
17. Frank P. Grad, "The Preamble of the Constitution of the World Health Organization", 80 (2002): 12, *Bulletin of the WHO*, 981-82, at 981.
18. J.M. Mann and Leary Gostin *et. al.*, "Health and Human Rights", *Health & Human Rights: An International Journal* 1:1 (1994), www.hsph.harvard.edu/fxbcenter/VINI/mannetal.htm. (Accessed on 30 January, 2009).
19. See, Webster Dictionary.
20. See Oxford English Dictionary.
21. WHO (1957), *Techn. Rep. Ser. No. 137.*
22. R. Dubos, *Man, Med. and Environment* (1968) quoted in K. Park, *op. cit.*, at 13.

function which results from its successful dynamic adjustment to forces tending to disturb it. It is not passive interplay between body substance and forces impinging upon it but an active response of body forces working toward readjustment".[23]

The WHO definition of health has been criticized as being too broad. Some argue that health cannot be defined as a "state" at all, but must be seen as a process of continuous adjustment to the changing demands of living and of the changing meanings we give to life. It is a dynamic concept. It helps people live well, work well and enjoy themselves. The WHO definition of health is, therefore, considered by many as an idealistic goal than a realistic proposition. It refers to a situation that may exist in some individuals but not in everyone all the time; it is not usually observed in groups of human beings and in communities. Some consider it irrelevant to every day demands, as nobody qualifies as healthy, i.e. perfect biological, psychological and social functioning. Inspite of the above limitations, the concept of health as defined by WHO is broad and positive in its implications, it sets out the standard, the standard of "positive" health. It symbolizes the aspirations of people and represents an overall objective or goal towards which nation should strive.[24]

The World Health Organization (WHO) definition of health is not an "operational" definition, i.e., it does not lend itself to direct measurement. Studies of epidemiology of health have been hampered because of our inability to measure health and well-being directly. In this connection an "operational definition" has been devised by a World Health Organization (WHO) study group.[25] In this definition, the concept of health is viewed as being of two orders. In a broad sense, health can be seen as "a condition or quality of the human organism in given conditions, genetic or environmental". In a narrow sense—one or more useful for measuring purposes health means: (a) there is no obvious evidence of disease, and that a person is functioning normally, i.e. conforming with normal limits of variation to the standards of health criteria generally accepted for one's age, sex, community and geographic region; and (b) the several organs of the body are functioning adequately in themselves and in relation to one another, which implies a kind of equilibrium or homeostasis—a condition relatively stable but which may vary as human beings adapt to internal and external stimuli.[26]

23. Perkins quoted in K. Park, *Ibid.*
24. K. Park, *op. cit.*, at 12.
25. *Ibid.*
26. *Id.*, at 13.

There are some negative aspects of health, which have been discussed by some scholars. According to them, health is considered as an absence of disease or illness, and also as an absence of sickness or suffering. Nevertheless, each of these aspects carry different conceptions. If medical conception of health as absence of disease relates to organic level of experience, identifying pathological abnormality in terms of sickness, a medical and psycho-social conception of "health as absence of illness", on the other hand relates to personal experience of pain and discomfort where one feels illness without having a disease. Similarly, a sociological conception of "health as absence of sickness" relates to status requiring two-fold professional attention namely exemption from normal social responsibilities and need for non-volitional attention for getting well. Further, the conception of "health as absence of suffering" is related to growth of hospitalization with a purpose of reducing suffering.[27]

A normative definition that "Health is optimum capacity to perform social roles" constitutes adequacy relative to capacities, feeling and biological functioning needed for performing social tasks. Functional fitness, which is the standard of positive health, is related to such capacity. Identification of health as status is a value-free approach to use statistical norms of fixing the health of the individual. At present, there is no agreed norms, i.e. the index of health status is sometimes social, sometimes non-social, sometimes biological and medical indices are preferred. The definition is, however, closely related to functional fitness. Health status can be normative as well as positive. When health is seen as a sick role, it signifies three characteristics of the individual: (i) he/she is exempted from normal social responsibilities; (ii) he/she cannot get well on his/her own; (iii) he/she should have the will and ask for getting well. All these necessitate professional intervention.[28]

According to the definition of health as "a functional requisite for the social system", its importance appears to be propagated through health education. The societal perspective on health is essential because it is related not only to illness or sickness or disease of individual but also to national defence and urban development. The stress is on functional efficiency and not just on functional fitness. Health forms part of social situation and not just of environment. The working norms, levels of living, distribution of health services and the health providing institutions, even health needs as determined by defence needs, composition of industrial production and population density comprise

27. Avanish Kumar, *op. cit.*, at 18-19.
28. *Id.*, at 19; also see Kulkarni, Health for Peace (New Delhi: Institute of Peace Research and Action, 1992), at 8.

social situation. The concept is essentially relativistic, i.e. society specific.[29]

Health as a social system is perhaps the widest conception of health in traditional sociology of health. Health is an important cog in the social machine. There has to be equilibrium in the social system. Poor health becomes dysfunctional and a cost to the society, therefore, the society should take care of the sick. The medical system should be viewed as a mechanism through which the restoration of health takes place. This approach is specially significant in times of resource scarcities. The extended meaning of health calls upon doctors to go beyond curing patients, collecting and interpreting data not only on clinical categories but also on health needs and utilization of health services. This conception helps in integrating health into the socio-economic system.[30] A healthy person continually participates in social functioning, but illness deprives him of this. Therefore, it is potentially disruptive to this social functioning of an individual. A state of perfect health is one which people strive for but do not expect to attain. The ideal state is the absolute state; it is static and in some sense negative. Critics have suggested that health should be viewed holistically, i.e. as a state of functional fitness comprising the negative as well as the positive aspects.[31]

III. MULTI-DIMENSIONS OF HEALTH

The concept of health is multi-dimensional. The World Health Organization (WHO) definition envisages three specific dimensions—the physical, the mental and the social. Besides these, many more dimensions may be added, such as spiritual, emotional, vocational and political. As the knowledge base grows, the list may be expanding. Although these dimensions function and interact with one another, each has its distinct nature.

(i) Physical, Mental and Social Dimensions

The physical dimension of health implies "perfect functioning" of the body in which every cell and every organ is functioning at optimum capacity and in perfect harmony with the rest of the body. At the community level, the state of health may be assessed by such indicators as death rate, infant mortality rate and expectation of life.[32]

29. *Ibid.*
30. *Ibid.*
31. *Ibid.*
32. K. Park, *op. cit.*, at 14.

Mental health is also an entirely different problem and equally important like physical health. Mental health is not mere absence of mental illness but it has been defined as a "state of balance between the individual and the surrounding world, a state of harmony between oneself and others, a coexistence between the realties of the self and that of other people and that of the environment.[33] Although mental health is an essential component of health, the scientific foundations of mental are not yet clear. Keeping in view the dignity and welfare of persons with mental illness the international forum did not leave this area untouched. In an effort to allow to persons with mental illness as integrated a life as possible, the General Assembly has made some principles providing protection of persons with mental illness and the improvement of mental health care.[34]

Social health is the third dimension and has been defined as the "quantity and quality of an individual's international ties and the extent of involvement with the community". In general, social health takes into account that every individual is a part of a family and of wider community and focuses on social and economic conditions and well-being of the "whole person" in the context of his social network.[35] Social well-being implies harmony and integration within the individual, between each individual and other members of society and between individuals and the world in which they live.

(ii) Vocational Dimensions

The vocational aspect of life is a new dimension. It is a part of human existence. When work is fully adapted to human goals, capacities and limitations, work often plays a role in promoting both physical and mental health. Physical work is usually associated with an improvement in physical capacity, while goal achievement and self-realization in work are a source of satisfaction and enhanced self-esteem.[36] Truly admitting that the importance of this dimension is exposed when individuals suddenly lose their jobs or faced with mandatory retirement. For many individuals, the vocational dimension may be merely a source of income. But to others, it represents the

33. N. Sartorius, "Mental Health in the Early 1980's: Some Perspectives" (1983), 61: 1, *Bulletin of WHO* (World Health Organization), 1-6, at p. 5.
34. K. Park, *op. cit.*, at 13; see also Furan Ahmad, "International Instruments and Health" in International Conference on Global Health Law held on 5-7 December, 1987, at 3.
35. K. Park, *ibid.*
36. *Id.*, at 15; see also WHO (1985), *Tech. Rep. Ser.*, 275.

culmination of the efforts of other dimensions as they function together to produce what the individual considers life "success".[37]

(iii) Other Dimensions

A few other dimensions have also been suggested, namely, (i) philosophical dimension which deals with issues like concept of health, value systems affecting health and attitude towards illness, pain, ageing or death which, in the final analysis, determine the nature and quality of the health services; (ii) cultural dimensions which deals with life styles of people which have far reaching consequences on the practice of health; (iii) socio-economic dimension deals with the social, economic and political organization of the society as a whole; (iv) environmental dimension deals with problems like public sanitation, pollution, water supply, housing or settlement patterns, with a view to protect health system; (v) nutritional dimension deals with the quantities and quality of food available to all; (vi) educational dimension deals with the role and responsibilities of individuals and families in maintaining a healthy society; (vii) preventive dimension deals with problems relating to the prevention of avoidable suffering, disease or untimely death; and, (viii) curative dimension deals with measure for the provision of adequate and appropriate treatment when, despite of all efforts, disease or ill-health does manifest itself.[38]

These dimensions symbolize a huge range of factors to which other sectors besides health must contribute if all people are indeed to attain a level of health that will permit them to lead a socially and economically productive life.

IV. DETERMINANTS OF HEALTH

Many factors combine together to affect the health of individual and communities. Whether people are healthy or not, is determined by their circumstances and environment. To a large extent, factors such as where we live, the state of our relationship with friends and family all have considerable impacts on health, whereas the more commonly considered factors such as access and use of health care services often have less of an impact. Health is multifactorial. The factors which influence heath lie both within the individual and externally in the society in which he or she lives. Thus, before analyzing the

37. R.M. Eberst, Jr. School Health, 54(3), 99-104 (1984).
38. Avanish Kumar, *op. cit.*, at 24; also see, Health For All: An Alternative Strategy (Pune: Indian Institute of Education, 1981) at 12. Report of a Joint Study Group of ICSSR and ICMR.

determinants of health, it is pertinent to examine the factors which influence the human health. These underlying influential factors become challenge to health and ultimately become the determinants of health. The declaration of *Alma-Ata* opened up a new era in public health thinking and practice. The Health-For-All strategy, rooted in a progressive implementation of primary health care, has led to the achievement of major health gains worldwide. To developed and developing nations alike, it has brought notable health benefits, a number of deadly diseases have been gradually conquered, overall mortality rates have declined significantly, access to health care has improved and, during the last decade of the 20th century, life expectancy has increased considerably worldwide.[39]

The influential factors, which affects human health (either positively or negatively) becomes a challenge to health and finally determine our health status. These factors, in a nut shell, are shown in the chart below:

Keeping in view the brief analysis of the selective significant factors that reduce or increase the burden of disease, it is clear that these factors become either positive or negative determinants of health status. Some of the health determinants are as follow:

(i) Biological Determinants

The physical and mental traits of every human being are to some extent determined by the nature of his genes at the moment of conception. The genetic make-up is unique is that it cannot be altered after conception. A number of diseases are now known to be of genetic origin, for example, chromosomal anomalies, errors of metabolism, mental retardation, some types of diabetes, etc. The state of health, therefore, depends partly on the genetic constitution of man. But now-a-days medical genetics offers hope for prevention and its treatment. This knowledge will help people achieve better health; the individual has the opportunity to assert greater control over his life and long lasting suffering can be reduced and some lines avoided. Inspite of it some times it gives birth to basic ethical, legal and social issues.[40]

---

39. K. Park., *op. cit.*, at 17; also see; Genevieve Pinet, "Health Challenges of the 21st Century: A Legislative Approach to Health Determinants" (1998) 49: 1 IDHL 131-177, at p.132.
40. Avanish Kumar, *op. cit.*, at 27; Control of Hereditary Diseases (Geneva: WHO 1996) at p.73. Report of a WHO Scientific Group (WHO Technical Report Series No. 865), see also K. Park, *op. cit.*, at 18.

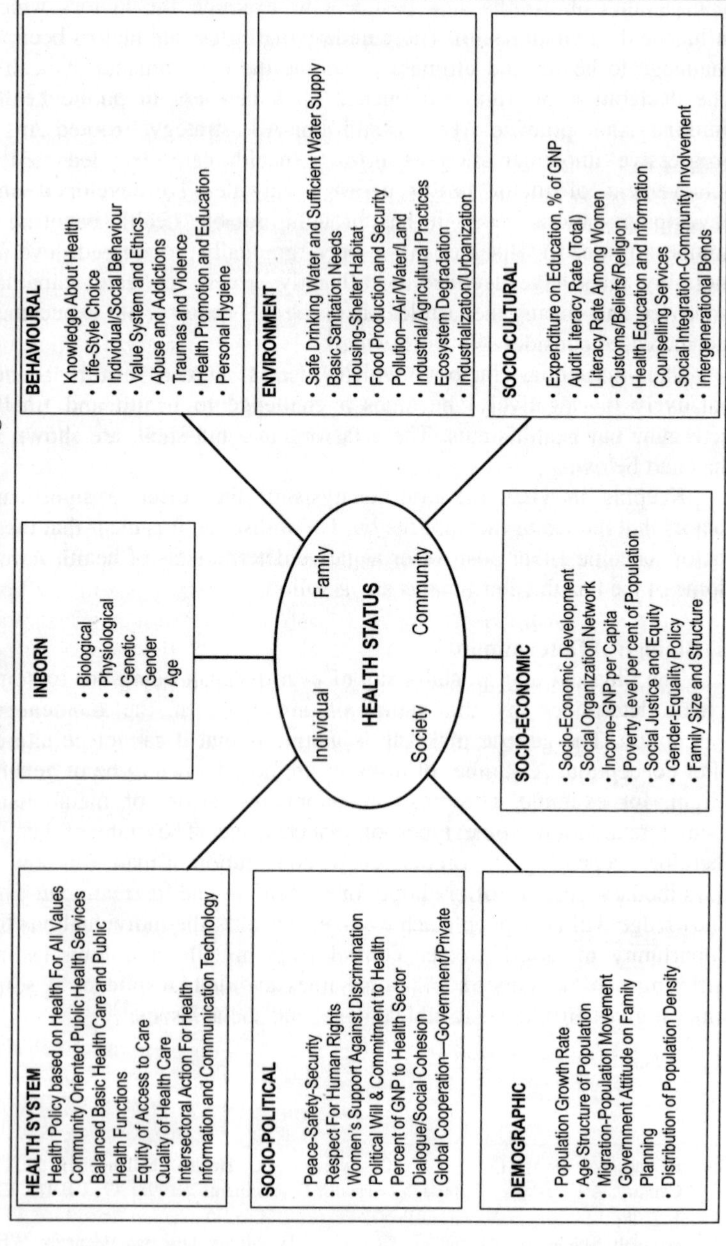

Figure 1: Selective Significant Factors Influencing Human Health

The European Convention on Human Rights and Biomedicine, signed by 22 member-States out of a total of 40 of the Council of Europe (CE) on 4 April 1997, is the first international legal instrument that specifically prohibits any discrimination against a person on the basis of his genetic heritage and only authorizes predictive testing for genetic disease with a medical objective.[41] The Universal Declaration on the Human Genome and Human Rights, adopted unanimously by the General Conference of UNESCO (United Nations Educational, Scientific and Cultural Organization) on 11 November 1997, strikes a balance between safeguarding respect for human dignity, freedom and HR (Human Rights) and the need to ensure freedom of research, while emphasizing the prohibition of all forms of discrimination based on genetic characteristic.[42]

The successful cloning of an adult sheep by a team of scientists in Scotland in March 1997, interesting opportunities to advance biomedical research on diagnosis and treatment of diseases affecting human beings raised great concern the world over because of the potential implications of cloning procedure is human reproduction. The same the World Health Assembly adopted by consensus resolution WHA (50.37) affirming that: "the use of cloning for the replication of human individuals is ethically unacceptable and contrary to human integrity and morality. But in October 1997, "Scientific and Ethical Review Group of WHO's Special Programme of Research, Development and Research Training in Human Reproduction" was convened with representatives of UNESCO (United Nations Educational Scientific and Cultural Organization), IARC and the CE (Council of Europe), as there was felt a need to develop international guidelines covering the technical and ethical issues of cloning in human health.[43] Now developments in the biological disciplines and future progress will together ensure that the 'inborn' determinants of health continue to increase its importance.

41. Avanish Kumar, *Ibid.* Also see, The European Convention on Human Rights and Biomedicine Adopted by the (CE) Council of Europe in April 1997. http://conventions.oe.int/treaty/treaties/html/164.htm. (Accessed on 28 June, 2008).
42. The Universal Declaration on the Human Genome and Human Rights: Adopted by the UNESCO in Nov., 1997. ww/.UMR.edu/humanrts/instree/ udhrhg.htm. (Accessed on 28 June 2005).
43. The Universal Declaration on the Human Genome and Human Rights Adopted by the UNESCO in Nov., 1997. www1.umn.edu/humanrts/ instree/udhrhg.htm. (Accessed on 28 June, 2008).

(ii) Behavioural Determinants

Behaviour is another factor which influences health. Behaviour is of great importance to health, either directly through learned life styles or indirectly in the environmental and socio-economic context. Health requires the promotion of healthy life style. During the last two decades or so considerable body of evidence has accumulated which indicates that there is an association between health and lifestyle of individuals.[44]

Many current-day health problems especially in the developed countries (e.g. coronary heart disease, obesity, lung cancer, drug addiction) are associated with lifestyles still persist, risks of illness and death are connected with lack of sanitation, poor nutrition, personal hygiene, elementary human habits, customs and cultural patterns. WHO's (World Health Organization) World Health Report 1995 corroborates these findings,[45] stating that lifestyle-related diseases and conditions are responsible for 70-80 percent of deaths in developed countries and about 40 percent in the developing world. Even in developing countries the situation is expected to worsen in the future with a growing number of lifestyle-related diseases, attributed to the rapid emergence in the middle class of unhealthy dietary and behavioural changes. The development process brings about changes in lifestyle which increases the risk of developing those so called "diseases of modern civilization" common in industrialized countries such as cardiovascular diseases, certain type of cancer and obesity.[46]

It may be noted that not all lifestyle factors are harmful. There are many that can actually promote health. Examples include adequate nutrition, enough sleep, sufficient physical activity, etc. In short, the achievement of optimum health demands adoption of healthy lifestyles. Health is both a consequence of an individual's lifestyle and a factor in determining it.

(iii) Environmental Determinants

Environment is the third factor which influences the health. It is usually defined as the aggregate of all external conditions and influences affecting the life and the development of an organism. It consist of those things to which man is exposed after conception. It is defined as "all that which is external to the individual human host".[47]

---

44. K. Park., *op. cit.*, at 18.
45. The World Health Report 1995: Bridging the Gaps (Geneva: WHO 1995), at 12; D.L. Wingard (1982). *Am. J. Epid*, 116 (5) 765.
46. Avanish Kumar, *op. cit.*, at 29; The World Health Report 1995: Bridging the Gaps. (Geneva: WHO 1995) at p.12; see also, Genevieve Pinet, *op. cit.*, at 138.
47. K. Park, *op. cit.*, at 18.

It was Hippocrates who first related disease to environment, e.g., climate, water, air, etc. Centuries later, Pettenkofer in Germany revived the concept of disease-environment association. Environment is classified as "internal" and "external". The internal environment of man pertains to "each and every component part, every tissue, organ or organ system and their harmonious functioning within the system". Internal environment is the domain of internal medicine. The external or macro-environment consists of those things to which man is exposed after conception. It is defined as "all that which is external to the individual human host".[48] One may divide it into physical, biological and psychological components, any or all of which can affect the health of man and his susceptibility to illness. Some epidemiologists have used the term "microenvironment" (or domestic environment) to personal environment which includes the individual's way of living and lifestyle, e.g., eating habits, other personal habits (e.g., smoking or drinking), use of drugs, etc. It is also customary to speak about occupational environment, socio-economic environment and moral environment.[49]

In the poor and least developed countries, the domestic environment remains a major factor of ill-health, linked with lack of access to safe water supplies and adequate basic sanitation, upon which the control of many infectious diseases largely depend. If the environment is favourable to the individual, he can make full use of his physical and mental capabilities. But in the industrialized countries, there is considerable concern about the adverse health effects of continuing environmental degradation, notably, pollution, the uncontrolled dumping of chemical wastes, and the transport and storage of potentially dangerous substances, especially nuclear wastes. Another environmental threat is the depletion of the ozone layer, predicted to result in global climate changes. Changes in climatic condition may have an impact on public health,[50] increasing the potential for transmission of infectious diseases through the extension of breeding areas for mosquitoes and other insect vectors of disease. Together with the WHO (World Health Organization) and UNEP (United Nations Environment Programme) has studied the impact of the depletion of the ozone layer on health and analyzed the potential impact of global climate change on the health.[51] Climate changes over recent decades

---

48. J.M. Last, A Dictionary of Epidemiology, 1983.
49. *Supra* n. 47.
50. The World Health Report, 1996: Fighting Diseases, Fostering Development (Geneva: WHO 1996), at 6.
51. Avanish, *op. cit.*, at 31; see also, Khanchit *et. al.*, "Climate Change and Infections Diseases: A Dimension of Global Health Security", *IJEC*, January-December, 2008, Vol. 4, Issues 7 & 8, pp. 48-53.

have probably affected some health outcomes. The potential impact of climate change, on health in developing countries, has not been sufficiently addressed may include the following:

- Acute deaths due to sudden heat waves, floods and droughts;
- Vector-borne diseases such as dengue, malaria and chikungunya;
- Water borne disease especially diarrhea;
- Malnutrition and its associated effects on child growth and development; and
- morbidity and mortality due to cardio-respiratory ailments.

The World Health Report, 2002[52] reported the estimates of climate change to worldwide diarrhea incidence approximately 2.4 percent and 6.0 percent of malaria in some middle income countries in 2000. Climate change is also projected to increase the proportion of the population exposed to dengue from 35 percent to 60 percent by the latter part of the country. However, casual attribution to climate change is difficult to confirm. There is a need to document similar observations in different population settings.

Although, the environmental policies for the protection of health occupies an important role but is not necessarily a predominant concern. So there is a need to strike a balance between the protection of environment and the public health. In order to exercise health responsibilities, health authorities need to carry out health impact assessment at the regional, national and local levels on the extent of severity of communicable disease as a consequence of climate change.

(iv) Health Services as Determinants

The term health and family welfare services covers a wide spectrum of personal and community services for treatment of disease, prevention of illness and promotion of health. The purpose of health services is to improve the health status of population. Health care system in the 21st century will continue to be confronted with a wide variety of challenges, such as demographic evolution, new patterns of diseases, escalating environmental degradation, changing economic and social structures and status, further developments in health technology and growing expectations of health care consumers. The purpose of health services is to improve the health status of population. This may be done by immunization of children, provision of safe water can prevent mortality and morbity from water borne disease. Further the case of pregnant

52. WHO: World Health Report, 2002, Reducing Risks Performing Life, Chapter 4: 47-97 (WHO, Geneva, 2002).

women and children would contribute to the reduction of maternal and child morbidity and mortality. The need of the hour is that the health services must reach the social periphery, equitably distributed, accessible at a cost the country and community can afford and socially acceptable.[53] Frankly admitting, all these are ingredients of what is now termed "primary health care", which is seen as the way to better health. To be effective, the health services must reach the social periphery, equitably distributed, accessible at a cost the country and community can afford and socially acceptable. Health services can also be seen as essential for social and economic development. In fact, health care does not produce good health, but the most we can expect from an effective health service is good care.[54]

(v) Socio-economic Determinant

It is a truism that the socio-economic situation of a country has a definite influence on the health of its population. A large body of evidence supports the view that the lower the socio-economic status, the higher the prevalence of disease. For the majority of the world's people, health status is determined primarily by their level of socio-economic development, e.g. per capita GNP (Gross National Product), education, nutrition, employment, housing, the political system of the country, etc. Poverty is the major single determinant of individual, family and community health,[55] and major challenge of present times. Director General of WHO (World Health Organization), Dr. H. Nakajima, in his message, presenting the 1995 World Health Report, cited poverty as the world's deadliest disease, stressing its role in contributing to the suffering and burden of illness, disability and death affecting many people worldwide. Extreme poverty – the world's most ruthless killer— is listed in WHO's (World Health Organization's) "International Classification of Diseases". Reduction of poverty is one of the four key priorities identified for future international health action in achieving the goals and targets defined in WHO's 'Ninth General Programme of Work' (1996-2001). In renewing its "Health For All" policy for the 21st century, WHO (World Health Organization) has chosen to combat against poverty as its first strategic line of action.[56]

To achieve the goal of 'Health For All', WHO (World Health Organization) has set the target of at least 5 percent expenditure of each country's GNP (Gross National Product) on health care. Political

53. WHO (1978), Health For All, Sr. No. 1.
54. Avanish Kumar, *op. cit.*, at 32.
55. *Ibid.*, also see, The World Health Report, 1995: Bridging the Gaps (Geneva: WHO, 1995), at 12.
56. Avanish Kumar, *op. cit.*, at 34; see also, World Health Report, 1995, at 81.

commitment and leadership is needed which is oriented towards social development, and not merely economic development. If poor health patterns are to be changed, then changes must be made in the entire socio-political system in any given community. Social, economic and political action is required to eliminate health hazards in people's working and living environments.[57]

(vi) Science and Technological Advances as Determinant

Advances in science and technology, medical sciences, engineering and communications in the last decade of the 20th century has offered untold opportunities to influence health. There is a need to consider the benefits as well as the potential risks of these new technologies in terms of health, integrity and dignity of the individual. Advances in fields such as genetic screening, assisted reproduction, organ transplantation and intensive care units have reaped considerable advantages. These refined instruments give man more and more power to manipulate life and come to question our values.[58] To be true, this inevitable technological evolution necessitates ongoing ethical reflection in order to prevent deviations or excesses and ensure the respect of identity, dignity and autonomy of the human beings. In fact, ethics and law complement each other. Hence, moving from ethics into law also depends on the capacity of the legislator to respond to a felt social need. This definitely requires precise identification of the need to be satisfied, the determination of feasible and desirable solutions, and the choice of the most relevant legal tool.

(vii) Gender as Determinant

The gender concept was first used in 1970's to describe those characteristics of men and women which are socially constructed in contrast to those which are biologically determined. WHO (World Health Organization) has estimated that in different countries unsafe abortion can cause from 25 to 50 percent of maternal deaths simply because women do not have access to family planning services they want and need or have no access to safe procedures or to humane treatment for the complication of abortion and because of costly contraceptive methods, lack of information and restrictive legislation. From a study, jointly carried out by World Health Organization and UNICEF (United Nations International Children Emergency Fund),

57. K. Park., *op. cit.*, at 17.
58. Avanish Kumar, *op. cit.*, at 36; also see, Genevieve Pinet, "Health Challenges of the 21st Century: A Legislative Approach to Health Determinants", (1998), 49: 1, *IDHL* 131-177, at 132. (International Digest of Health Legislation).

about 99 percent of pregnancy-related deaths occur in developing countries (55 percent in Asia and 40 percent in Africa) and by contrast, less than 1 percent in developed countries.[59] The rise of the AIDS (Acquired Immuno Deficiency Syndrome) epidemic has brought to our attention, the risk of sexually transmitted diseases and the vulner ability of women to HIV (Human Immuno Deficiency Virus) infection and AIDS (Acquired Immuno Deficiency Syndrome), in all parts of the world, related to their status in society, including social and cultural expectations about their sexuality.[60]

Health legislation has contributed substantially in promoting public health and could be used more vigorously to promote women's health. Laws that give women the right to control their fertility and provide access to such services tend to reduce mortality and morbidity related to pregnancy. Women themselves should be encouraged and supported to take advantage of the basic Human Right (HR) and freedoms that empower them to realize their own health goals, not only as regards the right to health care, the right to benefit from scientific progress and patient's rights with their important aspect of confidentiality and privacy, but also as regards a broader span of rights – for instance, the right to be free from discrimination, rights regarding survival and security, family and private life, information and education.[61] The 1990s have witnessed an increased concentration on women issues. In 1993, the Gobal Commission on Women's Health was established. The Commission drew up an agenda for action on women's health covering nutrition, reproductive health, the health consequences of violence, aging, lifestyle related conditions and occupational environment. It has brought about an increased awareness among policy-makers of women's health issues and encourages their inclusion in all development plans as a priority.

(viii) Human Right as Determinant

Equity in health and social justice are amongst the major determinants of health and will remain the foundation of World Health Organization's (WHO's) 'Health For All' policy in the 21st century. WHO was the first to recognize the right to health as one of the fundamental right of every human being, as stated in its Constitution. The World Health Organization (WHO) Constitution asserts that: "the enjoyment of the highest attainable standard of health is one of the

59. Avanish Kumar, *op. cit.*, at 39; also see, The World Health Report, 1997: Conquering Suffering, Enriching Humanity (Geneva: WHO, 1997), at 83.
60. See, the World Health Report, 1996: Fighting Diseases, Fostering Development. (Geneva: WHO, 1996), at 13.
61. *Ibid.*

fundamental right of every human being without distinction of race, religion, political belief, economic or social condition". The 'Health For All' movement launched in 1977 was based on the recognition of the close linkage between health, Human Right (HR) and social development. The resolution on "Health For All in the year 2000" reaffirmed that health is a basic Human Right and called for a social target of a standard of health to be attained by all citizens of the world by the year 2000 to 'permit them to lead a socially and economically productive life".[62] The Declaration of *Alma-Ata* reaffirmed that health is a fundamental Human Right but focused further on a specific approach concentrating on primary health care as the key to the attainment of that right and 'Health For All'. World Health Organization has developed a set of basic indicators of primary health care and 'Health For All Attainment', which further linked that goal with the fight against inequities in health. Indeed these indicators are the best measures of the "right to health" which exist in the world today. Although WHO did not explicitly link its health action with the Human Right promotion and protection, the organization has a long history of operationalizing the right to health. In order to develop the Human Right agenda of World Health Organization and engage in a broader cooperation among health and Human Right agencies, World Health Organization convened a "Consultation on Health and Human Rights" in December 1997.[63]

Thus, health is recognized as essential to the human in every condition. A health physique and mind, apart from being the concern of the individual, is also the concern of the entire community, because without a healthy population no sustainable economic, scientific and technological development is possible.[64]

However, the development of the concept of health as absence of disease and health as right to life has been determined the past experiences and vision for the future. Health is also a total sum of strengthening adequate nutrition, community support, education, safe environment and social cohesion. Rights are a mode to empower and mobilize the vulnerable and the disadvantaged, and this is the main concern of anxiety in different parts of the world. The language of a health creates consciousness and their existing condition, cause of oppression and the possibility of change.[65]

Health as a basic and fundamental right is indispensable for the existence of other human rights. Each and every human being is entitled

62. Pinet, *op. cit.*, at 166.
63. *Ibid.*
64. *Supra* n. 1.
65. Right to Health Care in India, http://www.manupatra.com.

to the attainment of adequate standard of health conducive to enjoy a life in dignity. The implementation of the right to health may be undertaken through a number of different approaches such as the formulation of health policies or the realization of health programmes initiated and developed by State bodies such as legislature, executive and the judiciary and international instruments.[66] Among the international bodies the WHO is an official agency of United Nations performing this task globally. Further, the right to health includes certain components which are legally enforceable. The right to health contains both freedoms and entitlement. The freedom includes the right to be free from torture, non-consensual medical treatment and human experimentation, and the right to control one's own health and body such as sexual and reproductive freedom.[67] Thus, freedom in this context means the possibility of choice, and consciousness about the consequences of choice, both in regard to both production and consumption of health inputs inviting people to design their own health-illness health-cycles. So the entitlement includes the right to a system of health protection which provides equality of opportunity for people to enjoy the highest attainable level of health, meaning the probability that one will not die from a disease pre-maturely, whether that premature death is brought about by misguided health care, wrong distribution, ecological imbalances and lack of self-reliance.[68]

V. HEALTH AND HUMAN RIGHTS LINKAGES

The right to health extends to all things which promote health and well-being and prevents illness and disease, not just access to medical care. This includes among many others, the right to education, food and shelter; freedom from discrimination and persecution; right to information and to the benefits of science. Keeping this in view, the

66. Universal Declaration of the Rights, 1948, International Covenant on Economic, Social and Cultural Rights, 1966; International Covenant on Civil and Political Rights, 1966; U.N. Declaration on Elimination of Discrimination of Women, 1967; Convention on the Elimination of All Forms of Discrimination Against Women, 1979; Convention Against Torture and other Cruel, Inhuman and Degrading Treatment or Punishment, 1984; Convention/Declaration on the Rights of the Child, 1989; Convention for the Protection of Human Rights and Dignity of Human Being with Regard to the Application of Biology and Medicine; Convention on Human Rights and Bio-Medicine, 1997. Declaration of the UN Conference on the Human Environment – 1972 (Stockholm Declaration), Convention concerning the protection of workers against occupational Hazards in the working Environment due to Air Pollution, Noise and Vibration, etc.
67. Avanish Kumar, *op. cit.*, at ii.
68. *Id.*, at iii.

complex linkage between health and human right is mainly based on three part framework, all of which are inter-connected and has definitely substantial consequences. First is the positive and negative impact of health policies, programmes and practices on human rights, which focuses on the use of state power in the context of public health. The second linkage is based on the understanding of human rights violations which again have health impact. This process engages health expertise and methodologies in helping to understand how well-being is affected by human rights violations. The third is based on the proposition that promotion and protection of human rights and protection of health are fundamentally linked. This internal linkage has strategic implications and potentially dramatic practical consequences for work in each domain.[69] The examples of the linkages between health and human rights can be understood by going through the following Fig. 2.

Therefore, an earnest attempt is made by the researcher to explain these three linkages in the following.

Figure 2:[70] Linkages Between Health and Human Rights

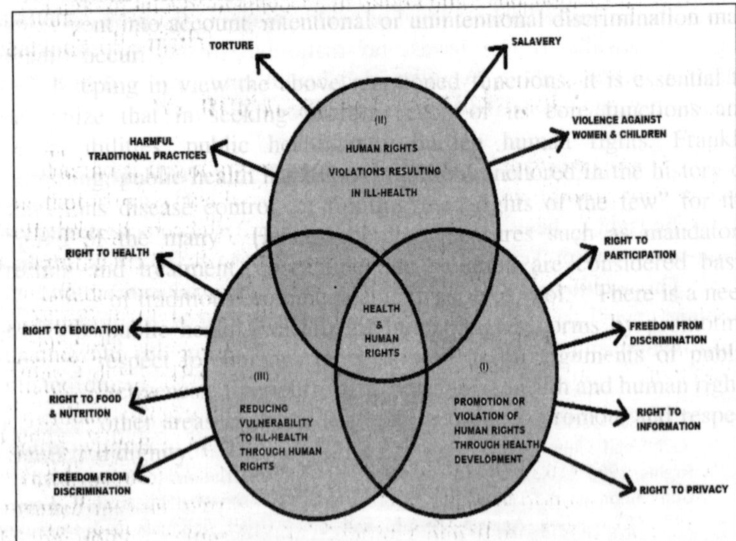

Source: 25 Questions & Answers on Health Rights (Geneva: WHO, 2002), at 8. (Health & Human Rights Publication Series, Issue No. 1, July 2002)

---

69. J.S. Mann and Leary Gostin *et. al.*, Health and Human Rights, *Health and Human Rights: An International Journal*, 1:1 (1994). www.hsph.harvard.edu/fxbcenter/VINI/mannetal.htm. (Accessed on 11 November, 2009).
70. 25 Questions and Answers on Health and Human Rights, (Geneva: WHO, 2002) at 8. *Health and Human Rights Publication Series*, Issue No. 1, July 2002.

(i) Impact of Health Policies on Human Rights

Truly admitting, health care is provided through many diverse public and private mechanisms all over the globe. However, the responsibilities of public health are carried out in large measure through policies and programmes promulgated, implemented and enforced by, or with support from, the state. The three central functions of public health include, viz., (a) assessing health needs and problems; (b) developing policies designed to address priority health issues; and (c) assuring programmes to implement strategic health goals.[71] The potential benefits to and burden on human rights may occur in the pursuit of each of these major areas of public health responsibility. Hence, a State's failure to recognize or acknowledge health problems that preferentially affect a marginalized or stigmatized group may violate the right to non-discrimination by leading to neglect of necessary services, and in so doing, may adversely affect the realization of other rights including the right to "security in the event of sickness (or) disability...", or to the "special care and assistance" to which mothers and children are entitled.[72] Thus, the right to freedom from discrimination is an important element of linkage between health and human right. Further, discrimination against ethnic, religious and racial minorities, as well as on account of gender, political opinion or immigration status, compromises or threatens the health and well-being of millions of people. This practice threatens physical and mental health and denies people access to care altogether, deny people appropriate therapies, or relegate them to inferior care. Similarly, the misuse of information about HIV infection status has led to: restrictions of the right to work and to education; violations of the right to marry and found a family; attacks upon honour and reputation; limitations on freedom of movement, arbitrary detention or exile; and even cruel, inhuman or degrading treatment.[73]

The another major task of public health is to develop policies to prevent and control priority health problems. No doubt, burdens on human rights may arise in policy-development process. It is worth to quote examples that if a government refuses to disclose the scientific basis of health policy or permit debate on its merits, or in other ways refuses to inform and involve the public in policy development, the right to "seek, receive and impart information and ideas... regardless of frontiers,[74] and "to take part in the government....directly or through

71. Mann and Gostin, *op. cit.*
72. UDHR: Article 25; ICCPR: Article 26; ACHR: Article 24; ECHR: Article 14.
73. Mann and Gostin, *op. cit.*
74. UDHR: Article 19; ICCPRR: Article 19; CEDAW: Articles 10, 14 and 16; CRC: Articles 13, 17 and 24.

freely chosen representative"[75] may be violated. Here the right to participation becomes another important element, linking health and human rights. Participation of individuals and groups in matters that affect them is essential to the protection of all human rights. Participation of individuals and groups in matters that affect them is essential to the protection of all human rights. The Declaration of *Alma-Ata* on Primary Health Care[76] states, "the people have the right and duty to participate individually and collectively in the planning and implementation of their health care. It is also to highlight that due to violation of right to information and participation, the prioritization of health issue may definitely result in discrimination against individuals, as and when the major health problems of a population defined on the basis of sex, race, religion or language are sympathetically given lower priority.

The last core function of public health is to assure services capable of realizing policy goals and is also linked with the right to non-discrimination. It is a truism that when health and social services do not take logistic, financial and socio-cultural barriers to their access and enjoyment into account, intentional or unintentional discrimination may readily occur.[77]

Keeping in view the above mentioned functions, it is essential to recognize that in seeking to fulfil each of its core functions and responsibilities, public health may burden human rights. Frankly admitting, public health has a long tradition, anchored in the history of infections disease control, of limiting the "rights of the few" for the "good of the many". Hence, coercive measures such as mandatory testing and treatment, quarantine and isolation are considered basic measures of traditional communicable disease control.[78] There is a need to adopt public health concern for human rights norms by promoting societal respect for human rights as well as on arguments of public health effectiveness. Every efforts to harmonize health and human rights goals in other areas are also desirable in order to promote and respect rights and dignity.

---

75. UDHR: Article 21; ICCPR: Article 25; ICESCR: Article 15; CEDAW: Articles 7, 8, 13 and 14.
76. Declaration of *Alma-Ata*: Article IV. Adopted at the International Conference on Primary Health Care, *Alma-Ata*, USSR, 6-12, September 1978. www.who.int/hpr/NPH/docs/declaation-almaata.pdf. (Accessed on 11 November 2009).
77. Emily Friedman, Money is not Everything: Non-financial Barriers to Access, *JAMA*, 271:19 (1994) at 1536.
78. Mann and Gostin, *op. cit*.

(ii) Impact of Human Rights Violation on Health

Health impacts are obvious and inherent in the popular understanding of certain severe human rights violations, such as torture, imprisonment under inhumane conditions, summary execution and 'disappearances'. It is for this reason, health experts are concerned about human rights and are making available their expertise in order to restrict such abuses.[79] There may be numerous examples of this type of medical human rights collaboration which includes: exhumation of mass graves to examine allegations of executions; examination of torture victims,[80] and entry of health personnel into prisons to assess health status.[81] Health impacts of rights violations go beyond these issues in two ways. First, the duration and extent of health impacts resulting from severe abuses of rights and dignity remain generally under-appreciated. Torture, imprisonment under inhuman conditions or trauma associated with witnessing summary executions, torture, rape or imprisonment of others have been shown to lead to severe, probably life long effects on physical, mental and social well-being. The researcher find that torture remains epidemic in dozens of countries around the world. Treatment and prevention programmes are emerging on every continent in response to this epidemic. Second, beyond these serious problems, it is apparently clear that violations of many, if not all, human rights have negative effects on health. The other violations of the right, with substantial health impacts, including governmental withholding of valid scientific health information about contraception or measures to prevent infection with a fatal virus (HIV)[82]

(iii) New Avenues for Human Well-Being

To promote and protect human right is inextricably linked with the challenge of promoting and protecting health derives in part from recognition that health and human rights are complementary approaches to the central problem of defining and advancing human well-being. The broad mention of health in the UDHR (Article 25) and specific health-related responsibilities of states listed in Article 12 of the ICESCR, including: reducing stillbirth and infant mortality and promoting healthy

79. H.R. Geiger and R.M. Cook Deegan, The Role of Physicians in Conflict and Humanitarian Crisis: Case Studies from the Field Missions of Physicians for Human Rights, *JAMA*, 270:5 (1993), 616-620 at 617.
80. R.F. Mollica and Y. Caspi Yavin, Measuring Torture and Torture-Related Symptoms, *Journal of Consulting and Clinical Psychology*, 1991, Vol. 3:4, pp. 581-587, at 582.
81. Timothy Harding, Prevention of Torture and Inhuman or Degrading Treatment: Medical Implications of a New European Convention, *The Lancet* (1989), 1, No. 8648, pp.1191-1193 at 1192.
82. Mann and Gostin, *op. cit.*

child development; improving environmental and industrial hygiene; preventing, treating and controlling epidemic, endemic, occupational and other diseases; and assurance of medical care. Much of the world is enmeshed in violent conflicts, either self-imposed or super-imposed. A great deal of the world's human and financial resources, which could have been used for constructive and welfare purposes of peace and prosperity, is wasted for destructive purposes. This is evidenced by the World Health Report for 2007, which, craving for "A Safer Future", highlights the health consequences of poverty, wars and conflicts and stresses the importance of strengthening health systems in building global public health security. According to the report many of the public health emergencies cold have been prevented or better controlled but for the weaker and ill-prepared health systems. Huge amounts of money are spent on defense sector compared to social service sector. In the year 2007-08 budget of Rs. 96,000 crore was allocated for defense while only Rs. 9,321 crore was allocated social services (which includes education, health care and broadcasting). The researcher find that modern concepts of health recognize that underlying 'conditions' establish the foundation for realizing physical, mental and social well-being. It is, therefore, submitted that from the human rights perspective, health experts and expertise may contribute usefully to societal recognition of the benefits and costs associated with realizing, or failing to respect human rights and dignity. This can be accomplished without seeking to justify human rights and dignity on health grounds. Rather, collaboration with health experts can help give voice to the pervasive and serious impact on health associated with lack of respect for right and dignity. In addition to this, the right to health can only be developed and made meaningful through dialogue between health and human rights disciplines. Finally, the importance of health as a pre-conditions for the capacity to realize and enjoy human rights and dignity must be appreciated.

The author divides this study in to eight chapters. Chapter 1 introduces the subject matter. This chapter is the conceptual study of health as human right, exploring the multi-dimensional nature and various determinants of health. It also analyzes the complex linkages between health and human rights. Chapter 2 is devoted to the gradual development of health status in the past. Chapter 3 is exclusively devoted to various provisions regarding the health care rights. The various articles like Articles of the Constitution namely, 41, 45, 48, etc. relating to health are explained with various judgments. Chapter 4 is devoted to the legal provisions relating to health under various laws like civil, criminal and miscellaneous Acts relating to medical health laws, child health laws occupational health laws, etc. In Chapter 5, various Five Year Plans, programmes and policies and their analysis on health care system are discussed. In Chapter 6, various judgments on the protection of health rights are discussed. Chapter 7 is brief summary of health planning in Himachal Pradesh and analysis of various issues like expenditure during various health plans, availability of infrastructure facilities, standards of health services and treatment patterns. In this chapter, an empirical study of the standards of health right in Shimla town is made. Chapter 8 deals with the conclusion of the study. Some suggestions for certain judicial and legislative action have also been submitted.

CHAPTER 2

Right to Health in Historical Perspective

I. INTRODUCTION

From time immemorial man has been interested in trying to control disease. The medicine man, the priest, the herbolist and the magicians, all undertook in various ways to cure man's disease and/or to bring relief to the sick. In an almost complete absence of scientific medical knowledge, it would not be fair to say that the early practitioners of medicine contributed nothing to the alleviation of man's suffering from disease. Chinese medicine claims to be the world's first organized body of medical knowledge dating back to 2700 BC.[1] It is based on two principles—the *yang* and the *yin*. The *yang* is believed to be an active masculine principle and the *yin* a negative feminine principle. The balance of these two opposing forces meant good health. Similarly, Egypt had one of the oldest civilizations about 2000 BC. In the realm of public health, the Egyptians excelled. They built planned cites, public baths and underground drains which even the modern might envy. Health is a common theme in most cultures. In fact, all communities have their concept of health, as part of their culture. India has also one of the most ancient civilizations in recorded history. Thousands of years before the Christian era, there existed a civilization in the Indus Valley, known as the Indus Valley Civilization. It showed relics of planned cities with drainage, houses and public baths built of baked bricks suggesting the practices of environment at sanitation, by an ancient people as far back as 3000 B.C.[2] India was invaded by the Aryans around 1400 B.C. It was probably during this period, the *Ayurveda* and

1. K. Park, Park's Textbook of Preventive and Social Medicine, 1 and 2 (2005).
2. Jayanti Sengupta, *The Trail*, 27-29 (2005).

the *Siddha* system of medicine came into existence. *Ayurveda* or the science of life developed a comprehensive concept of health.[3] The Manu Samhita prescribed rules and regulations for personal health, dietetics and hygienic ritual at the time of birth and death, and also emphasized the unity of physical, mental and spiritual aspects of Life.[4]

"*Sarve Jana Sukhino Bhavatu*" (May all men be free from disease and may all be healthy) was an ancient saying of the Indian Sages. This concept of happiness has its roots in the ancient Indian philosophy of life, which conceived the oneness and unity of all people wherever they lived. The post-vedic period (600 B.C.-600 A.D.) was dominated by the religious teaching of Buddhism and Jainism.[5] Medical education was introduced in the ancient Universities of Taxila and Nalanda, leading to the titles of *Pranacharya* and *Pranavishara*. A Hospital System was developed for men, women and animals and the system was continued and expanded by King Ashoka.

The next phase in Indian History (650-1850 AD) witnessed the rise and fall of Mughal Empire. The Muslim rulers introduced in India around 1000 A.D., the Arabic system of medicine popularly known as *Unani* system, the origin of which is traced to Greek medicine.[6] The *Unani* system since then became, part of Indian medicine. With changes in the political conditions in India, the torch which was lighted thousands of years ago by the ancient sages grew dim, medical education and medical services became static, and the ancient Universities and hospitals disappeared. After this by the middle of the 18th century, the British had established their rule in India which lasted till 1947.[7]

With the passage of time and development in the field of science and technology, study of health was neglected. But, however, during the past few decades, there has been a reawakening that health is fundamental human right and a worldwide social goal; that it is essential to the satisfaction of basic human needs and to an improved quality of life; and that it is to be attained by all people.[8]

3. Arjun Dev, *Social Science*, 4-6 (2005).
4. *Supra* n. 1 at 2.
5. Domink Wujastyk, *The Roots of Ayurveda* (1998).
6. M.R. Goyal, *Anatomy of Medical Education* (1986).
7. Urmila Thatte and Sharadini Dahanukar, *Ayurveda Unravelled*, 3 (1998).
8. Health Care in India—Indian Health Care Services & Health Industry Study, available on http://indianchild.com/health-care-in-india.htm.

II. RIGHT TO HEALTH DURING ANCIENT ERA

India had played a distinct role in the history of technology and science. The history of technology and science in India as per the present day archaeological evidence, begins with the Indus Valley Civilization which is often referred to as Harappan culture. Harappa along with Mohenjo-daro being the important cities of archaeological value in the Indus Valley. This period is usually called the pre-vedic period. Harappa had established commercial, as well as cultural link with the neighbouring countries in the Central and West Asian regions.[9]

This civilization flourished in Northern and Western India between 2500 B.C. and 1500 B.C. The evidence from the examination of the skulls discovered at Mohenjo-daro and Harappa show that the inhabitants of that time were of the aboriginal proto-australoid type. There are many representations on the seals from Mohenjo-daro and Harappa of a male God horned and three faced, sitting in the posture of a *Yogi*, his legs bent double heel to heel and surrounded by animals. This was perhaps, the proto-type of the *Siva* who is even now treated as the God of Yoga and Medicine.[10]

These excavations at Harappa and Mohenjo-daro bears ample testimony to the proficiency reached by the people of the Indus Valley civilization in matters of sanitation and housing. It appears that both the cities of Harappa and Mohenjo-daro were built after careful planning. Houses were provided with modern amenities like baths, lavatories, drains, fresh-water tanks, courtyards and bedrooms. The main drains could be cleared by lifting a specially made cover prepared of bricks. The whole concept of town-planning shows a remarkable concern for sanitation and public life which was, perhaps, without parallel in those days. All these point out to the high quality of medical science and the concern for the health prevalent at that time in India.[11]

The medical systems that are truly Indian in origin and development are the *Ayurveda* and the *Siddha* systems. *Ayurveda's* origin is traced far back to the vedic times, about 5000 B.C. During this period, medical history was associated with mythological figures, sages and seers. *Dhanvantari*, the Hindu God of medicine is said to have been born as a result of the churning of the oceans during a 'tug of war' between gods and demons. According to some authorities, the medical knowledge in the *Atharvaveda* gradually developed into the science of *Ayurveda*. In ancient India, the celebrated authorities in Ayurvedic medicine were *Atreya*, *Charaka*, *Susruta* and *Veghbhatt*. Atreya (about

9. Bhagwan Dash, *Fundamentals of Ayurvedic Medicine*, 6-7 (1978).
10. Jayanti Sengupta, *op.cit.*, at 27-29.
11. K. Park, *op.cit.*, at 2.

800 BC) is acknowledged as the first great Indian physician and teacher. He lived in the ancient University of Takshashila, about 20 miles west of modern Rawalpindi.[12] Among the many distinguished names in Hindu medicine, that of Susruta, the "father of Indian Surgery" stands out in prominence. He compiled the surgical knowledge of his time in his classic *'Susruta Samhita'*. It is believed that this classic was compiled between 800 BC and 400 AD.

The post-vedic period was also dominated by the religious teaching of Buddhism and Jainism. Ayurveda witnessed tremendous growth and development during the Buddhist time. King Ashoka and the other Buddhist Kings patronized Ayurveda as a state medicine and established schools of medicine and public hospitals.[13] Of significance in Ayurveda is the "*tridosha* theory of disease". The *doshas* or humors are: *Vata* (wind), *Pitta* (gall) and *Kapha* (Mucus). Disease was explained as a disturbance in the equilibrium of the three humors; when these were in perfect balance and harmony, a person is said to be healthy.[14] Hygiene was given an important place in ancient Indian medicine. The laws of Manu were a code of personal hygiene. Medical historians admit that Indian medicine has played in Asia the same role as the Greek medicine in the west.[15]

The broad objectives of medical education were well defined during this period. Although treatment of the sick was considered important and primary, due emphasis was also placed on preventive and promotive aspects of health care. Medicine was divided into two broad categories—one was for the promotion of vigour in the healthy and other for the destruction of disease in the ailing, as quoted in the Charaka Samhita. In the ancient scriptures surgery also formed part of the practice medicine. The practical skill for this used to be imparted through well-planned practical exercises mentioned in the writings of Sushruta.[16]

After the final qualifying examination, the students were granted licence to practice by the King. Sushruta (Sutra 10.10) tells us that requisite qualifications of the physician were "Having studied, the science, having fully grasped the meaning, having acquired practical skills, and having performed the operations on dummies, with ability to teach the science and with the King's permission, a physician should

12. J.N. Banerjee (1966), *Ind. J. Med. Edu.* 5, 79 quoted in K. Park, *Ibid.*
13. K. Park, *op. cit.*, at 2.
14. P. Kutumbiah (1956), *Ind. J. Hist. Med.*, 2, 70, quoted in K. Park, *op.cit.*, at 2.
15. Davis and Parke, *Great Moments in Medicine: A History of Medicine in Pictures* (1961).
16. *Supra* n. 5 at 4.

enter his profession".[17]

Thus, it is only a Ayurveda originated in India long back in pre-vedic period which deals with measure for hèalthful living and principles for maintenance of health, it has also developed a wide range of the therapeutic measures to combat illness. These principles of positive health and therapeutic measures relate to physical, mental, social and spiritual welfare of human beings.[18]

III. RIGHT TO HEALTH DURING MEDIEVAL ERA

In medieval era, the Muslim rulers introduced the Arabic system of medicine, popularly known as Unani system, the origin of which is raced to Greek medicine. With changes in the political conditions in India, the torch which was lighted thousands of years ago by the ancient sages grew dim, medical education and medical services became static, and the ancient Universities and hospitals disappeared.[19] During the Mughal period, Ayurveda declined due to lack of state support.

It was a period of compilation than of original contribution. Many works were destroyed during this period, either by invaders or also by quarrelling Hindu and Buddhist parties, who obviously had lost the true understanding of their faith. In many ways, this was a decadent period of Indian History, the consequences of which are still felt even today.[20] To reiterate, the Unani Tibb System of medicine, whose origin is traced to the ancient Greek medicine, was introduced into India by the Muslim rulers about the 10th century A.D. By the 13th century, the Unani system of medicine was firmly entrenched in certain towns and cities notably Delhi, Aligarh, Lucknow and Hyderabad.[21] It enjoyed State support under successive Muslim rulers in India, till the advent of the British in the 18th century.

During this period, there was no specific codes for medical treatment of physical illness in the Quran. Muslims have historically sought the Quran as a healing source in times of psychological and spiritual distress. When experiencing physical illness, Muslims have also been open to the rituals and medicinal practices of different traditions. The following sayings of the Prophet are used to encourage patients to seek proper treatment in times of illness that "There is no

17. Michael Dick, *The Ancient Ayurvedic Writings*, available on site http://www.fact-inder.com/sushruta.html.
18. Department of Ayurveda, Yoga & Naturopathy, Unani, Sidha and Homeopathy, http://indianmedicne.nic.in/html/ismh/annual/annual.htm.
19. K. Park, *op. cit.*, at 679.
20. Bhagwan Dash, Acarya Manfred M. Junius, A Hand Book of Ayurveda, 10 (1988).
21. J.N. Banerjee (1966) *Ind. J. Med. Edu.* 5, 79 quoted in K. Park, *op. cit.*, at 2.

disease that Allah has created except that he also has created its remedy".[22] "Taking proper care of one's health is the right of the body".[23] "The Prophet not only instructed sick people to take medicine, he himself invited expert physicians for this purpose".[24]

So in contrast to modern western civilization, the Islamic traditions does not separate science from religion. They thought that traditions of the prophet Muhammad are saturated with reference to learning, education observation and the use of reason in all realms of life-medicine and the health care included. Islam teaches individuals and societies how to live a physically, mentally legal system derived from the Quran and Sunnah (tradition of the Prophet) aims at creating a healthy environment that will have a positive effect on an individual's physical, mental and spiritual development. At a physical level, the Quran and Sunnah encourage healthy eating, at the same time forbid all substances that cause bodily harm; intoxicants, drugs and so forth. Fruits and vegetables, dates, yogurt, camel milk, natural honey, black seeds and the like are especially emphasized for their matritious quality and health benefits. The Quran also addresses various diseases, especially of the heart, which often lead to direct and indirect physical and mental ailments. It mentions blindness, deafness, lameness and leprosy as well as mental disorders including psychoses and neurotic diseases, such as sadness and anxiety. But its primary focus is on moral and ethical diseases.[25] The Quran itself is referred to as book of healing. Thus, during pre-modern era, Islamic medical and other sciences leaned heavily upon local medical practices, as well as on works translated from Greek. These influences resulted in the further advancement of medical sciences, especially in the 11th and 12th century.[26]

IV. RIGHT TO HEALTH DURING BRITISH PERIOD

By the middle of 18th century, the British had established their rule in India which lasted till 1947. The credit for introducing modern medicines goes to Britishers in this country. At first, the aim was largely to train apprentices to help the army medical personnel, the qualifications required of such trainees being of an elementary nature. In

22. Volume 7, Book 71, Number 58.
23. Bukhari as – Sawm.55, an-Nikah 89, Muslim as – Siyyam 183, 193, Nisai.
24. Do. H. p. 50, As-Suyutis Medicine of the Prophet, p.125.
25. Ahmad F. Yousif : Muslim Medicine and Health Care, www.truthandgrace.com/muslim medicine.htm.
26. Nayer Teheri, Pre-Modern Medicine in Islamic Experience : May 2008 : Deptt. of Spirtual Care Harborview Medical Centre Reviewed by Jamal Rahman, Muslim. Sufi Minister, Cominister at Inter Faith Community Church in Seattle, Washington.

the year 1825, the Quarantine Act was promulgated and in 1859, a Royal Commission was appointed to investigate the causes of the extremely unsatisfactory condition of health in British Army stationed in India. The Commission recommended the establishment of a 'Commission of Public Health' in each Presidency and pointed out the need for the protection of water supplies, construction of drains and prevention of epidemics in the civil population for safeguarding the health of the British Army. In 1864, sanitary Commissioners were appointed in the three major provinces, *viz.*, Bombay, Madras and Bengal. The Civil Surgeons/District Medical Officers became *ex-officio* District Health Officers. Further, Public Health Commissioner and a Statistical Officer were appointed with the Government of India in 1869. After that a plethora of legislations, namely, Birth and Registration Act, 1883; the Vaccination Act, 1880; Indian Factories Act, 1881; the Local Self-Government Act, 1885; the Epidemic Diseases Act, 1897; the Madras Public Health Act, 1939; the Drugs Act, 1940, etc. were enacted by the Britishers to improve the health conditions of the citizens.

It is also crystal clear that the Government of India in 1858 directed that sanitation should be looked after by the local bodies, but no local public health staff was created to look after sanitation. It is in the year 1912 that the Government of India decided to help the local bodies with grants, and also sanctioned the appointment of Deputy Sanitary Commissioners and Health Officers. In the Motague-Chelmsford Constitutional Reforms led to the transfer of public health, sanitation and vital statistics to the provinces under the control of an elected minister. This was the first step towards elected minister. This was the first step towards decentralization of health administration in India.

The Government of India in 1943 appointed the Health Survey and Development Committee under the Chairmanship of Sir Joseph Bhore to survey the existing position in regard to health conditions and health organization in the country, and to make recommendations for the future development. The committee laid emphasis on integration of curative and preventive medicine at all levels. It also suggested short term measure, that is, one primary health centre for a population of 40,000. Each Primary Health Centre was to be manned by two doctors, one nurse, four public health nurses, four midwives, four trained *dais*, two sanitary inspectors, two health assistants, one pharmacist and fifteen class IV employees. On the other hand, it suggested long term programme of setting up primary health units with 75 bedded hospitals for each 10,000 to 20,000 population and secondary units with 650 bedded hospital, again regionalized around district hospitals with 2500 beds.[27]

Besides this, in the middle of nineteenth century, three Universities, namely, Calcutta, Bombay and Madras were established in order to provide better health facilities to the subjects. In 1914, the Madras Medical College started training to First Class Health Officers. The medical education in this country continued to be guided for a long time by British pattern of medical education as laid down by the General Medical Council of Great Britain. It took one hundred years to establish 27 medical colleges which we inherited at the time of Independence in 1947.

V. RIGHT TO HEALTH IN POST-INDEPENDENCE ERA

India became independent in 1947. For the first time in India's long history, a democratic regime was set up with its economy geared to a new concept, the establishment of a "Welfare State". The burden of improving the health of the people, and widening scope of health measures fell upon the national government. The Bhore Committee's report and recommendations became the basis for most of the planning and measures adopted by the national government. In 1947, Ministers of Health were established at the Centre and States and in 1948 India joined the World Health Organization as a member-state. In 1949, the Constituent Assembly adopted the Constitution of India. Article 246 of the Constitution of India covers all the health subjects; these have been enumerated in the Seventh Schedule under three lists—Union List, Concurrent List and State List. Article 47 of the Constitution under the Directive Principles of State Policy states; "that the State; shall regard the raising of the level of nutrition and the standard of living of its people and the improvement of public health as among its primary duties."

Truly admitting that the public health during the 19th century was largely a matter of sanitary legislation and sanitary reforms aimed at the control of man's physical environment, e.g., water supply, sewage disposal, etc. clearly these measures were not aimed at the control of any specific disease, for want of the needed technical knowledge. However, these measures vastly improved the health of the people due to disease and death control.[28]

At the beginning of the 20th century, a new concept, the concept of "Health Promotion" began to take shape. It was realized that public

27. For more details see, Bhore Committee, 1946.
28. K. Park, *op. cit.*, at 7.

health had neglected the citizen as an individual, and that the State had a direct responsibility for the health of the individual. Consequently, in addition to disease control activities, one more goal was added to public health, that is, health promotion of individuals. It was initiated as personal health service; such as mother and child health services, school health services, industrial health services, mental health and rehabilitation services. Public health nursing was a direct off-shoot of this concept. Public health departments began expanding their programmes towards health promotional activities. (C.E.A.) Winslow, one of the leading figures in the history of public health, in 1920, defined public health as "the science and art of preventing disease, prolonging life and promoting health and efficiency through organized community effort". This definition summarizes the philosophy of public health, which remains largely true even today.[29]

Since the state had assumed direct responsibility for the health of the individual, two great movements were initiated for human development during the first half of the previous century, namely, (A) provision of "basic health services" through the medium of primary health centres and sub-centres for rural and urban areas. The evolution of health centres were an important development in the history of public health.[30] In 1981, the League of Nations Health Organization called for the establishment of health centres. The Bhore Committee (1946) in India had also recommended the establishment of health centres for providing integrated curative and preventive services. Many developing countries have given the highest priority to the establishment of health centres for providing basic health services.[31] (B) The second great movement was the Community Development Programme to promote village development through the active participation of the whole community and on the initiative of the community. This programme tried to do too much too quickly with inadequate resources. It was a great opportunity lost, because it failed to survive. However, the establishment of primary health centres and sub-centres provided the much-needed infrastructure of health services, especially in the rural areas.[32]

With the advances in preventive medicine and practice of public health, the pattern of disease began to change in the developed world.

---

29. *Ibid.*
30. M.I. Roemer, Public Health Papers (1972), No. 48, Geneva, WHO.
31. M.R. Goyal, *op. cit.*, at 6.
32. R. Fendall, World Health Forum (1984), p. 300, also see Health Care in India — Indian Health Care Services and Health Industry Study. (Data 1995. Courtesy Library of Congress), available on site http://indianchild.com/health-care-in-india.htm.

Many of the acute illness problems have been brought under control. However, as old problems were solved, new health problems in the form of chronic diseases began to emerge, e.g. cancer, diabetes, cardiovascular diseases, alcoholism and drug addiction, etc. especially in the affluent societies. These problems could not be tackled by the traditional approaches to public health such as isolation, immunization and disinfection nor could these be explained on the basis of the goom theory of disease.[33] A new concept, the concept of "risk factors" as determinants of these diseases, into existence. The consequences of these diseases, unlike the swift death brought by the acute infectious diseases, was to place a chronic burden on the society that created them. These problems brought new challenges to public health which needed reorientation more towards social objectives.[34]

Social and behavioural aspects of disease and behavioural problems. In this process, the goals of public heath and preventive medicine which had already considerable overlapping became identical, namely, prevention of disease, promotion of health and prolongation of life. In short, although the term "public health" is still used, its original meaning has changed. In view of its changed meaning and scope, the term "Community Health" has been preferred by some leaders in public health. Community health incorporates services to the population at large as opposed to preventive or social medicine.[35]

In 1950, the Planning Commission of India was set-up by the Government of India, which set to work immediately for drafting the First Five Year Plan. In the First Five Year Plan with a total outlay of Rs. 2356 crores, a sum of Rs. 140 crores (5.9 percent) was allotted for health programmes. In the year 1954, a number of Health Schemes and programmes were started, namely, Contributory Health Service Scheme; National Water Supply and Sanitation Programme; the National Leprosy Control Programme, etc. Similarly, the Second Five Year Plan (1956-61) was launched with an outlay of Rs. 4800 crores, out of which Rs. 225 crores (5.0 percent) were earmarked for health programmes.

In 1959, Mudaliar Committee was appointed by the Government of India to survey the progress made in the field of health since submission of the Bhore Committee's Report, and to make recommendations for future development and expansion of health services. The Committee submitted its report in 1962. This committee found the conditions of Primary Health Centres to unsatisfactory and suggested that the Primary Health Centres, already established should be strengthened before new

33. K. Park, *op. cit.*, at 8.
34. C.L. Anderson, Community Health, 148 (1978).
35. K. Park, *op. cit.*, at 8.

ones are opened. In 1960, the School Health Committee was constituted to assess the present standards of health and nutrition of school children and suggest ways and means to improve them.

The Third Five Year Plan (1961-66) was launched with an outlay of Rs. 7500 crores out of which 342 crores (4.3 percent) were provided for health programmes. During this plan, three committees were constituted, viz. Shantilal Shah Committee, 1964; Chadha Committee, 1963; and Mukherjee Committee, 1966. Chadha Committee suggested that the vigilance activity in National Malaria Eradication Programme should be carried out by basic health workers (one per 10,000 population), who would function as multipurpose workers.

The Shatilal Shah Committee was set-up with a view to study the question for legalising abortions. The Mukherjee Committee worked out the details of Basic Health Services which should be provided at the block level, and some consequential strengthening required at higher levels of administration. Another Committee, known as the "Committee on Integration of Health Services" was set-up in 1964 under the Chairmanship of Dr. N. Jungalwala. The Committee was asked to look into various problems related to integration of health services in the country. The Modhok Committee, 1967 was constituted to review the working of the National Malaria Eradication Programme and recommended measures for improvement.

In 1969, the Fourth Five Year Plan (1969-74) was launched with an outlay of Rs. 16,774 crores, out of which Rs. 840 crores were allocated to health and Rs. 315 crores to family planning. During this plan, three legislations, namely, the Central Births and Death Registration Act, 1969; The Drugs (Price Control) Order, 1970; and the Medical Termination of Pregnancy Act, 1972 were promulgated. In 1973, the Kartar Singh Committee submitted its report recommending the formation of a new cadre of health workers designated "Multi-purpose Health Workers" for the delivery of health, family planning and nutrition services to the rural communities, who will replace in course of time the basic health workers, family planning, health assistants, auxiliary-nurse-mid-wives etc.

The National Programme of Minimum needs was incorporated in the Fifth Five Year Plan. A provision of Rs. 2803 crores was made for this programme which covered elementary education, rural health, nutrition, rural roads and water supply, housing, slum improvement and rural electrification. The Fifth Five Year Plan was launched on April 1974 with a total outlay of Rs. 53,411 crores of which Rs. 37,250 crores were in the public sector and Rs. 16,161 crores in the private sector. A sum of Rs. 796 crores were allotted to health and Rs. 516 crores to family planning. Shrivastava Committee set-up in 1974 to reorient medical education with national needs and priorities. The committee submitted its report in 1975. The acceptance of the recommendations of the Shrivastava Committee in 1977 led to launching of the Rural Health Service.

In 1980, the Sixth Five Year Plan (1980-85) was launched and in 1982 the Government of India announced the National Health Policy. National Leprosy Control Programme to be called National Leprosy Eradication Programme. Guinea-worm eradication programmes was launched.

The Seventh Five Year Plans (1985-90) was launched in 1985. Under this plan, Universal Immunization Programme, National Diabetes Control Programme and National AIDS Programme were initiated. An "Expert Committee for Health Manpower Planning, Production and Management" was constituted in 1985 under Dr. J.S. Bajaj, the then Professor at AIIMS. The major recommendations are:

(i) Formulation of National Medical and Health Education Policy.
(ii) Formulation of National Health Manpower Policy.
(iii) Establishment of an Educational Commission for Health Sciences (ECHS) on the lines of UGC.
(iv) Establishment of Health Science Universities in various states and Union Territories.
(v) Establishment of Health Manpower Cells at Centre and in the States.
(vi) Vocationalization of Education at 10+2 levels as regards health-related fields with appropriate incentives, so that good quality paramedical personnel may be available in adequate numbers.
(vii) Carrying out a realistic health manpower survey.

In 1989, Blood Safety Programme was launched. In 1990, Control of Acute Respiratory Infection (ARI) Programme initiated as a pilot project in 14 districts. Eighth Five Year Plan (1992-97) was launched in 1992. During this plan, few legislations, namely the Infant Milk Substitute, Feeding Bottles and Infant Foods (Regulation of Production, Supply and Distribution) Act, 1992; Panchayati Raj Act, 1994; Transplantation of Human Organs, 1995; and Prenatal Diagnostic Technique (Regulation and Prevention of Misuse) Act, 1994 came into force.

In 1997, Ninth Five Year Plan was launched. During 1998-99, National Family Health Survey-2 undertaken covering 90,000 women aged 15-49 years and Phase II of National AIDS Control Programme became effective. In 2000, the Government of India declared guinea worm free country and National Health Policy 2002 was announced. Further, the Government announced National AIDS Prevention and Control Policy 2002. The Tenth Five Year Plan was launched in 2003.

Overall, the health sector budget has been increased marginally from Rs. 19,534 crore in 2009 fiscal to Rs. 22,300 crore this time—a raise of 14.15 percent. The National Rural Health Mission has managed Rs. 13,910 crore, up from Rs. 12,529 crore last time.[36] This little budgetary raise the health ministry has been for the construction of six new AIIMS—like institutes and the upgradation of 13 existing government medical colleges.

The Government of India is already aware of the positive role and contribution of the indigenous systems of medicine in providing health care to Indian masses. The Government had created necessary infrastructure in the Central Ministry of Health for the promotion of Indian System of Medicine. From the very beginning, it had established the colleges, hospitals and dispensaries under the various systems of medicine and had granted them a status equal to that of modern medicine by treating all practitioners of various systems on an equal footing in terms of employment, pay structure, etc.[37] The Government of India has also set-up a separate Council known as the Council for Indian Medicine to look after and regulate the indigenous medical education standards in the country. A separate Council on the pattern of ICMR (Indian Council of Medical Research) the Council for Research in Indian Medicine is Homeopathy has also been established to develop and promote basic and applied research in different systems of Indian medicine.[38]

Naturopathy, Homeopathy and yoga today is a rapidly growing system and is being practiced almost all over the world. Naturopathy nature care is a way of life of which we find a number of references in the Vedas and our ancient texts. It is a system of healing science stimulating the body's inherent power to regain health with the help of five great elements of nature—Earth, Water, Air, Fire, Ether or Space. Naturopathy is a call to "Return to Nature" and to resort to simple way of living in harmony with self, society and environment. This nature care deals with the drugless therapies like message, electrotherapy, physiotherapy, acupuncture and acupressure, magneto therapy, etc.[39]

---

36. *The Tribune*, February 27, 2010, pp. 1 and 9.
37. M.R. Goyal, *op. cit.*, at 9.
38. *Ibid.*
39. http://indianmedicine.nic.in//html/nature/nature.htm. (access on).

Homeopathy in India has become a household name due to belief in the safety of its pills and gentleness of its cure. A rough study indicates that about 10 percent of the Indian population solely depend on homeopathy for their health care needs. It is more than a century and a half now that homeopathy is being practiced in India. It has blended so well into the roots and traditions of the country that it has been recognized as one of the national system of medicine and plays an important role in providing health care to large number of people.[40]

The tradition of yoga was born in India several thousand years ago. Its founders were great saints and sages. The great yogis gave rational interpretation of their experiences about yoga and brought a practically sound and scientifically prepared method within every one's reach.[41] Yoga was systematized by the great Indian sage 'Patanjali' in the Yoga Sutra as a special Darshana. Yoga is a science as well as art of healthy living physically, mentally, morally and spiritually. All the systems of medicine at their best aim at curing the disease, whereas yoga aims at preventing the disease and promoting health by reconditioning the psycho-physiological mechanism of the individual. The approach of yoga is not confirmed to various disorders. It aims at bringing under perfect control of the mind senses and pranic energy and direct them towards healthier channels with a view to acquire mental purity, intellectual stability and spiritual bliss.[42]

Unlike earlier, Yoga today is no longer restricted to privileged minority of hermits; it has taken its place in our every day lives and have undergone a worldwide awakening and acceptance in the last few decades. The science of yoga and its techniques have now been re-oriented to suit modern sociological needs and lifestyle. Experts of various branches of medicine including modern medical science are realizing the role of these techniques in the prevention of disease and promotion of health.[43]

40. http://indianmedicine.nic.in/htm/homeopathy//homoe.htm. (accessed on).
41. http://indianmedicine.nic.in/htm/yoga/yoga.htm. (accessed on).
42. *Ibid*. Maharashi Patanjali called the 'Father of Yoga' advocated the eight-fold path of yoga, popularly known as "Ashtanga Yoga", for all round development of human personality. The practice of Yamas-Niyamas is harmlessness towards all living beings, truthfulness, honesty, celibacy, on-hoarding of wordly objects, cleanliness, contentment, austerity, control of lust anger and infatuation, study of holy books and practice of japa and selfless action—all these pave way for increasing the power of concentration, mental purity and steadiness. Karma yoga, the path of work, involves doing action in a skillful way. It can be said as a way of enjoying work, doing it effortlessly.
43. Today, Swami Ramdev has worldwide immensely contributed in spreading awareness about health benefits through yoga.

VI. SUM UP

The foregoing study clearly reveals that during early period, Ayurveda was perhaps the only system of overall health care and medicine which served well the people in such crucial areas as health, sickness, life and death. It also enjoy the support of the people. Then followed a long period of medieval history marked by unsettled political conditions and several invasions from outside the country and soon health system faced utter neglect.[44]

With the awakening of nationalism and movement for freedom the Indian culture values and way of life (including health care and sickness cure system) suffered again. After the country became free in 1947, the movement for revival gained additional momentum. The first Health Ministers' Conference resolved that health care system to the people should be developed. In due course of time this system got official recognition and became a part of the National Health Network of the country.[45]

Now, India has moved forward in advocating global usefulness of Ayurveda contemporary scenario of health care through global networks. As a result, many foreign countries have began looking to India for understanding Ayurveda and incorporating it through education, research and practice to meet the overwhelming desire of consumers to access complementary and alternative medicine. Indian Missions in USA, UK, Russia, Germany, Hungary, South Africa have played an effective role in channeling the information of Ayurveda and opening up new opportunities for the spread of Indian Medicine into foreign institutions and the general public awareness building about Ayurveda in the foreign countries has been identified as an important thrust area.

44. Department of Ayurveda, Yoga and Naturopathy, Unani, Sidha, and Homeopathy. Available on site http://indianmedicne.nic.in/html/ayurveda/ayurveda.htm.
45. *Ibid.*

CHAPTER 3

Constitutional Protection to Health Care Rights

I. INTRODUCTION

The right to health care is an age-old phenomenon. It is said that 'Health is Wealth' and a healthy body is the very foundation of all human activities. The proverb, "Health is Wealth" has assumed more significance in contemporary societies across the globe. Resurgence of scientific, technological, industrial and economic revolutions in the world have brought all-around development of societies. Alongwith it, they also posed threat to life, environment and health of people. No nation can develop and prosper unless a society is physically, morally and politico-legally sound and healthy.

Life of individual is a nature's gift to whole mankind, which is to be preserved, protected and prospered. Right to life as a natural, fundamental and human right has become an integral part of every positive legal order in the world. Right to Life is, in fact, dependent upon the health of an individual. In other words, right to health is a pre-requisite of right to life and live with human dignity. Universal achievement of 'Health for All' has gained importance among nations of the world, as health is declared to be an essential part of right to life.

Health, the once forgotten entity both at the National and International levels, is considered as a worldwide social goal today. It is supposed to be essential to the satisfaction of the basic human needs and to an improved quality of life. The International community is bound to face the denting task of assuring and providing adequate health care to its ever growing population. Although, the right to health has been internationally recognized as a fundamental basic human right, the national strategies adopted by the nation-states for its realization have not been adequate. 'Health Services' is not a mere charity or the privilege of a few but a right to be enjoyed by all.[1]

Although, right to health has not been explicitly stated as a separate fundamental right under the Indian Constitution. But the Preamble to the Constitution of India, 1950 establishes India as socialistic and welfare state. The basic framework of socialism is to provide a decent standard of life to the working people and especially provide security from cradle to grave.[2]

The Constitution of India not only provides for the health care of the people but also directs the State to take measures to improve the condition of health care rights of the people.[3] Thus, the Preamble to the Constitution of India, *inter alia*, seeks to secure for all its citizens justice—social and economic. It provides a framework for the achievement of the objectives laid down in the Preamble. The Preamble has been amplified and elaborated in the Directive Principles of State Policy. These Directive Principles of State Policy direct the government to promote health of all people in general and vulnerable sections of the society in particular. The only right that is relatable to the right to health is the right to life guaranteed in Article 21 of the Constitution. The Supreme Court by its innovative judicial interpretation has expanded the meaning and scope of the word 'life' in Article 21 of the Constitution and has brought the right to health under the purview of right to life. The Court has held that a healthy body is the very foundation for all human activities. In a Welfare State, therefore, it is the obligation of the State to ensure the creation and the sustaining of conditions congenial to the good health.

II. CONSTITUTIONAL RIGHT TO A HEALTHY LIFE

Constitutional law is the Supreme *lex* of a nation which prescribes fundamental principles to regulate the relations of government and its citizens, and also to chart out plan and method according to which the public affairs of the nation are to be administered. The Constitution also provides citizens rights and freedoms, which could also be enjoyed within the reasonable limits of the Constitution. It is true that life is glorious gift from God. It is the perfection of nature, a masterpiece of creation. It is majestic and sublime. Human being is the epitome of the

1. Butter Worths, Legal Framework for Health Care in India, 1 (2002).
2. Md. Zafar Mahfooz Nomani, Socio-Legal Dimensions of Right to Health, p. 56.
3. Articles 39 and 47.

infinite prowess of the divine designer.

In India, the members of the Drafting Committee of the Constitution were of the opinion that in any industry which making consumer goods or in a social service, like education or health, there is danger to monopolists creating strong private interest which it will never be in the interests of the country to tolerate. With regard to health or the production of drugs or making medicines, or the supply of surgical and other instruments and apparatuses there is a danger of our country being dominated by private monopolists, that is they wanted to give the power to the representative of the people.[4] The founding fathers of the Constitution intended to save women from exploitation, who works in factories and mines and for this they tried further to add the word 'health' alongwith word 'strength' of the worker in Article 31 clause (v) in the Draft Constitution.[5]

The State is under an obligation to take all steps for improvement of public health and safeguard the right to life of every person.[6] To further strengthen it, the State now has directed to ensure free and compulsory education to all children upto 14 years of age under Article 45.[7] In the wake of Human Rights the ambit and scope of this Constitutional right is ever widening. Now the State is mandated to provide to a person all rights essential for the enjoyment of the right to life in its various perspectives of late, the right to health and access to medical treatment has been included in the plethora of rights brought under the ambit of Article 21.

Article 21 of the Constitution of India is one of the articles where, the higher courts have constantly applied their minds and the scope of this article is growing year after year. Hence, as on today, right to life also includes right to good health and right to a reasonable health care

4. Constituent Assembly Debates of India, Draft Constitution, Vol. VII, January 4-8, 1948 at 510.

5. *Id.*, at 512. In the Draft Constitution, the clause reads as follows: "The State shall .... Direct its policy toward securing ... that citizens are not forced by economic necessity to enter avocations unsuited to their age or strength." It has been after deliberations embodied in the Constitution in Article 39(e).

6. In *M. Vijaya* v. *The Chairman and Managing Director Singareni Collieries*, AIR 2001 AP 502; para 52. The Andhra Pradesh High Court, held that it was necessary for the State to identify HIV+ve cases and any action taken in that regard could not be termed as unconstitutional, Chief Justice S.B. Sinha, alongwith Justices B. Subhashan Reddy, Dr. Motilal B. Naik, Bilal Nazki and V.V.S. Rao, delivered the judgment.

7. 86th Amendment Act, 2007 added Article 21A making education a fundamental right for all children in the age group 6 to 14 years old. Also under Article 51A(K) of Part IV, a duty is enjoined upon every parent or guardian to provide opportunities for education to his child or as the case may be, ward between the age of six and 14 years.

system that is, medical aid, health, insurance, while in service or after retirement was a fundamental right under Article 21.

With the recognition that both the Preamble of Constitution and the fundamental right to life in Article 21 emphasize the value of human dignity, the Supreme Court began to address the importance of health as a fundamental right.[8] The Constitutional directives contained in Articles 39(e), (f), 42 and 47 in Part-IV of the Constitution of India cast the obligation on the State to ensure the creation and the sustaining of conditions congenial to good health.

In the Directive Principles in Part IV of the Constitution, Article 47 declares that:

> "State shall regard the raising of the level of nutrition and the standard of living of its people and the improvement of public health as among its primary duties".[9] It bring about prohibition of the consumption, except for medicinal purposes, of intoxicating drinks and of drugs which are injurious to health. Under this article, the consumption of cigarettes and other tobacco products which are injurious to health and with a view to achieving improvement of public health are brought under its purview. Keeping this in view, the Cigarettes and other Tobacco Products Act, 2003 (COTPA) is drafted primarily to include demand-reduction strategies geared to prevent new entrants to tobacco use.

In addition to Article 47, the right to health also has its reference in Articles 38 (social order to promote the welfare of the people), 39(e) (health workers, men, women and children must be protected against abuse), 41 (right to public assistance in certain cases, including sickness and disability) and 48A (the State's duty to protect the environment) of the directive principles. In a series of cases dealing with the substantive content of the right to life the Court has found that the right to live with human dignity includes the right to good health.[10]

Compared to some of the other social rights, the right to health has been articulated and recognized as an integral part of the right to life, only from the mid-nineties by the Indian Supreme Court. It was in 1995

8. Jayna Kothari, *Social Rights and Constitution* (2004), 6 SCC (Journal section), p. 32.
9. See, Constitution of India; Article 47.
10. *Vincent Panikurlangara* v. *Union of India*, (1987), 2 SCC 165; *Paschim Banga Khet Mazdoor Samity* v. *State of W.B.*, (1966) 4 SC 37; *Murli S. Deora* v. *Union of India*, (2001) 8 SCC 765; *Consumer Education and Research Centre* v. *Union of India*, (1995), 3 SCC 42; *M.C. Mehta* v. *Union of India*, (1999) 6 SCC 9; *'X'* v. *Hospital 'Z'*, (2003) 1 SCC 500; *Parmananda Katara* v. *Union of India*, (1989), 4 SCC 286.

in *Consumer Education and Research Centre* v. *Union of India*,[11] that the Supreme Court for the first time explicitly held that "the right to health is an integral facet of (a) meaningful right to life".[12]

This case dealt with the occupational health hazards faced by workers in the asbestos industry. Reading Article 21[13] with the relevant Directive Principles guaranteed in Articles 39(e),[14] 41[15] and 43,[16] the Supreme Court held that the right to health and medical care is a fundamental right and it makes the life of the workman meaningful and purposeful with the dignity of person.[17]

This recognition established a framework for addressing health concerns within the republic of public interest litigation and in a series of subsequent cases, the Court held that it is the obligation of the State not only to provide emergency medical services but also to ensure the creation of conditions necessary for good health, including provisions for basic curative and preventive health services and the assurance of healthy living and working conditions.[18]

Very significantly, while adjudicating on the social right to health, the Supreme Court has specifically considered the issue of availability of resources and has rejected the argument that social rights are non-enforceable due to shortage of resources. In *Paschim Banga Khet Mazdoor Samity Case*,[19] the Court addressed the issue of adequacy and

---

11. (1995) 3 SCC 922. Timely medical aid has been recently, held by the Supreme Court to be a right guaranteed under Article 21 as a right to life. See, *Kirloskar Brothers Ltd.* v. *Employees State Insurance Corporation*, AIR 1996 SC 3261.
12. *Id.*, at SCC, p.70, para 24.
13. Article 21, "No person shall be deprived of his life or personally liberty except according to procedure established by law".
14. Article 39(e) provides: "The State shall, in particular, direct it policy towards securing that the health and strength of workers—men, and women, and the tender age of children are not abused and that citizens are not forced by the economic necessity to enter avocations unsuited to their age or strength."
15. Article 41 requires that "the State shall within the limits of its economic capacity and development, make effective provisions, for securing the right to work, to education and to public assistance in cases of unemployment, old age, sickness and disablement, and in other cases of undeserved want".
16. Article 43 provides: "The State shall endeavour to secure, by suitable legislation or economic organization or in any other way, to all workers, agricultural, industrial or otherwise, work a living wage, conditions of work ensuring a decent standard of life and full enjoyment of leisure and social cultural opportunities and in particular, the State shall endeavour to promote cottage industries on an individual or cooperative basis in rural areas."
17. J.N. Pandey, *The Constitutional Law of India*, 262-63 (2003).
18. *Ibid.*
19. *Paschim Banga Khet Mazdoor Samity* v. *State of W.B.*, (1986) SC 2426; see also, *Consumer Education & Research Centre* v. *Union of India*, AIR 1995 SC 922,

availability of emergency in medical treatment. In this case, Hakim Sheikh, a member of the Paschim Banga Khet Mazdoor Samity, fell-off a train and suffered serious head injuries. He was brought to a number of State hospitals, including both primary health centres and specialist clinics, for treatment of his injuries because of lack of bed space and trauma, and neurological services. He was finally taken to a private hospital where he received his treatment. Feeling aggrieved by the callous and insensitive attitude of the government hospitals in Calcutta in providing emergency treatment the petitioner filed a petition in the Supreme Court and sought compensation. The issue presented to the Court was whether the lack of adequate medical facilities for emergency treatment constituted a denial of the fundamental right to life under Article 21.[20]

It was held that Article 21 of the Constitution casts an obligation on the State to take every measure to preserve life. The Court found that it is the primary duty of a welfare state to ensure that medical facilities are adequate and available to provide treatment and for the violation of the right to life of the petitioner, compensation was awarded to him.[21]

In the instant case, the Supreme Court recognized that financial resources are needed for providing these facilities, but Justice S.C. Agrawal held:

> "But at the same time it can not be ignored that it is the Constitutional obligation of the State to provide adequate medical services to the people. The Court recognized that substantial expenditure was needed to ensure that medical facilities were adequate. However, it held that a State could not avoid this constitutional obligation on account of financial constraints. Whatever is necessary for this purpose has to be done. In the context of the constitutional obligation to provide free legal aid to a poor accused this Court has held that the State cannot avoid its constitutional obligation in that regard on account of financial constraints. The said observations would apply with equal, if not

---

Wherein the Supreme Court held that health insurance, while in service or after retirement, was a fundamental right under Article 21.

20. J.N. Pandey, *op. cit.*, at 228.

21. This was held following a previous case concerning emergency medical treatment in *Parmananda Katara* v. *Union of India*, (1989) 4 SCC 286. The case concerned the availability of emergency medical treatment for a seriously injured man at a local hospital. The hospital doctors refused to provide the man with emergency aid and sent him to another hospital twenty kilometers away. The injured man died en route to the other hospital. The Court required the State to remove legal impediments imposed on doctors and hospitals for providing emergency medical aid.

greater, force in the matter of discharge of constitutional obligation of the State to provide medical aid to preserve human life".[22]

Hence, not only did Agrawal, J. reiterate that the State has to strive towards enforcement and guaranteeing of social rights irrespective of financial constraints, but also that the need for resources arises also in the matter of enforcement of civil/political rights. The Court in *Paschim Banga Case*,[23] also required the State to ensure that primary health centres are equipped to provide immediate stabilising treatment for serious injuries and emergencies.

The Court have not only looked at the issue of emergency medical treatment as part of the right to health, but have also addressed the importance of providing preventive health services to the Indian population. In addition, the Court have observed that a healthy body is the very foundation for all human activities and measures should be taken to ensure that health is preserved. For example, in *Murli S. Deora* v. *Union of India*,[24] which was a public interest litigation, the Supreme Court prohibited smoking in public places in the entire country on the grounds that smoking is injurious to the health of passive smokers and issued directions to the Union of India, State Governments as well as the Union Territories to take effective steps to ensure prohibiting smoking in all public places. In another interesting PIL, the Supreme Court, taking into consideration the increasing pollution levels in New Delhi due to diesel emissions, and that such exposure to toxic air would violate the right to life and health of the citizens, directed all private non-commercial vehicles to conform to Euro II norms with a specified time period.[25]

Article 23: This article is indirectly related to health Article 23(1) prohibits traffic in human beings. It is well-known that traffic in women leads to prostitution, which, in turn, is a major factor in spread of AIDS. Prostitutes are known to be a very high-risk group for AIDS and other Sexually Transmitted Diseases (STD). Both prostitutes and their clients have thus a high risk of contracting and transmitting these diseases.[26]

Article 24 reads that "No child below the age of fourteen years shall be employed to work in any factory or mine or engaged in any other

22. *Paschim Banga Khet Mazdoor Samity* v. *State of W.B.* (1996) 4 SCC 37.
23. *Ibid.*
24. (2001) 8 SCC 765.
25. *M.C. Mehta* v. *Union of India*, (1999) 6 SCC 9.
26. Narender Kumar, Constitutional Law, 283 (2002). The expression traffic in human beings has been held to be a very wide expression including the traffic in women for immoral or other purposes, such as making them devadasi or Jogins; see in *Vishal Jeet* v. *Union of India*, AIR 1990 SC 1412.

hazardous employment". Thus, this article is of direct relevance to child health.[27] It may be mentioned that child labour is widely prevalent in India, and has adverse effect on the physical, mental and social health of children.[28]

On the other hand, Article 32 is the corner-stone between the rule of law on the one hand and the fundamental rights on the other. It states that the right to move the Supreme Court for enforcement of the fundamental rights is guaranteed.[29] The parallel article in respect of the High Courts is Article 226. These articles empower every citizen of India to move the courts for violation of the fundamental rights, the most important of which, in the context of health, is the right to life, with all its wider connotations guaranteed by Article 21.[30]

Another Article 38 of the Indian Constitution falls under chapter four, Directive Principles of State Policy. As such there is not much case law in relation to this Article. Poverty in itself is a major determinant of health, Article 38(2) enjoins upon the State to minimize in equalities not only in income but also in "facilities and opportunities". This would naturally cover facilities and opportunities for preventing disease, promoting health and curing illness. It would include facilities and opportunities for education. It is well to remember that there is a close linkage between education and health. Child mortality and maternal mortality are both significantly less in educated mothers. Education women have higher age at marriage, smaller family size and healthier and better nourished children. These associations stand out even when other variables like income are kept constant. The best example is Kerala where infant mortability rate is one-fourth of the national average. This is so in spite of the fact that economic status of people in Kerala is not very high. However, the State enjoys near 100 percent literacy.[31]

Kerala is the southern-most state of India. With a population of 31.83 million, and a population density of 819 sq.km., the State of Kerala is extremely crowded, perhaps more than Bangladesh. Its annual per capita income of Rs. 21,046 (2000-01) is little higher than the national average of Rs. 16,707. The daily per capita calorie intake of 2158 lacs is below the recommended daily allowance of 2400 lacs.[32] Nevertheless, Kerala has surpassed all the Indian States in certain

27. D.D. Basu, *Shorter Constitution of India* (2003), p. 327.
28. M.C. Gupta, "Child Labour: A Socio-gender Perspective," *Legal News and Views*, January-March, 1997.
29. M.C. Gupta, *Health and Law*, 327 (2002).
30. Narender Kumar, *op. cit.*, at 525.
31. *Ibid.*
32. National Institute of Nutrition (1986), *Nutrition News*, 7 (5) 1.

important measures of health and social development, as shown in Table 1.

Table 1: Comparison of Kerala and All-India Health Statistics

	Year	*Kerala*	*All-India*
Death Rate/1000	2002	6.4	8.1
Rural Birth Rate	2002	16.8	25.0
Infant Mortality Rate	2002	10	6.4
Annual Growth Rate (Percent)	2001	0.9	1.93
Life Expectancy at Birth (Projection)	2001-06	66.5	61.5
Male		71.7	64.1
Female		7.5	65.4
Literacy Rate (Percent)	2001	90.92	65.38
Female Literacy Rate	2001	87.86	54.16
Mean Age at Marriage Females	1999	22.1	19.5
Per Capita Income	2001	Rs.21046	Rs.16707
Doctor Population Ratio	1991	1:7213	1:2148

Kerala has demonstrated that, in a democratic system with a strong political commitment to equitable socio-economic development, high levels of health can be achieved even on modest levels of income. Kerala can, therefore, be considered a yardstick for judging health status in the country.[33]

Studies have shown that the efforts in the health field were simultaneously reinforced by development in other sectors, literacy (especially female literacy) has played a key role in improving the health situation, this was probably responsible for the high rate of utilization of health facilities. Longstanding programmes directed at social welfare raised not only educational levels of the population but also developed a social infrastructure, including a transport network which provided easy access to services. An effective programme of land reform had given poor people access to land resources for food production at the household level. Kerala has demonstrated that good health at low cost is attainable by poor countries, but requires major political and social commitment.[34]

Clauses (a), (d), (e) and (f) of Article 39 of the Indian Constitution are particularly relevant to health.[35] It reads: "The State shall, in

33. K.S. Jaya Rao, (1986), *Under the Lens, Medico-Friend Circle*, V.H. A.I., N.D.
34. Ratcliffe, John (1984). In: Practising Health for All, David Morley, *et. al.* (eds.), Oxford University Press.
35. D.D. Basu, *op. cit.*, at 448.

particular, direct its policy towards securing:

(a) that the citizens, men and women equally, have the right to an adequate means to livelihood;[36]

(d) that there is equal pay for equal work for both men and women;[37]

(e) that the health and strength of workers, even men and women and the tender age of children are not abused and that citizens are not forced by economic necessity to enter avocations unsuited to their age of strength;[38] and

(f) that children are given opportunities and facilities to develop in a healthy manner and in conditions of freedom and dignity and that youth are protected against exploitation and against moral and material abandonment.[39]

As regards clause (f), this clause would include legislation for protection of children and development of their personality and corrective measures relating to juvenile delinquents.[40]

Article 40 reads:

> "The state shall take steps to organize village panchayats and endow them with such powers and authority as may be necessary to enable them to function as units of self-government". This Directive Principle has now been translated into action through the 73rd Amendment Act, 1992, whereby Part IX of the Constitution titled "The Panchayats" was inserted. The Panchayats system has significant implications for the health sector. These will be discussed in relation to relevant Articles 243 and 243-A to 343-O contained in Part IX.[41]

Article 41 reads, "The state shall, within the limits of its economic capacity and development, make effective provisions for securing the right to work, to education and to public assistance in case of undeserved want". Its implications in relation to health are obvious.[42]

Article 42 reads, "the State shall make provision for securing just and humane conditions of work and for maternity relief." The implication of this article for health is obvious. Being a Directive Principle, it is not enforceable. However, the principle is being followed

36. *Ibid.*
37. *Id.*, at 450.
38. *Id.*, at 452.
39. *Ibid.*
40. *Sheela* v. *Union of India*, AIR 1986 SC 11773, paras 4 and 10.
41. D.D. Basu, *op. cit.*, at 454.
42. *Ibid.*

in actual practice. An example is the recent hike in the quantum of maternity leave from three months to four and a half months as available to Central Government employees.[43]

Article 48-A reads that "The State shall endeavour to protect and improve the environment and to safeguard the forests and wild life of the country". This Article was inserted by the Constitution (42nd Amendment) Act, 1976. It enjoins upon the State to protect and improve the environment, which has a direct bearing on health.[44]

Article 51-A is the solitary Article comprising Part IV-A of the Constitution, titled "Fundamental Duties" which was inserted by the Constitution (42nd Amendment) Act, on with the recommendations of the Swaran Singh Committee. This article lists various fundamental duties of a citizen. This article brings our Constitution in consonance with Article 29(1) of the Universal Declaration of Human Rights. Similar provisions exist in the Constitution of Japan, China and Russia. Clause (g) of this Article concerns environment.[45] Article 51(g) reads: "It shall be a duty of every citizen of India to protect and improve the natural environment including forests, lakes, rivers and wild life and to have compassion for living creature."[46]

Article 243-G falls under Part IX of the Constitution labeled, "The Panchayats". Part IX was inserted by "The Constitution (73rd Amendment) Act, 1992 and became effective on April 24, 1993. Article 243-G states that the legislature of a State may endow the Panchayats with necessary power and authority in relation to matters listed in the Seventh Schedule.[47] Under entry six of the State list contained in the Seventh Schedule to the Constitution, the State legislature is empowered to make laws with respect to public health and sanitation, hospitals and dispensaries. Entry fifty-two of Union list of the Seventh Schedule to the Constitution allows Parliament to make laws relating to industries, the control of which by the Union is declared by Parliament by law to be expedient in the public interest. The entries in this Schedule having direct connection to health are as follows:

11. Drinking water.
23. Health and Sanitation, including hospitals, primary health centres and dispensaries.
24. Family Welfare.
25. Women and Child Development.

---

43. *Id.*, at 455.
44. *Id.*, at 559.
45. *Id.*, at 465.
46. *Id.*, at 466.
47. *Id.*, at 1116.

26. Social Welfare, including Welfare of the handicapped and mentally retarded.

It is vital to note that the level of performance of the Panchayat system varies from State to State.[48] It has a relatively stronger footing in Maharashtra and Gujarat.

Article 243-W[49] finds place in Part IX-A of the Constitution titled "The Municipalities". It was inserted by the Constitution (74th Amendment) Act, 1992 and became effective on June 7, 1993. Article 243-W provides the power, authority and responsibilities of municipalities. A municipality may be of three types in terms of Article 243-Q.[50] These are Nagar Panchayat, Municipal Council and Municipal Corporation. The functions that may be entrusted to municipalities are listed in the Twelfth[51] Schedule. The entries in this Schedule having direct relevance to health are listed below:

5. Water supply for domestic, industrial and commercial purposes.
6. Public health, sanitation conservancy and solid waste management.
9. Safeguarding the interests of weaker sections of society, including the handicapped and mentally retarded.
16. Vital statistics including registration of births and deaths.
17. Regulation of slaughter-houses and tanneries.

---

48. *Id.*, at 1848.
49. 243-W provides that the legislature of a State, subject to the provisions of the Constitution, may by law endow—
    (a) the Municipalities with such power and authority as may be necessary to enable them to function as institutions of self-government and such law may contain provision for the devolution of powers and responsibilities upon Municipalities, subject to such conditions as may be specified therein, with respect to—
        (i) the preparation of plans for economic development and social justice;
        (ii) the performance of functions and the implementation of schemes as may be entrusted to them including those in relation to the matters listed in the Twelfth Schedule.
    (b) the committees with such powers and authority as may be necessary to enable them to carry out the responsibilities conferred upon them including those in relation to the matters listed in Twelfth Schedule.
50. Article 243-Q (1) provides for the establishment of the following three types of Municipalities in every State –
    (a) A Nagar Panchayat for a transitional area, that is to say, an area in transition from a rural area to an urban area. It may be called by any name.
    (b) A Municipal Council for a smaller urban area.
    (c) A Municipal Corporation for a large urban area.
51. D.D. Basu, *op. cit.*, at 1849.

Article 246[52] relates to the subject-matter of laws made by Parliament and by the legislatures of States. The Indian Union is quasi-federal in nature. The Indian Constitution envisages a scheme of distribution of legislative powers between the Parliament and the State Legislatures in such a manner as to give predominance to the former over the latter. This distribution is given in the Seventh Schedule of the Constitution and contains three lists which are as follow:

List I: Union List

It contains 97 items of national importance in respect of which only the Parliament can make laws. The matters include Defence, Foreign Affairs, Banking, Currency, Union Taxes, etc.

27. "Port Quarantine, including hospitals connected there with: Seamen's and marine hospitals".
55. "Regulation of labour and safety in mines and oil fields".
58. "Manufacture, supply and distribution of salt by Union agencies, regulation and control of manufacture, supply and distribution of salt by other agencies".
64. "Institutions for scientific or technical education financed by the Government of India wholly or in part and declared by Parliament by law to be institutions of national importance".
65. "Union agencies and institutions for professional, vocational or technical training...."
66. "Co-ordination and determination of standards in institutions for higher education or research and scientific and technical institutions".
67. "Census". This item is of special importance to health. National census is of great help in planning of health services at the regional level on the basis of regional disparities in relation to morbidity and mortality, etc. The age distribution of population, family size and age at marriage have important connotations in the context of the population problem and the national family welfare programme. Census reveal a gradual increase in the geriatric population with consequent need for appropriate health facilities for the old.
84. "Duties of excise on tobacco and other goods manufactured or produced in India except:

52. Article 246 provides that the Union Parliament may make laws with respect to the matters contained in Union list and a State Legislature may make laws with respect to the matters contained in the State List. As regards the matters contained in the Concurrent List, both Union Parliament and the State Legislatures are vested with concurrent powers of Legislations.

(i) alcoholic liquors for human consumption;
(ii) Opium, Indian hemp; and other narcotic drugs and narcotics, but including medical and toilet preparations containing alcohol or any substance included in sub-paragraph (b) of this entry".

List II: State List

It consists of 66 items of local or State interest in respect of which the legislature of the State is component to make laws. The matters include public order and police, health, agriculture, forests, etc. The following are the items—or entries—which are relevant to health:

6. "Public health and sanitation, hospitals and dispensaries".
8. "Intoxicating liquors, that is to say, the production, manufacture, possession, transport, purchase and sale of intoxicating liquors".
9. "Relief of the disabled and unemployable".
10. "Burials and burial grounds; cremations and cremation grounds".
15. "Preservation, protection and improvement of stock and prevention of animal diseases; veterinary training and practice".
17. "Water, that is to say, water supplies, irrigation and canals, drainage and embankments, water storage and water power subject to provisions of entry 56 of List I."

List III: Concurrent List

This list is not found in those constitutions that are truly federal in nature, such as that of the USA. In India, it contains 47 items in respect of which both the Parliament and the State Legislatures can legislate. The matters in this list include general laws, procedural laws, marriage, planning, education, etc. The following are the items or entries listed that are relevant to health and medical sciences:

16. "Lunacy and mental deficiency, including places for the reception or treatment of foodstuffs and other goods."
19. "Drugs and Poisons, subject to the provisions of entry 59 of list I with respect to opium."
20A. "Population control and family planning".
24. "Welfare of labour including conditions of work, provident funds, employer's liability, workmen's compensation, invalidity and old age pensions and maternity benefits."
25. "Education, including technical education, medical education

and Universities, subject to the provisions of entries 63, 64, 65 and 66 of List I, vocational and technical training of labour."

26. "Legal, medical and other professions."
30. "Vital statistics including registration of births and deaths."

Article 263: This Article provides for the formation of an Inter-State Council for:

"(b) investigating and discussing subjects in which some or all of the states, or the Union and one more of the states, have a common interest; or
(c) making recommendation upon any such subject and, in particular, recommendations for the better coordination of policy and action with respect to that subject."

An example of such Council is the Central Council of Health and Family Welfare. Coordination in matters related to health is achieved through a Central Health Council. All State Health Ministries are its members and the Union Minster of Health is the Chairman. It meets once in a year to draft policy matters. The Director General of Health Services acts as the Secretary. The State heads of health or medical departments are also present to advise their Ministers in technical matters.

III. RECOGNITION OF RIGHT TO HEALTH AS A FUNDAMENTAL RIGHT

Regarding 'Right to Health' many have argued that the phrase, it is inaccurate and misleading, because everyone cannot be assured good or perfect health.[53] However, as health is the optimum state of body and mind, the right to health can be interpreted to mean a right to the highest attainable standards of physical and mental health, and equal access of every human being to medical care facilities as well as to living conditions conductive to the maintenance of good health. The right to health has been defined as "Every woman, man, youth and child has the human right to the highest attainable standards of physical and mental health, without discrimination of any kind. Enjoyment of the human right to health is vital to all aspects of a person's life and well-being and is crucial to the realization of many other fundamental human rights and

53. Malika Ramachandran, "The Right to Health and the Indian Constitution", 1, *DLR (S)*, 2004, at 1.

freedoms."[54] The human right to health can be said to included among other rights like standard of mental and physical health, access to adequate health care services equitable distribution of food, safe drinking water and sanitation, safe and healthy environment, essential drugs are essential, the protection and maintenance of the health of persons, the Right to Health, in its true sense is not the provisions of health care facilities alone.

In India, the right to health and protection has been recognized since early times. India is a founder member of the United Nations and it ratified various international conventions[55] promising to secure health rights of individuals in society. In this context, Article 51A[56] of the Constitution of India provides for promotion of international peace and security. The Preamble to the Constitution of India, which strives to provide for a welfare state with socialistic pattern of society under Article 21 of the Constitution guarantees the right to life and personal liberty.[57]

"No one shall be deprived of his right to life and personal liberty except according to procedure established by law."

Though it does not expressly contain the right to health, it has now been well settled through a series of cases that this includes the right to health. Further, Articles 38[58], 42[59], 43[60] and 47[61] of the Constitution also

---

54. Vernellia Randall, http://www.academic.udayton.edu/health/07 Human Rights/health/health.htm.
55. M.C. Gupta, Health and Law, (2002), p. vii.
56. Narender Kumar, *op. cit.*, at 367.
57. *Id.*, at 228-29.
58. Article 38(1) provides: "The State shall strive to promote the welfare of the people of securing and protecting, as effectively as it may, a social order in which justice-social, economic, and political, shall inform all the institutions of national life". Clause (2) of Article 38 which was inserted by the Constitution (44th Amendment) Act, 1978 further requires: "The State shall, in particular, strive to minimize the inequalities in income, and endeavour to eliminate inequalities in status, facilities and opportunities, not only amongst individuals, but also amongst groups of people residing in different areas or engaged in different vocations".
59. Article 42 requires that "the State shall make provisions for securing just and humane conditions of work and for maternity relief.
60. Article 43 provides: "The State shall endeavour to secure, by suitable legislation or economic organization or in any other way, to all workers, agricultural, industrial or otherwise, work for a living wage, conditions of work ensuring adecent standard of life and full enjoyment of leisure and social and cultural opportunities and, in particular, the state shall endeavour to promote cottage industries on an individual or cooperative basis in rural areas".
61. Article 47 provides, "The State shall regard the raising of the level of nutrition and the standard of living of its people and the improvement of public health as among its primary duties, and in particular, the State shall endeavour to bring about

provide for the promotion of health of individuals in society.

Complaints of medical negligence have been made in the past of late. Such complaints have assumed a wider dimensions as the incidents have increased due to the opening of thousands of nursing homes, charitable hospitals, central government health services dispensaries, and employees, state insurance hospitals, etc.[62]

The Courts in India have played a significant role in realization of the right to health by recognizing it as a part of the fundamental right to life and issued suitable directions to the State authorities for fulfilment of their duties. They have also provided redressal by meaningful and just interpretation to the right to life and commanding enforcement of the duties of a welfare state.

The Supreme Court in *Paschim Banga Khet Mazdoor Samity & Ors.* v. *State of West Bengal & Anrs,*[63] while widening the scope of Article 21 and the governments responsibility to provide medical aid to every person in the country, held that in a welfare state, the primary duty of the government is to secure the welfare of the people. Providing adequate medical facilities for the people is an obligation undertaken by the government in a welfare state. The government discharges, this obligation by running hospitals and primary health centres which provide medical care to the persons seeking to avail of these facilities. In this case, the Court awarded a compensation of Rs. 25,000 to Hakim Sheikh who fell from a train and suffered severe head injuries but was refused treatment from as many as seven hospitals on the grounds of non-availability of bed, though it was an emergency case.[64]

In the instant case, apex Court held that failure on the part of a government hospital to provide timely medical treatment to a person in need of such treatment is a violation of the right to life. Other than compensation the Supreme Court directed that the State Government to take proper administrative action against medical officers. In order to avoid such cases of negligence in future, the apex Court laid down certain guidelines to ensure that adequate facilities are available so that patients can be given immediate treatment. In *Akhil Bhartiya Soshit Karamchari Sangh* v. *Union of India,*[65] the Supreme Court pointed out that fundamental rights are intended to foster the ideal of a political democracy and to prevent the establishment of authoritarian rule, but

prohibition of the consumption except for medicinal purposes of intoxicating drinks and of drugs which are injurious to health".

62. Butterworths, *Legal Framework for Health Care in India*, 15-16 (2002).
63. (1996) 4 SCC 37.
64. *Ibid.*
65. (1981) 1 SCC 246.

they of no value unless they can be enforced by resort to courts. The directive principles can not, in the very nature of things be enforced in the Court of law, but it does not mean that directive principles are less important than fundamental rights or that they are not binding on the various organs of the State.

(i) Professional Obligation to Protect: 'Life of Accident Victims'

In *Parmananda Katara* v. *Union of India*,[66] the apex Court called upon the doctors to render their professional services to save and preserve the life of the injured persons without waiting for the completion of legal formalities. The Court held that whether the patient be an innocent person or be a criminal liable to punishment under the law, it is the obligation of those who are in charge of the health of the community to preserve life so that innocent may be protected and the guilty may be punished. A governmental hospital doctor positioned to meet this state obligation is bound to extend assistance for preserving life. Every doctor, whether working in government hospital or otherwise, has a professional obligation to extend his services with the expertise and care for protecting life. No law or state action could intervene, the Court laid down, to delay the discharge of this paramount obligation of the members of medical profession. The Court held that a doctor in a Government hospital was duty bound to extend medical aid to the injured without delay in all cases, irrespective of the fact, whether they were medico-legal case or otherwise.

(A) Duty of a doctor when an injured person approaches him

Whenever on such occasions, a man of medical profession is approached by an injured person, and if he finds that whatever assistance he could give is not really sufficient to save the life of the person, but some better assistance is necessary it is the duty of the man in the medical profession so approached to render all the help which he could, and also see that the person reaches the proper expert as early as possible.[67] It has been held that the obligation of the doctor is total, absolute and paramount, and laws of procedure, whether in statutes or otherwise, which would interfere with the discharge of this obligation cannot be sustained and must, therefore, give way. The Court also directed that wide publicity be given to its decision to ensure that every doctor, wherever he is in the territory of India, should forthwith be aware of this position.

66. AIR 1989 SC 2039.
67. *Ibid.*

(B) Legal protection to doctors treating injured persons

A doctor does not contravene the law of the land by proceeding to treat an injured victim on his appearance before him, either by himself or with others. Zonal regulations and classifications cannot operate as fetters in the discharge of the obligation, even if the victim is sent elsewhere under local rules, and regardless of the involvement of police. The 1985 decision of the Standing Committee on Forensic Medicine is the effective guideline.[68]

(C) No legal bar on doctors from attending to the injured persons

There is no legal impediment for a medical professional, when he is called upon or requested to attend to an injured person needing his medical assistance immediately. The effort to save the person should be the top priority, not only of the medical professional, but even of the police or any other citizen who happens to be connected with the matter, or who happens to be connected with the matter, or who happens to notice such an incident or a situation.[69]

(D) No Harassment of Doctors

The Court has deprecated the tendency to harass the medical professionals. It has remarked that unnecessary harassment of the members of the medical profession either by way of request for adjournments, or by cross-examination should be avoided. In doing so, the apprehension that the men in the medical profession have, which prevents them from discharging their duty to a suffering person, is removed, and a citizen needing assistance of a man in the medical profession receives it. The Court, however, added that these apprehensions, even if with some foundation, should not prevent the persons in the medical profession, from discharging their duty as a medical professional, to save a human life, and to do all that is necessary.[70]

(E) Duty of a Doctor to Conduct Medical Examination of Rape Victims

The Supreme Court in *State of Karnataka* v. *Manjana*[71] deprecated the tendency of refusal to conduct medical examination of rape victims

68. *Ibid.*
69. *Ibid.*
70. *Ibid.* It is pertinent to read from the news reports that inspite of the Supreme Court's directives, doctors/hospitals in some of the cases have denied treatment to accident victims. This even led to the Constitution of an enquiry committee by the Delhi Medical Council, to probe into the incidence of denial of emergency treatment by one of the private hospitals in Delhi. (See *Hindustan Times*, dated 29 April, 2001).
71. AIR 2000 SC 2281.

by doctors in rural government hospitals unless referred to by the police. The Court observed:

> We wish to put on record our disapproval of the refusal of some government doctors, particularly in rural areas, where hospitals are few and far between to conduct any medical examination of a rape victim unless the case of rape is referred to them by the police.

The Court added that such a refusal to conduct the medical examination, necessarily results in a delay in the ultimate examination of victim, by which the evidence of rape may have been washed away by the complainant herself or be otherwise lost. The Court, therefore, directed that the State must ensure that such a situation does not reoccur in future.

In *Poonam Sharma* v. *Union of India and Ors.*[72], the petitioner is heir and legal representative of one Vinod Kumar Sharma who met with in an accident while allegedly driving in a drunken state. He suffered head injury and the doctor stitched the wound and gave Brufen tablet. Thereafter, he was arrested for commission of an offence under Motor Vehicle Act, 1988. When he complained of severe headache and was again taken to the same doctor. He was neither hospitalized nor was given further any treatment. His bail was obtained but his condition deteriorated. He was declared dead. The Delhi High Court held that a citizen of India is entitled to preservation of life not only at the hands of public authorities, which would include hospital authorities.

In *D.K. Joshi* v. *State of Uttar Pradesh and Other*,[73] the Supreme Court had taken notice of the distressing situation of public health in the state of Uttar Pradesh and inaction of the State Government to stop the menace of the unqualified and unregistered medical practitioners proliferating all over the State. The District Magistrates and District Medical Officer did not take effective steps to stop this menace which is hazardous to human life. The Court directed the Secretary, Health and Family Welfare Department, State of U.P. to take all necessary steps to stop the unqualified and unregistered medical practitioners in carrying on the medical profession, and also directed to the District Magistrates and the Chief Medical Officers to identify such persons within a time limit to fixed by the Secretary, Health and Family Welfare Department. All the District Magistrates and Chief Medical Officers were required to monitor the action taken against such persons. It was also directed that

72. AIR 2003 Del. 50.
73. (2000) 5 SCC 80. The Division Bench comprised of Justice S. Rajendra Babu and Justice S.N. Phukan.

the Secretary, Health and Family Welfare Department should give due publicity to the names of such unqualified/unregistered medical practitioners so that people do not approach such persons for medical treatment, also issue necessary directions from time to time to these officer so that such unauthorized persons could not pursue their medical profession in the State.[74]

The question of reimbursement of medical treatment of the employees was dealt by the Supreme Court in *State of Punjab* v. *Ram Lubhaya Bagga,* etc.[75] In this case the respondent Ram Lubhaya Bagga was suffered a severe heart attack on 13th March 1995 and was taken to the Escort Heart Institute and Research Centre in an emergency. On 27th March, he underwent coronary artery bypass surgery. Finally he was discharged on 10th April 1995. The entire expenses incurred for the treatment, surgery, post-operative check up, etc. came to Rs. 2,11,758.70. In May 1996, he had submitted the bill to the government for reimbursement. The Court recognized that when Government forms its policy, it is based on number of circumstances on facts, law including constraints based on its resources.[76] The Court held that:

> "... Where according to new government policy the employee was given free choice to get treatment in any private hospital in India, but due to financial constraints, the reimbursement was allowed to the level of expenditure as per the rate fixed by the Director, Health and Family Welfare, for a similar treatment package or actual expenditure whichever is less, a committee of technical experts was constituted by the Director, Health and Family Welfare to finalize the roles of various treatment packages...[77] No State of any country can have unlimited resources to spend on any of its project. That is why provision of health facilities cannot be unlimited. It has to be the extent finance permit. The principle of fixation of rate and scale under this new policy was justified and cannot be held to be violative of Article 21 or Article 47 of the Constitution of India."[78] The Court also stated that the treatment of a disease in a country abroad would be permitted in extremely rare cases where satisfactory treatment is not available in the country. Prior approval of the State Medical Board shall be a pre-requisite in such cases.[79]

74. *Id.*, at 82, para 6.
75. AIR 1998 SC 1703.
76. *Id.*, at 1704.
77. *Id.*, at 1711; paras 27 and 28.
78. *Ibid.*, para 29.
79. *Id.*, at 1709.

Commenting upon the right of the citizens and duty of the State, Hon'ble Mr. Justice A.P. Mishra observed:[80]

> "When we speak about a right, it correlates to a duty upon another, individual, employer government or authority. In other words, the right of one is an obligation to another. Hence, the right of a citizen to live under Article 21 casts obligation on the State. This obligation is further reinforced under Article 47, it is for the State to secure health to its citizen as its primary duty. No doubt, Government is rendering this obligation by opening Government hospitals and health centres, but in order to make it meaningful, it has to be within reach of its people, as far as possible, or reduce the queue of waiting lists, and it has to provide all facilities for which an employee looks for at another hospital... since it is one of the most sacrosanct and valuable rights of a citizen and equally sacrosanct sacred obligation of the State, every citizen of this welfare state looks towards the State for it to perform its this obligation with top priority including by way allocation of sufficient funds. This in turn will not only secure the right of its citizen to the best of their satisfaction but in turn will benefit the State in achieving its social, political and economical goal."

It is submitted that the learned Judge not only recognized right to health as a fundamental right under Article 21 of the Constitution but also imposed duty upon the State to secure health to its citizens. The learned Judge tried to establish a close relationship between Articles 21 and 47 of the Constitution and stated that best health of the citizen shall benefit the State in achieving its social, political and economical goal. Truly admitting the valuable observations of the learned judge would not only help to strengthen the right to health as a fundamental right under Article 21 of the Constitution but would also impose duty upon the State to make policies for the improvement of health of its citizens.

(ii) Workers' Right to Clean Environment and Health Care Facilities

It is basic right of all to live in a healthy environment. Healthy environment is a nature's gift. Air and water are essential for living and human being cannot survive for a moment without the air, hence the air

80. *Id.*, at 1710-11; in *N.D. Jayal* v. *Union of India* (2004) 9 SCC 362, Rajindra Babu, J. of the Supreme Court stated that right to health is a fundamental right under Article 21. Protection to this is inextricably linked with clean and healthy environment itself is a fundamental right.

should be pollution-free. Cry for a clean environment has now transformed into shriek sending jitters down the polluters' spine. Right to a healthy environment is now being acknowledged as a human right. The Supreme Court of India has developed the concept of the right to healthy environment as a part of the right to life under Article 21 of the Constitution. The term 'health' implies more than absence of sickness. Medical care and health facilities not only protect against sickness but also ensure manpower for economic development. Health is, thus, a state of complete physical, mental and social well-being and not merely the absence of disease or infirmity. In the light of socio-economic justice assured in our Constitution, right to health is fundamental human right. The maintenance of health is the most imperative constitutional goal whose realization requires interaction of many social and economic factors.

The Supreme Court has recognized the rights of the workers and their right to basic health facilities under the Constitution. The right to basic health facilities are also enshrined under the International Conventions to which India is a party. In its path-breaking judgment in *'Bandhua Mukti Morcha* v. *Union of India*,[81] the Court delineated the scope of Article 21 of the Constitution, and held that it is the fundamental right of every one in this country, assured under the interpretation given to Article 21 by this Court in *Francis Mullin's Case*,[82] to live with human dignity, free from exploitation, this right to live with human dignity enshrined in Article 21 derives its life breath from the Directive Principles of State Policy and particularly clauses (e) and (f) of Article 39 and Articles 41 and 42. It must include protection of: the health and strength of workers, men and women; and children of tender age against abuse; opportunities and facilities for children to develop in a healthy manner and in conditions of freedom and dignity; educational facilities; just and humane conditions of work and maternity relief. These are the minimum requirements, which must exist in order to enable a person to life with human dignity. No State, neither the central government nor any State Government, has the right to take any action which will deprive a person of enjoyment of these basic essentials.

In *CESE Ltd.* v. *Subhash Chandra Bose*,[83] the Court held that:

> "The health and strength of a worker is an integral facet of the right to life. The aim of fundamental rights is to create an egalitarian society to free all citizens from coercion or restrictions

81. AIR 1984 SC 802.
82. AIR 1980 SC 849.
83. (1992) 1 SCC 461.

by society and to make liberty available for all".[84]

The Court further held that the term health, implies more than an absence of sickness. Medical care and health facilities not only protect against sickness, but also ensure stable manpower for economic development. Facilities of health and medical care generate devotion and dedication, to give the worker's best, physically as well as mentally, in productivity. It enables the worker to enjoy the fruits of his labour, to keep him physically fit and mentally alert for leading a successful, economic, social and cultural life. The medical facilities are, therefore, part of social security, and like gilt-edged security, would yield immediate returns in the increased production, or at any rate reduce absenteeism on grounds of sickness, etc. Health is thus a state of complete physical, mental and social well-being and not merely the absence of disease or infirmity. In the light of Articles 22 to 25 of the Universal Declaration of Human Rights, International Convention on Economic and Cultural Rights, and in the light of socio-economic justice ensured in our Constitution, right to health is a fundamental right.

The Court while reiterating its stand for providing health facilities in *Vincent* v. *Union of India*,[85] held that a healthy body is the very foundation for all human activities, that is why the adage "*Sariramadyam Kholu Dharma Sadbanam*". In a welfare state, therefore, it is the obligation of the State to ensure the creation and the sustaining of conditions congenial to good health. The Court also observed that the maintenance and improvement of public health have to rank high as these are indispensable to the very physical existence of the community, and on the betterment of these, depends the building of society of which the Constitution-makers envisaged. In this case, the petitioner had sought directions from the Supreme Court for banning the import, manufacture, sale and distribution of drugs recommended for a ban by the Drugs Consultative Committee, and for cancellation of all licenses authorizing all such drugs. The Court observed:

> "The branch of health care of citizens involves an ever changing challenge. The problem is a shifting one and one cannot have a fixed process to deal with such situations that would arise from time to time." "...The Central Government on the basis of the expert advice can indeed adopt an approved national policy and prescribe an adequate number of formulations which would on the whole meet the requirement of the people at large. Obviously,

84. *Id.*, at 462, para 30.
85. AIR 1987 SC 994.

instant attention has to be bestowed to keep abreast of the changing situations and make proper and timely amends. While laying the guidelines on this score, injurious drugs should be totally eliminated from the market. Great care in this regard has to be taken... Such drugs as are found necessary should be manufactured in abundance and availability to satisfy every demand should be ensured. Undue competition in the matter of production of drugs by allowing too many substitutes should be reduced as it introduces unhealthy practice and ultimately tends to affect quality."[86]

The Court further held that in a series of pronouncements during the recent years this Court has called out from the provisions of Part IV of the Constitution several obligations of the State, and called upon it to effectuate them in order that, the results pictured by the fathers of the Constitution may become a reality. The importance of this judgment could be seen in the light of recent international agreement on TRIPS 14 Justice Raganath Mishra's observation regarding right to health *vis-à-vis* right to life in that case was as follows:

"Article 21 of the Constitution guarantees right to life and this Court has interpreted the guarantee to cover a life with normal amenities assuring good living which include medical attention, life free from diseases and longitivity upto normal expectations".[87]

The Supreme Court has also brought occupational health hazards to workers within the coverage of Article 21. The right to health and medical care to protect the health and vigour of a worker while in service or post-retirement has been held to be fundamental right under Article 21 read with the directive principles contained in Articles 39(e), 41, 43, and 47 and all fundamental human rights to make the life of workers meaningful and purposeful, with dignity of person.[88]

The Court in *Vincent* has directed the Central Government to compensate and reimburse the petitioner for the expenses of his recognition of his services for asking directions for maintenance of approved standard of drugs and banning of injurious and harmful drugs.

86. *Id.*, at 996; paras 19 and 20.

87. Due to the agreement on TRIPs, after 31st December 2004, the process patent system hither to used in India would be replaced by more restrictive product patent system. Foreign Pharmaceutical Companies (the primary manufacturers of drugs) would then monopolize the production, distribution, pricing and finally availability of new medicines. The Indian government needs to create legislation that would be favourable to its citizens' right to health.

88. *Supra* n. 1.

The Court further observed that attending to public health is of high priority-perhaps the one at the top.

A three judge bench of the Supreme Court in *Consumer Education and Research Centre & Ors.* v. *Union of India*,[89] ruled that right to health and medical care, to protect health and vigour while in service or post-retirement, is a fundamental right of a worker under Article 21, read with Articles 39(e), 41, 43 and 48-A. All related articles and fundamental human rights are intended to make the life of the workman meaningful and purposeful. Lack of health denudes him of his livelihood. Compelling economic necessity to work in an industry exposed to health hazards due to indigence to bread-winning for himself and his dependents, should not be at the cost of the health and vigour of the workman.[90]

In this case, the petitioner an accredited organization filed public interest litigation under Article 32 of the Constitution to issue guidelines for the protection of the health of the worker engaged in mines and asbestos industries. Speaking on behalf of the Court Ramaswamy, J. stated that in Karnataka, Andhra Pradesh and Rajasthan, there exists about thirty mines and the workmen employed therein are about 1061. There are about 74 asbestos industries in nine States, namely, Haryana, Delhi, Andhra Pradesh, Karataka, Rajasthan, Maharashtra, Kerala, Gujarat and Madhya Pradesh. It would also appear that as on August 1986 there were about 11,000 workmen employed in those industries.

Basing on Biswas Committee Report, the petitioner filed the writ-petition. The Central Government accepting the said report, framed model rule 123A of Factories Act and on its model relevant laws and rules were amended and are now brought into force. The Hon'ble Judge did not refer to the findings and recommendations of Biswas Committee as the "Asbestos Convention, 1986" covered the whole ground.

The Hon'ble Judge stated that in Convention 162 of the International Labour Conference (ILC) held in June 1986, it is adopted on 24th June, 1986, the Convention called "the Asbestos Convention, 1986". India is one of the signatories to the Convention and it played a commendable role suggesting suitable amendments in the preparatory conferences. It has come into force from June 16, 1989, after its ratification by the Member-States. The Court referred the provisions of Articles 5(2), 8, 9, 15, 16, 18, 19, 20, 21, and 22 of the Asbestos Convention, 1986 and stated that in Part VI-Final Provisions, Article 24

89. (1995) 3 SCC 42. The case was heard by a three Judges Bench consisting of A.M. Ahmadi, C.J., M.M. Punchhi and Ramaswamy, JJ. The decision of the Court was delivered by Ramaswamy, J.

90. *Ibid.*, paras 24 and 25.

is relevant for the purpose of this case and clause (1) thereof states that this convention shall be binding only upon those members of the International Labour Organization whose ratifications have been registered with the Director-General.

The Court observed:

> "Lack of health denudes his livelihood. Compelling economic necessity to work in an industry exposed to health hazards due to indigence to bread winning to himself and his dependents should not be at the cost of the health and vigour of workman… Health of the worker enables him to enjoy the fruit of his labour, keeping him physically fit and mentally alert for leading a successful life, economically, socially and culturally. Medical facilities to protect the health of the workers are, therefore, the fundamental and human rights to the workmen."[91]

The Supreme Court, while highlighting the importance of the directive principles, reiterated its stand *Kirloskar Brothers Ltd.* v. *Employees State Insurance Corporation.*[92] It observed that in expanding economic activity in a liberalized economy, Part IV of the Constitution enjoins not only the State and its instrumentalities but even private industries to ensure safety to the workman, and to provide facilities and opportunities for health and vigour of the workman assured in relevant provisions in Part IV, which are integral parts of the right to equality under Article 14 and right to invigorated life under Article 21.

In the instant case, the company had two factories in Maharashtra and in Madhya Pradesh. Only the factory situated in Madhya Pradesh was covered under the Act. It had regional officers, at several places. Accordingly those regional offices were required to contribute their share of the health insurance of the workmen. The contention of the company was that since the products of the factory covered under the Act constituted only 3 percent to 33 percent and not a predominant part, therefore, it was not liable to pay contribution. Rejecting this contention, the apex Court held that every human being has the right to live and to feed himself and his dependents. For welfare of the employees, the employer should provide facilities and opportunities to make their life meaningful." The Court further held:

> "health is thus a state of complete physical, mental and social well-being and right to health, therefore it is a fundamental and human right of the workman".[93]

91. AIR 1995 SC 922 at 940.
92. (1996) 2 SCC 682.
93. *Id.*, at 687; para 8.

The Court observed that the principal test was whether the employee was engaged in connection with the work of the factory. The test of predominant business activity was not relevant. The true test was the control exercised by the principal was not relevant. The true test was the control exercised by the principal employer over the employee. When there was connection between the factory and the finished products which were sold or distributed in the regional offices or establishment and principal employer had control over employee, the Act became applicable. Thus, the decision is just a contribution of human rights jurisprudence by the Supreme Court in the area of right to health.

In *State of Punjab* v. *Mohinder Singh Chawla*,[94] the respondent, a state employee, had heart ailment. Since the facility of the treatment was not available in the State Hospital of Punjab, permission was given by the Director, with the approval of Medical Board to get treatment outside the State. He was sent for treatment in All India Institute of Medical Sciences (AIIMS) at New Delhi. He submitted his medical bill for reimbursement. While granting reimbursement for the actual expenses incurred, the government rejected his bill for room rent paid to the hospital as inadmissible. The Supreme Court directed the State Government to pay not only medical expenses incurred by the employee, but also room rent of the hospital. The Court categorically observed: "It is now settled law that right to health is an integral to right to life. Government has constitutional obligation to provide the health facilities".[95]

The Court further held that if the Government servant had suffered an ailment which required treatment at a specialized approved hospital and on reference where at the Government servant had undergone such treatment therein, it was the duty of the State to bear the expenditure incurred by the Government servant. Expenditure thus incurred required to be reimbursed by the State to the employee.

(iii) Constitutional Right to Health Care for Convicts and Undertrials

The Supreme Court, while recognizing the custodial rights of individuals in *Supreme Court Legal Aid Committee through Hon. Secretary* v. *State of Bihar & Ors.*[96] ruled that it is the obligation of the police to ensure appropriate protection of the person taken in custody, including medical care if such person need it. The State of Bihar was

94. AIR 1997 SC 1225.
95. *Id.*, at 1227; para 4.
96. (1991) 3 SC 482.

directed to pay a compensation to the tune of Rs. 20,000 to the legal representative of the deceased.

(iv) Guidelines for Holding Eye Camps: Liability of Philanthropic Institutions for the Loss of Eye Right of Persons During the Conduct of Eye Camps

In *A.S. Mittal & Ors.* v. *State of Uttar Pradesh & Ors.*,[97] the Supreme Court, while dealing with a public interest litigation under Article 32 of the Constitution, alleging negligence on the part of the doctors in providing services at an eye camp organized by the Lions Club, observed that the whole programme at Khurja, however, laudable the intentions with which it might have been launched, proved a disastrous medical misadventure for the patients. The operated eyes of the patients were irreversibly damaged owing to a post-operative infection of the intraocular cavities. It is now undisputed that this terrible medical mishap was due to a common contaminating source. The suggestion in the report of the enquires that ensued, is that in all probability, the source of the infection was the 'normal saline' used on the eyes at the time of surgery. It was further observed that despite every care taken by the answering respondent and his associates and assistants, a large number of patients could not regain their vision in the Khurja Camp. It is extremely unfortunate that some 84 patient's vision could not be restored, despite every care bestowed by the answering respondent. The Court held that a mistake by a medical practitioner, which no reasonably competent and careful practitioner, would have committed, is a negligent one.[98]

> The Indian Medical Council constituted a sub-committee after the above proceedings, and submitted its recommendations before the Court. The Court gave suggestions to the ministry to incorporate the following guidelines under the revised guidelines:

(A) Staff

The operations in the camps should only be performed by qualified experienced ophthalmic Surgeons registered with Medical Council of India or any State Medical Council. The Camp should not be used as a training ground for post-graduate students, and operative work should not be entrusted to post-graduate students. There should be a pathologist to examine urine, blood sugar, etc. It is preferable to have a Dentist to check the teeth for sepsis and a physician for general medical check-up.

---

97. AIR 1989 SC 1571.
98. *Ibid.*

(B) Medication

All medicines to be used should be of standard quality duly verified by the doctor in-charge of the camp. The Court further held that maintenance of the highest standards of aseptic and sterile conditions at places where ophthalmic surgery or any surgery is conducted cannot be over-emphasized. It is not merely on the formulation of the theoretical standards, but the professional commitment with which the prescriptions are implemented that the ultimate results rests. The government, the states and the union, incur enormous expenditure of public money on health care. However, the standards of cleanliness and hygiene in public hospitals leave much to be desired. Maintenance of sterile aseptic conditions in hospitals, to prevent cross-infections should be a routine hospital activity, purity of drugs intended for human use should be ensured by prior tests and inspection.

But owing to a general air of cynical irreverence and complaisance, with the continuing deterioration of standards, the very concept of standards and the imperatives of their observance tend to be impaired. The remedy lies in a ruthless adherence to the virtue of method, and laying down practical procedures in minute detail and by exacting not merely expecting-strict adherence to these procedures.

In view the facts of the case, the Court observed that indeed, the factual foundations requisite for establishing the proximate casual connection for the injury, has yet to be established conclusively. The Court held that the State government should afford the victims some monetary relief, in addition to the sum of Rs. 5,000 already paid by way of interim relief. The State government was directed to pay a further sum of Rs. 12,500 to each of the victims.

(v) Role of Legal Aid and Advice Board

In *A.S. Mittal & Ors.* v. *State of Uttar Pradesh & Ors.*,[99] while awarding compensation on humanitarian grounds in case of damage caused to eyes during eye camps, held that if any of the victims are otherwise eligible for pension under any of the existing schemes now in force in the State, their cases shall be considered for such benefit. The Legal Aid and Advice Board of UP State was directed to take up this issue and process the claims of the victims, for such other benefits under any of the existing government schemes providing for aid to the aged, the disabled, and the destitute, subject to the condition that the victims otherwise satisfy the conditions of those schemes.

99. AIR 1989 SC 1571.

(vi) Right to Health *vis-à-vis* Privacy of HIV/AIDS Patients[100]

The right to health has acquired a new dimension due to spread of deadly disease AIDS across the world. AIDS has drawn the attention of the whole of the world community. It has now become an epidemic affecting millions of people including men, women and children. This life threatening disease has emerged as a serious public health problem. India has the second highest number of HIV/AIDS cases in the world after South Africa.

The Supreme Court has accepted the right to health as fundamental right under Article 21 of the Constitution. Constitutionally, an AIDS patient is entitled to get medical treatment, without any discrimination. He can also secure damages if he is denied medical treatment and as a result suffers any injury. However, the right to treatment continues to be denied to HIV/AIDS patients. A number of petitions have been filed before the Supreme Court asking the government to provide ARVs.[101]

HIV infected individual has a right to life which includes right to dignity as well as right to privacy and confidentiality. Right to life means right to enjoy life as a human being. He has a right to eat, drink, to socialize, to move in friends and also to enjoy sexual pleasure. But as soon as the fact of his being infected with AIDS come to the knowledge of other persons he is discarded from the society. The question arises whether the physician is duty-bound not to disclose the secrets of a patient or he has also some duty with respect to healthy people who can be infected if he does not disclose the confidentiality. In such situations, there is a conflict of duties as well as conflict of rights. Patient has a right to enjoy his life as well as healthy people also have right to life under Article 21 of the Constitution. In short, the doctor has duty towards patients to whom he treat on the one hand and towards world at large on the other.

---

100. The issue concerning HIV/AIDS were elaborately discussed during the three day UN Summit and the 189 member UN General Assembly adopted the Declaration of Commitment on HIV/AIDS on 27th June, 2001. The Summit noted with concern that nearly thirty-six million people today are living with HIV. It is estimated that nearly 75 percent of the infected population live in Sub-Saharan Africa. The session was mainly aimed at protecting women from exploitation and preventing them from being forced into unsafe sex. This said that women account for 52 percent of the 17.5 million adults who have died of AIDS since the epidemic began 20 years ago. Quite apart from this the Union Minister for Health and Family Welfare, Government of India expressed his doubts on the UN figure of 5,60,000 AIDS-related orphans in India. According to him, the number is between 60,000-70,000. (See, the *Times of India*, 29 June, 2001 at p. 1).
101. The AIDS Initiative, *Frontline*, 16 January 2004, p.107. ARV is anti-retroviral treatment provided to AIDS patients.

The Supreme Court of India held in *Mr. 'X'* v. *Hospital 'Z'*,[102] wherein the appellant contended that right to privacy was infringed by the respondents by disclosing the appellant as HIV positive. They were, therefore, liable for damages. The Court observed that the right to privacy has been culled out of the provisions of Article 21 and other provisions of the Constitution relating to fundamental rights read with Directive Principles of State Policy. The Supreme Court, in several judgments, has made attempts to trace the origin of the 'right to privacy' and a number of American decisions, including *Munn* v. *Illinois*,[103] and various articles were considered and it was ultimately laid down as under:

Depending on the character and antecedents of the person subjected to surveillance as also the Objects and the Limitation under which surveillance is made, it cannot be said surveillance by domiciliary visits would always be unreasonable restriction upon the rights of privacy. Assuming that the fundamental rights explicitly guaranteed to the citizen have penumbral zones and that the right to privacy is itself a fundamental right, that fundamental right must be subject to restriction on the basis of compelling public interest.

The Court observed that as one of the human rights, the right to privacy is not treated as absolute, and is subject to such action as may be lawfully taken for the prevention of crime or disorder or protection of health, or morals, or protections of rights and freedoms of others. The right to privacy may arise out of a particular specific relationship, which may be commercial, matrimonial, or even political. As already discussed above, the doctor-patient relationship, though basically commercial, is professionally a matter of confidence and, therefore, doctors morally and ethically bound to maintain confidentiality. In such a situation, public disclosure of even true private facts may amount to an invasion of the rights of privacy which may sometimes lead to the clash of one person's right to be alone with another person's right to be informed.

The Court held that disclosure of even true private facts, have the tendency to disturb a person, and ruled that the right to privacy is an essential component of the right to life envisaged by Article 21. The right, however, is not absolute and may be lawfully restricted for the prevention of crime, disorder, or protection of health, or morals, or protection of rights and freedoms of others. The Court further ruled that having regard to the fact that the appellant was found to be HIV positive, its disclosure would not be in violation of either the rule of

102. (1998) 8 SCC 296: AIR 1998 SC 3662.
103. (1877) 94 US 113.

confidentiality of the appellant's right to privacy, as MSW with whom the appellant was likely to be married, was saved in time by such disclosure. She would have been infected with the dreadful disease, had the marriage taken place and been consummated.

The Supreme Court of India has played a decisive role in realization of the right to health by recognizing it as a part of the fundamental right to life and issuing suitable directions to the State authorities for the discharge of their duties. The Courts have protected people with HIV/AIDS against discrimination in employment and services, but the issue of right to health of persons with HIV is a new and emerging area of adjudication. A decision of Andhra Pradesh High Court in *M. Vijaya*,[104] the Court observed that AIDS as a public health issue and one that needs to be articulated in terms of the constitutional guarantee to the right to life, making employers and health providers accountable for any negligence, omission or failure to conform to procedure. In this case, the Court awarded compensation as a public law remedy in addition to and apart from the private law remedy for tortuous damages.

In *Mr. "X"* v. *Hospital "Z"*,[105] the Supreme Court has partly overruled its earlier decision. The petitioner raised the question whether a person suffering from HIV positive contracting marriage with a willing partner after disclosing the factum of disease to that partner would be committing an offence within the meaning of Section 269 and 270 of the Indian Penal Code. In other words, the clarification was sought by the petitioner that there was no bar for marriage, if the healthy spouse consented to marry after knowledge of the HIV-positive status of the other spouse. The Court held that the earlier decision of the Court was based on the facts of the case that it was open to the hospital to reveal such information to persons related to the girl whom he intended to marry and she had a right to know about the HIV-positive status of the appellant. However, further observations of the Court to declare in general as to whether such persons were entitled to be married or not, or if they marry they would commit an offence, or whether right to marry was suspended during the period of illness, were unnecessary and uncalled for. This development is being seen as an affirmation by the highest court in the country of the rights-based response to HIV/AIDS.

In Public Interest Litigation, *Common Cause* v. *Union of India*,[106] serious deficiencies and shortcomings with respect to collection, storage and supply of blood through various blood centres were highlighted

104. *M. Vijaya* v. *Chairman, Singareni Collieries, Hyderabad*, 2001 (5) ALD 522 (LB).
105. AIR 2003 SC 664.
106. AIR 1996 SC 929.

before the Supreme Court. The Court constituted a committee to examine the various draft schemes suggested by the petitioner and the Union of India. After reviewing the report of the Court Committee, and that of the Experts Committee set-up by the Indian Red Cross Society, the Court held that the government should take suitable action as per the immediate and long-term implementation plans suggested by the Court Committee.

The foregoing discussion reveal that a proper balance must be established between social and individual interests. The fight against AIDS is also a fight against fear, against prejudice and against irrational action born of ignorance. The essence of the matter is that spreading awareness about HIV/AIDS will go a long way in correcting the existing misconceptions and removing the stigma associated with the disease in India. The protection and dignity of people living with HIV/AIDS is essential to prevention and control of HIV/AIDS. Thus, awareness of public is the only way to prevent the spread of AIDs. Sex is a private, individual decision. It is difficult to monitor it. The government can help by spreading awareness about the causes of the disease, making accessible healthcare and medicine, bringing HIV/AIDS into the public health agenda and developing an environment where people with HIV can live with dignity. It is encouraging that the government constituted a National Council on AIDS headed by the Prime Minster of India to pay greater attention to the campaign against AIDS.[107]

(vii) Public Health *vis-à-vis* HIV/AIDS Patients

In *Lucy R.D. Souza* v. *State of Goa*,[108] the question whether the Section 53(i)(viii) of Goa, Daman and Diu Public Health Act, 1985, which was amended in 1987 is reasonable and not violative of Articles 14, 19(1)(d) and 21 of the Constitution in case of the isolation of the HIV/AIDS patients. The Court held that the isolation of the patients has a scientific basis and it is one of the proper measures for the prevention of the AIDS-hence, the above said section is reasonable and not violative of the above mentioned articles of the Constitution. In a conflict between right of an individual and the public interest, the former must yield to the latter.

In *LX* v. *Union of India, Delhi High Court*,[109] LX, an undertrial, tested HIV-positive. A drop in his CD4 count necessitated his commencement on Anti-Retroviral Therapy (ART). Subsequently, LX

107. PM announces National AIDS Council, *Legal News & Views*, February 2005, at p. 7.
108. AIR 1990 Bom. 355.
109. Available at http://www.lawyerscollective.org. visited on 25 January, 2010.

ought to continue to provide him ART despite his release. In a series of interim orders, the Delhi High Court directed the Government to continue to provide ART to LX. Later, LX was directed to present himself at the All India Medical Sciences (AIMS) with his past records for the continuation of his treatment. Pursuant to the commencement of the ARV roll-out by the Government of India in April 2004, the High Court directed the government to provide ART to LX under the ARV roll-out programme and to reimburse AIMS for the costs incurred by them in providing treatment to LX.

In *Subodh Sharma & Anrs.* v. *State of Assam & Ors.*,[110] Public Interest Litigation was filed by the petitioners, namely, Subodh Sharma and Sabita Goswami on behalf of the miserable plight of a woman namely, Jahanbi Goswami Sharma, wife of an AIDS patient. The PIL was filed to espouse the cause of those who are infected or suspected to have been infected by HIV or AIDS, and the members of their family. The first HIV positive case was detected in Assam in 1990. Assam is surrounded by Manipur, Tripura, Nagaland, Meghalaya and Arunachal Pradesh and is the abode to a large number of floating populations. Therefore, special attention for HIV/AIDS intervention programme is necessary to spread awareness and impart information about the disease apart from effective steps in providing medical care.[111]

The grievances of the petitioners were that funds released for the project were deposited in the revenue deposit and was not utilized for the purpose it was allotted. The State is yet to constitute AIDS Control Society under the Societies Registration Act with representation from NGOs. In addition to constitution of the society, there must be a system to heck as to whether funds used in the project has been utilized properly. The Court disposed of the writ petition by directing the respondents to property implement the guidelines and strategies formulated by the National AIDS Control Organization (NACO) in letter and spirit. It also directed that not to divert the funds released by the Government of India to any other Heads of Account except for the purposes of implementation of the programme as per guidelines and strategies formulated by the NACO and the funds with held so far be released for the programme, if not already lapsed.[112]

(viii) To Secure Health to Its Citizen is Primary Duty of State under Articles 21 and 47 of the Constitution

According to the General Comment 14, Committee on Economic,

110. *Ibid.*
111. *Ibid.*
112. *Ibid.*

Social and Cultural Rights,[113] the right to health like all human rights, imposes three types or levels of obligations on State parties: the obligations to respect, protect and fulfil. The obligation to respect requires states to refrain from interfering directly or indirectly with the enjoyment of the right to health. The obligation to protect requires states to take measures that prevent third parties from interfering with what Article 12 guarantees. Finally, the obligation to fulfil requires states to adopt appropriate legislative, administrative, budgetary, judicial, promotional and other measures towards the full realization of the right to health. In turn, the obligation to fulfil contains obligation to facilitate provide and promote.

Article 21 of the Constitution makes it obligatory for the State to safeguard the right to life of persons.[114] The right to health, i.e. the right to the highest attainable standards of physical and mental health and access to health care facilities being an integral part of the right to life, it can be said that the State is under an obligation to safeguard the heath of persons.

The State is bound to provide medical aid and treatment to persons suffering from sickness, injury or disease and if it, through the hospitals and health centres established by it, fails to provide such care, it would be considered as a violation of Article 21. In *Paschim Bang Keth Mazdoor Samiti* v. *State of West Bengal*[115], the Court held that; Article 21 imposes an obligation on the State to safeguard the right to life of every person. Preservation of human life is thus of paramount importance. The Government hospitals run by the State and the Medical Officers employed therein are duty-bound to extend medical assistance for preserving human life. Failure on the part of a Government hospital to provide timely medical treatment to a person in need of such treatment results in the violation of his right to life guaranteed under Article 21.

Not only is the State under an obligation to provide facilities for medical care but if a government servant has to undergo treatment in any other hospital due to emergency or under reference from a government hospital, the State has to bear the expenses incurred by it.

In *State of Punjab* v. *Mohinder Singh Chawla*,[116] it was held that it is now well settled that the right to health is integral to the right to life. Government has the constitutional obligation to provide facilities. If a government servant has suffered an ailment which requires treatment

113. Ravi Duggal, "Operationalizing Right to Health Care in India", www.cehat.org./paper 7.htm.

114. *Paschim Bang Kheth Mazdoor Samiti* v. *State of West Bengal*, AIR 1996 SC 2426.

115. *Ibid.*

116. AIR 1997 SC 1225 at 1227.

therein, it is the duty of the State to bear the expenses incurred by the government servant.

Courts have recognized that it may not be possible for the government to provide for sophisticated hospitals in every village in the country. However, the Government has to assist persons to get treatment and at least, primary health centres can be established in villages.

In *Mahendra Pratap Singh* v. *State of Orissa*,[117] the Court observed that:

> In a country like ours, it may not be possible to have sophiscated hospitals but definitely, can within their limitations aspire to have a primary health centre. The Government is required to assist people to get treatment and lead a healthy life. Healthy society is collective gain and no government should make any effort to smother it. Primary concern should be primary health centre and technical fetters should not be introduced as subterfuges to cause hindrances in the establishment of health centres.

Thereby there is an implication that the enforcing of the right to life is a duty of the State and that duty covers the providing of primary health centres.[118] The Court has also laid stress on the point that the State cannot plead lack of financial resources to carry out the directions meant to provide adequate medical services to people.[119] However, in *State of Punjab* v. *Ram Lubhaya Bagga*,[120] the Court observed:

No right could be absolute in a welfare state. A man is a social animal. He cannot live without the co-operation of a large number of persons. Every article one uses is the contribution of many. Hence, every man's rights have to give way to the rights of the public at large. Every fundamental right under Part III of the Constitution is not absolute and it is to be permissible with a reasonable restrictions. This principle equally applies when there is any constraint on the health budget on account of financial stringencies. But we do hope that the government will give due consideration and priority to the health budge in future.

In *Confederation of Ex-Servicemen* v. *Union of India*,[121] a five Judges Bench of the Supreme Court held that to get free and full medical care/medical aid is not a fundamental right of ex-servicemen. The instant petition under Article 32 of the Constitution was filed by the

---

117. AIR 1997 Ori. 37, cited in "Legal Position Paper on Right to Health Care", Part II.
118. Legal Position paper on Right to Health Care, Part II, www.cehat, org./rthc/paper 3htm.
119. M.P. Jain, Constitution of India, 1317 (2003).
120. AIR 1998 SC 1703.
121. (2006) 8 SCC 399.

Confederation of Ex-Servicemen Associations seeking direction to the respondent Union of India to recognize the right of full and free medicare of ex-servicemen, their families and dependents treating such right as one of the fundamental rights guaranteed under the Constitution of India. Another prayer was made to direct the respondents to take necessary steps to ensure that full and free medicare was provided to ex-servicemen, their families and dependents on at par with in-service defence personnel. Justice C.K. Thakkar on behalf of the Court partly allowed the writ petition, and held that free and full medical aid/facilities are not a part of the fundamental right of ex-servicemen. Relying on a number of decisions of the apex Court, held that the policy decision in formulating contributory scheme for ex-servicemen is in accordance with the provisions of the Constitution and also in consonance with the law laid down by the Supreme Court. The five-judges bench settled the principles and held that to get free and full medical care is not a fundamental right of ex-servicemen. The Court was of the considered opinion that though the right to medical aid is a fundamental right of all citizens including ex-servicemen guaranteed by Article 21 of the Constitution, framing of scheme for ex-servicemen and asking them to pay "one-time contribution" neither violates Part III nor it is inconsistent with Part-IV of the Constitution.

In *Reliance Infocom Ltd.* v. *Chemanchery Grama Panchayat & Ors.*,[122] a Division Bench of the Kerala High Court has observed that the use of mobile phone is a common phenomenon throughout the country and has made drastic changes in the people's lifestyle. It has revolutionized the medium of communication throughout the world. Constant use of mobile phone, it is reported, may have its own adverse ill-effects on human health as well. The vital question that was posed for consideration in this case was not with regard to ill-effects of use of mobile phones but whether installation of mobile base station and its functioning would cause any health hazards to the people who are residing nearby. Apprehension had also been voice that radiation emanating from large telecommunication towers would expose human beings living within the magnetic field to fatel diseases like cancer, embryo disruption and changes in DNA structure.

Justice K.S. Radhakrishnan while delivering the judgment on behalf of the Court held the RF exposures from Mobile Base Stations are much less than from radio, FM radio and television transmissions and that the consensus of scientific community is that the radiation from mobile phone stations is far too low to produce health hazards if people are kept away from direct access to the antenna and the overall evidence

122. AIR 2007 Kerala 33.

indicates that they are unlikely to pose a risk to health. The Court conducted that permission granted for installation of Mobile Base station by the Panchayat would not cause health hazards to the people of the locality nor will it affect the fundamental rights guaranteed to citizens under Article 21 of the Constitution. However, Court gave a general direction to the TRAI to make periodical inspection to ascertain whether radiation emanated from the mobile base stations would cause any heath hazards to the people of the locality.

(ix) Right to Food and Public Health

Article 25 of the Universal Declaration of Human Rights, 1948 provides that "everyone has the right to a standard of living adequate for the health and well-being of himself and of his family, including food, clothing, housing and medical care and necessary social services". Similarly, Article 11 of the International Covenant on Economic, Social and Cultural Rights stipulates that "the States parties to the present covenant recognize the right of everyone to an adequate standard of living for himself and his family, including adequate food, clothing and housing, and to the continuous improvement of living conditions. And that recognizing the fundamental right to everyone to be free from hunger, they shall take the measures, for securing these rights."

The Heads of State and Government gathered in Rome at the World Food Summit at the invitation of Food and Agricultural Organization (FAO), reaffirmed on November 13, 1996, the right of everyone to access to safe and nutritious food, consistent with the right to adequate food and the fundamental right of everyone to be free from hunger. They considered it intolerable that more than 800 million people throughout the world and particularly in developing countries, do not have enough food to meet their basic nutritional needs, and pledged their political will and their common and national commitment to achieving food security for all and to an ongoing effort to eradicate and hunger in all countries.[123] The Second National Family Health Survey (1998-99) provides ample evidence of the catastrophic nature of nutritional problem in India. According to this survey, 47 percent of all Indian children are undernourished, 52 percent of all adult women are anaemic, and 36 percent have a Body Mass Index (BMI) below the cut-off of 18.5 commonly associated with chronic energy deficiency.[124]

123. Yogendra Kumar Srivastava, Right to Food: A Human Right, *The PRP Journal of Human Rights*, July-September 2001, p. 11.

124. International Institute for Population Sciences (2000), pp. 246, 250 and 270. The 'Child under Nutrition' figures are based on weight-for-age data for children under the age of three; see also Jean Dreze, Democracy and Right to Food, *Economic and Political Weekly*, April 24, 2004, Vol. 39(17), p. 1723.

These nutritional deficiencies have devastating consequences for the well-being and future of Indian people. The Noble Laureate Amartya Sen endorsed that India had more endemic hunger and regular undernourishment than any part of the world.[125] According to the Report of the FAO, the number of hungry people in India between 1998 and 2000 increased by 18 million and remained unchanged as a share of population at broadly one-fifth.[126] Moreover, a study by the UN World Food Programme and M.S. Swaminathan Research Foundation revealed that about one-third of people starve for want of food and some 160 million go without a square meal while granaries overflow.[127] The right to freedom from hunger is fundamental, which means that the State has an obligation to ensure, as a minimum, that the people do not starve. This right is closely linked to right to life itself. In addition, however, State should also take all the necessary steps possible towards the goal of full enjoyment of the right to adequate food. This means everyone must have physical and economic access at all times to food is adequate in quantity and quality to allow for a healthy and active life. By implication and in view of the Supreme Court interpretation, the right to life also includes the right to health. For healthy life, the food available should be adequate in quality as well as quantity to meet nutritional requirements. Henry Shue talks of the Right to 'subsistence', which will include food among other things as a means of leading a healthy and satisfactory life.[128] It is true that a prospective society must have healthy subjects and good health cannot be achieved without adequate good food.[129] The level of a country's progress and development is estimable based upon its ability to save its people from starvation.

In *Shaibya Shukla* v. *State of UP*,[130] the tenders were invited as regards auction of the chemically treated Soyabean which was unfit for human consumption. The tender notice as well as auction was held invalid when it was offered to the public in general. The Articles 21, 47 and 48 of the Constitution of India, as its offer for sale by auction in general market to anyone, is likely to create danger to the life and health of human being as well as animals also. The Court further held that Articles 47 and 48 of the Constitution respectively contain directions

125. B.N. Arora, Human Rights: Right to Food Eluding Millions in India, *Mainstream*, 6 December 2003, pp. 8-9.
126. *Frontline*, 22 November 2002, p. 113.
127. *Nation and the World*, 11 December 2002, p. 24.
128. Quoted by Atul Vishwanathan and Ketan Makhija, Arrest Hunger: The Right to Food, *The Lawyers' Collective*, February 2004, Vol. 19, p.13.
129. T.V. Subba Rao, Right to Food—Perspectives in Law, *The Academy Law Review*, 1995, Vol. 19: 1 & 2, p. 257.
130. AIR 1993 All. 171.

which impose duty on the state to raise level of nutrition and standard of living and improve public health.

Similarly, the matter came before the consideration of Supreme Court in *Tapan Kumar Sadhu Khan* v. *Food Corporation of India and Ors.*[131] The appellant Tapan Kumar Sadhukhan was proprietor of one M/s. Makali Trading Company dealing in manufacture and supply of cattle food, poultry food, manure, etc. as a registered contractor of respondent 1. His plea was that rice was unfit to human consumption was sought to be sold as substandard damaged rice, subject to upgradation by the purchasers. The appellant further claimed that the quality control manual issued by Respondent 1 relating to central legislation regarding food grains handling, made no provision for sale of substandard/damaged rice can be upgraded for making it fit for human consumption. The appellant expressed concern that while selling these rice respondent was not taking any responsibility. In the present case civil appeal arose out of the order of Division Bench of High Court of Calcutta. The Supreme Court has directed the Food Corporation of India to secure a commanding position in the foodgrains trade of the country. Being an agency of the State, it must confirm in the letter and spirit of Article 47 of the Constitution. The trading activity in rice and other foodgrains must be done keeping in view the obligation to improve public health. The stock that is found suitable cannot be immediately used for human consumption, for that can be so used only after being upgraded. If substandard rice is released and sold in open market, it would be highly injurious to the consumers. Public health would be jeopardized if such rice is consumed by members of the public. A mere undertaking is no guarantee that the dealer will upgrade the rice before marketing the same. The most ideal solution is that Food Corporation of India should itself upgrade the rice before sale.[132]

(x) Rehabilitation of Tsunami Victims and their Health

In *Kranti* v. *Union of India and Others*,[133] the division Bench of the Supreme Court held that the work of rehabilitation of tsunami victims in the Andaman and Nicobar Islands though has been taken up in all earnest, yet there is still a good deal which is required to be done to ameliorate the misery of the victims. Each of the problems elaborated by the writ petitioners need to be dealt with, to enable the victims of the tsunami families to cope with the disaster. The Court acknowledged that the monsoons are due at any time to add to the misery of those who

131. (1996) 6 SC 101.
132. *Id.*, at 102; paras 13 and 22.
133. (2007) 6 SCC 744.

were rendered homeless by the tsunami. Spread of diseases is a serious threat as also the spectre of hunger. Therefore, the Court directed that the immediate action must be taken for health facilities, lack of drinking water, and shortage of food. The Court also directed the local administration to arrange for preservation of the rainwater by means of rainwater harvesting and construction of ponds, where the rainwater could be collected and used. As far as the lack of health facilities are concerned, it was pointed out that where population was of about 6000 people there was only a male doctor, there was no lady doctor to treat women patients, and when the only doctor available goes on leave there was no replacement. The Court as suggested by the petitioner directed the administration to take immediate steps to arrange for more doctors who if necessary could be airlifted to the different islands in emergent situation.[134]

(xi) Faith Healing as a Form of Curing Ailments

In *Rajesh Kumar Srivastava* v. *A.P. Verma*,[135] the Lal Mahendra Sewa Shakti Samiti, Kotwa, Allahabad through its members and Sri Ajay Pratap Singh had no right to hold congregation in public parks, charge consideration and to profess and practice in public that the chanting of '*Om Namoh Shivai*' was cure to all ailments. Such a practice was illegal and violative of law as well as the right of citizen including those innocent persons suffering from various ailments, who participated in such congregation guaranteed under Article 21 of Constitution of India and which the State and the Court are obliged to protect. The Allahabad High Court held that the right to cure ailments through religious practices including "faith healing" cannot be claimed as fundamental right. No person has an absolute right to freedom of religion. Every form and method of curing and healing must have established procedures, which must be proved by known and accepted methods, and approved by experts in the field of medicines. It is only when a particular form, method of path is accepted by the experts in the field of medicines that can be permitted to be practiced in public. The right to health included in Article 21 does not come in conflict or overlap with the right to propagate and profess religion. These two are separate and distinct rights. Where the right to health is regulated by validly enacted legislation, the right to cure the ailment through religious practices including 'faith healing' cannot be claimed as a fundamental right.

To safeguard the public health, safety, and welfare, morality is one

134. *Id.*, at 747.
135. AIR 2005 All. 175 (popularly known as chanting of *Om Namoh Shivai* Case).

of the most basic of the governmental powers. Yet its exercise always raises serious questions because that exercise invariably involves a clash between the rights that are fundamental to a society. Incidentally, our Constitution does not provide explicit help in resolving these kinds of problems, whereas the liberal democratic society after all has real and fundamental interest in protecting individual liberty as well as public health, morals and safety as rightly said by Jagdish Swarup in his book. 'Constitution of India'.[136] Professing of 'health healing' in public on charging consideration was violative of constitutional and legislative scheme. The claim to cure ailments fall in the domain of right to health. A person has no right to induce others to believe in his faith in religion to cure others from ailments.

(xii) Implementation of International Standards in India

In *M/s. Cosmopolitan Hospitals & Anr.* v. *Smt. Vasantha P. Nair & Ors.*,[137] the Supreme Court reiterated its stand towards the Constitutional Right of an employee, to health and medical aid, and safety from occupational health hazards. It ruled that the employer is obliged to provide protective measures to workmen Asbestos industries are bound by the directions issued by the International Labour Organization (ILO) in "All Safety in the Use of Asbestos'. It is, therefore, necessary to issue appropriate directions in the light of the rules issued by the ILO and the same shall be binding on all the industries.[138]

(xiii) Processes and Remedies

Constitution is the basic law of land from which all other laws derive their authority. The Courts can declare any law or part of law, which violates the Constitution, as *ultra vires* the Constitution and, hence, invalid. A very important feature of the Indian Constitution is the fundamental rights guaranteed to every citizen which are listed in Part III of the Constitution. Any citizen whose fundamental rights have been violated or infracted can move the Supreme Court or the High Court, praying that the Court may issue a writ to appropriate authority against such violation. Besides this, any aggrieved party can file a civil or criminal complaint or suit against the other party in an appropriate complaint or suit against the other partly in an appropriate court having necessary territorial or pecuniary jurisdiction.

---

136. Jagdish Swarup, Constitution of India, 1106 (2006).
137. (1992) 1 CPR 820.
138. Butterworths, Legal Framework for Health Care in India, 24 (2002).

The Constitution of India under Article 32[139], 136,[140] 226,[141] and 227,[142] provides the right to move the Supreme Court or High Courts by appropriate proceedings for the enforcement of the rights conferred and guaranteed under the Constitution.

(A) Right to Move the Supreme Court

Any person whose rights have been infringed can move the Supreme Court under Article 32 of the Constitution. The Court in the recent past has liberalized the traditional private law rule that 'only a person who has suffered injury by reason of violation of his legal right or interest is entitled to seek judicial redress'. The Supreme Court has enlarged the rights of the citizens under this Article, for the purposes of dealing with public law. The Court in *Nilabati Behera's*[143] *case* entertained a letter as a petition and awarded compensation under clause (2) of Article 32 of the Constitution. The Supreme Court shall have the power to issue directions or orders or writs, including writs in the nature of *habeas corpus,*[144] *mandamus,*[145] *prohibition,*[146] *quo warranto*[147] and

139. Article 32 confers one of the "highly cherished rights". It is the right to move the Supreme Court for the enforcement of the fundamental rights.
140. The Supreme Court may, in its discretion, grant special leave to appeal from any judgment, decree, determination, sentence or order in any cause or matter passed or made by any Court or Tribunal in the territory of India.
141. Article 226(1) provides that notwithstanding anything in Article 32, every High Court shall have power, throughout the territories in relation to which it exercises jurisdiction to issue to any person or authority, including in appropriate cases, any government, within those territories, directions, orders or writs, including writs in the nature of *habeas corpus, mandamus, prohibition, quo warranto* and *certiorari* or any of them, for the enforcement of any of the rights conferred by Part II and for any other purpose. Clause (1) of Article 226 says that the High Court may issue writs, etc. to person or authority within those territories in relation to which it exercises jurisdiction.
142. Article 227 (1).
143. (1993) 2 SC 746.
144. Writ of *Habeas Corpus* is a Latin term which means "You may have the body", this writ is inform, an order, issued by the Court calling upon the person by whom another person is detained, to bring that person before the Court and to let the Court know, by what authority, he has detained that person. If the detention is found to be without legal justification, the person is ordered to be released. The main object of the writ is to provide quick and immediate remedy.
145. Writ of *Mandamus* means, "the order". This writ is thus a command issued by a Court asking a public authority to perform a public duty belonging to its office.
146. Writ of prohibition is issued primarily to prevent on in prior court or tribunal from exceeding its jurisdiction. It is to prohibit the inferior Courts or tribunals from exercising power or authority not vested in them.
147. Writ of *Quo Warranto* means, "what is your authority". The writ is issued to call upon the holder of a public office to show the Court, under what authority he is holding that office.

certiorari,[148] whichever may be appropriate, for the enforcement of any of the rights conferred by this part.

(B) Right to Move the High Court

The Constitution of India under Article 226 provides the right to move the High Court by appropriate proceedings for the enforcement of the rights conferred and guaranteed under the Constitution and other laws.[149]

Even after 62 years of independence no effective steps have been taken to implement the Constitutional obligation upon the State to secure the health and strength of the people. The Supreme Court in its land mark judgments[150] has brought the medical facilities to be a part of life and liberty and imposes a duty not only upon the State but also the private employees to provide the health services during and after employment but no effective steps have been taken to implement it except by legislative enactments.[151]

The Supreme Court of India in a series of cases played a significant role and has awarded compensation to the victims and their families for the violation of right to health and even right to life guaranteed under the Constitution. The Court in realization of the right to health by recognizing it as a part of the fundamental right to life and issued suitable directions to the State authorities for the fulfilment of their duties. Though, the Court in a series of judgments has declared the right to health as a fundamental right but it has not been given the recognition by the states.[152]

In view of the increasing number of AIDS patients, it is necessary to formulate some guidelines for protecting the right to privacy of these unfortunate victims, whereas some time protecting the right to privacy of these unfortunate victims, whereas some time protecting the lives of others by passing on the information to the person to be affected by non-disclosure of the said information.[153]

Most of the hospitals/dispensaries particularly in villages do not have even minimum infrastructure. Health care is basic need of the

---

148. Writ of *Certiorai* literally means, "to certify". Like prohibition, the writ of *certiorari* is also a jurisdictional writ and is issued against judicial or quasi-judicial authorities, on similar grounds, i.e., excess of jurisdiction, want of jurisdiction of violation of the principles of natural justice.
149. Narender Kumar, *op. cit.*, p.524.
150. *Parmananda Katara* v. *Union of India*, AIR 1989 SC 2039; *Paschim Bang Khet Mazdoor Samiti* v. *State of W.B.* (1996) 4 SCC 37, *Consumer Education and Research Centre* v. *Union of India* (1995) 3 SCC 42, etc.
151. Right to health: Limits of Recognition available on cite http://www.manuatra.com.
152. *Ibid.*
153. Mr. *'X'* v. *Hospital 'Z'*, AIR 1999 SC 495.

people and needs to be taken due care of.[154]

The time taken in the cases related to medical malpractice or negligence is also very alarming, taking the example of *Achutrao H. Khodwa* v. *State of Maharashtra*,[155] the case filed in 1963 and its Supreme Court judgment came in 1996.

It is also minimum requirement of the hospitals to provide basic hygiene to the patients during operations and other treatments so as to avoid losses like suffered by the victims in the case of *A.S. Mittal* v. *State of U.P.*[156]

IV. SUM UP

The foregoing study reveals that right to health is an age old phenomenon. The concept of right to health has much to offer apart from the protection and preservation of the health. Despite some gains, the binding legal obligations in relation to health have not been sufficiently recognized and emphasized. Constitutionally recognized right to health can only be fulfilled through rational planning, which in turn is dependent on accurate and regular information-gathering and timely statistics on health needs from the Government, which are often unavailable. This may lead to the charges that the right to health is no more than a rhetorical one. However, jurisprudence reveals that Courts and lawyers are not completely incapable of . working with and pronouncing on the social right to health.

The decided cases on the health to the late nineties clearly shows that the right to health and access to medical treatment has become part of Article 21. A corollary of this development is that while so long the negative language of Article 21 was supposed to impose upon the State only the negative duty not to interfere with the life or liberty of and individual without the sanction of law, judges have now imposed a positive obligation upon the State to take steps for ensuring to the individual a better enjoyment of his life and dignity.[157]

India is a signatory to the *Alma-Ata* Declaration of 1978. The National Health Policy, approved by Parliament in 1983 clearly indicates India's commitment to the goal of Health for All by 2000 AD. These trends have resulted in greater degree of State involvement in the management of health services, and the establishment of nation-wide systems of health services with emphasis on primary health care approach.[158]

154. Narender Kumar, *op. cit.*, at 238.
155. AIR 1996 SC 2383.
156. AIR 1989 SC 1571.
157. *Ibid.*
158. K. Park, *Preventive and Social Medicine*, 21 (2005).

Among the cooperation of mankind and government, national and international organizations are working for achieving our health goals. The cooperation covers supplies of drugs and communicable diseases and achievement of "Health for All" through primary health care. The TCDC (Technical Cooperation in Developing Countries), ASEAN (Association of South-East Asian Nations) and the recently established SAARC (South Asia Association for Regional Cooperation) are important regional mechanisms for such cooperation.[159]

The eradication of small pox, the pursuit of "Health for All" and the campaign against smoking and AIDS are a few recent examples of international responsibility for the control of disease and promotion of health. Today, more than ever before, there is wider international understanding on matters relating to health and "Social Injustices" in the distribution of Health Services. The WHO (World Health Organization) is a major factor in fostering international cooperation in health. In keeping with its Constitutional mandate, WHO (World Health Organization) acts as a directing and coordinating authority on international health work.[160]

159. WHO (1986), Seventh Report World Health Situation, Vol. 4, Evaluation of the Strategy for Health for All, WHO, SEARO.
160. K. Park, *op. cit.*, at 21.

CHAPTER 4

Legal Dimensions of Right to Health under Various Legislations

I. INTRODUCTION

In India, the government's concern for health and safety of its people is indicated by the legislations enacted for health care. Recently Article 21 of the Indian Constitution has been interpreted to incorporate the right to health in right to life and hence this right having now acquired a constitutional status through judicial activism, can be judicially enforced.[1] The Directive Principles of State Policy provided against the exploitation of weaker sections of society, including children, and mandate the state to raise the levels of nutrition, the standard of living and improve public health. Protection improvement of environment and safeguarding forests and wildlife is also an obligation of the State.[2] These are contained in Articles 39, 47, 48A in Part IV of the Constitution. Numerous statutory enactments also safeguard the health of those employed in factories, large scale industrial undertakings and mines, the health of women and children and also protect human environment. These statutory enactments cover a wide range[3] of area

1. Right to Health: Limits of Recognition, http://www.nliu.com/art1.htm.
2. Apart from the Constitutional obligations, the definition of health in the Preamble of the WHO Constitution, which defines health as a state of complete physical, mental and social well-being and not merely the absence of diseases or infirmity; in also the major obligatory force.
3. The Juvenile Justice Act, 1986; the Mental Health Act, 1987; the Epidemic Disease Act, 1948; the Consumer Protection Act, 1986; the Vaccination Act, 1888 and other later Vaccination Acts are the few examples which cover wide range of health care activities in various fields.

including food safety legislations,[4] labour laws,[5] and environmental legislations,[6] and in fact, accord with the spirit of the Constitution.

Furthermore, to make freedom disease effective, various statutory provisions have been enacted to protect the health interests of the people. These include: The Indian Penal Code, 1860; the Fatal Accidents Act, 1855; the Dangerous Drugs Act, 1930; Prevention of Food Adulteration Act, 1954; the Medical Termination of Pregnancy Act, 1975; and the Transplantation of Human Organs Act, 1994, etc. We have all over the country, several hospitals, consumer tribunals and plural process of healing, at the service of the people, some run by the State, charitable institutions and by various private agencies for health protection.

II. RIGHT TO HEALTH UNDER VARIOUS LEGISLATIONS

Human life is precious and every person has a fundamental right to live with dignity. It is the duty of a welfare state to protect and develop the life of every citizen. Every nation has evolved its own system of laws to ensure the health rights of every citizen. These laws aim to establish humane system of health care based on the principles of equity, justice and efficiency. Right to health and health care is a fundamental right under Article 21 of the Constitution of India. This has also been emphasized by the Supreme Court of India in several rulings. This Article of the Constitution casts a special obligation on the State to protect citizen's life from medical and other forms of negligence.[7] The State's concern for the health and safety of its people is indicated by the large number of legislators, especially on health and an equally large number of provisions on health in Miscellaneous Acts. The Indian Supreme Court has interpreted Article 21 of the Indian Constitution in the Marshallian spirit[8] and has broadened its scope repeatedly, relying

4. Sections 269-277 of the Indian Penal Code; Drugs and Cosmetics Act, 1940; the Drugs Control Act, 1950; the Drugs and Magic-remedies (Objectionable Advertisements) Act, 1954 and the Infant Milk Substitutes, Feeding Bottles and Infant Foods (Regulation, Production, Supply and Distribution) Act, 1992 deal with food safety and related issues.
5. The Factories Act, 1948; Mines Act, 1952; Plantation Labour Act, 1951; Beedi and Cigar Workers' Act, 1966; Dock Workers Act, 1986 and the Employees' State Insurance Act, 1948 are few of the important legislations.
6. The Environment (Protection) Act, 1986 and the Wild Life (Protection) Act, 1972; Air (Prevention and Control of Pollution) Act, 1986; the National Environmental Tribunal Act, 1995.
7. K.P.S. Mahalwar, Indian Constitution and the Weaker Sections, 98 (2007).
8. Chief Justice Marshall said the Constitution was "made for ages to come", and consequently had to be adopted to the various crises of affairs—*M.C. Cullah* v.

on general legal doctrines, international conventions[9] and fascinatingly, the Directive Principles of State Policy, thus making some of them enforceable. The Courts in India have shown keen interest in protecting the health of the people in the society and have accepted it in clear-cut manner that administrative as well as judicial wings of the State are under a duty not to adopt an indifferent attitude in this respect.[10] Right to health is one of the various indivisible rights[11] that have been recognized by the Supreme Court under Article 21.

(i) Medical Health Laws

In India, the right to practice in allopathic, homeopathic, ayurvedic, unani and other systems of medicine is regulated by central and state legislation. So it is the duty of the medical professionals to be aware about the basic laws. These requirements have become almost obligatory ever since the Supreme Court judgment of 1995 in the case of *Indian Medical Association* v. *V.P. Shantha*,[12] whereby the medical services have been brought under the purview of the Consumer Protection Act of 1986. Code of Medical Ethics, Dentist Act, 1948; the Pharmacy Act, 1948; the Pre-natal Diagnostic Techniques (Regulation and Prevention of Misuse) Act, 1994, etc. are some prominent Central Acts which provide minimum standards for medical education, enrolment of doctors and also regulate their professional conduct by formulating the Code of Medical Ethics. In order to understand the efficacy, functioning and regulation of medical professionals under the aforesaid Central Acts it is necessary to examine them. In *C.E.S.C. Limited* v. *Subhash Chandra Bose*,[13] in his minority judgment Ramaswami, J. referred Article 25(2) of the Universal Declaration of

Mayland, (1819) 4 Wheel 17 US 316.

9. *Jolly George Varghese* v. *Bank of Cochino*, (1980) 2 SCR 913; *Vellore Citizens' Welfare Forum* v. *Union of India* (1996) 5 SCC 647; *People's Union of Civil Liberties* v. *Union of India*, (1980) 2 SCR 913 and *Vishaka* v. *State of Rajasthan*; (1997) 3 LRC 361 are some of the cases in which Indian Courts have relied on the International Conventions.
10. *Municipal Corporation of Delhi* v. *Suraj Ram* (1995) 2 Cr.L.J. 571.
11. Right to Food, Right to Shelter, Right to Clean decent environment, Right Against Corruption, Right to Education, Right to Livelihood, Right to Education, Right to Privacy and Right to have proper roads are few of the rights which have been incorporated into Article 21 of the Indian Constitution. These rights shifted the focus of Article 21 from negative to positive obligations of the State.
12. (1995) 6 SCC 651.
13. AIR 1992 SC 573. The case was heard by the three Judges Bench of the Supreme Court consisting of Ranganath Mishra, C.J., M.M. Punchi and K. Ramaswami, JJ. Judges were differing in their views. The majority view was taken by Rangnath Mishra, C.J. and Punchhi, J. and the minority view by K. Ramaswami.

Human Rights, Article 7(b) of the International Covenant on Economic, Social and Cultural Rights, and Article 39(e) of the Constitution of India and held that the right to health and medical care is a fundamental right. Right to livelihood springs from the right to life guaranteed under Article 21. The health and strength of workers is an integral facet of right to life. The aim of fundamental rights is to create an egalitarian society to free all citizens from coercion or restrictions by society and to make liberty available for all. Right to human dignity, development of personality, social protection, right to rest and leisure as fundamental human rights to common man mean nothing more than the status without means. To the tillers of the soil, wage earners, labourers, wood-cutters, rickshaw pullers, scavengers and hut dwellers, the civil and political rights are mere 'cosmetic rights' socio-economic and cultural rights are their means and relevant to them to realize the basic aspirations of meaningful right to life.

In the following section an attempt has been made to give a brief survey of these legislations:

(A) Code of Medical Ethics[14]

Doctors have an onerous responsibility to the public. Their profession demands utmost devotion and sincerity. Since they deal with the lives of people, it is expected of them that they take the maximum care. Physicians should try to improve their medical knowledge and skill, and should make available to their patients and colleagues the benefit of their professional attainments. The honoured ideals of the medical profession imply that the responsibilities of the physician extends not only to individuals but also to society.[15] The press has been highly appreciative when the doctors really do their duty with devotion and dedication. When few bottles of highly contaminated bottles of life saving fluids were seized by the alert doctors at the capitals Ram Manohar Lohia hospital before they could be administered to critical patients, it was given wide publicity by the press.[16]

The report on Lok Nayak Jaiprakash Narain Hospital that its operation theatres are high risk zones speaks volumes about the health care being provided in one of the capital's prestigious hospitals. For lack of facilities critical patients are either being discharged or being

---

14. The Medical Council of India is empowered under Section 33 of the Indian Medical Council Act 1956 to formulate a Code of Medical Ethics for doctor. A copy of the Code along with a declaration is given to all the new entrants at the time of registration and the applicant is obliged to read and abide by the same. (A full text of the code of Medical Ethics formulated by the Medical Council of India).
15. Code of Medical Ethics, para 2.
16. M.P. Singh, *International Conference on Global Health Law*, 166 (1997).

kept on medicines so to be a recognized medical practitioner a person should possess a valid/recognized medical qualification or medical degree and should be registered with the relevant council or board.[17]

(B) Pre-Natal Diagnostic Techniques (Regulation and Prevention of Misuse) Act, 1994

The Act[18] provides for the regulation of the use of pre-natal diagnostic techniques for the purpose of detecting genetic or metabolic disorders, chromosomal abnormalities or certain congenital malformations and sex linked disorders and prevention of misuse of such techniques for the purpose of pre-natal sex determination leading to female foeticide. The Act bans the use of medical techniques and technologies for pre-natal diagnostics except in cases where the pregnant woman is above 35 years of age, has a history of two or more abortions or foetal loss, has a history of being exposed to potentially teratogenic drugs, radition, infection or hazardous chemicals or has a family history of mental retardation or physical deformities. The Act also declares illegal any advertisement regarding the availability of pre-natal sex detection facilities at clinics, laboratories or centres. The regulation of these centres is to be achieved through Governmental appointed bodies.

(C) The Medical Termination of Pregnancy (MTP) Act, 1971 and MTP Rules, 1975[19]

This law provides the liberalized conditions for women to seek abortion, and doctors to do it. Following conditions are mentioned in the law when a pregnant woman can get her aborted:

(a) Therapeutic: When the continuation of pregnancy endangers the life of women or may cause grave injury to her physical or mental health.

(b) Social: When economic and social environment is not suitable for continuation of pregnancy and secondly contraceptive failure.

(c) Humanitarian reasons (e.g. rape).

(d) Eugenic reasons: When there is a risk of the child born with serious physical or mental handicaps (e.g. congenital defects, etc.),

(e) When pregnant women is mentally not sound (e.g.

17. *Ibid.*
18. For detail see Pre-Natal Diagnostic Technique (Regulation and Prevention of Misuse) Act, 1994.
19. For detail see Medical Termination of Pregnancy (MTP) Act, 1971 and MTP Rules, 1975.

Schizophrenia, mania, etc.), written consent of the guardian is necessary for abortion of such women.

Medical termination of pregnancy can be done by registered medical practitioner registered under the MCI (Medical Council of India) Act only and those who have undergone 6 months housemenship or 3 years post-graduate training in obstetric and gynecology or any register medical practitioners who have conducted 25 cases of medical termination of pregnancy in approved institution, not by the practitioners of other system of medicine. When pregnancy is less than 12 weeks duration then one medical practitioner can perform the (MTP) Medical Termination of Pregnancy Act, 1971, but if the duration of pregnancy is more than 12 weeks but less than 20 weeks then two medical practitioners should consult each other and certify that if pregnancy is not terminated may endanger the life of that woman or mental on physical injury or pregnancy will give rise to congenital defect in child.

The Medical Termination of Pregnancy (MTP) can be conducted in governmental hospital/nursing homes/centre approved the Directorate of Health Services, or by Chief Medical Officer of district.

(D) Transplantation of Human Organs Act, 1994[20]

This Act repeals the Ear Drums and Ear Bones (Authority for use of Therapeutic Purposes) Act, and Eyes (Authority for Use for Therapeutic Purposes) Act, 1982.

Various terms are defined in detail, some of the important terms are as follows:

(a) Brain-stem death[21]—the stage at which all functions of the brain-stem have permanently and irreversibly ceased and is so certified by registered medical practitioners or board of experts, or any authority which have power to do so.

(b) Deceased Person[22]—a person in whom permanent disappearance of all evidence of life occurs, by reason of brain-stem death or in a cardiopulmonary sense, at any time after life birth has taken place.

(c) Donor[23]—any person, not less than eighteen years of age, who voluntarily authorizes the removal of any of his human organs for therapeutic purpose.

20. For detail see Transplantation of Human Organs Act, 1994.
21. Section 2.
22. See Section 2; *ibid.*
23. *Ibid.*

Other terms like human organs, near relatives, therapeutic purpose, transplantation, and payment are also defined. Any person more than 18 years authorizes the removal, before his death, of any human organ of his body. Any written authority given before his death or willingly given authority to any of his near relatives can be accepted or he doesn't showed unwillingness before death, of any human organ of his body. Any written authority given before his death or willingly given authority to any of his near relatives, can be accepted or he doesn't showed unwillingness before death, then person possess in his dead body is authorized for removal of organs. Before removal of body organs, at least registered medical practitioner should certify that life or brain-stem function have ceased.

A dead body lying in a hospital or prison and not claimed by any of the near relatives within forty-eight hours from the time of the death of concerned person, a person incharge of any other authorized person who strongly believe that body will not be claimed authorizes for removal of body organs. No hospital or place is legally authorized to remove the human organs unless appropriate authority like state or central government authorizes and register it.[24]

Any illegal supply or giving commitment or publishing/ advertisement to supply or human organs or giving human organs on payment by an individual or society, or organization, or agent are considered as an offence and punishment may be awarded.[25]

(E) Mental Health Act, 1987

Under the Mental Health Act, 1987,[26] a "Mentally Ill Person" means a person who is in need of treatment by reason of any mental disorder other than mental retardation.[27]

Mental hospitals and nursing homes can be established or run only on obtaining a licence from State or Central authority for mental health services, and would be regulated for proper functioning and care of the mentally ill. Psychiatric services provided from a general hospital or nursing home would not be covered by the licensing and regulating rules.[28]

Any person aged eighteen and above can voluntarily get admission for inpatient treatment. In case of minor (less than 18 years of age) mentally ill can be presented for admission by the guardian as a voluntary patient. The medical office in charge, should be satisfied

24. Sections 10-12 and 14-17; *ibid.*
25. Sections 18-22; *ibid.*
26. For detail see "Mental Health Act".
27. Sub-section (1) of Section 2; *ibid.*
28. Sections 3-10; *ibid.*

about the need of inpatient treatment.[29]

Patients admitted on voluntary basis, if they request for discharge, are obligated to be discharged by the medical officer-in-charge within 24 hours of receiving the request, provided the medical officer is convinced that the discharge will not harm the interest of the voluntary patient. In such case, the medical officer would constitute a Board of two medical officers and seek their opinion. If the Board is of the opinion that such voluntary patient needs further treatment in the mental hospital or mental nursing home, the medical officer shall not discharge the voluntary patient but continue his treatment for a period not exceeding 90 (ninety) days at a time.[30]

Admission to mental hospital can also be made on request of a relative or friend of the patient if the patient is not in a position to express willingness for admission as voluntary patient, provided the medical officer-in-charge is satisfied, that is in the interest of the patient to do so. This application should be accompanied by two medical certificates (one from a medical officer who is working in governmental service) stating that the person has such mental illness and it requires inpatient observation and treatment.[31]

No person admitted on the request of another person can be kept in the Mental Hospital for than 90 days unless admitted under a Reception Order.[32]

Apart from voluntary admission, a mentally ill person can be admitted through reception order. An application for reception order may be made by the Medical Officer-in-Charge of a mental hospital, by the spouse or by any other relative of the mentally ill patient for admission to the Magistrate. The application should be accompanied by two medical certificates from two independent medical practitioners certifying the need for admission for treatment, and that is in the interest, for personal safety of the patient, or that of others. The medical practitioners should have seen the patient within the last ten days prior to the application. The Magistrate can pass the Reception Order or Rejection to the application, after personally reviewing the documents and personally examined the alleged mentally ill (unless for reasons which he considers expedient not to personally examine). The consideration of the application should be made in the presence of applicant, the allegedly mentally ill person, and the person appointed by the allegedly mentally ill to represent him.[33] A reception order is valid

29. Sections 15, 16, 17; *ibid.*
30. Sub-section 3 of Section 18; *ibid.*
31. Sub-sections 1 and 2 of Section 19; *ibid.*
32. Sub-section 2 of section 19; *ibid.*
33. Section 22; *ibid.*

upto 30 days only or till discharged.[34] A mentally ill patient admitted by relative or friend can also apply to the Magistrate for discharge.[35] Detailed procedures are laid down for being taking into custody by the police, confinement and security of mentally ill persons or prisoners in mental hospital.[36]

Detailed procedures are laid down for ensuring proper care and custody to a mentally ill person by his legal relatives, through the police stations.[37]

The Act provides for regular, thorough supervision of mental hospitals and nursing homes by monthly joint inspection of three visitors designated by the State authority for mental health services.[38]

Any person (other than a prisoner) admitted to a mental hospital who feels he has recovered from his illness can apply for discharge to the Magistrate, supported by a medical certificate from the medical officer-in-charge of the hospital;[39] he can be allowed to take leave from the hospital on request of his relatives or friends for a specified period.[40]

Detailed procedures of safety in hospital, or during leave of absence or transfer to the another hospital has been laid down in Sections 45, 46, 47. Similarly, safe custody and protection of property of the patients has been defined in Sections 50-77.

Physical or mental cruelty of mentally ill patients is forbidden. Similarly, conduct of research on a mental patient is forbidden, unless voluntarily consents is obtained. The human rights of a mentally ill person are protected under Section 81. Penalties and fines for contravening the provisions are enlisted in the Act.[41]

(F) The Epidemic Diseases Act, 1897

The Act[42] was passed to enable State governments to take measures to contain and to prevent the spread of any dangerous epidemic diseases if the existing laws are found to be inadequate to meet such contingencies. Hence, such orders and regulations are usually applicable while the danger of the epidemic exists or is perceived to exist.

This is a very brief legislation consisting of four sections. Section 1 makes the Act applicable to whole of India. Section 2 concerns special

34. Section 31; *ibid.*
35. Sub-section 3 of Section 19; *ibid.*
36. Sections 23 and 25; *ibid.*
37. Section 25; *ibid.*
38. Section 37; *ibid.*
39. Section 43; *ibid.*
40. Section 46; *ibid.*
41. Sections 82 and 87; *ibid.*
42. For detail see "The Epidemic Diseases Act, 1897".

measures for control of epidemic diseases. Under Section 2 of this Act, if the state government is satisfied that an epidemic disease has occurred in any part of the State or the State is threatened by such an epidemic and considers that the provisions of the existing laws are insufficient to meet the requirements, it may take or empower any of its officers to take/prescribe such suitable measures after duly notifying the public. It may also determine the manner and by whom any expenses incurred shall be paid including compensation, if any. All measures are to be observed by the public or a person or a class of persons as it shall deem necessary to prevent the outbreak or spread of such disease. Any person disobeying any order or regulation made under this Act shall be deemed to have committed an offence is punishable.[43]

The State government may also take measures without prejudicing the provisions of the Epidemic Act and prescribe regulations for inspection of persons traveling by road, rail, air or sea or other means and consider segregation of persons suspected of being infected with any such disease either in a hospital, temporary accommodation or other suitable means. Section 2(a) of the Act empowers the central government to take similar action when an epidemic occurs in India or a part of it. In *Shiv Charan Das* v. *State*,[44] the High Court observed that Section 2 of the Epidemic Diseases Act authorizes the Government not only to promulgate a regulation itself but also to require or empower any other person to take such measures as may be necessary. It is, therefore, permissible under that section for the Government to authorize the Medical Officer of Health or the Chairman of a Municipal Board to issue the necessary regulation to prevent epidemic diseases, and that is done, no difficulty can arise in the strict compliance with the provisions of Section 195(1)(a) of the Criminal Procedure Code, 1973 (2 of 1974), in case the regulation is broken by any one." Section 3 lays down penalty for violation of the Act and reads as follows:

> "Penalty—Any person disobeying any regulation or order made under this Act shall be deemed to have committed an offence punishable under Section 188 of the IPC (Indian Penal Code) 45 of 1860."

The last section[45] provides protection to persons acting under the Act. It states that no suit or other legal proceeding shall lie against any person for anything done or in good faith intended to be done under this Act.

---

43. Section 188 of the Indian Penal Code.
44. 1958 ALJ 617 at 618-19.
45. Section 4 of the Epidemic Diseases Act, 1897.

(G) The Drugs and Cosmetic Act, 1940

The Drugs and Cosmetic Act[46] is mainly aimed to regulate the import, manufacture, distribution and sale of Drugs and Cosmetic, presumably for maintaining high standards of medical treatment.

All medicines (*Ayuvedic*, *Sidha* and *Unani*) for internal or external use of human beings or animals and all substances (other than food) intended to be used for or in the diagnosis, treatment, mitigation or prevention of any disease or disorder in human beings or animals including preparation applied on human body or to destroy insects.[47] The central or state governments have power to make rules and appoint inspector to control or inspect any drug or cosmetic for its standardization and safety which can be tested in the Central or State Drug laboratory.[48] The Government can prohibit manufacturing, importing or selling of any drug or cosmetic. Violation of law by any person or corporate manager or owner is liable for punishment for a term which may extend to 3-10 years and shall also be liable to fine which could be five hundred to ten thousand rupees or with both.[49]

(H) The Drugs and Magic Remedies (Objectionable) Advertisement Act, 1954[50]

Advertisement includes publication of the visual and written material in the press and other popular media including notices, circulars, labels, wrappers; as also audio/audio visual transmissions announcing and/or displaying the subject-matter. Drugs include medicines for internal and external use for humans and animals, substances used for diagnosis, mitigation or prevention of diseases and any article other than food intended to affect or influence in any way the structure or any organic function of the body.[51]

The Act provides for prevention of advertisements which may be exploited by unscrupulous and commercially oriented personnel for including people for self-medication of fraudulent, or exploitative or dangerous and harmful nature.[52]

The Act prohibits taking part in the publication of any advertisement relating to a drug which directly or indirectly gives a false impression regarding its true character or makes a false claim or is

46. For detail see Drugs and Cosmetic Act, 1940.
47. Section 3; *ibid.*
48. Section 7; *ibid.*
49. Sections 27 to 30; *ibid.*
50. For detail see "The Drugs and Magic Remedies (Objectionable) Advertisement Act, 1954".
51. Section 2(b).
52. *Ibid.*

otherwise misleading.[53]

Any person who has read, seen or heard such an advertisement is empowered to lodge a complaint with the police or the Court at the place where such an advertisement was encountered and the offence is cognizable wherein the advertiser, publisher, printer and editor or anyone directly involved are all individually liable.[54] Penalty for violation of the Act for the first offence is imprisonment upto six months or fine or both. For subsequent conviction, imprisonment may extend to one year.[55]

(I) The Patent Act, 1970[56]

The Government of India initiated to amend the Patent Act, 1970 to introduce product patent protection to drug, medicine or food. A Patent Amendment Bill was introduced to this effect in the 13th Lok Sabha but the Bill lapsed due to the dissolution of Lok Sabha. In the last week of August 2004, the cabinet decided to refer the Bill to a Group of Ministers (GOM) to study the implications of contentious issues in the Bill. The provisions of the referred bill were identical to the lapsed bill. This was a matter of concern as the Bill in its present form seriously compromised on the accessibility and availability of medicines, two important components of right to health. The right to life and health is a fundamental right guaranteed to every person living in India and is non-negotiable. As the health is one of the fundamental basic needs of all human beings. In legal terms, fundamental human rights treaties recognize the right to the enjoyment of the highest attainable standard of physical and mental health. Health policies encompass a number of elements from prevention to cure and access to drugs.

(ii) Food Laws

Food is the basic necessity. The growth of a human being depends upon and is governed by the quantity and purity of food that he eats. Food can be solid and liquid. The most important food law is the Prevention of Food Adulteration Act, 1954.[57] Food being a basic need, certain items of food are also covered under the Essential Commodities Act. Adulteration of food stuff has become so rampant and the evil is so

53. Section 4; *ibid.*
54. Section 9(a); *ibid.*
55. *Ibid.*
56. For detail see "The Patent Act, 1970".
57. The subject of adulteration of food-stuffs and other goods was included in the Concurrent List as item No. 18 of list 3 of 7th Schedule to our Constitution where after a Central Act named "Prevention of Food Adulteration Act, 1954" was enacted to ensure uniformity, which extends to whole of India.

wide-spread and persistent that drastic remedy was required to remedy the cancerous growth of anti-social behaviour. Everyday the newspapers are full of incidents involving death or hospitalization because of large scale adulteration in water, milk, meat and cooked food.

(A) The Prevention of Food Adulteration Act, 1954

The Act[58] provide the protection from adulteration/ contamination of food that may lead to the health risk of consumers. The Act deals with the frauds also that can be perpetrated by the dealers by supplying cheaper or adulterated foods. The Act regulates the use of chemicals, pesticides, flavours and other additives in food preparation. Through this Act there is a control over dumping of sub-standard foods. Enrichment of flour, bread, or other cereals with vitamins or minerals, iodization of salt, vitaminization of vanaspati oil, addition of vitamin "C" in certain foods can be done under the provision made in this Act. Different definitions of food, adulteration, misbranding, etc., are described in the Act.[59] Centre is empowered to appoint an Advisory Committee called the Central Committee for Food Standard.[60] In any dispute and adulterated sample need to examined by the Court. The Central Food Laboratories gives its final opinion on the subject. These laboratories are located in Calcutta, Ghaziabad, Mysore and Pune. There are approximately 84 Food Laboratories in the country at district/regional/state level working for the purpose of the prevention of Food Adulteration Act, 1954. Powers are given to the State Governments to appoint Public Analyst and Food Inspectors who control the food supply, and marketing of foods. It is the duty of inspector to draw and dispatch samples to a laboratory. Central Government is empowered to define the standards of quality, control over production, distribution and sale of food, packing labeling, licensing and controlling the food additives.[61] There is a provision of penalty if anybody break the law for a maximum imprisonment of 1 year or a minimum fine or Rs. 2000 in the first instance and for imprisonment of 6 months which may extend 6 years and cancellation of license on the second of subsequent offence. There is a penalty for violation of rules with regard to seized article subsequently found adulterated and contaminated with injurious substances when consumed food adulterated food is likely to cause death or injury to the body or amount to grievous hurt can be punished according to Section 320 of the

58. For detail see, "The Prevention of Food Adulteration Act, 1954".
59. Section 2; *ibid.*
60. Section 3; *ibid.*
61. Section 11; *ibid.*

Indian Penal Code. There is an imprisonment of not less than 3 years but which may extend to the life term and with the fine which shall not be less than Rs. 5000.[62]

(iii) Occupational Health Laws

The Joint International Labour Organization/World Health Organization Committee on occupational Health has stated that the general aims of occupational health should be the promotion and maintenance of the highest degree of physical, mental and social well-being of workers in all occupations, the prevention among workers of departures from health caused by their working conditions, the protection of workers in their respective employments from risks resulting from factors adverse to health, the placing and maintenance of the workers in an occupational environment adapted to their physiological and psychological needs.[63]

With increase in the number of industries and the absence of any legislation to look into the basic needs of the workers and also having realized that it was the man behind the machine who was more important in maximizing the profits of the organization, a number of occupational health laws were framed.[64] Among the various laws which govern the conditions in the industry and also safeguarded the health and welfare of the workers, the few significant ones are the following:

(A) The Factories Act, 1948

The Factories Act is the principal legislation, which governs the health, safety and welfare of workers in factories. The Act extends the whole of India except Jammu & Kashmir. The Act addressed the issues of safety, health, and welfare. Many amendments were aimed to keep the Act in tune with the developments in the field of health and safety. However, it was not until 1987 that the element of occupational health and safety, and prevention and protection of workers employed in hazardous process, got truly incorporated in the Act.[65]

A factory under the Act is defined as a place using power, employs 10 or more workers or 20 or more workers without power. However, under Section 85, the state governments are empowered to extend the provision of the Act to factories employing fewer workers also. This section has been used to extend the coverage of the Act to work places like power looms, rice mills, flour mills, oil mills, saw mills, pesticide

62. Section 16; *ibid.*
63. M.C. Gupta, *Health and Law*, 131 (2002).
64. *Ibid.*
65. Sections 11 to 20 of the Factories Act.

formulating units and other chemical units where hazards to health are considered to put workers at risk. The Act does not permit the employment of women and young in a dangerous process or operation. Children, who have not attained an age of 15 years, are not permitted to be hired.[66] The Act deals with provision of environmental sanitation that protect the worker from hazardous environment.[67] Cleanliness of the working place, privy benches, stairs, walls, etc. are explained.[68] Disposal of wastes and effluents should be without any risk.[69] Ventilation, temperature inside factory, dust and fumes emission, lighting, artificial humidification, over crowding (minimum of 50 cubic metres per person) are specified.[70] There should be a provision for safe and cool drinking water and provision for safe and cool drinking water and provision of water in the latrine and urinal. One latrine for 25 female workers but one for 25 male workers upto 100 and one for 50 thereafter one urinal for 50 persons upto 500 men and after that one for every 100 more. Safety measures like fencing of machines, protection of eyes by use of goggles, precautions against fire, dangerous fumes, etc. are defined.[71]

Facilities for washing, and sitting, canteens, crèche (one for more than 30 women) and first and appliances are provided.

One Welfare Officer for 500 or more workers is suggested. There is provision for one weekly holiday, and not more than 48 hours in a week an adult worker should work. There is at least half an hour rest after a stretch of 5 hours of continuous work. No women should be employed between 7 p.m. and 6 a.m. No person less than 14 years of age should work in the factory. No child should work more than 4 hours a day and should not work in the night between 10 p.m. and 6 a.m. one full wage leave should be given to an adult worker for every 20 days of work and one for every 15 days to the child worker. 12 weeks of maternity leave should be given to a woman. If an accident occurs in any factory causing death or bodily injury or prevents a worker from working for more than 48 hours, the manager must immediately send notice to the prescribed authority (i.e. Labour Commissioner). Following are the Notifiable Diseases:

1. Lead poisoning or its sequelae
2. Land tetra-ethyl poisoning

---

66. Section 11; *ibid.*
67. Section 12; *ibid.*
68. Sections 13-17; *ibid.*
69. Sections 21-40; *ibid.*
70. Section 42-48; *ibid.*
71. Section 49.

3. Phosphorus poisoning or its sequelae
4. Mercury poisoning or its sequelae
5. Manganese poisoning or its sequelae
6. Arsenic poisoning or its sequelae
7. Poisoning by nitrous fumes
8. Carbon bisulphite poisoning
9. Benzene and its derivatives poisoning
10. Chrome Ulceration or its sequelae
11. Anthrax
12. Silicosis
13. Poisoning by halogens or its derivatives of hydro carbons
14. Pathological manifestation due to radium, radio active substances, or x-ray
15. Primary epitheliomatous cancer of the skin
16. Toxic anemia
17. Toxic jaundice due to poisonous substances
18. Oil acne or dermatitis due to mineral oil or its derivatives in any form

However, the Act do not have provision for some important places of work like hospitals, fire stations, and others where serious health and safety risks may exist. The process of automation and the industrial revolution heralded by micro-electronics is which has resulted in computer-based production methods, increasing use of robots, lasers, and new welding technologies have totally transformed the workplace. Consequent up on this change, the role of labour inspection has also changed and needs reorientation. Inspectors needs additional skills and expertise and a new approach when assessing and evaluating workplace hazards. This has not happened in India. The increasing complexity of workplace and transfer of technologies due to a burst in economic activities requires that inspectors should possess reasonable amount of knowledge of occupational safety and health.

In the case of *Consumer Education and Research Centre*[72] Ramaswami, J. held that the right to health, medical aid to protect the health and vigour of a worker while in service or post-retirement is a fundamental right under Article 21, read with Articles 39(e), 41, 43, 48-A and all related to Articles and fundamental human rights to make the life of the workman meaningful and purposeful with dignity of persons. Articles 1 and 25(2) of the Universal Declaration of Human Rights, the

72. *Consumer Education and Research Centre* v. *Union of India*, AIR 1995 SC 922. The case was heard by a three Judges Bench consisting of A.M. Ahmadi, C.J., M.M. Punchhi, and Ramaswamy, JJ. The decision of the Court was delivered by Ramaswami, J.

Charter of United Nations, Articles 21, 38(1), 46, 39(e), 42, 43, 48-A of the Constitution of India, Article 2(b) of the International Covenant on Economic, Social and Cultural Rights, and relied on a number of decisions of the Supreme Court.[73] Relying on a number of decisions of the apex Court,[74] the learned judge stated that in an appropriate case, the court would give appropriate directions to the employer, be if the state or its undertaking or private employer to make the right to life meaningful; to prevent pollution of work place; production of the environment; protection of the health of the workman or to preserve free and unpolluted water for the safety and health of the people. The authorities or even private persons or industry are bound by the directions issued by the Court under Article 32 and Article 142 of the Constitution.

(B) The Maternity Benefit Act, 1961

This Act[75] came into force in November 1963 and has undergone six amendments since then i.e., during 1970, 1972, 1973, 1976, 1988 and 1995. As the number of women employees was increasing, this legislation was passed with the object of doing social justice to women workers employed in factories, mines and plantations. It is basically meant to provide maternity leave and benefits to women employees. This Act applies to every establishment, be it a factory, mine or plantation including any such establishment belonging to Government and to every establishment wherein persons are employed for the exhibition of equestrian, acrobatic and other performances. It also applies to every shop or establishment within the meaning of any law for the time being in force in relation to shops and establishments in a State, in which 10 or more persons are employed, or were employed on any day of the preceding 12 months. No employer shall knowingly employ a woman in any establishment six week immediately following the day of her delivery nor shall a woman work in any establishment during this period including miscarriage or medical termination of pregnancy.[76] Similarly, no pregnant woman will be subjected to work of an arduous nature or which involves long hours of standing during the period of one month immediately preceding the period of six weeks before her expected date of delivery or during any period during the six weeks for which the pregnant woman does not avail leave of absence.[77]

73. *Consumer Education and Research Centre* v. *Union of India*, AIR 1995 SC 992 at 940.
74. *Nilabati Behera* v. *State of Orissa*, (1993) 2 SCC 746.
75. For detail see Maternity Benefit Act, 1961.
76. Section 4; *ibid.*
77. Section 6; *ibid.*

Women employees are entitled to maternity benefits amounting to a period of 12 weeks of wages of which not more than six weeks shall precede the date of her expected delivery subject to the fact that she has served for a minimum period of 80 days in the 12 months immediately preceding the date of her expected delivery. In case of death of either the mother or the child prior to delivery, the maternity benefits are available upto and including the date of death. However, in case of the death of the mother during her delivery, the child is entitled to the complete maternity benefits for the whole period or till the period of his death within the period.[78]

The woman entitled to maternity benefit under this Act is required to give a notice regarding the same as per the prescribed form to her employer for payment to her or her nominee and will undertake not to work in any establishment during the period.[79] She will also notify the date from which she will be absent from work; which should not exceed a duration of six weeks from her expected date of delivery. Initial payment for the absence prior to the delivery will be paid in advance and the remaining payment will be affected on furnishing proof of delivery. Further, failure to give notice does not disentitle a woman to the maternity benefits and she may give the notice as soon as possible after her delivery.[80]

If the employer has not provided for the pre and post-natal care free of charge, the woman employee is entitled to receive medical bonus of Rs. 250 which may be revised from time to time in keeping with the cost of living.[81] In case of miscarriage a woman is entitled to six weeks leave with pay at the rate of maternity benefit immediately following the day of her miscarriage/MTP (Medical Termination of Pregnancy) on production of proof thereof.[82] Section 9A provides for leave with wages for a period of two weeks immediately following tubectomy.

A woman suffering from illness arising out of pregnancy, delivery, premature birth of child, miscarriage, MTP (Medical Termination of Pregnancy) tubectomy operation and the like is entitled to one months additional leave with wages at the rate of maternity benefit independent of her entitlements under Sections 6 and 9.[83]

On rejoining after her delivery, a woman is entitled to two breaks in her day's schedule for nursing the child until the child attains the age of

78. Section 5; *ibid.*
79. Section 6; *ibid.*
80. Section 7; *ibid.*
81. Section 8; *ibid.*
82. Section 9; *ibid.*
83. Section 10; *ibid.*

15 months independent of the normal breaks.[84] A woman cannot be dismissed during the period of her pregnancy nor can any retrograde steps be initiated with regard to the term and conditions of service. The only exception being on account of gross misconduct where the employer may by order in writing communicated to the woman, deprive her of maternity benefit and/or medical bonus. The woman, however, has the right to appeal to the prescribed authority within a period of 60 days.[85]

The employer cannot deduct the wages of a woman entitled to maternity benefits because of the nature of work assigned to her by virtue of the provisions contained in Section 4(3) or for breaks allowed for nursing the child under Section 11.[86]

(C) The Atomic Energy Act, 1973[87]

X-rays have a potential of causing cancers, genetic mutations and congenital malformations and hence they should be used very judiciously and with the utmost of safety precautions to prevent harm to patients and others who may receive radiation during a diagnostic procedure. The rules framed under the Atomic Energy Act provide for the Atomic Energy Regulation Board (AERB) to prescribe a safety code and regulations for diagnostic X-Ray units in the country. Accordingly, the Atomic Energy Regulation Board was constituted by Government of India in November,1983 and the rules framed by it for diagnostic X-Rays are as follows:

AERB[88] Code No. SC/MED2: "Safety Code for Medical Diagnostic X-Ray Equipment and Installations". The Code was issued on 30 December, 1986. This safety code details the mandatory requirement for the equipment layout, operation, safety procedures, appointment of safety officer, minimum qualifications and experience of the personnel, etc. The State Government is to create a stipulated implementing agency for enforcement of the provisions. The Code has different sections dealing with introduction, definition, built-in safety specifications for medical diagnostic X-Ray equipment, specifications for radiation protection devices, X-Ray Room layout, operational safety, patient protection, radiation protection programme, personnel required and responsibilities and regulatory control.

84. Section 11; *ibid.*
85. Section 12; *ibid.*
86. Section 13; *ibid.*
87. For detail see The Atomic Energy Act, 1973.
88. Atomic Energy Regulation Board.

(D) The Employee's State Insurance Act, 1948

The Act[89] to provide for certain benefit to employees in case of sickness, maternity and employment injury and to make provisions for certain other matters. The scheme covers all employees in respect of wages not exceeding Rs. 3000 per month excluding over time wages. It is financed by contributions payable by the employer and the employees at the rate of 4 percent and 1.5 percent respectively of the wages. An employee has normally to contribute for a minimum number of days in contributory period to be entitled to benefits in the corresponding benefit period except in case of Disablement and Dependant's Benefits.[90] Sickness benefit, extended sickness benefit, maternity benefit and medical care are subject to fulfilment of contributory conditions, whereas disablement and dependant's benefit for an employment injury are payable without regard to satisfaction of contributory conditions. The duration of benefit is 91 days, two consecutive benefit periods in case of sickness benefit, 124 days in case of extended sickness benefit and 3 months in case of maternity benefit. Disablement and Dependant's benefits are payable at the rate of about 70 percent of wages. Funeral expenses are payable as a lump sum not exceeding Rs. 1000.

(E) The Dangerous Machines (Regulation) Act, 1983

A large number of accidents occur every year during the threshing season injuring persons operating power threshers, many of whom are permanently disabled. A major contributory factor is the unsafe design of power threshers and lack of safety features. It was therefore considered necessary to regulate trade and commerce in production, supply distribution and use of power threshers to ensure that they conform to prescribed standards of safety. The Act seeks to achieve that object.

(F) The Dock Workers (Safety, Health and Welfare) Act, 1986

The objective of this Act is the safety, health and welfare of dock workers in respect of all parts and all ships. There is also a provision for the appointment of Chief Inspectors and Inspectors of dock safety with appropriate powers for enforcing the provisions of the Act and holding inquiries into cases of accidents and disease. Obligations are also imposed on dock workers to follow certain safety practices. Punishments for offences against the Act, with provision for enhanced punishment in case of second and subsequent conviction, is provided.

89. For detail see The Employee's State Insurance Act, 1948.
90. Benefits afforded by the Scheme are, sickness benefit, extended sickness benefit, maternity benefit, medical care, disablement benefit, dependants benefit, funeral expenses.

(G) The Public Liability Insurance Act, 1991

The Act is to provide for public liability—insurance for the purpose of providing immediate relief to the persons affected by accident occurring while handling any hazardous substance and for matters connected these with or incidental thereto. This act made it mandatory for occupiers of hazardous activity to do public liability insurance to provide minimum relief to the victims. Few important provisions under the said Act are as follow:[91]

Section 3(1) of the said Act provides, "where death or injury to any person (other than a workman) damage to any property has resulted from an accident or the owner shall be liable to give such relief as is specified in the schedule for such death, injury or damage.

Section 4(1) of the Act reads, "Every owner shall take out, before he starts handling any hazardous substance one or more insurance policies providing for contracts of insurance thereby he is insured against liability to give relief under sub-section (1) of section 3.

Provided that ally owner handling any hazardous substance immediately before the commencement of this Act shall take out such insurance policy or policy as soon as may be and in any case with in a period of one year from such commencement".

Section 14(1) of the Act provides, "wherever contravenes any of the provisions of section 4 or fails to comply with any direction issued under section 12, he shall be punishable with imprisonment for a term which shall not be less than one year and six months but which may extend to six years, or with fine which shall not be less than one lakh rupees or with both."

(2) Whoever, having already been convicted of an offence under sub-section (1) is connected for the second offence, he shall be less than two years but which may extend to seven years and with fine which shall not be less than one lakh rupees".

In terms of transparency requirements and public involvement in the regulatory process there are drawbacks in the Act. There is operational and institutional structure problems while considering the application of these legislations. We know that in practice, whenever the accident takes place, it takes years to fix the liability and the quantum of compensation is very small. The officers of the insurance companies do not pay any attention unless they are given bribes. In such a situation the Government should keep a close watch on it. Only the enactment of law will not serve any purpose. It is also the duty of Government to ensure proper implementation of the Act.

91. The Public Liability Insurance Act, 1991 contains 23 sections and one schedule.

(iv) Child Health Laws

Only healthy children make healthy adults. About three-fourths of Indian children are malnourished. One-third of children are born underweight. All India infant mortality rate is around 70 per 1,000 live births compared to around 10 in the developed countries.[92]

Child health does not function in isolation. It is a part of the overall health scenario. If the general quality of life and health of population, especially women, improves, child health will automatically improve. In case of consumption of alcohol and cigarettes during pregnancy is harmful to the unborn child causing congenital deformity and even miscarriage.[93] Those who both drink and smoke have 50 stillbirths per 1,000 deliveries, compared to half this rate in those who only drink but do not smoke.[94] But legal action against such women is difficult in the absence of specific substantive and procedural provisions.[95] The same is true of alcohol excessively give birth to children with fetal alcohol syndrome women addicted to cocaine and marijuana give birth to babies having drug withdrawal syndrome and congenital defects.[96] The enormity of the problem is evident from the fact that in US alone, 7.5 million children are born annually with such defects. India still has unacceptably high infant mortality rate. A major cause of infant mortality is malnutrition and diarrhea. Both are closely related to lack of breast-feeding and improper quality and use of breast milk substitutes.

The following three legislative measures in this regard are important:

- The Infant Milk Substitutes, Feeding Bottles and Infant Foods (Regulation of Production, Supply and Distribution) Act, 1992;
- The Infant Milk Substitutes, Feeding Bottles and Infant Foods (Regulation of Production, Supply and Distribution) Rules, 1993; and
- Prevention of Food Adulteration (Fifth Amendment) Rules, 1991.

The main aim of the Infant Milk Substitutes, Feeding Bottles and Infant Foods (Regulation of Production, Supply and Distribution) Act,

92. M.C. Gupta, *Health and Law*, 187, (2002).
93. UNICEF: Children and the Environment, 20, (1990).
94. Newland, K., 1984, *Infant Mortality and the Health of Societies*, World Watch Paper No. 47.
95. S.M. Rashid: Protection of the Life and Health of Unborn Children. In Souvenir of the International Conference on Global Health and Law, pp. 153-70, Delhi: Indian Law Institute, Dec., 5-7, 1997.
96. *Ibid.*

1992[97] is the protection and promotion of breast feeding and ensuring the proper use of infant foods. The rules under Infant Milk Substitutes, Feeding Bottles and Infant Foods (Regulation of Production, Supply and Distribution) Rules, 1993[98] have been made by the Central Government in pursuance of Section 26(1) of the Infant Milk Substitutes, Feeding Bottles and Infant Foods (Regulation of Production, Supply and Distribution) Act, 1992. They came into force on August 1, 1993.

The Prevention of Food Adulteration Rules,[99] 1991 as amended by Prevention of Food Adulteration (Third Amendment) Rules, 1999 contain special provisions related to infant foods.

(A) The Child Labour (Prohibition and Regulation) Act, 1986

The main aim of the Act[100] is to prohibit the engagement of children in certain employment and to regulate the conditions of work of children in certain other harmful employment. This repealed the Employment of Children Act, 1938. It extends to the whole India. According to this Act Child means a person who has not completed his 14 years of age.[101] No child shall be employed in any occupation, transport, railways, catering establishment at a railway station or in train, construction or port, railways, catering establishment at a railway station or in train, construction or port, biddi-making, carpet-making, cement factory, cloth printing, dyeing, weaving, mica-cutting and splitting, soap tanning, wood-clearing, matches, explosives and firework.[102]

The Central Government shall form "Child Labour Technical Advisory Committee" to advise the Central Government for the purpose of addition of any other occupations or process.[103] No child shall work for more than 6 hours per day and three hours continuous before he has had an interval for rest for at least one hour. He will neither be allowed to work between 7 p.m. and 8 a.m., nor allowed to do overtime. He will be given a weekly full wage holiday.[104] If any establishment has children as the workers should inform the inspector who will inspect the conditions and nature of work and also certify age of the child.[105] Each

97. For detail see Infant Foods (Regulation of Production, Supply and Distribution) Act, 1992.
98. For detail see Infant Milk Substitutes, Feeding Bottles and Infant Foods Regulation of Production, Supply and Distribution) Rules, 1992.
99. For detail see Prevention of Food Adulteration Rules, 1991.
100. For detail see Child Labour (Prohibition and Regulation) Act, 1986.
101. Section 2; *ibid.*
102. Section 3; *ibid.*
103. Section 5; *ibid.*
104. Sections 7-8; *ibid.*
105. Sections 9-10; *ibid.*

establishment where a child is working make sure for his health and safety. Any violation of the Act may lead to the punishment with imprisonment or fine or both.

(B) The Juvenile Justice Act, 1986

The Act[106] provides for the care, protection, treatment, development and rehabilitation of neglected or delinquent juveniles, and for the adjudication of certain matters relating to, and disposition of delinquent juveniles. In the Act, Juvenile means a boy who has not attained the age of 16 years or a girl who has not attained the age of 18 years. Neglected juvenile means a juvenile who—(i) is begging, (ii) lives in brothel, or with a prostitute, (iii) who is being abused or exploited, or (iv) destitute. Delinquent juvenile means a juvenile who has found to have committed an offence.[107]

It is the responsibility of the state to look into the problem for juvenile social maladjustment and make special efforts to mobilize all possible resources of the family, the community, and social organization. Any juvenile, who is likely to be abused, exploited and inducted into criminogentic life and is need of legal support to be appropriately rehabilitated. The Act has also described special offences in respect of juvenile like, punishment of cruelty to juvenile, employment for begging, giving intoxicating liquor or narcotic drug or psychotropic substance and exploitation of juvenile employee.

(C) The Child Marriage Restraint Act, 1929

The aim of the Act[108] is to prevent child marriage so that child can get an opportunity to fully develop before getting the responsibility of marriage in their adulthood. The child marriage is also linked with population control that is why it was necessary to increase the age of marriage. Child means a person who, if male, has not completed 21 years of age and if a female, has not completed 18 years of age. Being a male above eighteen years of age and below twenty-one, contract of marriage shall be punishable with simple imprisonment which may extend to fifteen days or with fine which may extend to one thousand rupees, or with both. Parents or guardian or in any other capacity, lawful or unlawful, who does any act to promote the marriage or permits it to be solemnized or negligently fails to prevent it from being solemnized, shall be punishable with simple imprisonment which may extend to three months and shall also be liable to fine. The Act do not provide punishment to the woman.

106. For detail see Juvenile Justice Act, 1986.
107. Section 2; *ibid.*
108. For detail see Child Marriage Restraint Act, 1929.

(D) Children as Victims of Drugs

Children, because of their tender age, are particularly prone to be swayed into addiction under unhealthy influences and to be used as an instrument in drug trafficking. There is widespread use of illicit drugs among street children. Even amongst children in educational institutions, use of drugs is increasing. There are innumerable documented instances to show that children of the poor are introduced and addicted to drugs only to be manipulated as tools in drug trafficking by organized criminal syndicates.[109]

Under the Juvenile Justice (Care and Protection of Children) Act, 2000, it is an offence to give or cause to be given to any juvenile or child, any intoxicating liquor or any drug or psychotropic substance except upon the order of a duly qualified medical practitioner or in case of sickness. The punishment for this offence is imprisonment for a term which may extend to three years and fine.[110]

There are several lacunae found in the Act. Although the Act gives the members of the Child Welfare Committee (CWC) power to function as a magistrate, and pronounce punishments, but members of the CWC have hardly ever used this opportunity. Though the formation of the Commissions is a step forward in recognizing child rights. Despite the 2006 amendment in the said Act mandating that every district in the country must have a CWC and Juvenile Justice Board (JJB) within one year from the notification of the new Act, the Government itself admits that many states and UTs have not established any. Some states do not have enough JJBs to deal with the number of children coming in conflict with law. There is lack of implementation because of lack of

109. Today drug abuse has become a menace as it is prevalent amongst children belonging to all strata's of the society. The district mental health programme is throwing up increasing evidence of inhalant drug abuse in the Chandigarh city. Camps conducted under the programme in different colonies show that children as young as five years are inhailing drugs like eraser fluids, solvents like taulene (used for fixing punctures), petrol, diesel. This is happening, despite the ban on sale of correction fluids in Chandigarh. Experts demand curbs on easy and cheap availability of inhalants like whiteners. Visit http://www.tribuneindia.com/2007/20070411/cth1.htm. (accessed on September 27, 2009).

110. Section 25: The Juvenile Justice (Care and Protection of Children Act), 2000. This Act deals with the law relating to juveniles in conflict with law and children in need of care and protection, by providing for proper care, protection, and treatment by catering to their development needs, and by adopting a child friendly approach in the adjudication and disposition of matters in the best interest of children, and for their ultimate rehabilitation through various institutions established under the Act. The said Act received the assent of the President of India on December 30, 2000. The Act contains total 70 sections. The said Act also amended in 2006, known as the Juvenile Justice (Care and Protection of Children) Amendment Act, 2006, No. 33 of 2006 (22 August, 2006).

role clarity within the judiciary, administration and lack of resources. Another problem with the said Act is that its members have a dual role of counseling children as well as awarding punishments. Since the implementation of Juvenile Justice Laws by most states was tardy. The National Human Rights Commission (NHRC) is playing a more proactive role in ensuring the monitoring of the implementation. The amended law makes it mandatory for the states to set-up Juvenile Justice Boards and protection homes at district levels. But states are dragging their feet on implementation of the Juvenile Justice (Care and Protection) Amendment Act, 2006.[111]

(E) National Plan of Action for Children, 2005[112]

Further, to secure and strengthen the health status of children the National Plan for Children was initiated in the year 2002 by inviting comments and inputs from all concerned Ministries, Departments at the Centre level, from the State Governments and UT Administrations. An Advertisement was also published in the newspapers to invite comments from the public as well, resulting in framing of the National Plan of Action for Children 2005. This plan commits itself to ensure all rights to all children upto the age of 18 years. This calls for collective commitment and action by all sectors and levels of government and partnership with families, communities, voluntary sector and children themselves. This plan will be implemented throughout the country through national measures and through State Plans of Action for Children. In recognition of the fact, that 41 percent of India's population is below 18 constituting, a significant national assets, the plan re-affirms the nation's commitment wisely, effectively, and efficiently invest its national resources to fulfil its commitment to children.[113] The National Plan of Action for Children, 2005 is divided into following four sections:

Guiding Principles of National Plan of Action, 2005 are:

(a) to regard child as an asset and a person with human rights;
(b) to address issues of discriminations emanating from biases of gender, class, caste, race, religion and legal status in order to ensure equality;

---

111. See also http://www.thehindu.com/2006/03/28/stories.http:enews. toxicslink. org/report-view-php?id=14.http://www.indianexpress.com/ news/soon-nhrc-norms-for-the-missing/22557. (accessed on September 2, 2009.
112. http://www.wcd.nic.in/NAPAug 16Apdf (accessed on May 20, 2006).
113. Ibid.

Figure 1: National Plan for Action for Children, 2005

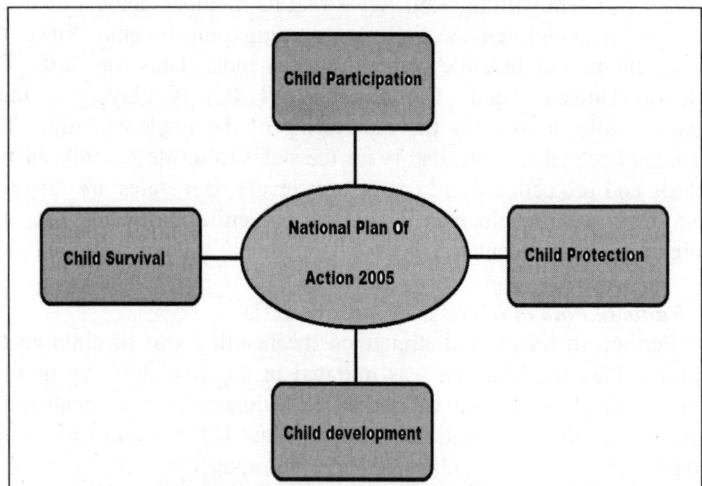

(c) to accord utmost priority to the most disadvantaged, poorest of the poor and least served child in all policy and programmatic interventions; and

(d) to recognize the diverse stages and settings of childhood and address the needs of each, providing to all children the entitlements that fulfil their rights and meet their needs in each situations.

(a) Child Health

The goals relating to health lay down in the plan are:[114]

- To reduce infant mortality rate to below 30 per 1000 live births by 2010.
- To reduce child mortality rate to below 31 per 1000 live birth by 2010.
- To reduce neonatal mortality rate to below 18 per 1000 live births by 2010.
- To explore possibilities of covering all children with plan for health insurance.
- To reduce Maternal Mortality Rate (MMR) to below 100 per 1,00,000 live births by 2010.
- To prevent and progressively eliminate child marriage and under age child bearing by enforcing the Child Marriage

114. *Ibid.*

(Restraint) Act, 1929, now it is amended in 2006 known as the prohibition of Child Marriage Act, 2006.[115]

- To eliminate child malnutrition as a national priority.
- To reduce five malnutrition and low birth weights by half by 2010.
- To ensure adequate neonatal and infant nutrition.
- To reduce moderate and severe malnutrition among preschool children by half.
- To reduce chronic under nutrition and stunted growth in children.
- To effectively implement the Infant Milk Substitutes, Feeding Bottles and Infant Foods (Regulation of Production, Supply and Distribution) Act, 1992 as amended in 2003.
- Universal equitable access to and use of safe drinking water and improved access to sanitary means of excreta disposal by 2010.
- All households to have sustained access to potable drinking water by 2012, to be undertaken in a phased manner with annual targets.
- 100 percent of rural population to have access to basic simulation by 2012.
- To cover 100 percent urban population with low cost sanitation and safe water disposal facilities by 2010, and build an enabling environment for sanitation and hygiene that promotes prevention of pollution of all fresh water bodies.

The health of child has been taken by the government as a serious issue under different policies, i.e. National Population Policy, 2000 and National Health Policy, 2002.

(b) Child Development

The goals lays down under this head are:[116]

- To universalize early childhood services to ensure children's physical, social, emotional cognitive development.
- To ensure that care, protection and development opportunities are available to all children below 3 years.

115. It provides for the prohibition of the solemnization of child marriages and for matters connected with child marriages. The act makes an offence punishable, cognizable and non-bailable. Despite the existence of legislation banning it, child marriage continues to be social reality in India today. Visit www.unicef.org.india/chld-protection_1536.htm. (accessed on September 24, 2009).
116. *Ibid.*

- To ensure integrated care and development and pre-school learning opportunities for all children aged 3 to 6 years.
- To provide day-care and crèche facilities to parents in rural and urban areas.
- Assurance of equality status for girl child as an individual and a citizen in her own right through promotion of special opportunities for her growth and development.
- To ensure survival, development and protection of girl child and to create an environment wherein she lives a life of dignity with full opportunity for choice and development.
- To stop sex selection and female foeticide and infanticide.
- To ensure the girl child's security and protect her from abuse, exploitation, victimization and all other forms of violence.
- To protect the girl child from deprivation and neglect and to ensure the girl child equal share of care and resources in the home and community and equal access to services.[117]
- To take measures to protect girl children from any treatment which undermines their self-esteem and causes their enclose on from social mainstream and also to break down persistent gender stereotype.
- To ensure equal opportunity for free and compulsory elementary education to all girls.
- To ensure full opportunities to all adolescents girls and boys in the age group of 13 to 18 years to realize their rights and develop their full potential as human beings.[118]
- To provide the adolescents with education and development opportunities so that they can participate in the life and progress of community as productive citizens.
- To eliminate child marriages by 2010.
- To ensure right to survival, care, protection and security for all children with disability.

---

117. In Haryana, State Government has introduced a new scheme for the girls child which is named 'LADLI'. The objective of the scheme is to raise the status of the girl child in the family and in society and to change the mindsets of the people for proper rearing of the girl children and enduring their right to birth and survival. Under the scheme all parents residents of or domiciled in Haryana will be provided financial incentive @ Rs. 5000 per year for upto five years if their second girl child is born on or after 20th August 2005. National Report on 'A World fit for Children', Ministry of Women and Child Development, Government of India, 2007.
118. The Government has also started Rashtriya Swasthya Bima Yojna under the women and children labour welfare schemes, transportation of pregnant women and children during emergency from the village to CHC/district. The scheme of Kishori Shakti Yojana for adolescent girls has also been started to raise the level of nutrition. http://www.delhiplanning.nic.in/pd/2008-09. (accessed on July 19, 2009).

- To ensure the right to development with dignity and equality creating an enabling environment where children can exercise their rights, enjoy equal opportunities and full participation in accordance with the UN Convention on the Rights of the Child, and other laws dealing with Child Rights in India.
- To ensure inclusion and effective access to education, health, vocational training along with specialized rehabilitation services to children.
- To eliminate disability due to poliomyelitis by 2007.
- To conserve and protect the natural environment and safeguard natural resources, for the good and well-being of all children.
- To ensure children's survival, health and food security through conservation and safe use.
- To create and uphold a safe, supportive and protective environment for all children within and outside the home.
- To prevent children from getting into conflict with law.
- To recognize, promote and protect the rights of children in conflict with law through preventive, protective, reformative and rehabilitative policies, laws, plans, strategies, programmes and interventions.
- To protect all children, both girls and boys from all forms of sexual abuse and exploitation.
- To prevent use of children for all forms of sexual exploitation including child pornography.
- To develop new and strengthen existing legal instruments to prevent sexual abuse and exploitation of children.
- To stop sale of children and all forms of child trafficking, including for sexual purpose, marriage, labour, adoption, sports entertainment and illegal activities like organ trade, begging and drug peddling.
- To eliminate child labour from hazardous occupations by 2007 and progressively move towards complete eradication of all forms of child labour.
- To protect children from all kinds of economic exploitation.
- To stop the growth of HIV/AIDS and sexually transmitted infections by 2010.
- To reduce the proportion of infants infected with HIV by 20 percent by 2007 and by 50 percent of all such children by 2010.

(c) Child Participation: The goals laid down under this section are:

- To promote within the family, community, schools and institutions as well as in judicial and administrative proceedings, respect for the views of all children, including the views of the most marginalized, especially girls, and facilitate their participation in all matters affecting them in accordance to their age and maturity.
- To make all children aware of their rights and provide them opportunities to develop skills to form and express their views, build self-esteem, acquire knowledge, from aspirations, build competencies in decision-making and communication, and gain confidence which will empower them to become actively involved in their own development and all matters concerning and affecting them.
- To empower all children as citizens by promoting their participation in decisions that affect their lives, the lives of their families communities and the larger section of society in which live.

(d) Mobilizing Resources, Implementation of the Plan and Monitoring

The National Plan of Action for Children, 2005 commits the allocation of required financial, material, technical and human resources from the central and the state government to ensure its full implementation, investing in children lays the foundation for a just society, a strong economy and a world free from poverty.[119]

- To secure financial, material, technical and human resources from all international organization civil society, private sector and non-governmental organization will be involved to ensure the rights and well-being of all Indian children.
- The primary responsibility for the implementation of this National Plan of Action for children, 2005 and for ensuring on enabling environment for securing the rights and well-being of children rests with the Central, State and local governments.
- Ensure inter-sectoral coordination and convergence of all departments, Ministries and programmes affecting children.
- Ensure that efforts are made by Government agencies for creating awareness and multimedia publicity through mass-communication in the print and electronic media, for promoting child rights.

119. *Ibid.*

- The National Plan of Action, 2005 shall be monitored by the National Coordination Group created for implementation and monitoring of the convention on the Rights of Child.
- The Department of Women and Child Department shall create suitable mechanisms to ensure this by establishing:
  (a) National Commission for the Protection of Child Rights including the setting up of State Commissions.
  (b) Central Nodal Authority for combating trafficking for commercial sexual exploitation, including the setting up of the State authorities.
  (c) Creations of other needs-based mechanisms for child protection as and when required.
- This plan will be regularly monitored at the National, State and District levels to assess progress towards the goals and targets. A comprehensive system would be developed and operated to collect and analyze disaggregated data on children, based on age, gender, cultural and socio-economic grouping.
- Efforts will be made to strengthen the existing data collection mechanisms so that quality data on various measurable development is generated.
- Periodic and annual reviews will be conducted at the national and state level in order to more effectively address the obstacles and accelerate progress on the NPA goals.
- Appropriate mechanisms for effective monitoring and evaluation will be set-up at the national, state, district block and village level for reporting and periodic review of the targets.

(v) Women's Health Laws

When we discuss law related to women's health, it needs to be emphasized that we have to deal with health in its comprehensive meaning. Thus, not only laws specifically related to women's physical, mental or social health are important, but even the laws that empower women are relevant. This is because women's empowerment is an undisputed determinant of women's health.

The Beijing Declaration on Women[120] gives a wider dimension to the right to health. It states:

"Women have the right to the enjoyment of the highest attainable

120. Beijing Declaration and Platform for Acton, Adopted by the Fourth World Conference on Women, Beijing, September 1995, A/CONF. 177/20 (1995) & A/CONF. 177/20/Add.1 (1995).

> standard of physical and mental health. The enjoyment of this right is vital to their life and well-being and their ability to participate to all areas of public and private life. Health is a state of complete physical, well-being and not merely the absence of disease or infirmity. Women's health involves their emotional, social and physical well-being and is determined by the social, political and economic context of their lives, as well as by biology.[121]
>
> Thus, women health should also involve their emotional, social and physical well-being and is determined by the social, political and economic context of their lives, as well as biology. Prevailing laws, and their implementation to ensure the well-being of women and granting them equal status in the society. To reiterate, when we discuss laws relating to women's health, it needs to be emphasized that we have to deal with health in its comprehensive meaning. Thus, not only laws specifically related to women's physical, mental or social health is important, but even the laws that empower women are relevant. This is because women's empowerment is an undisputed determinant of women's health.[122]

(A) The Medical Termination of Pregnancy Act, 1971

The Act[123] is essentially designed to ensure safeguarding of women's health and specifies the conditions under which medical termination of pregnancy is permissible, personnel who are legally authorized to perform the terminations and the statutory facilities in which the process can be undertaken. The MTP (Medical Termination of Pregnancy Act) has been discussed earlier. The implementation of the Act has resulted in saving the life and health to innumerable women who were earlier forced to fall into the clutches of quakes for seeking illegal abortions.

The issue of reproduction has always been central to women's lives. In all cultures and ages women have sought ways and means to either prevent conception, or get rid of an unwanted pregnancy, to voluntarily remain child free, or to deal with involuntary childless. Intervention in reproduction is not of recent origin. Contraception and abortion have been known for long time. Up until the Middle Ages in Europe (and in developing countries to some extent even until this day), women practicised as healers and midwives, providing contraceptive measures,

121. Mohammed Hussain, K.S., "World Trade Organization and the Right to Health: An Overview," *Indian Journal of International Law*; Vol. 43, No. 2, April-June, (2003).
122. Mahalwar, K.P.S., *Indian Constitution and the Weaker Sections*, 2007 at p. 96.
123. For detail see the Medical Termination of Pregnancy Act, 1971.

performing abortions and offering concoctions to ease the pain of labour, according to methods and skills handed down from generation to generation.

An extremely significant development took place with the passing of "The Medical Termination of Pregnancy (MTP) Act" in 1971 which became effective from April, 1972. Until then the abortion laws in India had been very restrictive. The most important reason given for liberalization was to counter the hazard of the large number of illegal abortions. Since the concept of family planning was already accepted, it was assumed that the liberalization of the abortion law would meet with support rather than opposition from religious and professional groups. The legislation provided recourse to abortion under broad health (physical and mental) grounds on eugenic indications, under juridical conditions (such as incest or rape), and for social reasons such as mental or social injury to the mother. The law did not have population control as its stated objective. However, the provisions of the law were liberal enough for those who wished to avail themselves of it to do so. The Commission stated: '…abortion also can be used as a means to control family size as is being done currently in several countries. In which family planning or contraception and abortion are in two parallel categories, both of which lead to population control' (Government of India: 1966). It is noteworthy that Indian women obtained the right to abortion without a struggle or even a campaign on this issue, whereas it is still an explosive issue in many countries, predominantly Catholic countries as well as in the US where the opposition to abortion is the strongest and is organized in a pro-life lobby. The population control motive is likely to have played an important role in the liberalization of abortion in India. The easy availability of abortion did not make it an issue of 'self-determination' for women in India.

During the past three decades, there has been liberalization of abortion laws throughout the world. In India, abortions were governed exclusively by the Indian Penal Code and the Code of Criminal Procedure. It was considered a crime except when performed to save the life of a pregnant woman.

The Medical Termination of Pregnancy Act (MTPA) is a health care measure which helps to reduce maternal morbidity and mortality resulting from illegal abortions. It also affords an opportunity for motivating such women to adopt some form of contraception.

MTPA was enacted purely to safeguard the rights of women and the doctors who performed abortion. Previously, abortion was an offence under the Indian Penal Code except when it was done to save the life of woman. This led to illegal abortions. According to the objects and reasons of the MTPA, doctors had often been confronted with gravely ill or pregnant women whose uterus has been tempered with a view to causing an abortion who consequently suffered very severely. The legislation was conceived, (1) as a health measure—where there is a danger to life or risk to physical or mental health of the woman, and (2) on humanitarian grounds such as when a lunatic woman was raped, etc. and (3) eugenic grounds where there is a substantial risk that the offspring would suffer from deformities and diseases.

The MTPA allows abortion if the doctor is of the opinion that the continuance of the pregnancy would endanger the life of the pregnant woman or involve grave injury to her physical or mental health; or there is a substantial risk that the child would suffer from disabling physical or mental abnormalities. The anguish caused by pregnancy as a result of rape, or as a result of failure of any device limiting the number of children may be presumed to constitute a grave injury to the woman's mental health. The medical practitioner can take into account the pregnant woman's actual or reasonable foreseeable environment to determine the advisability of abortion. If the pregnancy is twelve weeks old, the opinion of one registered medical practitioner is required. In theory, the law recognizes women's right, as the medical practitioner is required. In theory of the law recognizes women's right, as the medical practitioner has to consider only her consent. The matter is thus purely between the two and even the husband's consent becomes unnecessary. In reality, however, a woman's right to abortion is very restricted, and mostly, it turns out to be a family decision. Various court judgments have hold that abortion of a foetus without the husband's consent would amount to cruelty under the Hindu Marriage Act and hence is a ground for divorce.

Under the MTPA, the pregnancy of a girl below 18 years of that of a lunatic can be terminated only with the consent in writing of her guardian. The MTPA permits the pregnancy of a 'lunatic' (as defined under the Lunacy Act and hence will include the mentally ill and mentally disabled) with the written consent of her guardian provided the doctor is of the opinion that the pregnancy will cause injury to the woman's physical or mental health. No law permits sterilization to be performed on the mentally ill or disabled. The issue is complex, involving a woman's right over her body. Besides, given over utter callousness towards the under-privileged, any such freedom to perform sterilization will be misused. Besides, there are degrees of retardation and some women are capable of taking care of themselves through in a limited way. At the same time, there is genuine anguish of many parents that their mentally retarded daughters might become victims of pregnancy due to sexual abuse and about their daughter's hygiene after their lifetime.

MTPA recognizes 'failure of contraceptives' as a ground for seeking abortion. This relief is restricted, however to married women. Unwed pregnant women are forced to mention rape or grave injury to mental or physical health in order to seek abortion. Since the rules in government hospitals are rigid, such women prefer to go to private clinics or quacks.

In India, merely the fact that abortion legislation is liberal does not guarantee that women have access to legal abortion facilities. Incidence of illegal abortions is alarmingly high. It is 10 times as many as illegal abortions are carried out as legal ones and at least 80 percent of women admitted to hospital with complications have had abortions performed by unqualified people. Around one-tenth of maternal deaths in the country are due to septic abortions. About seven million induced abortions take place every year. Abortion is advocated openly by government authorities. One hoarding spotted in Bombay read: 'Carrying again? You need not worry. Get your pregnancy terminated. Abortion is legal'. It is clear that abortion is regarded by the authorities as a family planning method. On paper, however, abortion is not part of the family planning programme and programme ostensibly only a health measure. Studies show that high percentage of women seeks help for abortion at a late stage of pregnancy. This is due to reasons of their legal rights to abortion, ignorance regarding the availability of legal abortion facilities and above all due to inadequate health care services. Mainly the better educated/informed and economically well-off women find their way to legal abortion clinics, while women services, providers of which also have a generally low educational level and many not themselves understand the instructions for correct use of the abortion pill. These women could use it without the supervision of trained health workers. They are less likely to have access to the necessary information. When complications occur, medical help will often be inaccessible to them.

Although induced abortion was legalized in India in 1971. The number of legal abortions in India has risen rapidly since 1972, but it has leveled off at about 600,000 annually. The fact that many legal abortions performed in private facilities are probably not reported may affect the data. In addition, a number of illegal abortion procedures are in use, from modern surgical techniques carried out by private practitioners without the requisite licenses to a variety of folk methods. The actual numbers of illegal, unsafe abortions performed and the extent of associated morbidity and mortality are unknown. In one hospital study, infection resulting from abortion was the single highest cause of death (26 percent of direct obstetric deaths and 18 percent of deaths from all causes). In community-based studies of Andhra Pradesh and Karnataka, illegal abortions were estimated to be responsible for about 6 and 3 percent of total maternal deaths, respectively. The studies indicated that about two-thirds of all abortions deaths involved induced abortions and the other one-third miscarriages. According to the Andhra Pradesh study, roughly one-half of the abortion deaths were caused by hemorrhage and the other half by infection. The Indian Council of Medical Research carried out a study of induced abortion in the states of Haryana, Orissa, Rajasthan, Tamil Nadu, and Uttar Pradesh in 1983-84. It found that for the five states combined, 6 of each 1,000 pregnancies ended in legal abortions and 213 per 1,000 in illegal abortions. Assuming this relationship holds for subsequent years for the rest of India, the approximately 600,000 legal abortions reported in 1990 indicate that a total of about 1.3 million illegal abortions are performed annually in the country. For the five states combined, only about 55 percent of the abortions were carried out in the first trimester, and of these only about one-quarter were provided by doctors (government or private) or other health staff. A study funded by the Ford Foundation argues that previous research seriously underestimates the magnitude of illegal abortion and suggests that nearly 7 million induced abortions occur annually. These figures imply that for every legal abortion in India, 10 more are performed illegally. The study also estimates that the number of abortion-related deaths is significantly higher than was previously reported, accounting for at least 15 percent of all maternal deaths. Thus, it is clear that medical terminations performed by qualified personnel, which are often performed at facilities distant from women's homes and may be prohibitively expensive, are competing with more convenient, less expensive alternatives performed locally, which many believe are less dangerous for women than surgical techniques. The constraints involved in delivering medical terminations suggest that increasing the number of procedures performed at public sector facilities will require an increase in the number of procedures performed at public sector facilities will require an increase in the number of approved facilities, improvements in the quality of services provided, and public education. Devolving authority from specialists and training a wider range of health providers to perform terminations in the first trimester can also associated with unsafe practices, particularly in rural areas. The complications of unsafe abolitions should be promptly referred and treated. The high levels of abortion in India underscore the need to make contraceptives more widely available so that women can avoid unwanted pregnancies in the first place.

(B) Pre-Natal Diagnostic Techniques (Regulation and Prevention of Misuse) Act, 1994

This Act[124] provides for regulation of the pre-natal diagnostic techniques for the purpose of detecting any genetic or metabolic disorder, chromosomal abnormalities or certain congenital malformations and sex linked disorders and prevention of misuse of such techniques for the purpose of pre-natal sex determination for female foeticide. The Act thus aims at preventing the killing of baby girls even before they are born. However, it is doubtful whether the practice of pre-natal sex determination followed by abortion in case of female child has decreased to any significant extent.

Maharashtra was the first State to pass the Pre-natal Diagnostic Techniques Act in 1988 under public pressure. The Act bans the use of medical techniques and technologies for pre-natal diagnostics except in cases where the pregnant woman is above 35 years of age, has a history of two or more abortions or foetal loss, has a history of being exposed to potentially teratogenic drugs, radiation, infection or hazardous chemicals declares illegal any advertisement regarding the availability of pre-natal sex detection facilities at clinics, laboratories or centres. The regulation of these centres is to be achieved through government appoint bodies.

Informed consent of the pregnant woman has to be taken and also a copy of the same to be given to her before such tests can be conducted. Act also prohibits disclosure of the sex of the foetus to the woman or her relatives by words, signs or any other manner.

The Act defines offences and lay down penalties for contravention of the provisions of the Act. A significant aspect is that under Section 24, unless the contrary is proved, the court shall presume that the pregnant woman has been compelled by her husband or the concerned relative to undergo pre-natal diagnostic tests and such person shall be liable for punishment for abetment of the offence. The Act makes an offence under the Act cognizable, non-bailable and non-compoundable.

Five million missing girls later, the country has seen its first ever conviction for foetal sex determination. After 12 years of existence of PNDT Act, first time in Haryana a doctor and his assistant has been given two years imprisonment and a fine of Rs. 5,000 each for violating the Pre-Natal Diagnostic Technique (Regulation and Prevention of Misuse) Act, 1994. Another conviction was in Punjab for improper

124. For detail see Pre-Natal Diagnostic Techniques (Regulation and Prevention of Misuse) Act.

maintenance of records and the doctor got away with a fine. According to Sabu George, "sex selection is a high volume, low risk business. Volumes have to be high because one or two cases do not get the errant doctor much money and the risk low because hardly anyone is caught. According to Dr. Bedi, "It is a Rs. 500-1000 crore industry if you take into account that five to seven lakh fetuses are aborted in the country every year at a cost of Rs. 10,000-15,000 each. So doctors won't stop conducting ultrasound tests till there is deterrent." The deterrent will also come in the form of convicted doctor losing his/her registration. Debarring is inherent in the law.

(C) Drugs and Cosmetic Act, 1940

While this Act[125] is not primarily related to women, yet is relevant to their health. This is so because the use of cosmetics is more widespread among women. Cheaper cosmetic of poor quality are known to cause various types of allergy and toxicity, including lead toxicity. To that extent, this Act is related to women's health.

(D) Maternity Benefit Act, 1961[126]

As the number of women employers are increasing, this legislation was passed with the object of doing, social justice to women workers employed in factories, mines and plantations. It is basically meant to provide maternity leave and other benefits to women employees and enabling them to fulfil their commitment to nursing their babies till attainment of an age of 15 months.

The Act prohibits the employer from engaging or making a woman work for six weeks after her delivery or miscarriage. The employer is also required not to engage a woman in an arduous task, one which involves hours of standing on or which in any way is likely to interfere with her pregnancy, the normal development of the foetus or is likely to cause miscarriage or otherwise adversely affect her health provided she requests the employer to this effect. This stipulation applies to one month before the date of her expected delivery, or any six weeks before the expected delivery. Woman has a right to payment of maternity benefit for the three months. To claim this benefit of wages, however, she must have been in employment for at least eighty days in the twelve months immediately preceding the date of their expected delivery. A woman is also entitled to medical bonus of Rs. 250 if no pre-natal confinement and post-natal care is provided free of charge by the employer. This applies also to a woman who has miscarriage, she is

125. For detail see Drugs and Cosmetic Act, 1940.
126. For detail see "Maternity Benefit Act", 1961.

entitled to leave for a month for any illness arising out of the pregnancy, delivery, premature delivery or miscarriage. The medical bonus may be revised from time to time in keeping with the cost of living.

In case of miscarriage of MTP, a woman is entitled to six weeks leave with pay at the rate of maternity benefit immediately following the day of her miscarriage/MTP on production of proof thereof. Section 9A provides for leave with wages for a period of two weeks immediately following tubectomy. A woman suffering from illness arising out of pregnancy, delivery, premature birth of child, miscarriage, MTP, tubectomy operation and the like is entitled to one months additional leave with wages at the rate of maternity benefit of her entitlements under Sections 6 and 9.

The Act also stipulates that she is allowed two nursing breaks in the course of her work till the child attains fifteen months independent of the normal breaks. Woman cannot be dismissed during the period of her pregnancy nor can any retrograde steps be initiated with regard to the term and conditions of service. The only exception being on account of gross misconduct where the employer may by order in writing communicated to the woman, deprive her maternity benefit and/or medical bonus. The woman, however, has the right to appeal to the prescribed authority within a period of 60 days. The employer can not deduct the wages of a woman entitled to maternity benefit because of the nature of work assigned to her by virtue of the provisions contained in Section 4(3) or for breaks allowed for nursing the child under Section 11.

The Act is applicable to factories, mines and plantations. Government can also by certification extend its applicability to other classes of establishment—industrial, commercial, agricultural or otherwise.

The Government of India has recently increased the maternity leave entitlement from 90 days to 135 days. Fifteen days paternity leave to fathers has now also been provided for.

Strangely, the statute provides for forfeiture of maternity benefit. If a woman works in the establishment during the period of authorized absence, her claim to maternity benefit can be forfeited. In the prevailing unequal situation some employers force their employees to work and take refuge under this provision. The Act provides for inspectors empowered to examine its violation. A few years ago a circular was issued to Central Government employees restricting the benefits to married women. This caused various protests and the circular was withdrawn. Such a move was clearly against the spirit of the Act which recognizes the women's right to health and does not concern itself with existing norms of morality and is truly a welfare legislation. The Act also mentions about the provision of crèches for children have any provision of crèche. Act also provides a clean work environment, effective ventilation and temperature, and all other amenities. Conversely, in most of the establishments the laws are blatantly violated.

(a) Family Planning Methods: The use of condoms to prevent conception has been known for a long time. As well as abstinence, withdrawal and other traditional sexual practices which contributed to birth control. Research in animal and human reproduction made great strides in the twentieth century. With the development of the contraceptive pill in the early 1990s, and later, other contraceptive methods, fertility management through medical technology became more efficient and reliable.

According to guidelines of the Helsinki Declaration, in any research on human beings, each potential subject must be adequately informed of the aims, methods, anticipated benefits and potential hazards of the study and the dis-comfort if any entail. This is to prevent human beings from guinea pigs. Various methods of family planning like pills, injectable contraceptives, implants and sterilization are discussed below for the purpose of women's health issues.

(b) Pills: The one area where there is a need to examine a legislation is in the field of family planning. The pill, which has been in the market since the 1960s, was considered safe for long, as the side-effects came to be known much later. Unlike in the West where it is not available without a doctor's prescription. In India pills like Mala-D advertising campaign by the government sponsored media. While this will be no doubt beneficial to woman as she would be examined on an individual basis, in reality medical facilities are unavailable or difficult to reach for a large number of people. In such a case a rigid rule might make even the existing facilities inaccessible to the average woman who does not want a pregnancy.

(c) The Injectable Contraceptive: One of the injectable is Net-en and its import has been permitted since late 1984. Net-en is a bimonthly injection that inhibits the production of gonadotropin. It does not need any chart as in the case of Pill or periodic check-us as in IUDs.

In March 1985, research trials of Net-en were held at a Rural Health Centre in Patancheru, Street Shakti Sangathana got word of it. They tried to dissuade the doctors from conducting trail as they had read about the side effects of the drugs and the lack of adequate long-term studies with it. They would not conceive if they took the drug, but were not told about its side effects nor that they were participating in a trial, the case is still in the Court. Depo Provera is another injecable contraceptive that is available without a prescription. Both these drugs are the subject matter of litigation. In the absence of any legislation to define and regulate such contraceptives (many of them prohibited in the countries of their origin or sold under strict conditions) activist groups have been forced to take these issues to Court. Depo Provera has been approved for use. Earlier it was contraceptive was banned in the country of origin. The government gave its approval in 1994 and launched in India. There are number of contradictions for the use of these drugs, but primary health centres in India have hardly any facilities for such large-scale investigation and maintenance. Moreover, the staff is often poorly-trained callous or careless, and under compulsion to meet impossible targets, which creates a great potential for abuse.

(d) Implants: Work on contraceptives in the form of implants first began in the 1960's. The idea was to find a way to put hormones in some kind of capsule that would gradually release them into the body over a period of time to prevent pregnancy. A number of different hormones and different types of capsules were tested, as well as different sites on the body for places to implant. The most widely used in Norplant. Norplant has been tested and used mainly in less developed countries.

A small study done by the Forum for Women and Health Bombay that Norplan is effective for a certain period. Otherwise it have also a lots of side effects.

(e) Sterilization: The most common method of contraception used in many developing countries such as India (besides abortion) is sterilization, and of this the major share is that of female sterilization. Laparascopic sterilizations are often done in sub-optimal conditions, either in institutional or mobile settings. In rural areas, camps are organized in temporary locations such as school buildings or some other public facility on special occasions. In these camps, a single surgeon performs 300-500 laparoscopies in 10 hours per day, which works out to one operation every two minutes. With the minimal care that is necessary for such an operation, only a maximum of 50 a day would be possible. There was a report from Kumbakonam that 1,225 women were operated upon in one day. In such a setting, it must be expected that the attitude of the health personnel would be callous. Obviously, follow-up care is not part of such mass programme which provides the facility of sterilization and move on. Often these areas do not have hospitals or clinics where women have problems can go for help.

(f) Reproductive Technology: Reproductive technologies designed to intervene in the process human reproduction for the prevention of conception and birth which includes contraceptives as well as methods of pregnancy termination. Since prevention and termination of pregnancy has been analysed under family planning method, therefore, the reproductive technology which helps in aiding or stimulating reproductive process. Reproduction technology is used for assisting reproduction in terms of aiding or stimulating reproduction like artificial insemination, in vitro fertilization, etc. Reproductive technologies are also used for genetic purposes and for prenatal diagnosis which includes sex-detection and sex-pre selection. The uses of technologies for assisting reproduction are extremely controversial; different interest groups in society have contributed to the debates with regard to their own sets of values, norms and interests. Childless individuals and couples see in these technologies a possibility to realize their desire for a child, which they expect to be supported by the providers for the technology and health care facilities. Researchers in human reproduction see it as an opportunity to do fundamental research in studying the processes of conception, the beginning of human life, and perhaps to manipulate and have more these technologies are concerned with their repercussions on society and see in these developments the potential so far reaching manipulation of the beginning of life, eugenic selection and increase in the control of women's bodies and lives.

(g) Artificial Insemination: Although non-medical artificial insemination has been around for a long time, the first known attempts date from 1799. The successful use for artificial insemination in hums dates from the 1870s. In artificial insemination a woman is inseminated with a man's sperm, produced after masturbation, without having sexual intercourse. It is a simple procedure entailing sperm being deposited in woman's vagina close to the cervix. The sperm used could be that of her husband or partner—referred to as Artificial Insemination by a Donor sperm (AID). The latter is resorted to when the husband/partner is infertile, has a law sperm count, or a genetic disorder which the parents do not want to pass on to the offspring.

(h) In-Vitro Fertilization (IVF): In Vitro Fertilization (IVF) of eggs from mammals began to be developed in the 1930's, however, research in eggs taken from women took long to develop. IVF (In-Vitro Fertilization) is at basis of a number of other techniques, making possible other manipulations, such as pre-implantations, such as pre-implantation diagnosis of embryo for genetic disorders and sex-selection, Durga Agarwal, born on 3rd October, 1978, was hailed as the first India 'test tube baby' and second in the world, but her claim to birth through IVF was contested, leading to suicide by Subhash Mukherjee, the doctor who claimed credit for it. Until the mid-1980s infertility treatment basically consisted of trying to diagnose the cause of infertility, rather than providing a way out. Then came corrective surgery in the form of tuboplasty, lately microscopic tuboplasty. Generally, it ended with the doctor giving up and the couple having to resign themselves to their fate, accepting childlessness or going in for adoption wither within the family, or through an adoption agency.

(i) Surrogacy: In the joint family system surrogate mothering (social, not biological) is common; widowed family members and older daughters also 'mother' children. The fulfilment is stressed rather than the biological process of child birth. The extraordinary and rapid advance of biological and genetic technology is going to give rise to new and complicated issues in the future that were unknown in our country. The status of children born by artificial insemination, the legal status of surrogate mother, is just some of the issues that might come to the courts in the future.

(E) Equal Remuneration Act, 1976[127]

The main provisions of the Act is to provide equal remuneration to men and women workers for the same or similar nature of work and prohibition of discrimination against women in the matter of employment. Appointment of authorities by the appropriate government to hear and decide claims and complaints, to hear appeal and to investigate whether the provisions of the Act are being complied with.

(F) Immoral Traffic (Prevention) Act, 1956[128]

India is a signatory to the International Convention for the Suppression of Immoral Traffic of May 1950. Accordingly, India passed the Suppression of Immoral Traffic in Women and Girls Act in 1956 (SITA) which was passed in Parliament and enforced since 1958. The object of this Act is to give effect to the declaration contained in Article 23 of the Constitution which prohibits traffic in human beings and makes any contravention of the prohibition an offence, punishable in accordance with the law. The Act prevents an offence, punishable in accordance with the law. The Act prevents sexual exploitation of women and girls for commercial purposes. However, it does not abolish, forbid, prohibit or ban prostitution but prohibits soliciting, reducing, etc. in public places. In 1986, a major amendment incorporated in 1986 to

127. For detail see "Equal Remuneration Act", 1976.
128. For detail see "Immortal Traffic (Prevention) Act, 1976".

include male prostitutes, the Act was renamed as Immoral Traffic (Prevention) Act.

(G) Dowry Prohibition Act, 1961[129]

This Act was made more stringent in 1985 and 1986 and corresponding amendments were made in the IPC and the Indian Evidence Act. However, the dowry problem continues and even has spread to communities where the system did not exist, thereby putting the efficacy of the law in doubt.

(H) National Commission for Women Act, 1990[130]

Successive Commissions on Women have noted in their reports the unequal status of women in every sphere of life and had suggested the setting up of an agency to fulfil the surveillance functions as well as to facilitate redressal of grievances of women. The country cannot progress as long as inequality persists with reference to half of its population. As a result, the National Commission for Women was set-up consisting of a Chairperson and six members. The main task of the Commission shall be to study and monitor all matters relating to the constitutional and legal safeguards provided for women, to review the existing legislations and suggest amendments, wherever necessary. It will also look into the complaints and take *suo moto* notice of the cases involving deprivation of the rights of women in order to provide support, legal or otherwise, to helpless women.

(I) The Child Marriage Restraint Act, 1929[131]

It was amended by Act 2 of 1978, which raised the minimum age of marriage to 18 for girls and 21 for boys. This had indeed been very progressive since earlier the minimum age of marriage for girls and boys was 14 and 18 respectively. This was subsequently amended in 1949 to raise the age to 15 for girls while no change was affected in case of boys.

(vi) Health Rights of Persons with Disabilities

The Constitution of India contains provisions in the form of directives to the States for the protection and empowerment of the disabled. India is a founder member of the United Nations and has ratified various conventions for the protection of the rights of the people. The adoption of declarations at the international level had a

129. For detail see "Dowry Prohibition Act, 1976".
130. For detail see "National Commission for Women Act, 1990".
131. For detail see "The Child Marriage Restraint Act, 1929".

tremendous impact on the Indian Legislature. The Government for the first time in 1987 has made an effort by enacting the Mental Health Act. During the 1990s the government had come out with 3 comprehensive legislations for the protection and rehabilitation of persons with various forms of disabilities. The enactment of the Rehabilitation Council of India Act, 1992; the Persons with Disabilities (Equal Opportunities, Protection of Rights and Full Participation) Act, 1995; The National Trust for Welfare of Persons with Autism, Cerebral Palsy, Mental Retardation and Multiple Disabilities Act, 1999, are steps in the right direction. While recognizing the plight of children especially juveniles the government has enacted the Juvenile Justice (Care and Protection of Children) Act, 2000.[132]

(vii) Environment Laws

Environment means our surroundings. The concept is to whatever object that is surrounding us. Einstein once remarked, "The Environment is everything that is not me. The term 'Environment' is derived from the French word 'environ' or 'environner' meaning "around", "roundabout", "to surround". Etymologically, environment is that of surroundings which influences an organism. Thus, environment may be defined as "sum total of all condition and influences that effect development and survival of life of organism.[133]

Environment of Pollution is natural as well as made by men. Pollution of air and water is man-made and is serious than the natural pollution. Over population, faulty drainage system, seepage from improperly constructed or improperly placed septic tanks, cesspools, leaking sewer lines, industrial wastes and dumping and covering of vegetable materials in garbage, etc. are the main cause for making the air as well as water polluted through human excreta. Though, we have Air (Prevention and Control of Pollution) Act, 1974, still air and water pollution has not been controlled to the desired extent. An enactment namely, Employment of Manual Scavengers and Construction of Dry Latrines (Prohibition) Act, 1993 has been made for the purpose of ensuring a healthy environment and to provide right to live with dignity. The main aim of this is to analyse the law relating to healthy environment *vis-à-vis* human excretion.[134]

A clean environment is a pre-requisite for good physical health. The U.N. Conference on the Human Environment held at Stockholm in

132. Butterworths, *Legal Framework for Health Care in India*, 264, (2002).
133. Rakesh Kumar, "Environment Protection *vis-à-vis* Right to Health: Judicial Approach," *Chotanagpur Law Journal*, Vol. 1, No. 1, 2008-09.
134. *Id.*, at 371-72.

June, 1972 in which India also participated decided that appropriate steps be taken for the protection and improvement of human environment pursuant to this decision, the Parliament enacted the Environment (Protection) Act, 1986.[135] The idea behind enacting this Act is to coordinate activities of various regulatory agencies, creation of authorities with adequate powers for environmental protection, regulation of discharge of environmental pollution and handling of hazardous substances, speedy response in the event of accidents threatening environment and deterrent punishment to those who endanger human environment, safety and health.

The Employment of Manual Scavengers and Construction of Dry Latrines (Prohibition) Act,[136] 1993 is another legislative measures which seeks to eliminate the dehumanizing practice of employment of manual scavengers and protect human health and environment. The Act prohibits the construction or continuance of dry latrines.

In the light of socio-economic justice assured in our Constitution, right to health is fundamental human right. The maintenance of health is constitutional goal whose realization requires interaction of many social and economic factors.[137] *Pt. Parmanand Katara* v. *Union of India*,[138] the Supreme Court directed private doctors or hospitals to extend services to protect the life of the patient, be an innocent or a criminal liable to extend services to protect the life of the patient, be an innocent or a criminal liable for punishment in accordance with law. In *K.C. Malhotra* v. *State of M.P.*[139], the Court observed:

> "... the inhabitants of the locality may be of backward class or weaker sections of the society or community at large have got fundamental right under Article 21 of the Constitution entitling them to live as human being in the area. The nalla must be covered and there should be proper lavatories for public conservancy, which should be regularly cleaned. Public health and safety cannot suffer on any count and all steps are to be taken for the improvement of public health as among its primary duties".[140]

In *Niyamakendram, Blue Mountain Building, Kochi* v. *Secretary,*

135. The term 'environment is defined widely enough to include water, air and land and the inter-relationship which exists among and between water, air and land, and human beings and other living creature, plants, micro organisms and property.
136. *Workers of C.E.S.C. Limited* v. *Subhash Chandra Bose*, (1992) 1SSC 441.
137. AIR 1994 M.P. 48.
138. *Id.*, at 51-52.
139. AIR 1997 MP 191.
140. *Ibid.*

Corporation of Kochi,[141] the Kerala High Court decided to step in and bale out corporation from its precarious position in order to protect health of the citizens, which is part of the fundamental right to life and liberty. The matter was related to mosquito menace and no tangible action on part of the officer to combat mosquito menace by tackling it at war footing was taken. Court observed:

> "…. A stage has come for this Court to abnegate its role as an umpire to enter the play ground assuming the role of salutary player to protect human right … The Court has assumed to role of a "garbage supervisor, but the burnt of that cross is worth bearing, having regard to the ultimate benefit it may bring to the people. It is high time to remind the public authorities to shed their ego about the Court verdicts passed in public interest which must be accepted in the right spirit bearing in mind the paramount consideration of the health and well-being of the people as imperatively implicit in the right to life guaranteed under Article 21 of the Constitution."[142]

In *Murli S. Deora* v. *Union of India*,[143] the Supreme Court has held that passive smoking in public places is indirect deprivation of life without any process of law. The statement of objects and reasons of the Cigarettes and other Tobacco Production, Supply and Distribution Act, 1975 and the Cigarettes and other Tobacco Products (Prohibition and Advertisement and Regulation of Trade and Commerce, Production and Distribution) Bill, 2001 intends to protect the environment and control the pollution. The Bench comprising M.B. Shah and R.P. Sethi, JJ. observed:

> "Fundamental Right guaranteed under Article 21 of the Constitution of India, *inter alia*, provides that none shall be deprived of his life without due process of law. There is no reason why a non-smoker should be afflicted by various diseases including lung cancer or of heart, only because he is required to go to public places. It is indirectly depriving him of his life without any process of law. Undisputedly, smoking injurious to health and may affect the health of smokers but there is no reason that health of passive smokers should also be injuriously affected. In any case, there is no reason to compel non-smokers to be

141. AIR 1997 Ker. 152.
142. *Id.*, at 152.
143. (2001) 8 SSC 765; *Murli S. Deora* v. *Union of India*, 2003 (5) Scale 31A ; Murli S. Deora v. *Union of India*, 2003 (5) Scale 346; *K. Ramana Krishnan* v. *State of Kerala*, AIR 1999 Ker. 385.

helpless victims of air pollution."[144]

Besides, these Miscellaneous Acts there are some other civil laws like law of torts and Civil Procedure Code, Contract Act, 1872 and criminal laws like Indian Penal Code and Criminal Procedure Code which contains the provisions of health and punishments in the violation of health protection laws.

The history of the development of tort[145] litigation, especially with regard to medical negligence cases, is of recent origin in India. It has its roots in the English Common Law,[146] of *ibi remedium ibi jus* (Where there is a remedy, there is a right) to *ibi jus ibi remedium* (where there is a right there is a remedy). Its transplantation in India by Courts, to exercise their power to administer law according to 'justice, equity and good conscience' indicate that the torts are primarily those wrongs for which either statutory remedies are not available or, if available, are inadequate or inappropriate. Further, in formulating the concept of actionable wrong, courts are in fact not only identifying the interests which require protection but also the circumstances under which they need to be protected. With changes in social, political and economic conditions, there inevitable changes in the nature and extent of the protected interests. Finally, the interests are preserved and promoted through the grant of civil right of action for unliquidated damages to the aggrieved person. Further, in a tort of medical negligence, the cause of action is personal against the person who has been negligent in discharging his duties, and that the cause of action does not survive against his estate or the legal representative.[147] There has been steady growth of tort litigation in India in the area of medical negligence.[148] This is primarily due to lack of awareness about ones own rights, the

144. *Ibid.*, obtained from *Ganesh Chandra Bhat* v. *Distt. Magistrate, Almora*; AIR 1993 All. 291, 298.

145. Sir John Salmond defined 'tort' as a civil wrong for which the remedy is an action for damages and which is not exclusively the breach of a contract or breach of a trust or other merely equitable obligation.

146. With the passage of time and to meet the emerging situations and demands the legislature in UK has resorted to enactment of legislations such as the Fatal Accidents Act, 1846, 1959, 1976; the Workmen's Compensation Act, 1897, Law Reform (Miscellaneous Provisions) Acts, 934 and 1971; Law Reform (Contributory Negligence) Act, 1952, Law Reform (Husband & Wife) Act, 1962; Congenital Disabilities (Civil Liability) Act, 1976; Unfair Contract Terms Act, 1977; Civil Liability Contribution.

147. *Balbir Singh Makol* v. *Chairman, M/s. Sir Ganga Ram Hospital & Ors.* (2001), 1 CPR 49.

148. *State of Madhya Pradesh* v. *Asharam* (1997) ACJ 1224 (MP); *State of Haryana* v. *Santra* (2000) 5 SCC 182; *Ram Bihari Lal* v. *J.N. Shrivastava*, AIR 1985 MP 158; *Achutrao H. Khadwa* v. *State of Maharashtra*, AIR 1996.

spirit of tolerance, the expenses involved and the delay in disposal of cases in Civil Courts etc.

There are more than 200 Central and State Legislations (enactments) that have some bearing on the environmental protection. However, in substantial number of these statutes, the environment concern appears to be incidental in nature. The following are some Acts which have some bearing on environmental protection:

1. The Air (Prevention and Control of Pollution) Act, 1981
2. The Ancient Monuments and Archaeological Sits and Remains Act, 1958
3. The Atomic Energy Act, 1962
4. The Code of Criminal Procedure, 1973
5. The Damodar Valley Corporation Act, 1948
6. The Easement Act, 1882
7. The Environment Protection Act, 1986
8. The Factories Act, 1948
9. The Forest (Conservation) Act, 1980
10. The Insecticides Act, 1968
11. The Indian Boiler's Act, 1923
12. The Indian Fisheries Act, 1897
13. The Indian Forest Act, 1927
14. The Indian Penal Code, 1860
15. Indian Ports Act, 1908
16. The Industries (Development and Regulation) Act, 1951
17. The Merchant Shipping Act, 1958
18. The Mines and Minerals (Regulation and Development) Act, 1957
19. The Motor Vehicles Act, 1988
20. The Northern India Canal and Drainage Act, 1873
21. Obstruction in Fairways Act, 1981
22. The Poison Act
23. The Prevention of Food Adulteration Act, 1954
24. The Police Act, 1861
25. The Public Liability Insurance Act, 1991
26. The River Boards Act, 1956
27. The Sarais Act, 1867
28. The Urban Land (Ceiling and Regulation) Act, 1976
29. The Water (Prevention and Control of Pollution) Act, 1974
30. The Water (Prevention and Control of Pollution) Less Act, 1977.
31. The Wild Life (Protection) Act, 1972
32. The Employment of National Scavengers and Construction of

Dry Latrines (Prohibition) Act, 1993.

33. The Bio-Medical Waste (Management and Handling) Rules, 1998 (further amended w.e.f. 17th September 2003 by the Bio-Medical 2008; Waste (Management and Handling) Amendment Rules, 2003.
34. Employment of Manual Scavengers and Construction of Dry Latrines (Prohibition) Act, 1993.

(viii) Emerging Issues

With the advancements in Medical Science and Technology several issues in health and medicine have emerged which require legislative intervention and control. To take some examples, the pre-natal diagnostic techniques were developed to detect genetic and other abnormalities at a fetal stage. However, because of the preference for a male child in our society, these tests were misused for gender detection followed by abortion if the test revealed a female foetus. Despite the law, however, sex detection tests continue. The procedure being extremely simple and private, it is very difficult to trace out the cases of female foeticide. Social awareness along with improvement in the social and economic status of girls alone can make the idea behind this law Pre-natal Diagnostic Techniques (Prevention of Misuse) Act meaningful.[149]

Another fall out of medical advancement which necessitated the enactments of the Transplantation of Human Organs Act of 1994.[150] This Act is enacted to provide for the regulation of removal, storage and transplantation of human organs for the therapeutic purposes and for the prevention of commercial dealings in human organs and for matters connected therewith on incidental thereto.

Another emerging issue is the increasing popularity of assisted reproductive techniques by couples who have difficulty in procreating in the normal natural way. Artificial insemination, surrogate motherhood, test tube babies and in-vitro fertilization are known to be in practice though there are no guidelines nor any law on the same so far. The Delhi Government has however, passed the Artificial Insemination (Human) Act, 1995.[151]

This Act is to provide for the regulation of donation sale and supply of human semen and ovum for the purpose of artificial insemination and for matters connected therewith or incidental thereto. The Act also provides for strict testing of the semen against (HIV) H infection and

149. International Conference on Global Health Law, 62, (1997) (Dec.).
150. For detail see Transplantation of Human Organs Act, 1994.
151. For detail see Artificial Insemination (Human) Act, 1995.

also prohibits the segregation of XX or YY chromosomes so that pre-conception sex selection is not possible.

(A) The Prohibition on the (Advertisement and Sale of Tobacco) Act, 2003[152]

Even though the ITC and the Hotel and Restaurant Association have challenged the Indian smoke-free law, to come into effect from October 2, a survey has shown that a majority of Indians are in favour of the law. The survey conducted between August 9 to 24, 2008 shows that 97 percent respondents want smoke-free public and workplaces, restaurants and bars. Importantly, 84 percent Urban Indians believe exposure to second-hand smoke is serious, something the new Indian smoke-free law hugely recognizes. Presenting new evidence, Monica Arora of HRIDAY, which works with the Health Ministry on anti-tobacco campaign said: We are not concerned about the outcome of petitions challenging the smoke free law. Supreme Court while hearing a similar matter in 2001 had held that a person's right to life is supreme, right to life include right to health."[153] Indian Smoke-free law defines public place as any place which general public can visit, as a matter of right or not.

(B) Bio-Medical Waste (Management and Handling) Rules, 1998[154]

Bio-Medical Waste (also popularly called as health care waste) is a by-product of health care and includes sharps, on-sharps, blood, body parts, chemicals, pharmaceuticals, medical devices and radioactive materials. Generation of bio-medical waste in sizeable quantities, depending upon the number of patients and the nature of activity, is an unavoidable side effect of health care delivery which primarily and predominantly takes within its fold processes like diagnosis, treatment, surgical intervention, post-operative care, rehabilitative care, clinical research, clinical trials, etc. Inadequate and poor handling or management of this waste exposes health-care workers, waste handlers, patients and the community in general to infections, toxic effects and serious fatal consequences as well.[155]

152. For detail see The Prohibition on the (Advertisement and Sale of Tobacco) Act, 2003.
153. Additi Tandon, 97% Indians want public places smoke-free, *Tribune News Service*, 29/9/2008 at pp.1 & 20.
154. For detail see Bio-Medical Waste (Management and Handling) Rules, 1998.
155. Jogo Rao, *Bio-Medical Waste & the Law*, 1, (2004).

(C) Mental Health Act, 1987

The Mental Health Act[156] is a comprehensive legislation which provides for the creation of Mental Health Authorities,[157] establishment and regulation of psychiatric hospitals and nursing homes,[158] rules governing admission and detention of patients,[159] liability of the government to meet cost of maintenance of mentally ill persons detained in psychiatric hospitals and nursing homes most importantly for the protection of human rights of mental ill persons.

(D) Rehabilitation Council of India Act, 1992

The Rehabilitation Council of India Act[160] was enacted by the government in 1992, providing for the setting up of the Rehabilitation Council at the National level with the specific objective of recognition and regulation of the conduct of the institutions providing education and other facilities. The Council under Section 18 of the Act is mandated to prescribe minimum standards of education required for granting a recognized rehabilitation qualification.

(E) Persons with Disabilities (Equal Opportunities, Protection of Rights and Full Participation) Act, 1995

This Act[161] is enacted to take certain steps for the prevention of occurrence of disabilities within the limits of their economic capacity and development by the appropriate government. The appropriate governments shall by notification make schemes to provide aids and appliances to persons with disabilities. Apart from the above Act contains provisions for regulating the establishment of Institutions,[162] provisions for social security including rehabilitation measures.[163]

(F) The National Trust for Welfare of Persons with Autism, Cerebral Palsy, Mental Retardation and Multiple Disabilities Act, 1999[164]

The government has enacted the legislation providing for the setting up of a body at the national level for the welfare of persons with Autism Cerebral Palsy, Mental Retardation and Multiple Disabilities

156. For detail see Mental Health Act, 1987.
157. Sections 3 and 4; *ibid.*
158. Sections 5-14; *ibid.*
159. Sections 15-36; *ibid.*
160. For detail see Rehabilitation Council of India Act, 1992.
161. For detail see Persons with Disabilities (Equal Opportunities, Protection of Rights and Full Participation) Act, 1995.
162. Sections 51-56; *ibid.*
163. Sections 66-68; *ibid.*
164. For detail see The National Trust for Welfare of Persons with Autism, Cerebral Palsy, Mental Retardation and Multiple Disabilities Act, 1999.

and matters connected therewith or incidental thereto. The Hon'ble Minster for Social Justice and Empowerment in a recently held conference organized by the Indian Law Institute at New Delhi, gave an assurance to set-up the National Trust with appropriate powers.[165]

Except this, another emerging issues increasing these days are mobile phone, computer application which are recent scientific achievements in modern era, but studies shows that mobile phones users may be placing their health at risk. The study done in several cities of U.S. among nearly 30,000 mobile phone users revealed that the cause of accidental death had been the increasing minutes of use of the mobile phone.[166] One research conducted in UK showed that the mobile phone exposure an hour before sleep adversely affects deep sleep. It also could result in lack of concentration and confusion. There is also a rising fear regarding human health getting affected due to exposure to electromagnetic fields. One of the big concerns regarding the effects from exposure to non-ionizing electromagnetic fields is the cancer and related syndromes.[167]

In mid-1992 a lawsuit was filed in an US Court in Florida by David Reynard alleging that using a cell phone had caused his wife a fatal brain cancer. But, the suit was dismissed by the Federal Court in 1995 for lack of valid scientific evidence.[168] In addition to the radiation caused by the mobile phone, base stations and associated antennas are another source of radiation. The radiated energy is restricted to certain safe margin indicated by the International Commission on Non-Ionising Radiation Protection. A survey study in France dealt with individually reported symptoms from people living within 300 meter radius of towers in rural areas and 100 meter in urban areas. Symptoms reported were fatigue, headache, sleep disturbance and loss of memory. Many people believed that the towers in the radio mobile systems caused symptoms such as anxiety, nausea and tiredness. Some users of mobile phones reported feeling of several unspecified symptoms during and after the phone use, ranging from burning and tingling sensations in the skin of the head, fatigue dizziness, loss of mental attention, disturbed reaction time and memory retentiveness, headaches, disturbance of the digestive system.[169] All of these feelings were typical of electrical sensitivity and attributed to psychological stress.

165. The National Trust under the 1999 Act was accordingly constituted in June 2000.
166. 'Mobile Phone Radiation Hazards'. http://www.ntc.org.sd/download/ mobile %20%20hazard.pdf. (accessed on July 19, 2008).
167. *Ibid.*
168. *Ibid.*
169. *Ibid.*

In the light of this, WHO issued in the year 2000,[170] guidelines to be strictly adhered worldwide so to protect everyone in the population: mobile phone users, those who work near or live around base stations, as well as people who do not use mobile phones. It recommended adoption of precautionary measures by governments of each nation and individuals like limited use of cell phones, use of "handfree" devices so to keep phones away from the head and body, not to use mobile phones while driving and reduction of exposure to RF fields, etc.[171]

Mobile phones may also interfere with certain electro-medical devices, such as cardiac pacemakers and hearing aids. In hospital intensive care departments, mobile phone use can be a danger to patients and should not be used in these areas. Similarly, mobile phones should not be used in aircraft as they may interfere with its navigation systems.[172]

Guidelines also suggested need for fences or barriers or other protective measures for some base stations (principally, those located on building rooftops) so to preclude unauthorized access to areas where exposure limits may be exceeded. Setting base stations near kinder gardens, schools and playgrounds should need special consideration. Also an open communication and discussion between the mobile phone operator, local council and the public during the planning stages for a new antenna can help create public understanding and greater acceptance of a new facility.[173]

Cell phones are an inevitable part of our lifestyle and work environment. At the same time, it is not logical to eliminate the radiation of these systems, radiation is an inherent characteristic thereof. The Indian courts are also giving attention to the mobile phone health hazards.

In *Reliance Infocom Ltd.* v. *Chemanchery Grama Panchayat & Others*,[174] the Kerala High Court gave a general direction to the TRAI to make periodical inspection to ascertain whether radiation emanated

---

170. Electromagnetic fields and Public Health: Mobile telephone and their base stations; WHO facts sheet No. 193, June 2000. http//www.who.int/media centre/factsheet/fs193/en (accessed on July 19, 2008.)
171. *Ibid.*
172. *Ibid.*
173. *Ibid.*
174. AIR 2007 Kerala 33. The Division Bench comprised of K.S. Radhakrishanan and K. Padmanabhan Nair, J.J. (In the instant case, in para 8 at 37) it was pointed out that the licence granted be cancelled by the panchayat on the basis of an apprehension that the radiation might cause health hazards to the people of the locality. The Court said that if the installation of tower and the emission of electromagnetic waves causes any air pollution, affecting human health, the pollution board can take appropriate measures under Air (Prevention and Control of Pollution) Act, 1991.

from the mobile base stations would cause any health hazards to the people of the locality. This judgment shows that radiation hazards posed by mobile handsets are real and in a way justifies the growing international concern and the expensive and costly researches ongoing for more than a decade in this regard.

Indeed, an effective system of health information and communications among scientists, governments, industry and the public is needed to raise the level of general understanding about mobile phone technology and reduce any mistrust and fears, both real and perceived. This information should be accurate and at the same time be appropriate in its level of discussion and understandable to the intended audience.

Similarly, there are several health problems associated with computer use which in the present times has become indispensable and one of the health hazard resulting from its use is called Cumulative Trauma Injuries (CTD's).[175] As with any task done repeatedly, working on a computer for long periods of time can cause inflammation of tendons, nerve sheaths and ligaments and damage to soft tissues. Depending on an individual's sensitivity to the repeated movements of keyboarding, the cumulative effect can be disabling. Resulting conditions are called Cumulative Trauma Disorders (CTD's). Different types of forearm and wrist CTDs from computer use are carpal tunnel syndrome,[176] tenosynovitis,[177] epicondylitis,[178] tendonitis,[179] and ganglionic cysts.[180] If you experience pain, numbness, tingling, or weakness in muscles or movement of arms, hands and fingers, it could be a sign or symptom of a CTD.

175. http//www.nysut.org/files/hs_070828_computer fact sheet.pdf. (accessed on July 19, 2008).
176. The syndrome may be associated with repetitive occupational trauma (cumulative trauma disorders); writs injuries, rheumatoid arthritis, pregnancy and other conditions. Symptoms include burning pain impairment of sensation in the distribution of the median nerve may occur. http://ctd.mdibi.org/detail.go?type=disease&ab=MESH & acc = D002349 (accessed on July 2, 2009).
177. It is an unusual manifestation of leprosy even though musculoskeletal swelling, and difficulty in moving the particular joint where the inflammation occurs. (http://medind.nic.in/jaa/to2/3/jaat0213p69.pdf. (accessed on July 2, 2009).
178. It is also referred as "tennis elbow". It is a very common cause of elbow pain that occurs overtime from repeated use of the muscles of the arm and forearm, leading to small tears of the tendons (a structure that connects muscle to bone). (http://en.wikipedia.org/wiki/) accessed on July 2, 2009).
179. It is a common condition that can cause significant pain. Tendonitis occurs when there is inflammation of tendons—the point where a muscle attaches. It can affect all parts of body. (http://en.wikipedia.org/wiki/) (accessed on July 2, 2009).
180. It is a swelling that often appears on or around joints and tendons in the hand or foot. It is most frequently located around the wrist and on the fingers. (http://en.wikipedia.org/wiki/-Ganglion-cyst). (accessed on July 2, 2009).

Neck and shoulder pain and stiffness can occur from improper placement of the computer monitor, mouse or document you are working from. Many people who use computers for prolonged periods of time complain of eyestrain, eye fatigue, eye irritation and blurred vision. Computers give off very low frequency and extremely low frequency radiation. Radiation is strongest at the back of the computer machine. The backs of computer monitors should be at least three to four feet from the user.[181] Unfortunately, there are no regulatory mechanism or guidelines issued either by the WHO or any nation including India to deal with various health hazards resulting from excess use of computers.

Another emerging issue popular these days are the hazards of plastic bags. Before the advent of poly-bags, people did shop, buy things, bring eatables from the market, and did the same marketing as is done now. The raw material for the bag was decided by its usage, such as cloth bags for lighter items, Gunny bags/Jute bags for voluminous and heavier goods. The bags were washable and reusable.[182] But the onset of the use of plastic bags[183] gradually, exposed its numerous health hazards. From mega grocery store chains and retain outlets to pushcart vendors, eateries and restaurants, the plastic bag is found to be the wonder solution to storage and cartage. Hence, plastic bags are ubiquitous in cities, towns and hill stations.

The land littered by plastic bag garbage not only presents an ugly and unhygienic seen but also this "Throw away culture" resulting from their use has found their way into the city drainage system, resulting in blockage as well as erosion of soil, creating unhygienic environment resulting in health hazard and spreading of water borne diseases. The waste materials collected are of all types including plastic materials. In the form of plastic cups, plastic bottles, etc. indiscriminately are burnt on the roadside polluting the area with thick smoke which produce toxic gases posing a health hazard. Inhaling of such gases causes lung diseases and even cancer.

Whereas burning of waste material in public is a serious offence and violation of municipal corporation bylaws. Use of plastic bags has resulted in killing of hundred of thousands of birds, whales, and turtles every year the world over.[184]

Surprisingly, the world annual average usage of plastic is alarming 18 Kg per year. And average Indian uses one kilogram of plastic per

181. *Ibid.*
182. http://www.vigyanprasar.gov.in/comcom/plsticbags.htm. (accessed on July 7, 2008).
183. The first plastic sandwich bags were unveiled in 1957 in US. http://www.alternet.org/environment/61607 (accessed on July 2, 2009).
184. *Ibid.* "Unfriendly packaging", *The Times of India*, July 7, 2009.

year.[185] And more than a 100 million tones of plastic is produced world-wide each year.[186]

The Plastics Committee of Pollution Control Board said that the daily use of grocery bags for sundry purposes is the real culprit as far as the volume and dispersing is concerned. In Bangalore, an estimated 500,00 polybags are used per day every day forming about 25 percent of all forms of plastics used.[187]

Consequential harmful effects of poly bags can be following:[188]

- Rag pickers are prone to skin infections, respiratory ailments while collecting polybags for recycling.
- Recycled polybags are not suitable to carry food.
- Polybags being non-biodegradable accumulate in the soil suffocating the plant and animal life.
- Animals may eat/swallow the polybags. Recently a local newspapers carried a cover story "Polybags kill 18 deer in the national park in Bangalore". On post-mortem, passage with polybags eaten caused the death.
- Polybags are silent killers.
- Drains clogged by plastic bags
- Soil life suffocated by menace of polybags.
- Therefore, non-biodegradable plastic accumulation has become a growing monster.

Polythene bags dumped near residential houses are breeding places for mosquitoes which causes dengue fever, filariasis and malaria.[189] Use of polythene bags less than 40 micron thickness cause more harm not only to the environment, but public health as well.

In brief, the plastic hazard caused due to non-judicial usage of plastic polybags and their subsequent disposal into water bodies, land and burning, results in the gradual loss of the existing ecological balance and causes related health hazards.

Keeping in mind, the environmental pollution caused due to extensive use of used polythene packaging material, many states in

185. *Ibid.*
186. Though plastics have opened the way for a plethora of new inventions and devices. It has also ended up threatening the public health. India is the fourth highest Asian importer of plastic waste behind Hong Kong, Philippines, Indonesia. http://ww. plastmart.com/upload/literature/plastic-weating_unit_profile.asp. (accessed on July 7, 2008).
187. http://little ecofriends.org/polybag.htm. (accessed on July 7, 2008).
188. *Ibid.*
189. http://www.ecologycenter.org. (accessed on March 13, 2005).

India[190] including the Union Territory, Chandigarh has imposed a ban on the use of plastic bags.[191]

Further, it can be stated that plastic recycling can be used as an alternative method to prevent plastic from entering our environment and thus reducing the menace.[192] The plastic weaving concept or recycling technology is based on the fact that plastic bags which are thin and have average life time of 2 to 3 hours and are discarded. They are responsible for clogging, choking, flooding death and destruction. Instead if they are collected, even from roads, they can be washed cleaned, dried out into strips and woven into the basic plastic textile fabric which can then be stitched into various products like mats, folders, handbags and purses. In this manner, plastic waste becomes more manageable and less destructive.[193]

As we know, science has spared no field untouched, it has discovered a treatment for wrinkles too. Botox injection is the most common cosmetic operation. Botox is a drug made from a toxin produced by the bacterium clostridium botulinum. It is the same toxin that causes a life threatening type of food poisoning.[194] A new study warned in London that Botox injections can lead to depression. Scientists have found that they also stop people from being able to express their feelings visually that leads to them keeping emotions bottled up inside and perceiving the world in a negative way.[195] There

190. The name of states which includes ban of plastic bags use are: Andhra Pradesh, Delhi, Goa, Himachal Pradesh, Orissa, Nagaland, Pondichery, Punjab, Tripura, U.P., Mumbai, H.P., Bangladesh ban its use in 2002 to solve the problem of blocked drains and flooding. Infact, the three R's of polythene use, i.e. reuse, reduce and recycle which is a popular mantra amongst school children, must be taken seriously now by each one of us along with total ban on its use or at least use of thin polybags. http:cesorissa.org/pdf/newletter6.pdf. (accessed on July 2, 2009).
191. The Chandigarh administration has imposed a complete ban on the use and sale of polythene bags in the city. The date of notification is 30th July, 2008. It is imposed from 2nd October, 2008. The orders have strictly banned the use, storage import, selling, transportation and disposal of polythene and plastic carry bags by any person in the city. No shopkeeper, vendor, wholesaler, retailer, trader or hawker can use polythene anymore. Violators of this act can be given rigorous imprisonment extended upto five years or fine of Rs. One lakh or both depending on the extent of violators. For the habitual violators, an additional fine of Rs. 5,000 per day shall be imposed and there are provisions of imprisonment upto seven years depending upon the violation. http://www.igovernment.in/site/Chandigarh_imposes_complete_ban_on_using_polybags. (Accessed on August 20, 2009).
192. http://www.plastmart.com/upload/literature/plastic-weaving_unit_profile.asp. (Accessed on July 7, 2008).
193. *Ibid.*
194. http://www.nlm.nih.gov/medlineplus (accessed on July 3, 2009).
195. http://www.expressindia.com/latest-news/Botox-injections-can-cause-depression/435104/. (Accessed on July 3, 209).

are other risks of Botox like headache, temporary eyelid droop, nausea, squint/double vision, facial pain, redness at the injection site and muscle weakness. Pregnant women and people having any problem related to nervous system are not advised to take Botox.[196] Sometimes it gives temporary relief of spasticity but may cause paraesthesias and muscle damage if used repeatedly.[197] Again, till today, there is no regulatory mechanism or laws/guidelines to check the abuse of Botox either under any Central Law or under ICMR guidelines.

There are also the hidden hazards of microwave cooking. Although microwave ovens are an important cooking and food heating tool in many modern homes. But the research shows that microwave oven cooked food suffers severe molecular damage. When eaten, it causes abnormal changes in human blood and immune system. Persons working in microwave fields have reported headaches, eyestrains, over all fatigue and disturbance of sleep. These effects have been associated with the interaction of the microwave fields with the central nervous system of the body.[198] The heating of milk in a microwave actually destroys much of the milk's nutritional value; and the milk's natural immunity and disease fighting qualities are negated. Other negative effects from microwave ovens include brain damage by causing electrical impulses in the brain to become confused or simply "short out" due to eating the reduced or altered nutritional content of "micro waved" food. Eating microwaved food have also been linked to heart attacks and cancers and can result in memory loss, lack of plastic microwavable containers being noted to cause cancers.[199] And, again, there is no law or guidelines of the governments of the world to monitor the use of microwave cooking.

Briefly speaking, the rapid industrialization, unsafe working environment, improper installation and incorrect handling of mechanical devices generating electromagnetic waves at home and exposure to cooking fuel, has resulted in escalating environmental pollution and deterioration in the quality of indoor air.[200] This exposes even the foetus to many known and unknown pollutants with recognized harmful effects. So, the foetus is no longer sheltered in the mother's womb. It is

196. http://www.Lifestyle.iloveindia.com/lounge/botox-treatment-in-india-518.html. (accessed on July 3, 2009).
197. http://www.udaan.org/butulinum/botulin.html. (accessed on July 3, 2009).
198. http://www.ccohs.ca/oshanswers/phys/microwave-ovens.html. (accessed in July 6, 2009).
199. http://www.greenprophet.com/2008/08/12/.../microwave-oven-health/. (accessed on July 6, 2009).
200. Ranjit Singh, *The Threat to the Foetus from Environmental Degradation,* 13 KULR at 352 (2006).

threatened by the noxious environmental pollutants generated by modern agricultural and industrial practices crossing the physical barrier between a mother and her foetus. Noxious environmental pollutants generated by agriculture and industrial variants are playing havoc with the growth of the foetus.[201]

We must remember that science does not exist in isolation from the larger community that feels effect of its research. The complex sensitive issue like when human life actually deems to begin, i.e. at the conception or at the time of birth can only be addressed if scientific research is in congrument with fundamental values. In the end, it can be said that both law and science without conscience ultimately result in the death of the soul, and this has to be avoided for better future of mankind.[202]

On the other hand, liability of health professional under the Contract Act, 1872 mainly depends on the express or implied terms agreed upon by the patient or his representatives and the doctor or hospital. Consent for treatment on payment of fees on the part of a patient can be treated as an implied contract with the doctor who by undertaking treatment on acceptance of fees, promises to exercise proper care and skill. The Indian Contract Act, 1872 contains detailed provisions with regard to offer, acceptance, proposal, vicarious liability, etc. A detailed review and examination of the cases reveals that, though the provisions have a direct bearing on the services being provided by doctors and hospitals, it has a very limited application to medical negligence.[203]

There is also a legal provisions in the Consumer Protection Act, 1986 for the protection of health. Although these provisions are of recent origin in India but such a laws are very necessary to protect the consumers from hazard to their health and safety, and to make available to them consumer justice that is speedier and cheaper. Products injurious to health have also increased over the years. Laws were therefore, enacted mandating, regulating and overseeing health care establishments and institutions.[204] During the last two decades, attention has turned to the quality of the health services.[205] Consumers have not only been conferred a right to access health care but also to receive quality

---

201. *Ibid.*
202. *Supra* n. 70 at 173.
203. *Matheson* v. *Smiley* (1932) 2 DLR 781, *Indian Medical Association* v. *V.P. Shantha* (1995) 6 SCC 651; *Syed Abdul Khader* v. *Rani Reddy* (1979) 2 SCC 601; *Kalyani* v. *Tirkaram*, AIR 1938 Nag. 255, *Joseph alias Pappachan & Ors.* v. *Dr. George Moonjely & Anrs.*, AIR 1994 Ker. 289.
204. Butterworths, *Legal Framework for Health Care in India*, 95, (2002).
205. *Cosmopolitan Hospitals* v. *Vasantha P. Nair*, (1990).

treatment. Consequently, closer attention is being provided. In many developed and developing countries powerful consumer organizations have been instrumental dealing with the consumer protection laws and in expanding the horizon of such laws.[206]

In Indian Penal Code, 1860 there are many sections[207] which relates to the Criminal Liability of Health providers and standards of Health care. Any aggrieved person or his family members may lodge a complaint with the police for registration of the First Information Report (FIR). He may seek the assistance of police by dialing 100 or any other specific number. There is no fixed format for writing the complaint one can write accurately in a language of his choice, give full details as to names of the accused, place of commission of offence, date and time, etc. The complaint may be submitted either orally or in writing and in both the events it is the responsibility of the police officer to register his complaint. One should avoid delay in registering the complaint. If there is any delay the reasons for the delay may be stated in the complaint. The complainant is also entitled to have a copy of First Information Report (FIR) and can demand for the same. If a police officer refuses to register a complaint he can approach the higher officials or send the same by registered post or otherwise he can move a private complaint under Section 200[208] of the Code of Criminal Procedure, 1973 before a

---

206. Cases define service, *State of Orissa* v. *Divisional Manager LIC Sanor* (1996) 3 CPR 221, *Indian Medical Association* v. *V.P. Shantha* (1995) 6 SCC 651, *Vasantha P. Nair* v. *M/s. Cosmopolitan Hospitals (P) Ltd. & Ors.* (1991) 11 CPJ 444, *Yashwantbhai Harikrishankar Pandya & Anrs.* v. *Dr. K.C. Parikh & Ors.* (1992) 2 CPR 517; *Dr. A.S. Chandra* v. *Union of India* (1992) 1 Andhra LT 713; *C.S. Subramanian* v. *Union of India* (1994) 1 Mad LJ 438 (DB); *Prem Chand Sharma* v. *Director, Central Government Health Scheme* (1992) 2 CPR 51; *Additional Director CGHS, Pune* v. *Dr. R.L. Butan* 1 (1996) 1 CPR 136; *Consumer Unity and Trust Society of Jaipur* v. *State of Rajasthan & Ors.* (1991) 11 CPJ 56 (NC); *Fakir Mohan Bhuyan* v. *Dr. G.C. Pothal's Case* (1999) 1 CPR 140; *Laxman Thamappa Kotgiri* v. *Union of India & Ors.* (1998) CPR 674; *Harbhajan Singh* v. *Dayanand Medical Collage & Anrs.* (1994) 1 CPR; *M/s. Cosmopolitan Hospital* v. *Vasantha P. Nair* (1993) CCJ 198; *Yasmin Sultana's Anrs.* v. *Dr. Rupaben D. Patel & Anrs.* (1994) 1 CPR 407; *Shri Chandra Sagar D. Rajput Ors.* v. *Dr. Dinesh J. Shah* (1999) 1 CPR 434; *Narsinhbhai Bhimi Rajput* v. *Dr. J.K. Patel* (1994) 3 CPR 28; *Dr. Ravinder Gupta & Ors.* v. *Ganga Devi & Ors.* (1993) 3 CPR 255; *Rao* v. *Ministry of Health* (1954) 2 All ER 181; *M. Jeeva* v. *R Lalitha* (1994) 2 CPR 517 etc.
207. For instance, one Section related to health provisions under Indian Penal Code 1860 is Section 268. A person is guilty of a public nuisance, who does any act, or is guilty of an illegal omission, which causes any common injury, danger, or annoyance to the public or to the people in general who dwell or occupy property in the vicinity or which must necessarily cause injury, obstruction, danger or annoyance to persons who may have occasion to use any public right. A common nuisance is not excused on the ground that it causes some convenience or advantage.
208. Section 200 of Cr.P.C. (Code of Criminal Procedure, 1973) lays down the

Magistrate or a petition may be filed before the High Court in the concerned State under Article 226 of the Constitution for appropriate directions. A complaint may also be lodged with the Executive Magistrate under Sections 133 to 135[209] of the Code of Criminal Procedure 1973. The aforesaid provisions can be invoked to eliminate 'quacks' or persons practicing unauthorisedly in any area and are a threat to the lives of the public.[210]

III. SUM-UP

The States concern for the health and protection of its people depend on the large number of legislations and provisions on health in other legislations and their implementation. A major health hazard today is adulteration of food stuffs, drugs and environment pollution. Apart from provisions in the Penal Code and Constitution there are special laws to prevent adulteration of food, production of spurious and substandard drugs and on environment protection.

There are also laws to protect the health and safety of women, workers and children under the labour laws, certain kind of hazardous jobs are prohibited for women. There are also various Acts for the betterment of the children. But with the advancements in medical science and technology several issues in health and medicine have emerged which require legislative invention and control.[211]

---

preliminary procedure which a Magistrate shall follow on receiving a complaint.

209. Section 133 lays down the conditional order for removal of nuisance under six categories: (1) the lawful obstruction or nuisance to any way river or channel, lawfully used by the public or to public place; (2) the conduct of any trade occupation or the keeping of any goods or merchandise, injurious to the health or physical comfort of the community; (3) the construction of any building or the disposal of any substance as is likely to occasion conflagration or explosion; (4) a building, tent or structure or a free as is likely to fall and cause injury to persons; (5) an unfenced tank, well or excavation near a public way or place; and (6) a dangerous animal requiring destruction, confinement or disposal. Section 134 deals with service or notification of order served and section 135 deals with person to whom order is addressed to obey or show cause.

210. *Pt. Parmanand Katra* v. *Union of India & Ors.*, AIR 1989 SC 2039; *Juggankhan* v. *State of M.P.*, AIR 1985 SC 831; *Ram Niwas* v. *State of Uttar Pradesh* (1968) Cr.L.J. 635 (All.); *Sukaroo Kobiraj* v. *The Express* (1877) ILR 14 Cal. 566; *Dr. Khusaldas Pammandas* v. *State of Madhya Pradesh*, AIR 1960 MP 50 etc.

211. M.P. Singh, *International Conference on Global Health Law*, 59-62, (1997).

CHAPTER 5

Promotion and Protection of Right to Health through Health Plans

I. INTRODUCTION

The evolution and development of health policies and law in India centres during the endemic diseases and reprisal of remedial strategies.[1] Now the definition of health is not merely concentrated on the absence of disease but extend to the complete physical, mental and social well-being.[2] It has until recently tended to focus on infective micro-organisms, which were seen as the major source of human morbidity and mortality in India, as in most countries at the commencement of the epidemiological transition. Water and food-borne diseases in particular have been the target of a long sustained, widespread and still ongoing sanitary campaign.[3] In the British India, general death rate was 22.4, infant mortality rate was 162 per thousand, expectation of the life at birth was 26.91 for males and 26.56 for females. Nearly half of the total number of death were among children under 10 years.[4]

Endemic diseases like leprosy, tuberculosis etc. caused considerable morbidity. There was a wide prevalence of unsanitary conditions in rural and urban areas. Provision for protected water supply and drainage was totally inadequate. Food consumed was both

1. J. Bhore, Govt. of India, Report of the Health Survey and Development Committee, (1946).
2. Nomani Zafar, Socio-Legal Dimension of Right to Health, (2002), p. 1.
3. *Ibid.* Also see Sumit Guha, Health and Environmental Sanitation in Twentieth Century India, Monica Das Gupta, Health, Poverty and Development in India, (1996).
4. *Ibid.* Also see, Report of the Public Health Commissioner, Govt. of India (1934).

insufficient and ill balanced.[5] But, today 'The Report on Health'[6] examines the progress made in the health sector, identifies the constraints in providing universal access and provides options and future strategies. In terms of life expectancy, child survival and maternal mortality, India's performance has improved steadily. Life expectancy is now 63.5, infant mortality rate is now 53 per 1000 live births, maternal mortality ratio is down to 254 per lakh live births and total fertility rate has declined to 216. However, there are wide divergences in the achievements across states. There are also in equities based on rural-urban divides, gender imbalances and cast patterns.

II. NATIONAL FIVE YEAR PLANS

Since "health" is an important contributory factor in the utilization of manpower, the Planning Commission gave considerable importance to health programmes in the five year plans. For purpose of planning, the health sector has been divided into the following sub-sectors:[7]

(a) Water supply and sanitation;
(b) Control of Communicable diseases;
(c) Medical education, training and research;
(d) Medical care including hospitals, dispensaries and primary health centres;
(e) Public health services;
(f) Family planning; and
(g) Indigenous system of medicine.

All the above sub-sectors have received due consideration in the five year plans. However, the emphasis has changed from plan to plan depending upon the felt needs of the people and technical considerations. To give effect to a better coordination between the Centre and the State Governments, a Bureau of Planning was constituted in 1965 in the Ministry of Health, Government of India. The main function of this Bureau is compilation of National Health Five Year Plans. The Health Plan is implemented at various levels, e.g. Centre, State, District, Block and Village.[8]

5. E.H.C. Government of India, Report of the Environmental Hygiene Committee, 1949, (1950).
6. Annual Report to the People on Health, Government of India, Ministry of Health and Family Welfare, September 2010, p. 1.
7. J.B. Shrivastava, (1972), *Indian J. Med. Edu.*, Vol. XI, p. 99.
8. S.L. Dhir, (1972), *NIHAE Bulletin*, 5, pp.179-86.

The five year plans were conceived to rebuild rural India, to lay the foundations of industrial progress and to secure the balanced development of all parts of the country. Recognizing 'health' as an important contributory factor in the economic condition of the country, the Planning Commission gave considerable importance to health programmes in the five year plans.[9] The broad objectives of the health programmes during the five year plans have been:

(a) control or eradication of major communicable diseases;
(b) strengthening of the basic services through the establishment of primary health centres and sub-centres;
(c) population control; and
(d) development of health manpower resources.[10]

Today, India has a vast network of governmental voluntary and private health infrastructure manned by large number of medical and paramedical persons. During the Tenth Plan, efforts were intensified to improve the health status of the population by optimizing coverage and quality of care by identifying and rectifying the critical gaps infrastructure, manpower, equipment, essential diagnostic reagents and drugs.[11] The approach during the Tenth Plan was to improve access to, and enhance the quality of primary health care in urban and rural areas by providing an optimally functioning primary health care system as a part of Basic Minimum Services and to improve the efficiency of existing health care infrastructure at primary, secondary and tertiary care setting through appropriate institutional strengthening, and improvement of referral linkages. The monitorable targets for the Tenth Five Year Plan and beyond were as follows:

(a) Reduction of poverty ratio by 5 per cent points by 2007, and by 15 per cent points by 2012;
(b) All children in school by 2003; all children to complete 5 years of schooling by 2007;
(c) Reduction in gender gaps in literacy and wage rates by at least 50 per cent by 2007;
(d) Reduction in the decadal rate of population growth between 2001 and 2011 to 16.2 percent;
(e) Increase in literacy rate to 75 per cent within the plan period;

9. Government of India, Planning Commission (1974), Draft Fifth Five Year Plan, 1974-79, Vols. I & II, Controller of Publications, Delhi.
10. Government of India (1987), India A Reference Annual, 1986, Director Publications Division, Ministry of Information & Broadcasting.
11. Tenth Five Year Plan (2002-07), Volume II, Planning Commission, Govt. of India, New Delhi, pp. 81-82.

(f) Reduction of maternal mortality ratio to 2 per 1000 live births by 2007 and to 1 by 2012; and

(g) All villages to have sustained access to potable drinking water within the plan period.

These targets reflect the concern that economic growth alone may not lead to the attainment of long-term sustainability and of adequate improvement in social justice. Earlier plans have had many of these issues as objectives, but in no case specific targets were set. As a result, these were viewed in terms of being desirable but not essential. However, in the Tenth Plan, these targets are considered to be as central to the planning framework as the growth objective.

III. NATIONAL HEALTH PROGRAMMES

Technological improvements and increased access to health care have resulted in a steep fall in mortality, but the disease burden due to communicable diseases and non-communicable diseases, environment pollution and nutritional problems continue to be high inspite of the fact that norms for creation of infrastructure and manpower are similar throughout the country, there remains substantial variation between states and districts within the states, in availability and utilization of health care services and health indices of the population. During Tenth Plan there is continued commitment to provide essential primary care, emergency life saving services, services under national disease control programme free of cost to individuals, based on their needs, and not on their ability to pay.

Government has set targets in the Tenth Five Year Plan to control certain diseases like HIV/AIDS, tuberculosis, leprosy, malaria, and blindness, etc. through various National Health Programmes. Among this various international agencies like WHO, UNICEF, UNFPA, World Bank as also a number of foreign agencies like SIDA, DANIDA, NORAD, and USAID have been providing technical and material assistance in the implementation of these programmes. A brief account of these programmes which are currently in operation is given below:

(i) Vector Borne Disease Control Programme

Directorate of National Anti-Malaria Programme (NAMP) is the national nodal agency for prevention and control of major vector borne diseases of public health importance namely malaria, filaria, Japanese encephalitis, kala-azar and dengue/dengue haemohagic fever. Till 2002-03, the centrally sponsored schemes viz. National Anti-Malaria Programme, national filaria control programme and kala-azar control programme, had been operative in the country on the cost sharing basis between Cetnre and States. There was no specific centrally sponsored programme for J.E. and dengue/DHF, and the states were managing these diseases out of their own resources and with limited need-based support and technical guidance from the Directorate of NAMP. However, in pursuance of the concept of convergence, the Government of India has approved a National Vector Borne Disease Control Programme (NVBDCP) from the year 2003-04 by inclusion of Japanese Encephalitis (JE) and dengue/Dengue Hemorrhagic Fever (DHF) with other three ongoing programmes.[12]

National Malaria Control Programme (NMCP) was launched in India in April 1953. It was based on indoor residual spraying with DDT (1 gm per sq. metre of surface area) twice a year in endemic area where spleen rates were over 10 percent. The National Malaria Control Programme (NMCP) was in operation for 5 years (1953-58). The results of the programme were highly successful in that the incidence of malaria had declined sharply from 75 million cases in 1953 to 2 million cases in 1958, an estimated 80 percent reduction of the malaria problem. It also paid rich dividends to the country in different fields like agriculture, lane projects and industry. Encouraged by these spectacular results Government of India in the Ministry of Health changed the strategy from malaria control to eradication, and launched the more ambitious National Malaria Eradication Programme (NMEP) in 1958.[13] According to international standards, the programme was divided into preparatory, consolidation and maintenance phases. In the beginning, malaria eradication programme was highly successful. But very soon setbacks appeared in the form of focal outbreaks. The annual incidence of malaria cases in India escalated from 50,000 in 1961 to a peak of 6.4 million cases in 1976.[14]

(ii) National Filaria Control Programmes

The National Filaria Control Programme (NFCP) has been in operation since 1955. According to recent estimates about 420 million people are exposed to the risk of infection. 19 million manifest the disease, and 25 million have filarial parasites in their blood. The strategy follows the World Health Organization (WHO)[15]

12. Government of India (2004), Annual Report, 2003-04, Ministry of Health and Family Welfare, New Delhi.
13. Government of India (2004), Annual Report, 2003-04, Ministry of Health and Family Welfare, New Delhi.
14. K. Park, Preventive and Social Medicine, 227, (2005).
15. WHO (World Health Organization), also see *Swasth Hind National Health Programmes* (1996), Vol. XI (8-9), p. 139.

recommendation of annual single dose mass drug therapy with DEC/DEC with albondazole as a supplement of existing National Filaria Control Programme (NFCP) strategy 13-30 highly endemic districts to reduce transmission of filaria to a very significant low level. During 2003-04, central assistance of Rs. 19.5 crores was provided to the endemic States for supporting lymphatic filariasis elimination operations in the endemic districts.[16]

(iii) Kala-Azar Control Programme

Kala-Azar Control Programme was launched in 1990-91. This has brought down the incidence and death rate of the disease by 75 percent by the year 2002.[17]

The strategy for Kala-Azar Control includes three activities: interruption of transmission for reducing vector population by undertaking indoor residual insecticidal spray twice annually; early diagnosis and complete treatment of Kala-Azar cases; and health education for community awareness.[18]

In view of the success achieved so far, National Health Policy envisages Kala-azar elimination by the year 2010. The Tenth Five Year Plan targets are: Prevention of death due to Kala-azar by 2004 with annual reduction of at least 25 percent; zero level incidence by 2007 with at least 20 percent annual reduction using 2001 as the base year, and elimination of Kala-azar by year 2010. To achieve these goals, Government of India has decided to provide 100 percent central support from the year 2003-04.[19] An estimated population of 130 million is exposed to the risk of Kala-Azar in the endemic areas. The annual incidence of disease has come down from 77,099 cases in 1992 to 31,217 cases in 2005 and deaths from 1419 to 157, respectively.

(iv) Japanese Encephalitis Control Programme

Japanese Encephalitis is a disease with high mortality rate and those who survive do so with various degrees of neurological complications. During the last few years it has become a major public heath problem. States of Andhra Pradesh, West Bengal, Assam, Tamil Nadu, Karnataka, Bihar, Haryana, Kerala and Uttar Pradesh are reporting maximum number of cases.[20]

16. K. Park, *op. cit.*, p. 332.
17. Government of India (2004), Annual Report, 2003-04, Ministry of Health and Family Welfare, New Delhi.
18. *Ibid.*
19. *Ibid.*
20. Park's Textbook of Preventive and Social Medicine, Eighteenth Edition, 332, (2005).

The strategies for control of Japanese include: (a) care of the patient; (b) development of a safe and standard indigenous vaccine; (c) sentinel surveillance including clinical surveillance of suspected cases; (d) studies to identify the high risk groups by measuring the blood level of antibodies; and (e) epidemiological monitoring of the disease for effective implementation of preventive and control measures.[21]

Technical support is provided, on request by the State health authorities for the outbreak investigations and control. Insecticides used under the National Anti-Malaria Programme are used for the control of Japanese Encephalitis (JE) outbreaks where required.[22]

(v) Dengue Fever Control Programme

During 1996, an outbreak of dengue was reported in Delhi. Since then dengue has been reported from other states also. In view of this major outbreak of the disease a "Guideline of Preparation of Contingency Plan in case of outbreak/epidemic of Dengue/Dengue Hemorrhagic fever" was prepared and sent to all the states. It includes all the important aspects of control measures like identification of outbreak, delineation of affected area, containment of outbreak, case management vector control, Information-Education-Communication (IEC) activities about Do's and Don'ts for prevention of dengue, monitoring and reporting etc. Technical assistance for investigation, prevention and control of Dengue/Dengue Hemorrhage Fever (DHF) outbreak is provided to the State through Directorate of National Anti-Malaria Programme.[23]

(vi) National Leprosy "Eradication Programme"

The National Leprosy Control Programme (NLCP) has been in operation since 1955 as a centrally aided programme to achieve control of leprosy through early detection of cases.[24]

The (NLCP) National Leprosy Control Programme moved ahead initially a slow pace, presumably for want of clear-cut policies on operational objectives for nearly two decades.[25]

The availability of Dapsone monotherapy for Leprosy laid the

---

21. J. Kishore, National Health Programmes of India, Second Edition 40, (1999).
22. Park, *op. cit.*, at 332. Also see NICD (1997), Investigation & Control of Outbreak, Japanese Encephalitis.
23. Government of India (2004), Annual Report, 2003-04, Ministry of Health and Family Welfare, New Delhi.
24. Government of India National Leprosy Eradication Programme—Status Report, 1992, Leprosy Division DGHS, Ministry of Health and Family Welfare.
25. *Swasth Hind* (1996), Vol. XL (8-9), p.141.

foundation of National Leprosy Control Programme in 1955 with the main objective of controlling leprosy through domiciliary treatment with Dapsone. Social obstacles, non-availability of drugs, lack of primary prevention (vaccination) and lepral resistance to Dapsone caused programme failure. In 1981, Government of India asked the Indian scientists to develop a leprosy eradication strategy and subsequently launched the National Leprosy Eradication Programme (NLEP) in the year 1983 with health problem by the year 2000 A.D.[26] Later World Health Organization (WHO) in 1991 adopted a reduction calling for elimination of leprosy as a public health problem by the year 2000 A.D. (reducing prevalence to less than one case per 10,000 population).[27] The goal of leprosy elimination at national level (<1case/10000 population) as set by National Health Policy (2002) was achieved in the month of December 2005. Even though the disease came down to a level of elimination, still it is prevalent with moderate endemicity in about 20 percent of the district. During 2005-06 a total of 1.61 lakh new leprosy cases were detected.

(vii) National Tuberculosis Programme

National Tuberculosis Programme (NTP) has been in operation since 1962. India accounts for nearly one-third of global burden of tuberculosis. Every year, approximately 1.8 million persons develop tuberculosis of which about 0.8 million are new smear positive highly infectious cases and about 4.17 lakh people die of Tuberculosis (TB) every year, one person die every minute, and about 1006 people die every day.[28]

Since 1993, India has successfully implemented Revised National Tuberculosis Control Programme (RNTCP) using directly observed treatments (DOTS) strategy. As of March 2004, this programme covered about 76 per cent of Country's population (more than 851 million persons) in 466 districts and belongs to category 3 of Directly Observed Treatment (DOT) strategy. Tuberculosis remains a public health problem, with India according for one-fifth of the world incidence. Every year 1.8 million people in India develop tuberculosis, of which 0.8 million are infetectious smear positive cases the emergence of (HIV-TB).

26. Government of India, Annual Report, 1997-98, Ministry of Health and Family Welfare, New Delhi.
27. Government of India & WHO-SEARO, India, National Leprosy Eradication Programme. Report of the Mid-terms appraisal of World Bank NLEP supported project (7-9 April 1997). Also see Kishore J., *op. cit.*, p. 48.
28. Government of India (2004), Annual Report, 2003-04, Ministry of Health and Family Welfare.

Co infection and multi-drug resistant tuberculosis has increased the severity and magnitude of the problem. RNTCP has achieved nation-wide coverage in March 2006. Since the inception of the programme, over 6.3 million patients have been initiated on treatment and the programme has achieved all the proposed goals in terms of expansion of directly observed treatment, short course (DOTS) services, case finding, and treatment success during the Tenth Plan.

Table 1: The Tuberculosis Estimates for India (2002)

Population	049 million
Global Rank (by estimated number of cases)	1
Incidence (all cases/100000 population)	168
Incidence (New Smear +ve cases/100000 population	75
Prevalence (Smear +ve/100000 population	156
TB Mortality per 100000 population	37
Percentage of adults (15-49 years) TB Cases HIV Positive	4.6
Percentage of New cases multi-drug resistant	3.4

Source: WHO (2004), Global Tuberculosis Control, Surveillance, Planning Financing, WHO Report 2004.

The 4.4 per cent death rate in Revised National Tuberculosis Programme (RNTCP) area is substantially lower than the 29 percent mortality document among treated smear positive tuberculosis patients in non-RNTCP areas.[29]

(viii) National AIDS Control Programme

The first (AIDS) case in India was recorded in May 1986. Since then, many hundred of cases of AIDS have been reported from every State of the country.[30] Realizing the gravity of epidemiological situation of (AIDS) prevailing in the country, the Government of India has launched a comprehensive plan of action the National (AIDS) Control Programme since 1987.[31] The programme is assisted financially by the World Bank and the World Health Organization in eighth five year plan. The World Bank loan became effective from 1992 onward.[32]

The Government of India launched a 5 year HIV/AIDS Control Project from September 1992 to September 1997 as 100 per cent centrally sponsored project for all States/Union territories. The project

29. *Ibid.*
30. National AIDS Control Programme in India: Country Scenario, Dec., 1997. NACO Ministry of Health & Family Welfare, Govt. of India.
31. K. Benerjee, K. Dutta, HIV/AIDS—Issues and Challenges, *Indian Journal of Public Health*, 1997, pp. 155-56.
32. J. Kishore, *op. cit.*, p.12.

was later on extended time to time with new plans.[33] According to statistics released on 6 July, 2007, by National AIDS Control Organization (NACO) supported by UN AIDS and WHO, indicated that national adult HIV prevalence in India is 0.36 per cent, which corresponds to an estimated 2 million to 3.1 million people living with HIV/AIDS in India. The overall HIV/AIDS budget for NACO for the year 2005-06 was US$ 103 million and for the year 2006-07, it was US$ 138 million. To ensure sustainability, NACO is instrumental in promoting HIV/AIDS prevention and care activities into the ongoing governmental programmes of the government.

(ix) National Programme for Control of Blindness

The National Programme for control of blindness was launched in the year 1976 as a 100 percent centrally sponsored programme and incorporates the earlier trachoma control programme started in the year 1968. The National Survey on Blindness (2001-03) shows an estimated 1.1 per cent prevalence of blindness in general population with 62.6 per cent share, cataract continues to be the main cause of blindness. Uncorrected refractive errors were responsible for 19.7 per cent, glaucoma 5.8 per cent, posterior segment pathology for 4.7 per cent, corneal opacity for 0.9 per cent of blindness. Other causes were responsible for 6.2 per cent of blindness.[34]

The findings of the survey conducted during 2001-02, in randomly selected districts of the States covered by World Bank Project shows that dependence on eye campus has now reduced, except in remote and tribal areas; involvement of Primary Health Centres/Community Health Centre's doctor in the programme has increased; higher percentage of cataract operated persons consult the doctor at an early stage; there is increase in demand for modern techniques like intra-ocular lenses and suture-less surgeries; and about 84 per cent of cataract operated persons receive free spectacles from the health facilities.[35]

It is global initiative to reduce avoidable (Preventable and Curable) blindness by the year 2020. India is also committed to this initiative. The plan of action for the country has been developed with following main features:

33. Government of India, Annual Report, 1999-2000, Ministry of Health and Family Welfare, New Delhi.
34. Government of India, National Programme for Control of Blindness Course Material for Training in District Programme Management (Revised, 1996). Ophthalmic Section, Ministry of Health and Family Welfare, Nirman Bhavan, New Delhi.
35. Government of India (2004), Annual Report, 2003-04, Ministry of Health and Family Welfare, New Delhi.

Figure 4: Shows the Proposed Structure for Primary, Secondary and Tertiary Eye Care

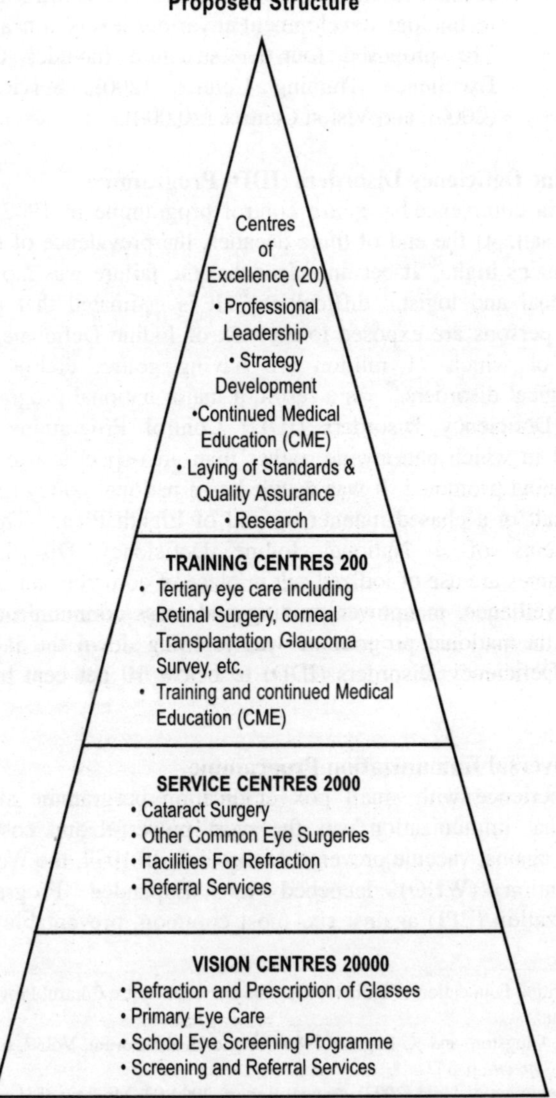

Source: Government of India (2004), National Programme For Control of Blindness in India, Ministry of Health and Family Welfare, New Delhi.

(a) Target diseases are cataract, refractive errors, childhood blindness, corneal blindness, glaucoma, diabetic retinopathy.

(b) Human resource development as well as infrastructure and technology development at various levels of health system. The proposed four-tier structure includes Centres of Excellence Training Centres (200), Service Centres (2000), and Vision Centres (20,000).

(x) Iodine Deficiency Disorders (IDD) Programme

India commenced a goitre control programme in 1962, based on iodized salt. At the end of three decades, the prevalence of the disease still remains high.[36] It became clear that the failure was mostly due to operational and logistic difficulties.[37] It is estimated that nearly 167 million persons are exposed to the risk of Iodine Deficiency Disorder (IDD), of which 71 million are having goitre, cretins and mild neurological disorders.[38] As a result, a major national programme—the Iodine Deficiency Disorders (IDD) Control Programme has been initiated in which nationwide, rather than area-specific use of iodized salt is being promoted. It was decided as a national policy to fortify all edible salt in a phased manner by end of Eighth Plan.[39] The essential components of a National Iodine Deficiency Disorders (IDD) Programmes are use of iodized salt in place of common salt, monitoring and surveillance, manpower training and mass communication.[40] The aim of the national programme was to bring down the incidence of Iodine Deficiency Disorders (IDD) to below 10 per cent by the year 2012.

(xi) Universal Immunization Programme

Experience with small pox eradication programme showed the world that immunization was the most powerful and cost effective weapon against vaccine preventable diseases. In 1974, the World Health Organization (WHO) launched its "Expanded Programme on Immunization (EPI) against six, most common, preventable childhood

36. Nutrition Foundation of India (1983), The National Goitre Control Programme, New Delhi.
37. G.A. Clugston, and K. Bagchi (1986), World Health Forum, Vol. 7, p. 33, also see Park, *op. cit.*, p. 342.
38. Government of India (2003), Annual Report, 2002-03, Ministry of Health & Family Welfare.
39. Government of India, Annual Report, 1993-94, Ministry of Health & Family Welfare.
40. Park., *op. cit.*, p. 342.

diseases, viz. diphtheria, pertursis (whooping cough), tetanus, polio, tuberculosis and measles. From the beginning of the programme UNICEF has been providing significant support to EPI (Expanded Programme on Immunization).[41] The Government of India launched its EPI in 1978 with the objective of reducing the mortality and morbidity resulting from vaccine-preventable diseases of childhood, and to achieve self-sufficiency in the production of vaccines.[42]

Significant achievements have been made in India under this programme. At the beginning of the programme in 1985-86, Vaccine coverage ranged between 29 per cent for BGC and 41 per cent for DPT. By the end of 2002, coverage levels had gone up significantly to about 82.9 per cent for Tetanus Toxoid for pregnant women, about 81 per cent for BGC, 70 per cent for DPT and 70 per cent for OPV. Since then, there is a significant decline in the reported incidence of the vaccine preventable diseases as compared to their incidence in 1987, as shown in Table 2.

Table 2: Percentage Decline in Vaccine Preventable Diseases from year 1987 to 2001

Disease	*1987*	*2001*	*%age Decline*
Poliomyelitis	28257	286	99.05
Diphtheria	12952	4954	61.75
Pertussis	163786	28900	82.36
NNT	11849	1354	95.75
Measles	247519	45301	81.70

Source: Government of India (2003) Annual Report, 2002-03, Ministry of Health and Family Welfare, New Delhi.

Pulse Polio Immunization Programme was launched in the country in the year 1995. Under this programme children under-five years of age given additional oral polio drops in December and January every year on fixed days. Since then there is a significant decline in the incidence of poliomyelitis following the success of the polio eradication programme, the next likely diseases for elimination are measles and neonatal tetanus.[43] India has the target number of Infants who reach their first birthday not fully immunized the (UIP) Universal Immunization Programme has also developed a multi year plan for 2005 to 2010 to reduce infant mortality rate to below 30 per 1000 live births

41. J.P. Grant (1987), World Health, Jan.-Feb., 1987, p. 10.
42. UNICEF (1987), The State of the World's Children, Oxford University Press, Oxford.
43. Government of India, Annual Report, 1992-93, DGHS, New Delhi.

and secondly, to achieve universal immunization of children against all vaccine preventable diseases.

(xii) National Guinea—Worm Eradication Programme

India launched its National Guinea—worm eradication programme in 1984. From the very beginning the programme was integrated into the national health system at village level. With well defined strategies, an efficient information and evaluation system, intersectional coordination at all levels and close collaboration with World Health Organization (WHO), United Nations International Children's Emergency Fund (UNICEF), India was able to significantly reduce the disease in affected areas. The country has reported zero cases since August 1996. In February, 2000, the International Commission for the certification of Drawnculiasis Eradication recommended that India be certified free of dracunculiasis transmission.[44] Globally the Guinea Worm Eradication Program has attracted much less political support than polio eradication. The lack of comparable urgency to publicize and complete this campaign is regrettable.

As 40,000 Guniawarm cases were occurring annually in 12,840 indemic villages across 89 districts of the then indemic states, viz. Andhra Pradesh, Gujarat, Karnataka, Madhya Pradesh, Maharashtra and Rajasthan. The State of Tamil Nadu remained free from Guniawarm (GW) since 1982. The last case was reported in July 1996 in Jodhpur in Rajasthan. The country was certified by "International Commission for Certification of Disease Eradication (ICCDE), World Health Organization as disease free on February 15, 2000. Routine Surveillance and IEC in all former endemic states was recommended to be continued till global eradication of disease is achieved, is being carried out.[45]

(xiii) National Cancer Control Programme

In India, it is estimated that there are about 2 million cancer cases at any given point of time with about 0.7 million new cases coming every year. The Government of India started the National Cancer Control Programme in a limited form during the year 1975-76 when central assistance of Rs. 2.5 lakh was provided to institutions for purchase of Cobalt Therapy units for treatment of cancer patients. This scheme continued during the Sixth and Seventh Plan period. During the Eighth Five Year Plan emphasis was on prevention, early detection of cancer and augmentation of treatment facilities in the country.[46] Cancer has

44. WHO, Weekly Epidemiological Record, No. 22 and 2nd June, 2000.
45. http://www.nicd.nic.in. (accessed on 12 Oct., 2010).
46. Government of India (2003), Health Information of India, 2000-2001, Ministry of Health & Family Welfare, New Delhi.

become an important public health problem in India with an estimated 7 to 9 lakh cases occurring every year. At any time of point, it is estimated that there are nearly 25 lakh cases in the country. The strategy under the National Cancer Control Programme (NCCP) was revised in 1984-85 and further in 2004 with stress on primary prevention and early detection of cancer cases. In India tobacco-related cancers account for about for half the total cancers among men and 20 percent among women. About one million tobacco related deaths occur each year, making tobacco-related health issues major public health concern.

(xiv) National Mental Health Programme

The National Mental Health Programme was launched during seventh Five Year Plan with a view to ensure availability of Mental Health Care services for all, especially the community at risk and underprivileged section of the population, to encourage application of mental health knowledge in general health care and social development. A National Advisory Group of mental health was constituted under the chairmanship of the secretary, Ministry of Health and Family Welfare for the effective implementation of the National Health Programme.[47]

(xv) National Programme for Prevention and Control of Diabities, CVDs and Stroke

The National Diabetes Control Programme was started on a pilot basis during Seventh Five Year Plan in some districts of Tamil Nadu, Karnataka and Jammu and Kashmir, but due to paucity of funds subsequent years this programme could not be expanded further. The main objectives of the programme are (i) identification of high risk subject at an early stage and imparting appropriate health education, (ii) early diagnosis and management of cases, (iii) Prevention, arrest or slowing of acute metabolic as well as Chronic Cardiovascular—renal complications of the diseases.[48]

Common risk factors for both CVD and diabetes are unhealthy diet, physical inactivity and obesity. There is evidence-based information that NCDs (Non-Communicable Diseases) are preventable through integrated and comprehensive interventions. Cost-effective interventions exist and have worked in many countries. The most successful one have employed a range of population wide approaches combined with interventions for the individuals. Thus, the programme will aim to prevent and control common national communicable diseases (NCDs) risk factors through an integrated approach and to reduce premature

47. Park, *op. cit.*, p. 347.
48. *Ibid.*

morbidity and mortality from diabetes, CVD, and stroke. Up scaling based on pilot results will be done during the Eleventh Five Year Plan.

(xvi) Controlling the H1N1 Pandemic

In recent times, Influenza a H1N1 virus created a scare by affecting birds/poultry in more than 60 countries including India. The speed and virulence with which the novel H1N1 virus spread in 2009 in over 200 countries, including India took the public health system by surprise and created a public health crisis. Containment of epidemics and rapid response to disease out breaks through a nation-wide networking of public health resources including public health laboratories is one of the major problems today. In an important policy shift during 2008-09, the Government of India decided to provide the services of epidemiologists in all district headquarters and state headquarters and entomologists and microbiologists and 23 entomologists have joined. However, integrated disease surveillance is still faced with inadequately trained professionals, ill-equipped public health labs and inadequate capacity for rapid response to disease outbreaks in many states. The ongoing initiative of upgrading the National Institute of Communicable Diseases into National Centre of Disease Control with responsibility of enhanced capabilities for lab-based surveillance of communicable diseases and rapid response for minimizing the effects of disease outbreaks is a major development in this field.[49]

(xvii) National Water Supply and Sanitation Programme

The National Water Supply and Sanitation Programme was initiated in 1954 with the object of providing safe water supply and adequate drainage facilities for the entire urban and rural population of the country.

The Government of India launched the International Drinking Water Supply and Sanitation Decade Programme in 1981. Targets were set on rural, 80 per cent for urban sanitation and 25 per cent for rural sanitation.

The latest assessment indicates that population and 16 per cent population has access to adequate sanitation facilities (out of which 2 per cent are in rural areas). Water supply and sanitation in India continued to be inadequate, despite longstanding efforts by the various level of Government and countries at improving coverage. The level of investment in water and sanitation, albeit law by international standards, has increased during the 2000's. Access has also increased significantly.

49. The Annual Report to the People on Health, Government of India, Ministry of Health and Family Welfare, September 2010, p. 17.

For example, in 1980 rural sanitation coverage was estimated at 1 percent and reached 21 percent in 2008. Also, the share of Indians with access to improved sources of water has increased significantly from 72 per cent in 1980 to 88 per cent in 2008. At the same time, local government institution in charge of operating and maintaining the infrastructure are seen as week and lack the financial resources to carry out their functions. In addition, no major city in India is known to have continues water supply and an estimated 72 per cent of Indians still lack access to improve sanitation facilities.

The number of innovative approaches to improve water supply and sanitation have been tested in India, in particular in the year 2000's. These include demand-diven approaches in rural water supply since 1999, community and—lack total sanitation, a public-private partnerships to improve the continuity of urban water supply in Karnataka and the use of micro-credit to women in order to improve access to an improved water source, but only 31 percent had accessed to improve sanitation.[50]

(xviii) National Family Welfare Programme

One of the important indices of population concentration is the density of population. In the Indian census, density is defined as the number of persons, living per square kilometer. The trends of the density in the country from 1901 onwards are as shown in Table 3.

Table 3: Density of Population in India, 1901-2001

Year	*Per Sq. Km*
1901	77
1911	82
1921	81
1931	90
1941	103
1951	117
1961	142
1971	177
1981	216
1991	267
2001	324

Source: Government of India (2001), World Health Report, 1997, Conquering Suffering, Enriching Humanity Report of the Director General, WHO.

While in common parlance, family size refers to the total number of persons in a family, in demography, family size means the total number

50. http.//en.wikipedia.org./ on 12 October, accessed on 2010.

of children a woman has borne at a point in the time.[51] The completed family size indicates the total number of children borne by a woman during her child bearing age, which is generally assumed to be between 15 and 45 years. The total fertility rate gives the appropriate magnitude of completed family size.[52]

The question of family size is important from the demographic point of view. The family planning programme's campaign is currently based on the theme of a "two child" family norm, with a view to reach the long-term demographic goal of (NRR = 1). Family planning involves both decision regarding the "desired family size" and the effective limitation of fertility once that size has been reached. Table 4 shows the total fertility rates (completed family size) in India and selected countries. The decrease in family size does not appear to be due to any reduction in fertility; rather it appears to be due to the result of deliberate family planning.

Table 4: Total Fertility Rates in Selected Developed and Developing Countries 1990 and 2002

Country	*1990*	*2002*
India	3.9	3.1
Bangladesh	4.6	3.5
Nepal	5.2	4.3
Sri Lanka	2.6	2.0
Myanmar	4.0	2.9
China	2.2	1.8
Pakistan	6.0	5.1
UK	1.8	1.6
USA	2.0	2.1
Japan	1.6	1.3
Switzerland	1.5	1.4

Source: UNICEF (2004), The State of World's Children, 2004.

India launched a nation-wide family planning programme in 1952. During the Third Five Year Plan (1961-66) family planning was declared as "the very centre of planned development". During the Fourth Five Year Plan (1969-74) the Government of India gave "top priority" to the programme. During the Fifth Five Year Plan (1975-80) there have been major changes. In April 1976, the country framed its first "National Population Policy".

Although the performance of the programme was low during 1977-

51. Government of India (2000), Annual Report, 1999-2000, Ministry of Health and Family Welfare, New Delhi.
52. *Ibid.*

78, it was a good year in as much as the programme moved into new healthier direction. The 42nd Amendment of the Constitution has made "population control and family planning" a concurrent subject, and this provision has been made effective from January 1977. The Sixth and Seventh Five Year Plans were set to achieve these goals. During 1992 these programmes were integrated under Child Survival and Safe Motherhood (CSSM) Programme.[53]

The Government of India have evolved a more detailed and comprehensive National Population Policy, 2000 to promote family welfare.[54]

The investment on family welfare programme during successive plan-periods is tabulated below. It can be seen that from a modest sum of 0.65 crores during the First Plan, the investment has reached a colossal amount of Rs. 27,125 crores during the Tenth Plan Period.

Table 5: Expenditure under the Programme from the First to Tenth Five Year Plan

(Rs. in Crore)

Period	*Expenditure*
First Plan (1951-56)	0.65
Second Plan (1956-61)	5.00
Third Plan (1961-66)	27.00
Annual Plan (Inter Plan 1966-69)	82.90
Fourth Plan (1969-74)	285.8
Fifth Plan (1974-79)	285.6
Annual Plan (1978-79)	101.8
Annual Plan (1979-80)	116.2
Sixth Plan (1980-85)	1309.00
Seventh Plan (1985-90)	2868.00
Annual Plan (1990-91)	675.00
Annual Plan (1991-92)	749.00
Eighth Plan (1992-97)	6195.00
Ninth Plan (1997-2002)	14170.00
Tenth Plan (2002-2007)	27125.00
Eleventh Plan	

Source: Government of India (2003), Health Information of India 2000 and 2001, DGHS, New Delhi.

The Family Welfare Programme in India has come a long way and holds forth the promise that in the not very distant future it may be accepted as a way of life by most people. Although birth control continues to occupy the same important position in the programme as it used to be in the earlier days the programme now aims at achieving a

53. Government of India (2004), Annual Report, 2003-04, Ministry of Health and Family Welfare, New Delhi.
54. Government of India (2003), Health Information of India, 2000 and 2001.

higher end—and that is, to improve, in conjunction with other development programmes, the quality of life of the people.[55]

(xix) Minimum Needs Programme

The Minimum Needs Programme (MNP) was introduced in the First Year of the Fifth Five Year Plan (1974-78). The objective of the programme is to provide certain basis minimum needs and thereby improve the living standards of the people. It is the expression and economic development of the government of the "social and economic development of the community particularly the underprivileged and under-served population."

(xx) 20 Points Programme

In addition to the Five Year Plans and Programmes, in 1975, the Government of India initiated a special activity. This was the 20-point programme—described as an agenda for national action to promote social justice and economic growth.

On August 20, 1986, the existing 20-point programme was restructured. Its objectives are spelt out by the Government as "eradication of poverty, raising productivity, reducing inequalities, removing social and economic disparities and improving quality of life." At least 8 of the 20 points are related, directly or indirectly, to health. These are:[56]

Point 1 - Attack on rural poverty
Point 7 - Clean drinking water
Point 8 - Health for all
Point 9 - Two child norm
Point 10 - Expansion of education
Point 14 - Housing for the people
Point 15 - Improvement of slums
Point 17 - Protection of environment

The restructured 20 point programme constitutes the charter of the country's socio-economic development. The vision, goals and objectives as well as broad strategies as articulated in the XIth Five Year Plan for the years 2007-12 and the Framework of Implementation of its flagship programme the National Rural Health Mission currently provide the guiding principles for the health sector. These are as briefly summarized

55. Veena Soni (1983), International Family Planning Perspectives, Vol. 9 (2), p. 35.
56. http://www.nicd.nic.in on 12 Oct., 2010.

below.[57]

- Health as a right for all citizens is the goal that the plan will strive towards.
- A comprehensive approach that encompasses individual health care, public health, sanitation, clean drinking water, access to food, and knowledge of hygiene, and feeding practices.
- To transform public health care into an accountable, accessible, and affordable system of quality services.
- Convergence and development of public health systems and services that are responsive to the health needs and aspirations of the people.
- Public provisioning of quality health care to enable access to affordable and reliable health services, especially in the context of preventing the non-poor from entering into poverty or in terms of reducing the suffering of those who are already below the poverty line.
- Reducing disparities in health across regions and communities by ensuring access to affordable health care.
- Good governance, transparency, and accountability in the delivery of health services that is ensured through involvement of Panchayati Raj Institutions (PRIs), community, and civil society groups.
- To raise public speeding on health from 0.9 per cent of GDP to 2-3 per cent of GDP, with improved arrangement for community financing and risk pooling.
- To undertake architectural correction of health system to enable it to effectively handle increased allocations and promote policies that strengthen public health management and service delivery in the country.
- Reduction in child and maternal mortality.
- Universal access to public services for food and nutrition, sanitation and hygiene.
- Universal access to public health care services, integrated comprehensive primary health care, with emphasis on services addressing women's and children's health and universal immunization.
- Prevention and control of communicable and non-communicable diseases, including locally endemic diseases.
- Population stabilization, gender and demographic balance.

57. The Annual Report to the People on Health, Government of India, Ministry of Health and Family Welfare, September 2010.

- Revitalize local health traditions and mainstream AYUSH.
- Promotion of healthy lifestyles.

The time bound objectives set out for the Eleventh Five Year Plan for achievement by the year 2012 are:

- Reducing Maternal Mortality Ratio (MMR) to 1 per 1,000 live births.
- Reducing Infant Mortality Rate (IMR) to 28 per 1,000 live births.
- Reducing Total Fertility Rate (TFR) to 2.1.
- Providing clean drinking water for all by 2009 and ensuring no slip-backs.
- Reducing malnutrition among children in the age group 0-3 years to half its present level.
- Reducing anaemia among women and girls by 50 percent.
- Raising the sex ratio in the age group 0-6 years to 935 by 2011-12, and to 950 by 2016-17.
- **Malaria Mortality Reduction Rate:** 50 per cent up to 2010, additional 10 per cent by 2012.
- **Kala Azar Mortality Reduction Rate:** 100 per cent by 2010 and sustaining elimination until 2012.
- **Filaria/Microfilaria Reduction Rate:** 70 per cent by 2010, 80 per cent by 2012 and elimination by 2015.
- **Dengue Mortality Reduction Rate:** 50 per cent by 2010 and sustaining at the level until 2012.
- **Contract operations:** Increase to 46 lakhs by 2012.
- **Leprosy Prevalence Rate:** Reduce from 1.8 per 10,000 in 2005 to less than 1 per 10,000 thereafter.
- **Tuberculosis DOTS series:** Maintain 85 per cent cure rate through entire mission period and also sustain planned case detection rate.

In terms of systems improvements the NRHM targets were:

- Upgrade all PHCs into 24x7 PHCs by the year 2010.
- Upgrading all Community Health Centres to Indian Public Health Standards.
- Increase Utilization of first referral units from bed occupancy by referred cases of less than 20 per cent to over 75 per cent.
- Engaging 4,00,000 female Accredited Social Health Activities (ASHAs).

IV. NATIONAL HEALTH POLICIES

The evolution and development of health policies culminated into a comprehensive National Health Policy in 1983. The policy laced with ancient and modern heritage of health care and constitutional objective of health and well-being of the citizens of the country. The policy admitted that the existing situation has come about because of the almost wholesale adoption of public health policies and establishment of curative centres based on the western models which are really not suitable for our conditions. The present system is largely curative, benefiting the upper crust of society especially those residing in the urban areas. The preventive promotive and rehabilitative aspects of health care have been neglected.[58] The community has not been involved in the identification of their health needs and priorities as well as in the implementation and management of the various health related programmes. The policy targeted 'Health for All' by 2000 A.D. through the universal provision of comprehensive primary health care services. The policy stated small family norms voluntary for population stabilization and thrashing of a National population policy, and National Medical and Health Education Policy.[59] For restructuring the health services the policy health services for provision of a well dispersed network of comprehensive primary health care services, integrally linked with the extension and health education approach.[60] The major focus of attention would be on comprehensive primary health care, attention would also have to be given to establishment of centres to provide services. To reduce governmental expenditure, efforts should be made to encourage private investments in such fields to that the majority of such centres within the government set-up can provide treatment to those entitled to free care, the affluent sector being looked after by the paying clinics.[61]

The policy feels that the country has a large number of private practitioners in various systems like *Ayurveda, Unani, Sidha, Homeopathy, Yoga, Naturopathy*, etc. and regards that these resources have not so far been adequately utilized. It calls upon the necessity to initiate organized measures to enable each of these various systems of medicine and health care to develop and integrate their services in the overall health care delivery system by a meaningful phased integration

58. Government of India, Health Statistics of India, Annual Publications, Report of the Health Survey and Planning Committee, (1959-61), p. 234.
59. *Id* at p.235.
60. *Id* at pp.235-236.
61. *Ibid.*

of the indigenous and the modern systems.[62] The policy identified nutrition prevention of food adulteration, maintenance of the quality of drugs; water supply and sanitation; environmental protection; immunization programme; maternal and child health services; school health programme; and occupational health services as special areas of attention.[63] The policy stress health education, child family education information system management and health insurance scheme. The National Health Policy is progressive and comprehensive document. For implementation of the goals set out in the policy, the need for urgent action and implementation deserves serious attention.[64] The progress of National Health Policy leaves a lot to be desired and National Medical and Health Education Policy as well as the National Population Policy are to formulation in the high of pollution policy.[65]

Since then there has been significant changes in the determinant factors relating to the health sector, necessitating revision of the policy, and a new National Health Policy, 2002 was evolved. The main objective of this policy is to achieve an acceptable standard of good health amongst the general population of the country. The approach would be to increase access to decentralized public health system by establishing new infrastructure in the existing institutions overriding importance would be given to ensure a more equitable access to health services across the social and geographical expense of the country. Primacy will be given to preventive and first line curative initiatives at the primary health level.[66]

The policy is focused on those diseases which are principally contributing to disease burden such as tuberculosis, malaria, blindness and HIV/AIDS.[67] Emphasis will be laid on rational use of drugs within the allopathic system. To translate the above objectives into reality, the health policy has laid down specific goals to be achieved by year 2005, 2007, 2010 and 2015.[68] These are as given in Table 6. Steps are already under way to implement the policy.

---

62. *Id.* at pp.236-237.
63. *Id.* at p.237-238.
64. *Ibid.*
65. *Id.* at 267-68.
66. Government of India (2002), National Health Policy—2002, Department of Health, Ministry of Health and Family Welfare, New Delhi.
67. HIV/AIDS.
68. Government of India (2002), National Health Policy—2002, Department of Health, Ministry of Health and Family Welfare, New Delhi.

Table 6: National Health Policy—2002

Goals to be Achieved by 2015

Eradicate Polio and Yaws	2005
Eliminate Leprosy	2005
Eliminate Lymphatic Filariasis	2010
Achieve Zero Level Growth of HIV/AIDS	2015
Reduce Mortality by 50% on account of TB, Malaria and other vector and water borne diseases	2007
Reduce Prevalence of blindness to 0.5%	2010
Reduce IMR to 30/1000 and MMR to 100/Lakh	2010
Increase Utilization of public health facilities from current level of <20% to 75%	2010
Establish and integrated system of surveillance, national health accounts and health statistics	2005
Increase health expenditure by government as a % of GDP from the existing 0.9% to 2.0%	2010
Increase share of central grants to constitute at least 20% of total health spending	2010
Increase state sector health spending from 5.5% to 7% of budget	2005
Further increase to 8% of the budget	2010

Source: Government of India (2002), National Health Policy, 2002, Department of Health, Ministry of Health and Family Welfare, New Delhi.

V. NATIONAL HEALTH COMMITTEES

(i) Bhore Committee, 1946

The Government of India in 1943 appointed the Health Survey and Development Committee with Sir Joseph Bhore as Chairman, to survey the then existing position regarding the health conditions and health organization in the country, and to make recommendations for the future development. The committee which had among its members some of the pioneers of public health, met regularly for 2 years and submitted in 1946 its famous report which runs into 4 volumes. The committee put forward, for the first time, comprehensive proposals for the development of national programme of health services for the country. The committee observed: "if the nation's health work and that such activities should proceed side by side with those concerned with the treatment of patients" some of the important recommendations of the Bhore Committee were:

(a) Integration of preventive and curative services at all administrative levels;

(b) The Committee visualized the development of primary health centres in 2 stages:

* as a short-term measure, it was proposed that each primary

health centre in the rural areas should cater to a population of 40,000 with a secondary health centre to serve as a supervisory, coordinating and referral institution. For each Primary Health Centre (PHC), two medical officers, 4 public health nurses, one nurse, 4 midwives, 4 trained dais, 2 Sanitary Inspectors, 2 health assistants, one pharmacist, and 15 other class IV employees were recommended.

* a long-term programme (also called the 3 million plan) of setting up primary health units with 75 bedded hospitals for each 10,000 to 20,000 population and secondary units with 650-bedded hospital again regionalized around district hospitals with 2500 beds; and
* major changes in medical education which includes 3 month's medicine to prepare "social physicians".

Although the Bhore Committee's recommendations did not form part of a comprehensive plan for national socio-economic development, the committee's report continues to be a major national document and has to provided guidelines for national health planning in India.

(ii) Mudaliar Committee, 1962

By the close of the Second Five Year Plan (1956-61), a fresh look at the health needs and resources was called for to provide guidelines for national health planning in the context of the Five Year Plans. In 1959, the Government of India appointed another committee known as "Health Survey and Planning Committee", popularly known as the Mudaliar Committee (after the name of its Chairman, Dr. A.L. Mudaliar) to survey the progress made in the field of health since submission of the Bhore Committee's Report and to make recommendations for future development and expansion of health services.

The Mudaliar Committee found the quality of services provided by the primary health centres inadequate, and advised strengthening of the existing primary health centres before new centres were established. It also advised strengthening of sub-divisional and district hospitals so that they may effectively function as referral centres.

The main recommendations of the Mudaliar Committee were: (a) consolidation of advances made in the first two five year plans; (b) strengthening of sub-divisional and district hospitals with specialist services to serve as central base of regional services; (c) regional organizations in each state between the headquarters organization and the district in charge of a Regional Deputy or Assistant Directors—each to supervise 2 or 3 district medical and health officers; (d) each primary health centre not to serve more than 40,000 population; (e) to improve the quality of health care provided by the primary health centres; (f) integration of medical and health services as recommended by the Bhore Committee; and (g) Constitution of an All India Health Service on the pattern of Indian Administrative Service.

(iii) Chadah Committee, 1963

In 1963, a committee was appointed by the Government of India, under the Chairmanship of Dr. M.S. Chadah, the then Director General of Health Services to study the arrangements necessary for the maintenance phase of the National Malaria Eradication Programme.

The Committee recommended that the "Vigilance" operations in respect of the National Malaria Eradication Programme should be the responsibility of the general health services, i.e. primary health centres at the block level.

The committee also recommended that the vigilance operations through monthly home visits should be implemented through basic health workers, one basic health worker per 10,000 population was recommended. These workers were envisaged as "multipurpose" workers to look after additional duties of collection of vital statistics and family planning, in addition to malaria vigilance. The Family Planning Health Assistants were to supervise 3 or 4 of these basic health workers. At the district level, the general health services were to take the responsibility for the maintenance phase.

(iv) Mukerji Committee, 1965

Within a couple of years of implementation of the Chadah Committee's recommendations by some states, it was realized that the basic health workers could not function effectively as multipurpose workers. As a result, the malaria vigilance operations had suffered and also the work of the family planning programme could not be carried out satisfactorily. This subject came up for discussion at a meeting of the Central Health Council in 1965. A committee known as "Mukerji Committee, 1965" under the Chairmanship of Shri Mukerji, the then Secretary of Health to the Government of India, was appointed to review the strategy for the family planning programme. The committee recommended separate staff for the family planning programme. The family planning assistants were to undertake family planning duties only. The basic health workers were to be utilized for purpose other than family planning. The committee also recommended to delink the malaria activities from family planning so that the latter would receive undivided attention of its staff. The recommendations were accepted by the Government of India.

(v) Mukerji Committee, 1966

As the states were finding it difficult to take over the whole burden of the maintenance phase of malaria and other mass programmes like family planning, small pox, leprosy, trachoma, etc. due to paucity of funds, the matter came up for discussion at a meeting of the Central Council of Health held in Bangalore in 1966. The Council recommended that these and related questions may be examined by a committee of Health Secretaries, under the chairmanship of the Union Health Secretary, Shri Mukerji. The committee worked out the details of the BASIC HEALTH SERVICE which should be provided at the block level, and some consequential strengthening required at higher levels of administration.

(vi) Jungal Walla Committee, 1967

The Central Council of Health at its meeting held in Srinagar in 1964, taking note of the importance and urgency of integration of health services, and elimination of private practice by government doctors, appointed a committee known as the "Committee on Integration of Health Services" under the chairmanship of Dr. N. Jungalwalla, Director, National Institute of Health Administrator and Education, New Delhi to examine the various problems including those of service conditions and submit a report to the Central Government in the light of these considerations. The report was submitted in 1967.

The committee defined, "integrated health services" as: (a) a service with a unified approach for all problems instead of a segmented approach for different problems; and (b) medical care of the sick and conventional public health programmes functioning under a single administrator and operating in unified manner at all levels of hierarchy with due priority for each programme obtaining at a point of time.

(vii) Kartar Singh Committee, 1973

The Government of India constituted a committee in 1972 known as "The Committee on Multipurpose Workers under Health and Family Planning" under the Chairmanship of Kartar Singh, Additional Secretary, Ministry of Health and Family Planning, Government of India. The terms of reference of the committee were to study and make recommendation on: (a) the structure for integrated services at the peripheral and supervisory levels; (b) the feasibility of having multipurpose, bipurpose workers in the field; (c) the training requirements for such workers; and (d) the utilization of mobile service units set-up under family planning programme for integrated medical, public health and family planning services operating in the field. The Committee submitted its report in September 1973. Its main recommendations were: (a) that the present Auxiliary Nurse Midwives to be replaced by the newly designated "Female Health Workers", and the present-day Basic Health Workers, Malaria Surveillance Workers, Vaccinators, Health Education Assistants and the Family Planning Health Assistants to be replaced by "Male Health Workers"; (b) The programme for having multipurpose workers to be first introduced in areas where malaria is in maintenance phase and small pox has been controlled, and later to other areas as malaria passes into maintenance phase or small pox controlled; (c) For proper coverage, there should be one primary health centre for a population of 50,000; (d) Each primary health centre should be divided into 16 sub-centres each having a population of about 3,000 to 3,500 depending upon topography and means of communications; (e) Each sub-centre to be staffed by a team of one male and one female health worker; (f) There should be a male health supervisor to supervise the work of 3 to 4 male health workers; and a female health supervisor to supervise the work of 4 female health workers; (g) The present-day lady health visitors to be designated as female health supervisors; and (h) The doctor in charge of a primary health centre should have the overall charge of all the supervisors and health workers in his area. The recommendations of the Kartar Singh Committee were accepted by the Government of India to be implemented in a phased manner during the Fifth Five Year Plan.

(viii) Shrivastav Committee, 1975

The Government of India in the Ministry of Health and Family Planning had in November 1974 set-up a 'Group on Medical Education and support manpower' popularly known as the Shrivastav Committee: (a) to devise a suitable curriculum for training a cadre of health assistants so that they can serve as a link between the qualified medical practitioners and the multipurpose workers, thus forming an effective team to deliver health care, family welfare and nutritional services to the people; (b) to suggest steps for improving the existing medical educational process as to provide due emphasis on the problems particularly relevant to national requirements, and (c) to make any other suggestions to realize the above objectives and matters incidental thereto.

The group submitted its report in April 1975. It recommended immediate action for: (a) creation of bands of para-professional and semi-professional health workers from within the community itself (e.g., school teachers, postmasters, gram sevaks) to provide simple, primitive, preventive and curative health services needed by the community, (b) establishment of 2 cadres of health workers, namely multipurpose health workers and health assistants between the community level workers and doctors at the Primary Health Centres (PHC); (c) development of a 'Referral Services Complex' by establishing proper linkages between the Primary Health Centre (PHC) and higher level referral and service centres, viz. taluka/tehsil, district, regional and medical college hospitals, and (d) establishment of a Medical and Health Education Commission for planning and implementing the reforms needed in health and medical education on the lines of the University Grants Commission.

The committee felt that by the end of the Sixth Plan, one male and one female health worker should be available for every 5,000 population. Also there should be one male and female health assistant for 2 male and 2 female health workers respectively. The health assistants should be located at the sub-centre, and not at the Primary Health Centre (PHC).

VI. RURAL HEALTH SCHEME, 1977

The most important recommendation of the Shrivastava Committee was that primary health care should be provided within the community itself through specially trained workers so that the health of the people is placed in the hands of the people themselves.

The basic recommendations of the committee were accepted by the Government in 1977, which led to the launching of the Rural Health Scheme. The programme of training of community health workers was initiated during 1977-78, steps were also initiated: (a) for involvement of medical colleges in the total health care of Selected Primary Health Centres with the objective of reorienting medical education to the needs of rural people; and (b) reorientation training of multipurpose workers engaged into uni-purpose workers. This "Plan of Action" was adopted by the joint meeting of the Central Council of Health and Central Family Planning Council held in New Delhi in April 1976.

VII. HEALTH FOR ALL (HFA)

In 1977, it was decided in the World Health Assembly to launch a movement known as "Health for All by the year 2000"—The fundamental principle of HFA strategy is equity, that is an equal health status for people and countries, ensured by an equitable distribution of health resources. The Member-Countries of WHO at the 30th World Health Assembly defined Health for All as:

> "Attainment of a level of health that will enable every individual to lead a socially and economically productive life".

In 1978, the *Alma-Ata* International Conference on Primary Health Care reaffirmed health for all as the major social goal of governments, and stated that the best approach to achieve the goal of HFA is by providing primary health care, especially to the vast majority underserved rural people and urban poor. It was envisaged that by the year 2000, at least essential health care should be accessible to all individuals and families in an acceptable and affordable way, with their full participation.[69]

The *Alma-Ata* Conference caused on all governments to formulate national policies. Strategies and plans of action to launch and sustain primary health care as part of a national health system. It is left to each country to develop its norms and indicators for providing primary health care according to its own circumstances. In 1981, a global strategy for HFA was evolved by World Health Organization. The global strategy provides a global framework that is broad enough to apply to all Members-States and flexible enough to be adapted in national and regional variations of conditions and requirements. This was followed by individual countries developing their own strategies for achieving HFA and synthesis of national strategies for developing regional strategies.[70]

VIII. NATIONAL STRATEGY FOR HEALTH FOR ALL/2000

As a signatory to the *Alma-Ata* Declaration in 1978, the Government of India was committed to taking steps to provide Health For All (HFA) to its citizens by 2000 A.D. In pursuance of this objective various attempts were made to evolve suitable strategies and approaches. In this connection two important reports appeared:

(i) Report of the Study Group on "Health for All—an Alternative Strategy", sponsored by ICSSR and ICMR.[71]

(ii) Report of the Working Group on "Health for All by 2000

69. WHO (1981), Global Strategy for Health for All by the Year 2000, HFA Ser. No. 3.
70. *Ibid.*
71. *Ibid.*

A.D." sponsored by the Ministry of Health and Family Welfare, Government of India.[72]

Both the groups considered in great detail the various issues involved in providing primary health care in the Indian Context. These reports formed the basis of the National Health Policy formulated by the Ministry of Health and Family Welfare, Government of India in 1983 which committed the government and people of India to the achievement of Health for All (HFA).[73]

The National Health Policy echoes the World Health Organization (WHO) call for Health For All (HFA) and the *Alma-Ata* Declaration. It had laid down specific goals in respect of the various health indicators by different dates such as 1990 and 2000 A.D. Foremost among the goals to be achieved by 2000 A.D. were:

(i) Reduction of Infant Mortality from the level of 125 (1978) to below 60.
(ii) To raise the expectation of life at birth from the level of 52 years to 64.
(iii) To reduce the crude death rate from the level of 14 per 1000 population to 9 per 1000.
(iv) To reduce the crude birth rate from the level of 33 per 1000 population to 21.
(v) To achieve a Net Reproduction Rate of one.
(vi) To provide potable water to the entire rural population.[74]

IX. THE MILLENNIUM DEVELOPMENT GOALS

In September 2000, representatives from 189 countries met at the Millennium Summit in New York, to adopt the United Nations Millennium Declaration. The goals in the area of development and poverty eradication are now widely referred to as "Millennium Development Goals" (MDGs). The MDGs place health at the heart of development and represent commitments by governments throughout the world to do more to reduce poverty and hunger and to tackle ill-health; gender inequality; lack of education; access to clean water; and environmental degradation. They were an integral part of the road map

72. ICSSR and ICMR (1980), Health for All: An Alternative Strategy, Indian Institute of Education, Pune.
73. Government of India (1981), Report of the Working Group on Health for All by 2000 A.D., Ministry of Health and Family Welfare, New Delhi.
74. Government of India (1983), Statement on National Health Policy.

towards the implementation of the UN Millennium Declaration.[75] Three of the 8 goals, 8 of the 18 targets required to achieve them, and 18 of the 48 indicators of progress, were health related. They assist in the development of national policies focusing on poor and help track the performance of health programmes and systems. Although, the Millennium Development Goals (MDGs) do not cover the whole range of public health domains, a broad interpretation of the goals provides an opportunity to tackle important cross-cutting issues and key constraints to health and development.[76] Governments have set a date of 2015 by which they would meet the Millennium Development Goals, i.e. eradicate extreme poverty and hunger; achieve universal primary education; promote gender equality; improve material health; combat HIV/AIDS, malaria and other communicable diseases; ensure environmental sustainability; and develop a global partnership for development.[77] Table 7 shows the detailed information regarding the indicators of health-related (MDGs) Millennium Development Goals in India, i.e. the base line (1990) and current level data.

Table 7: Health Related Millennium Development Goals in India

Indicator	*Year*	*India*
Goal 1: Eradicate Extreme Poverty and Hunger Target 2: Halve, between 1990 and 2015, the proportion of people who suffer from Hunger Goal 1. Target 2.14—Prevalence of under-weight children (under-five years of age) Goal 1. Target 2.15—Proportion (%) of population below minimum level of dietary energy consumption	1990 2001 1991 1999	53.4 47.0 25 24
Goal 4: Reduce Child Mortality Target 5: Reduce by two-thirds, between 1990 and 2015, the under-five mortality rate Goal 4. Target 5.113—Under-five mortality rate (Probability of dying between birth and age 5) Goal 4.Target 5.114—Infant Mortality Rate Goal 4.Target 5.115—Proportion (%) of 1 year old children immunized for measles	1990 2002 1990 2000 1990 2001	112.0 90.9 80.0 68.0 32.7 56.0
Goal 5: Improve Maternal Health Target 6: Reduce by three-quarters, between 1990 and		

75. WHO (2003), The World Health Report, 2003, Showing the Future.
76. UNDP (2003), Human Development Report, 2003, Millennium, Development Goals: A Compact Among Nations to end human poverty.
77. UNICF (2004), The State of World's Children, 2004.

2015, the maternal mortality ratio Goal 5. Target 6.116—Maternal Mortality Ratio	1990 2001	42.0 4.07
Goal 5. Target 6.117—Proportion (%) of births attended by skilled health personnel	1990 2001	89/36 42.3
Goal 6: Combat HIV/AIDS, Malaria and Other Diseases Target 7: Have halted by 2015, and begun to reverse, the spread of HIV/AIDS Goal 6. Target 7.118—HIV Prevalence Among Young People 15-24 years age group 15-49 years age group Goal 6. Target 7.119—Condom Use in High Risk population	1990 2001(M) 2001 (F) 2001 1990 2001 (F)	NA 0.22 0.46 0.8 NA 39.8
Goal 6. Target 7.120—Radio of Children Orphaned/Non-Orphaned in Schools	1990 2001	NA NA
Target 8: Halve halted by 2015, and begun to reverse the incidence of malaria and other major diseases		
Goal 6. Target 8.121—Malaria death rate per 100,000 in Children (0.4 years of age)	1990 2000	NA 6
Goal 6. Target 8.121—Malaria death rate per 100,000 (all ages)	1990 2002	NA 29
Goal 6. Target 8.121—Malaria death rate per 100,000	1990	NA
Goal 6. Target 8.121—Malaria prévalence rate 100,000	2002 1990	14 NA
Goal 6. Target 8.122—Proportion (%) of 5 population under age in malaria risk areas using insecticide—treated bed nets	2002 1990 2000	NA NA NA
Goal 6. Target 8.122—Proportion (%) of population under age 5 with fever being treated with antimal arial drugs.	1990 2000 1990	NA NA NA
Goal 6. Target 8.123—Tuberculosis Death Rate per 100,000.	2002 1990	40.4 NA
Goal 6. Target 8.123—Tuberculosis prevalence rate per 100,000	2002 1990	426 NA
Goal 6. Target 8.124—Proportion (%) of Semar-positve pulmonary tuberculosis cases detected and put under directly observed treatment short course (DOTS)	2001	22.7
Goal 6.Target 8.124—Proportion (%) of Semar-positive pulmonary tuberculosis cases detected and put under directly observed treatment short course (DOTS).	1990	NA
Goal 6.Target 8.124—Proportion (%) of Smear-positive pulmonary tuberculosis cases detected cured under directly observed treatment short course (DOTS)	2000	84
Goal 7: Ensure Environmental Sustainability Target 9: Integrate the principles of sustainable development into country policies and programmes and		

reverse the loss of environmental resources		
Goal 7. Target 9.129—Proportion (%) of population using biomass fuels	1990 2000	NA 81
Target 10: Halve, by 2015, the proportion of people without sustainable access to safe drinking water		
Goal 7. Target 10.130—Proportion (%) of population with sustainable access to an improved water source, rural	1990 2000	61 79
Goal 7. Target 10.130—Proportion (%) of population with sustainable access to an improved water source, urban		
Target 11: By 2020 to have achieved a significant improvement in the lives of at least 100 million slum dwellers	1990 2000	88 95
Goal 7. Target 11.131—Proportion (%) of Urban population with access to improved sanitation	1990 2000	44 61
Goal 8: Develop global partnership for development		
Target 17: In cooperation with pharmaceutical companies, provide access to affordable, essential drugs in developing countries.		
Goal 8. Target 17.146—Proportion (%) of affordable essential drugs on a sustainable basis	1990 1997	NA 80

Source: UNICF (2004), The State of World's Children, 2004. WHO (2003) Basic Indicators, 2002, Health Situation in South-East Asia.

The concepts and definitions of Millennium Development Goals (MDGs) are as follows. Here G denotes goal number, T-target number and I-indicators number prevalence of under weight children (under-five years of age) (Goal 1.Target 2.14): Proportion of children of under-five years with low weight for—age, as measured by percentage of children in moderate and severe malnutrition—those falling below 80 per cent of the median weight for reference value or below 2 standard deviations of national or international reference population, such as growth charts of the US National Center for Health Statistics.

Proportion (%) of population below minimum level of dietary energy consumption (Goal 1.Target 2.15): since there is no specific data available, proxy indicator proportion of population under nourished is used. It is the proportion in percentage of persons whose food intake falls below the minimum requirement of food intake that is insufficient to meet dietary energy requirements continuously.

Under-five mortality rate (Goal 4. Target 5.113): Probability of dying between birth and exactly five years of age, infant mortality rate (Goal 4. Target 5.114): Probability of dying between birth and exactly one year of age, expressed per 1,000 live births.

Infant mortality rate (Goal 4. Target 5.114): Probability of dying between birth and exactly one year of age expressed per 1,000 live births.

Proportion (%) of 1 year old children immunized for measles (Goal 4. Target 5.115): The percentage of infants reaching their first birth day fully immunized against measles (1 dose).

Maternal Mortality Ratio (Goal 5. Target 6.116): Annual number of maternal death per 100,000 live-births. A maternal death is the death of a woman while pregnant or within 42 days of termination of pregnancy, from any cause related to or aggravated by the pregnancy or its management, but not from accidental or incidental causes.

Proportion (%) of births attended by skilled health persons (Goal 5. Target 6.117): The proportion in percentage of births attended by skilled personnel per 1000 live births. Skilled health personnel refer exclusively to those health personnel (for example, doctors, nurses, midwives) who have been trained to proficiency in the skills necessary to manage normal deliveries and diagnose or refer obstetric complications. Traditional birth attendants trained or untrained, are not included in this category.

HIV prevalence among young people (Goal 6. Target 7.118): Since the relevant data is not available, the proxy indicator as proposed by UNAIDS/WHO is used. The proxy indicator is "HIV prevalence among 15-24 years old by sex" which is the estimated number of young people (15-24 years old) living with HIV/AIDS as per proportion of the same population and sex.

These country-specific estimates are expressed as a range generated by regional modeling. The other proxy indicator is "HIV prevalence rate among population 15-49 years of age".

Condom use in High-Risk Population (Goal 6. Target 7.119)

Since the data is not available, it has been proposed to use, "condom use among 15-24 years old by sex". This is the percentage of young men and women of age 15-24 years, who said that they used a condom the last time they had sex with a non-marital, non-cohabiting partner, of those who have had sex with such a partner in the last 12 months.

Ratio of children orphaned/non-orphaned in schools (Goal 6. Target 7.120)

Since the data is not available, the proxy indicator is used as "AIDS Orphans currently living" which is the estimated number of children (0-14) in a given year, having lost their mother or both parents to AIDS.

Malaria Death Rate per 100,000 in Children (0-4 years of age) (Goal 6. Target 8.121)

Proportion of children (0-4 years of age) died due to malaria in a given year. Malaria death rate per 100,000 in all age groups (Goal 6. Target 8.121): Proportion of people of all age groups died due to malaria in a given year. It is malaria crude death rate.

Malaria Prevalence Rate per 100,000 Population (Goal 6. Target 8.121)

Proportion of notified or reported cases of malaria per 100,000 population in a given area. It is malaria crude prevalence rate.

Proportion (%) of population under age 5 in malaria risk areas using insecticide treated bet nets (Goal 6. Target 8.122)

The percentage of children under-give years of age who are using insecticide treated bet nets among the same population living in malaria risk area, in a given year.

Proportion (%) of population under age 5 with fever being treated with anti-malarial drugs (Goal 6. Target 8. 122)

The percentage of children under five years of age who are with fever being treated with anti-malarial drugs among the same population living in malaria risk area in a given year.

X. SUM UP

Health is a positive state of well-being in which the harmonious development of physical and mental capacities of the individual lead to the enjoyment of a rich and full life. It is not a negative state of mere absence of disease. Health further implies complete adjustment of the individual to his total environment, physical and social. Health involves primarily the application of medical science for the benefit of the individual and of society. But many other factors, social, economic and educational have an intimate bearing on the health of the community. Health is thus, a vital part of a concurrent and integrated programme of development of all aspects of community life.[78]

78. Planning Commission, Government of India, 10th Five YEAR PLAN (2002-07), Vol. II, p. 1.

CHAPTER 6

Right to Health as a Right to Life: Judicial Approach in India

I. INTRODUCTION

Mental and Physical Health is the very basis of human personality. Diseases and mishaps must have had their grip over humans ever since they came into existence. The disablement, disfigurement and loss of life caused due to illness has alarmed human race. The multiple sources causing such agonies are both external and internal ranging from nature's wrath to lack of proper hygiene. If the human race is to survive and progress, preservation of good health is a must. Though personal hygiene can to a large extent ward-off ordinary ailments caused due to lack of hygienic, there are many factors, over which an individual can have no control, which causes health problems. The state agencies are in such areas better equipped to prevent the causes and deal with the ailments in a more regulatory, effective and authoritative manner. The legal responsibility of the State agencies to take care of the individual's right to health in a welfare state. Every sovereign state has plenary power to do all things which promote the health, peace, morals, education and good order of the people and tend to increase the wealth and prosperity of the State. Maintenance and improvement of public health have to rank high as these are indispensable to the very physical existence of the community and on the betterment of these depends the building of the society which the Constitution-makers envisaged.

II. CONSTITUTION VERSUS HEALTH

The apex Court in India has played a decisive role in realization of the right to health by recognizing the right as a part of the fundamental right to life and issuing suitable directions to the State authorities for the discharge of their duties. The Court has recognized that maintenance of health is a most imperative constitutional goal whose realization requires interaction of many social and economic factors. Article 25 of the Universal Declaration of Human Rights States:

(i) Everyone has the right to a standard of living for the health and well-being of himself and of his family, including food, clothing, housing and medical care and necessary social services, and the right to security in the event of unemployment, sickness, disability, widowhood, old age or other lack of livelihood in circumstances beyond his control.

(ii) Motherhood and childhood are entitled to special care and assistances.[1]

In the Constitution of India, in Article 47 of the Directive Principles of State Policy, there is a duty of the State to raise the level of nutrition and the standard of living and to improve public health. "The State shall regard the raising of the level of nutrition and the standard of living of its people and the improvement of public health as among its primary duties and, in particular, the State shall endeavour to bring about prohibition of the consumption except for medical purposes of intoxicating drinks and of drugs which are injurious to health."[2]

Nobel laureate, Dr. Amartya Sen has named illiteracy, malnutrition and lack of health care as the three unfreedoms in developing countries. In the 5th International Workshop on National Institutions for the promotion and protection of Human Rights held at Rabat, on 15th April, 2000, Mrs. Mary Robinson, UN High Commissioner for Human Rights stated:

> "The challenge is to translate the theory into reality and in a very large measure that can only happen at the national level; hence, the importance of national institutions and of their integrity and effectiveness. I urge you to continue and expand your role as human rights advocates for the most vulnerable and disadvantaged groups in your societies—inspite of the opposition you will inevitably encounter."

1. See Article 25 of Universal Declaration of Human Rights, 1948.
2. Articles 47, 39(e), 41, 43 of the Constitution of India.

Subsequently on 18th April, 2000 at Geneva, addressing the International Coordinating Committee of National Institutions of Human Rights, she said:

> "National Human Rights Institutions have the full range of human rights in the remit… An area which we have not touched on, and which I would like to mention here for further consideration is the right to health… Weakness in the delivery of proper health care ties into a broader theme of the Rabat Declaration".

The Rabat Declaration made on 15th April, 2000, called upon national institutions to continue their activities to promote and protect women's and children's rights in accordance with existing international treaties and conventions… They would like national institutions to remain vigilant to continue the fight against the abuse of the rights of the women, children and persons with disabilities, who are very often among the most vulnerable groups in the society. They wish to see these national institutions are capable of assisting political and legislative bodies in the development of appropriate law and practices. NHRC's (National Human Right Commission's) concern covers the entire range of human rights issues facing our country. Among them include assuring free and compulsory education upto the age of 14 years and essential public health and nutritional standards as also the special needs of persons affected by HIV/AIDS and related preventive measures. And everything which affects the human dignity is perceived by the Commission as having a bearing on human rights and this perception is receiving general acceptance.[3] The judiciary has also, on many occasions, emphasized the relevance of health to human life. In *State of Punjab* v. *Ram Lubhaya Bagga*,[4] the Court said that it has time and again emphasized to the government and other authorities for focusing and giving priority to the health of its citizens, as it (health) not only makes one's life meaningful and improves one's efficacy, but in true, it gives optimum output. While courts have recognized the importance of health to persons in general, in some cases, the significance of health to workmen in particular has been highlighted. Maintenance of health has been held to be of the greatest priority. *Vincent Panikurlangara* v. *Union of India*,[5] it was observed:

> "…. Maintenance and improvement of public health have to rank high as these are indispensable to the very physical existence of

3. Verma, J.S., *The New Universe of Human Rights*, 233-34 (2004).
4. AIR 1998 SC 1703, 1706 (para 6).
5. AIR 1987 SC 990.

the community and on the betterment of these depends the building of the society which the Constitution envisages. Attending to public health, in our opinion is, therefore of high priority—perhaps one at the top".

The Courts have also repeatedly underline the obligation of the state to protect the life and health of persons by providing adequate health care facilities and creating conditions congenial to the sustenance of good health. The judiciary has not only recognized the right to health as a basic component of the right to life, it has also in some cases, issued directions to the government or other appropriate authorities to take step towards fulfilling its obligation of protecting human life and promoting public health. In *Rakesh Chandra* v. *State of Bihar*,[6] a letter by two citizens of Patna regarding the conditions at a mental hospital near Ranchi was treated as a 'Public Interest Litigation' and was admitted under Article 32. On the visit of the Chief Judicial Magistrate, it was found that there was acute shortage of water, improper sanitation, unhygienic environment, non-availability of light, less number of beds, no doors in wards, improper bedding clothes and diet for the inmates, no account of stock of medicines, etc. Despite orders by the Court, defects were not being remedied. The Court was of the view that it was difficult for the Court to monitor the management of the hospital and a committee of management should be appointed with full powers to look after all aspects of the hospital and constituted the committee.

In *Common Cause* v. *Union of India*,[7] a petition was filed by means of public interest litigation in which the petitioners highlighted serious deficiencies and shortcomings in matter of collection, storage and supply of blood through the various blood centers operating in the country. From the report of M/S AF Frguson and Co., which was entrusted by the Ministry of Health, Govt. of India with the study of blood banks, it was found that there were a number of deficiencies such as no medical checkup of blood sellers (who included alcoholics and drug addicts), unhygienic conditions of the location of blood banks storage of blood, non-availability of trained personnel in blood-banks, etc. In this case, the Court appointed a committee to examine the matters and give certain directions such as for the setting up of a National Council of Blood transfusion and state councils, the activities of which would cover the entire range of services related to the operation and requirements of blood banks. This included launching of effective motivation programs through utilization of all media for stimulating voluntary blood donations, launching programs for blood

6. AIR 1989 SC 348.
7. AIR 1996 SC 929.

donations in education institutions, among the labour industry and trade, training of personal in relation to all operations of blood collection; storage and transport, quality control and archiving system, cross matching of blood between donors and recipients, etc. It directed the National Council to set-up an institute for research in the collection, processing and storage, distribution and transfusion of whole human blood and components of human blood and also directed the Council to undertake training programmes for training of technical personnel, etc. The Court has not only recognized the importance of maintenance of hygienic conditions within hospitals, it has also recognized that cleanliness had to be maintained in the hospital surroundings and upheld the removal of certain risks from the hospital premises as they posed health hazards.

In *N. Jagdeesan* v. *District Collector, North Arcot*,[8] the members of an association had established certain bunks/kiosks within the premises of hospitals and on road margins. The petitioners complained that they were being evicted other than in accordance with law. It was found that insofar as the bunk/kiosks located within hospitals were concerned, the Department of Health and Family Welfare of the Government of Tamil Nadu had ordered their removal as they posed a hazard to the health and well-being of patients and others visiting the hospitals as they created unhygienic conditions by littering the place and the food items provided by them were being consumed by the in-patients and other patients visiting the hospital which was providing to be delirious to their health and treatment. The Court found that the Appellants-petitioners had no genuine grievance and removal was due to health hazards. The court expressed concerned over the unhygienic conditions in hospitals in the case of *A.K. Mittal* v. *State of Uttar Pradesh*,[9] wherein it observed, the necessity of maintenance of the highest standards of aseptic and sterile conditions at places where ophthalmic surgery or any surgery—is conducted cannot be overemphasized. It is not merely on the formulation of theoretical standards but really on the professional commitment with which the prescriptions are implemented that the ultimate result rests. Government, States and Union, incur enormous expenditure of public money on health care. But, the standards of cleanliness and hygiene in public hospitals unfortunately, leave much to be desired. The maintenance of sterile, aseptic conditions in hospitals to prevent cross-infections should be ordinary, routine and minimal incidents of maintenance of hospitals, purity of drugs and medicines intended for mass use would have to be ensured by prior test inspection.

8. AIR 1997 SC 1197.
9. AIR 1989 SC 1570.

But, owing to a general air of cynical irreverence towards values that has, unfortunately developed and to the mood of complacence with the continuing deterioration of standards, the very concept of standards and the imperatives of their observance tend to be impaired. This is a disturbing feature. The remedy lies in a ruthless adherence to the virtue of method and laying down practical procedures in the minutes of detail and by exacting not merely expecting-strict adherence to procedures. The *Workmen of State Pencil Manufacturing Industries of Madhya Pradesh Case*,[10] a case concerning the death of workers at young age in the State pencil manufacturing industries, due to the accumulation of soot in their lungs, was one of the first health-related public interest litigation to be filed in the Supreme Court. The Court required the State to ensure installation of safety measures in the concerned factories, failing that it could close down the same. The increasing role of the Court from the recognition of right to health at the first level and then to managerial role could be understood by the gradual development from the *Parmanand case* to *Dr. Chandra Prakash case*.[11]

In *A.S. Mittal* v. *State of Uttar Pradesh*,[12] the Supreme Court ordered the State government of Uttar Pradesh to pay compensation, as it had not followed the norms prescribed for the eye-camp and caused serious injuries to 84 patients. In *Vincent Panikurlangara* v. *Union of India*[13] the Supreme Court observed that in a welfare state it is the obligation of the State to ensure the creation and the sustaining of conditions congenial to good health. Directions were sought from the Supreme Court for banning the import, manufacture, sale and distribution of drugs recommended for a ban by the Drugs Consultative Committee, and for cancellation of all licences authorizing all such drugs. The importance of this judgment could be seen in the light of recent international agreement on TRIPS.[14]

Justice Ranganath Mishra's observation regarding right to health *vis-à-vis* right to life in the instant case was as follows:

> "Article 21 of the Constitution guarantees right to life and this court has interpreted the guarantee to cover a life with normal amenities assuring good living which include medical attention,

10. CWP No. 5143 of 1980.
11. *Dr. Chandra Prakash* v. *Ministry of Health*, AIR 2002, Delhi, 188.
12. AIR 1989 SC 1570.
13. AIR 1987 SC 990.
14. Due to the agreement on TRIPS, after 31st December 2004, the Process patent system hitherto used in India would be replaced by a more restrictive product patent system. Monopolize the production, distribution and pricing and finally availability of new medicines. The Indian government needs to create legislation that would be favourable to its citizen's right to health.

life free from diseases and longitivity upto normal expectations".[15]

The Supreme Court has also brought occupational health hazards to workers within the coverage of Article 21. The right to health and medical care to protect the health and vigour of a worker while in service or post-retirement has been held to be fundamental right under Article 21 read with the Directive Principles contained in Articles 39(e), 41, 43 and 47 and all fundamental human rights to make the life of workers meaningful and purposeful, with dignity of person.[16]

In *Murali S. Deora* v. *Union of India*,[17] the Supreme Court recognizing Right to Health under Article 21 of the Constitution held that smoking is injurious to health and banned smoking at public places.[18] In *State of Punjab & Others* v. *Mohinder Singh Chawla*,[19] a Government official was reimbursed the expenses incurred on his treatment.

In *Hamid Khan* v. *State of M.P.*,[20] a practicing advocate of Mandla filed petition for apathy of the State Government or rather a gross negligence on part of the State Government in taking proper measures before supplying drinking water from hand pumps which has resulted in colossal damage to the population of Mandla district. The Court held that it is the duty of the State towards every citizen of India to provide pure drinking water and it is the State which is responsible for not taking proper precaution to provide pure drinking water to the citizen. In *Madarsa Road Residents Association* v. *Lt. Governor*,[21] the High Court upheld the validity of putting barriers on busy roads passing through silence zone to control the noise pollution which endangers the life and safety of the residents. In *Citizen Council, Jamshedpur* v. *State of Bihar*,[22] the petitioner made allegation in the writ petition to the effect that holding of exhibition on Aam Begum Maidan, Jamshedpur would cause health hazards, create traffic and law and order problems. But the Court declined to interfere in the speculation that "when the writ petition was heard, the exhibition has already commenced and it is

15. *Vincent Panikurlangara* v. *Union of India,* AIR 1987 SC 990.
16. *Bandhua Mukti Morcha* v. *Union of India* (1984) 3 SCC 161; *Consumer Education and Research Centre* v. *Union of India* (1995) 3 SCC, 42.
17. AIR 2002 SC 40.
18. This decision once again shows the conflicts between the right to health and problem of allocation of resources. Inspite of the Supreme Court verdict, smoking is continuing at the public places.
19. AIR 1997 SC 1225.
20. AIR 1997 MP 191.
21. AIR 1995 Del. 95.
22. AIR 1999 Pat. 1.

expected that it might have been over by now. In *Almitra H. Patel* v. *Union of India*,[23] the matter was related to solid waste disposal in class 1 cities. The Supreme Court held the programme like '*Swachha Bangalore*' involving separation of recyclable waste or non-bio-degradable waste as well as domestic hazardous waste at source by means of door to door collection by municipal workmen or through private contractors should be role model for other cities, particularly, Delhi. Further the Court directed NCTD to appoint Executive Magistrate under Sections 20 and 21 of the Cr.P.C. (Criminal Procedure Code) to try offences relating to littering, nuisance, sanitation, and public health. In *Murli Deora* v. *Union of India*,[24] the Supreme Court has held that passive smoking in public places is indirect deprivation of life without any process of law. The statement of objects and reasons of the Cigarettes (Regulation of Production, Supply and Distribution) Act, 1975 and the Cigarettes and other Tobacco Products (Prohibition and Advertisement and Regulation) Bill, 2001 intends to protect the environment and control the pollution. The Bench comprising M.B. Shah and R.P. Sethi, JJ. observed: "fundamental right guaranteed under Article 21 of the Constitution of India, *inter-alia* provides that none shall be deprived of his life without due process of law. There is no reason why a non-smoker should be afflicted by various diseases including lung cancer or of heart, only because he is required to go to public places.

It is indirectly, depriving him of his life without any process of law. Undisputedly, smoking is injurious to health and may affect the health of smokers but there is no reason that health of passive smokers should also be injuriously affected. In any case, there is no reason to compel non-smokers to be helpers victims of air pollution". Realizing the gravity of the situation and considering the adverse effect of smoking on smokers and passive smokers, the Court directed that smoking be prohibited in public place, i.e. namely: (1) Auditoriums, (2) Hospital buildings, (3) Health Institutions, (4) Educational Institutions, (5) Libraries, (6) Court Buildings, (7) Public Offices, (8) Public Conveyance including railways.

Right to life includes right to live with human dignity as the High Court of Madhya Pradesh held in the case of *Dr. K.C. Malhotra* v. *State of M.P.*[25] that right to live is the fundamental right to people, state has to provide at least minimum conditions ensuring human dignity. Right to

23. (2002) 2 SCC 679.
24. (2001) 8 SSC 765; *Murli S. Deora* v. *Union of India*, 2003 (5) Scale 349; *Murli S. Deora* v. *Union of India*, 2003 (5) Scale 346; *K. Ramana Krishnan* v. *State of Kerala*, AIR 1999, Ker. 385.
25. AIR 1994 M.P. 43.

life enshrined in Article 21 cannot be restricted to mere animal existence. It means something much more than just physical survival. Right to life includes right to live with human dignity, namely, the bare necessities of life such as adequate nutrition, clothing, shelter, facilities of reading, writing, expressing oneself in diverse forms, freely moving about the mixing and commingling with fellow human beings. The right to life and personal liberty includes the right to live with decency and dignity,[26] however person employed to scavenge the human excreta is denied right of decency and dignity. In spite of the existence of this legislation, the dehumanizing practice of manual scavenging of human excreta still continues in many parts of India.

The right to live in healthy environment *vis-à-vis* scavenging of human excretion is a double edged weapon which imposes duty upon the government as well as citizens to protect and maintain the healthy environment, as the Himachal Pradesh High Court held in the case of *Kinkri Devi* v. *State*.[27] More than the implementing authorities under E.M.S. and C.D.L. people may held in saving the environmental pollution from the human excretion.

In the case of *Kirloskar Brothers Ltd.*,[28] a three judge Bench of the Supreme Court consisting of K. Ramaswamy, S. Saghir Ahmad and G.B. Patnaik, JJ. held that health is a state of complete physical, mental and social well-being and right to health, therefore is a fundamental right of the workmen. In this case the appellant-company had two factories in the State of Maharashtra and one in Madhya Pradesh. Only one of these factories, viz. that situated in Madhya Pradesh was covered under the Employees' State Insurance Act, 1948. The appellant company had its registered head office at Poona for sale and distribution of its products from the three factories. It had also regional offices at several places. The Government of Andhra Pradesh and Karnataka applied the provisions of the Act to the appellant companies' regional offices situated at Secunderabad and Bangalore. Accordingly, the said regional offices were required to contribute their share of the health insurance of the workmen. On behalf of the appellant company it was argued that the products of the factory covered under the Act contributed only to 3 percent to 33 percent and not a predominant part of the business transacted by the said regional offices and therefore, the appellant company was not liable to pay compensation. The Supreme Court rejected the argument of the appellant company and held that in

26. *Maneka Gandhi* v. *Union of India*, AIR 1973 SC 597.
27. AIR 1988 HP 4.
28. *Kirloskar Brothers Ltd.* v. *Employees' State Insurance Corporation*, AIR 1996 SC 3261.

view of the provisions of Sections 2(9), 2(15) and 2(17) of the Employee's State Insurance Act, 1948, the person who keeps control or is responsible for the supervision of the establishment of the respective regional offices in connection with the factory whose finished products are distributed or sold would be the principal employer for the purpose of the Act. The person appointed for sale or distribution of the products in the regional office is the employee covered under the Act.

In *N.D. Jayal* v. *Union of India*,[29] Rajendra Babu, J. of the Supreme Court stated that right to health is a fundamental right under Article 21. Protection of this is inextricably linked with clean and healthy environment itself is a fundamental right. In *Rajesh Kumar Srivastava* v. *A.P. Verma*[30], Mr. Sunil Ambwani, J. of the Allahabad High Court held that the fundamental right to profess, practice and propagate religion gets controlled and is subservient to the powers of the State to regulate such practice. No person has a right to make a claim of curing the aliments and to improve health on the basis of his right to freedom of religion. Every form and method of curing and healing must have established procedures, which must be proved by known and accepted methods, and verified and approved by experts in the field of medicines. It is only when a particular form, method or path is accepted by the experts in the field of medicine that it can be permitted to be practicised in public. The right to health included in Article 21 does not come in conflict on overlap with the right to propagate and profess religion. These two are separate and distinct rights. Where the right to health is regulated by validly enacted legislation the right to cure the ailment through religious practices including 'Faith-Healing', cannot be claimed as a fundamental right. The freedom of conscience supplemented by freedom of unhampered expression of free conviction to practice rituals and ceremonies are part of religion or subject to public order, morality and health. There is no conflict between the two. The faith in any religion to practice rituals and observance of such religion is not to be confused with right to conscience and to practice and propagate the religion. The claim to cure ailments falls in the domain of right to health. A person has no right to induce others to believe in his faith in religion to cure others from ailments. The Court held that the propagation, practice and profession of 'faith healing' in public on charging consideration is violative to the Constitutional and Legislative scheme, and that such 'faith healing' based on a person's faith in the religious practices, in public for consideration is not permitted and is violative of the legislations. In the instant case the Lal Mahendra Sewa

29. (2004) 9 SCC 362.
30. AIR 2005 All. 175.

Shakti Samiti, Kotwa Kotwa, Allahabad through its members Sri Ajay Pratap Singh had no right to hold congregation in public parks, charge consideration and to profess and practice in public that the chanting of '*Om Namoh Shivai*' was cure to all ailments. Such a practice is illegal and violative of law as well as the right of citizen including those innocent persons suffering from various ailments, who participated in such congregation guaranteed under Article 21 of the Constitution of India and which the State and the Court are obliged to protect. Thus, the learned Judge expressly held that the right to health is regulated by validity enacted legislation. Right to cure ailments through religious practices including 'health healing' could not be claimed as a fundamental right. Professing of 'health healing' in public on charging consideration was violative of constitutional and legislative scheme. The claim to cure ailments falls in the domain of right to health. A person has no right to induce others to believe in his faith in religion to cure others from ailments.

In case of *Confederation of Ex-servicemen* v. *Union of India*,[31] a five Judges bench of the Supreme Court held that to get free and full medical care/medical aid is not a fundamental right of ex-servicemen. The present petition under Article 32 of the Constitution was filed by the confederation of ex-servicemen associations seeking direction to the respondent union of India to recognize the right of full and free medicare of ex-servicemen, their families and dependents treating such right as one of the fundamental rights guaranteed under the Constitution of India. Another prayer was made to direct the respondents to take necessary steps to ensure that full and free medicare was provided to ex-servicemen, their families and dependants on a par with in-service defence personnel. Speaking on behalf of the Court C.K. Thakkar, J. partly allowed the writ petition, and held that to get free and full medical aid/facilities is not a part of the fundamental right of ex-servicemen. He relied on a number of decisions of the apex Court[32] and held that the policy decision in formulating contributory scheme for ex-servicemen is in accordance with the provisions of the Constitution and also in consonance with the law laid down by the Supreme Court. The Learned Judge observed:

> "In our considered opinion, though the right to medical aid is a fundamental right of all citizens including ex-servicemen guaranteed by Article 21 of the Constitution, framing of scheme for ex-servicemen and asking them to pay" one time contribution neither violates Part-III nor is it inconsistent with Part IV of the

31. (2006) 8 SCC 399 at 430.
32. Consumer Education and Research Centre v. Union of India, AIR (1995) SC 922.

> Constitution. Ex-servicemen who are getting pension have been asked to become members of ECH by making "one time contribution" of reasonable amount (ranging from Rs. 1800 to Rs. 18,000. To us, this cannot be held illegal, unlawful, arbitrary or otherwise unreasonable".[33]

It is submitted that the learned Judge laid down principles regarding medicare/medical aid to ex-servicemen. The five Judges Bench settled the principles and held that to get free and full medical care is not a fundamental right of ex-servicemen. The learned Judge followed the principles laid down by the apex Court and stated that the right to medical aid is a fundamental right to life and personal liberty under Article 21 of the Constitution, framing of scheme for ex-servicemen and asking them to pay one time contribution is not violative of Part III and Part IV of the Constitution. [34]

In case of *Reliance Ltd.* v. *Cheman Chery Grama Panchayat & Ors.*[35] a Division Bench of the Kerala High Court stated that use of mobile phone is a common phenomenon throughout the country and has made drastic changes in the people's lifestyle. Users range from a common man to a multi-millionaire and this tiny instrument has revolutionized the medium of communication throughout the world. Constant use of mobile phone, it is reported, may have its own adverse ill effects on human health as well. The question that was posed for consideration in this case was not with regard to ill effects of the use of mobile phones but was not with regard to ill effects of the use of mobile phones but whether installation of mobile base station and its functioning would cause any health hazards to the people who are residing nearby, apprehension had also been voice that radiation emanating from large telecommunication towers would expose human beings living within the magnetic field to fate deceases like cancer, embryo distribution and changes in DNA structure. Delivering the judgment of the Court K.S. Radhakrishnan, J. held that RF exposures from mobile base stations are much less than from radio, FM radio and television transmissions and that the consensus of scientific community is that the radiation from Mobile Phone Base Stations is far too low to produce health hazards if people are kept away from direct access to the antenna and the overall evidence indicates that they are unlikely to pose

33. *Reliance Ltd.* v. *Chemanchery Grama Panchayat & Ors.*, AIR 2007, Kerala 33. The case was heard by a Division Bench consisting K.S. Radhakrishnan and K. Padmanabhan Nair, JJ. However, the Judgment of the Court was delivered by Radhakrishnan, J.
34. The National Human Rights Commission, Annual Report, 2001-02 at pp. 58-62.
35. AIR 2007, Kerala 33.

a risk to health. Therefore, it could be concluded that the permission granted for IS installation of Mobile Base Station by the Panchayat would not cause as such any health hazards nor will it affect the fundamental rights guaranteed to citizens under Article 21 of the Constitution. Cancellation of licence by the Panchayat based on an apprehension that the radiation may cause health hazards to the people of the locality was therefore not proper. However, court gave a general direction to the TRAI to make periodical inspection to ascertain whether radiation emanated from the Mobile Base station would cause any health hazards to the people of the locality. It is submitted that the approach of the learned Judge was proper and justified. He made the correct interpretation of the Section 4 of the Telegraph Act (1885) and Article 21 of the Constitution. He stated that installation of Base stations of Mobile Telephone service provider did not cause health hazards to people residing nearby nor infringe fundamental right to life enshrined in Article 21. It can be concluded that permission granted for installation of Mobile Base station by the Panchayat would not cause as such any health hazards nor will it affect the fundamental rights guaranteed to citizens under Article 21 of the Constitution.

The Supreme Court, while examining the issue of constitutional right to health care under Article 21, observed that in Article 21 "No person shall be deprived of his life or personal liberty except according to procedure established by law". Thus, right to life is fundamental right guaranteed by the Constitution.[36] But what is the meaning and scope of life and right to life? The Courts have held that "Right to live means something more than 'mere animal existence' and includes the right to live with human dignity and decency".[37]

The Supreme Court in *Paschim Banga Khet Mazdoor Samithy & Ors.* v. *State of West Bengal & Anrs.*,[38] while widening the scope of Article 21 and the governments responsibility to provide medical aid to every person in the country, held that in a welfare state, the primary duty of the government is to secure the welfare of the people. Providing adequate medical facilities for the people is an obligation undertaken by the government in a welfare state. The government discharges this obligation by providing medical care to the persons seeking to avail of those facilities. Article 21 imposes an obligation on the State to safeguard the right to life of every person. Preservation of human life is thus, of paramount importance. The government hospitals run by the

36. *The Times of India*, New Delhi, January 28, 1997.
37. *Sunil* v. *Delhi Admn*, 1978 SC 1675; *Vikram* v. *State of Bihar*, (1988), Supp. SCC 734 (para 2).
38. (1996) 4 SCC 37. Also see Sujit Das, Right to Emergency Medicare, A Landmark Judgment, *Economic and Political Weekly*, October 26, 1996.

State are duly bound to extend medical assistance for preserving human life. Failure on the part of a government hospital to provide timely medical treatment to a person in need of such treatment, results in violation of his right of life guaranteed under Article 21. The petitioner should therefore, be suitably compensated for the breach of his right guaranteed under Article 21 of the Constitution. After due regard to the facts and circumstances of the case compensation of Rs. 25,000 was given.

The decision of the Supreme Court was not confined to only providing remedy to the petitioner. The fact that emergency patients are daily turned away from the doors of the government hospitals in the country may not be exactly known to the Supreme Court, but the predicament of innumerable potential *Hakim Seikhs* has not escaped the notice of the Court. In order to initiate "remedial measures to rule out recurrence immediate medical attention and treatment to person in real need", the Supreme Court accepted the recommendations to this end made by an enquiry committee appointed by the State government in the course of the trial, took into consideration the steps taken by the government to implement those recommendations and further issued the following directions to the government to carry out in the government hospitals for the purpose of dealing with emergency patients:

(1) Adequate facilities be made available at the primary health centres where the patient can be given immediate primary treatment so as to stabilize his condition.

(2) Hospitals at the district and sub-divisional levels be upgraded so that serious cases can be treated there and their facilities for giving specialist treatment be increased having regard to the growing need.

(3) A 'central bureau' with centralized communication system be set-up through which a hospital unable to accommodate an emergency patient may send him to another hospital having vacant bed.

(4) Ambulance adequacy provided with necessary equipment patients from primary health centre to sub-divisional to district to state hospitals.

(5) The health centres, hospitals and their medical personnel be geared to deal with larger number of emergency patients on account of higher risks of accidents on certain occasions and in certain seasons.

For the purpose of restoration of minimum norms of work procedure in the hospitals, the Court accepted the recommendations of the enquiry committee to direct that in respect of Admission/Emergency Attendance Registers, the authorities should take the following steps:

(a) Clear recording of the name, age, sex, address, disease of the patient by the attending medical officer;
(b) Clear recording of date and time of attendance/examination/ admission of the patient;
(c) Clear indication whether and where the patient has been admitted, transferred, referred;
(d) Safe custody of the registers; and
(e) Fixing of responsibility of maintenance and safe custody of registers.

For the purpose of identifying the concerned individual medical officers dealing with particular patients, following procedure was directed to be adopted:

(A) A copy of the Duty Roster of Medical Officers should be preserved in the office of the superintendent incorporating the modifications done for unavoidable circumstances;
(B) Each department shall maintain a register for recording the signature of attending medical officers denoting their arrival and departure;
(C) The attending medical officer shall write his full name clearly and put his signature in the treatment document;
(D) The superintendent of the hospital shall keep all such records in his safe custody; and
(E) A copy of ticket issued to the patient should be maintained or the relevant data in this regard should be noted in an appropriate record for future guidance.

Whenever complaints of inadequacy, negligence malpractice in hospital services appear in public the authorities usually take shelter under the plea of financial stringency—poor exchequer and hence poor service. The Supreme Court felt that this point should be dealt with openly and clearly. Again a quote from the judgment:

It is no doubt true that financial resources are needed for providing these facilities. But at the same, it cannot be ignored that it is the constitutional obligation of the State to provide adequate medical services to the people. Whatever is necessary for this purpose has to be done. In the context of the constitutional obligation to provide free legal aid to a poor accused this Court has held that the state cannot avoid its constitutional obligation in that regard on account of financial constraints.[39] The said observations would apply with equal, if not greater, force in the matter of discharge of constitutional obligation of the state to provide medical aid to preserve human life. In the matter of allocation of funds for medical services the said constitutional obligation of the state has to be kept in view. It is necessary that time-bound plan for providing these services be chalked out keeping in view the recommendations of the committee as well as the requirements for ensuring availability of proper medical services in this regard as indicated by us and steps should be taken to implement the same.

It may thus appear that the State of West Bengal under a progressive Left Front government has been isolated by a vagary of litigation and has abruptly been called upon to discharge its constitutional obligation though its record may be none the worse compared to rest of the vast India. The Supreme Court, however, makes no such discrimination. The judgment went on to direct.

The State of West Bengal alone is a party to these proceedings. Other states, though not parties, should also take necessary steps in the light of the recommendations made by the committee, the direction contained in the Memorandum of the government of West Bengal dated August 22, 1995 and the further directions given herein. The Union of India is a party to these proceedings. Since it is the joint obligation of the centre as well as the states to provide medical services it is expected that the Union of India would render the necessary assistance in the improvement of the medical services in the country on these lines.[40] No doubt the judgment is unique on several counts. Non-party progressives have for some time been raising the slogan of health care as a fundamental right of the people. Health care or for that matter, any welfare service as an effective fundamental right of the people will necessarily be a very expensive business for the state. Except for the socialist countries no state has ever made any pledge to provide it for all people as a state enterprise. In many richer countries of the world, however, the state has performed a crucial role to provide almost universal medical care coverage for the population. Here also the Supreme Court dealt with medical care, not health care, and that also involving only emergency/serious patients needing hospitalization for life-saving medical aid, i.e., a very small percentage of sick people. Emergency medicare has not actually found a place in Part III of the Constitution as one of the fundamental rights. The Supreme Court Justices, S.C. Agarwal and G.T. Nanavati had to offer some arguments

39. See *Khatri (II)* v. *State of Bihar*, 1981 (1) SCC 627 at 631.
40. Sujit Dass, "Right to Emergency Medicare—Landmark Judgment," *Economic & Political Weekly*, Oct. 26, 1996 at pp. 2851-52.

to establish that the fundamental right to life guaranteed in Article 21 included the right to life-saving emergency medicare in the state hospital and held that right justiciable by granting financial compensation to a victim deprived of such right. This is undoubtedly a new decision in Indian judicial practice. This is also a step forward from the earlier Supreme Court decision on Consumer Protection Act, 1986 where the Court exempted those hospitals rendering free medicare to everybody from the purview of the Act. Perhaps it has not escaped the notice of the court that whatever might have been the intention of the Constitution-makers and whatever might have been the actual practice, national governments since independence and the leaders of the nation, big and small, have rarely defaulted in proclaiming through their all and sundry speeches government's policy of providing medicare to all. Under the circumstances, one can hardly fault the judgment if the Supreme Court took the leaders speeches at face value. But how far can the governments be pressurized?

The most significant elements of the judgment are:

(A) Right to admission in a State hospital of an emergency patient is a fundamental right guaranteed in Article 21.

(B) Non-availability of a vacant bed is not a valid pleas to deny such admission. The admissible patient, in such situation, will have to be kept on the floor or a trolley bed and thereafter the bed position may be adjusted by taking a loan from the cold war or by way of transfer/discharge.

(C) Financial stringency of state exchequer is not a valid plea for not complying with the Supreme Court's directions.

(D) Not only the government hospitals but the medical officers employed therein are also liable to a charge of violating fundamental right if they deny such admission.

(E) Not only West Bengal, but the judgment is applicable of all other States including the Centre.

Any one can now approach the nearby appropriate court on behalf of an emergency patient who is denied admission in a state hospital, with a reference to this judgment for judicial remedy. This legal remedy is obtainable for every victim if one is ready to take the trouble and spend a certain amount of money in the process. It is not known to everybody that in order to seek such remedy appointment of a lawyer or a petition in some special proforma or legal jargon, etc., are not mandatory. Any citizen putting his grievance on plain paper in ordinary language can approach a court and argue his own case. There will be, in fact, not much argument to offer if the fact of admissibility and denial of admission is established.

Who determines the admissibility of a patient? Whether his condition is an emergency/serious or not? In the case of Hakim Seikh this question was not raised since the emergency medical officers diagnosed him as admissible in the attendance tickets. Considering the circumstances surrounding medical practice in the country the authority to determine admissibility should reasonably be left to the attending doctor but the judgment clearly stipulated that in such exercise he should consult the specialist on duty in the emergency department. Every patient or his escort, therefore, should take care in insisting on the doctor to write his categorical opinion on admissibility on the attendance ticket. It is a patients' admissibility status what constitutes his fundamental right. Further, if a hospital is now found to have neglected in arranging for the provisions for emergency medicare as stipulated in the judgment, a cause of action for contempt of court will ensue.[41]

In *State of Punjab* v. *Ram Lubhaya Bagga*,[42] the Supreme Court while considering the Articles 21,[43] 41,[44] and 47[45] of the Constitution observed that rights and duties are correlated with each other. Hence, the right of a citizen to live under Article 21 casts on obligation on the State. So it is for the State to secure health to its citizen under Article 47. The Court further held that the State can neither urge nor say that it has no obligation to provide medical facilities. If that were so it would be the violation of Article 21. No State or country can have unlimited resources to spend on any of its projects. That is why it only approves projects that appear feasible. The same holds true for providing medical facilities to its citizens. Provision of facilities cannot be unlimited. It has to be to the extent that finances permit. If no scale or rate is fixed then in case private clinics or hospitals increase their rate to exorbitant scales, the state would be bound to reimburse the same. The principle of fixing of rate and scale under such a policy is justified, and can not be held to violate Article 21 or Article 47 of the Constitution.

---

41. *Ibid.*, at p. 2853.
42. (1988) 4 SCC 117.
43. Article 21 of the Constitution says that no person shall be deprived of his life or personal liberty except according to procedure established by law.
44. Article 41 directs the State to ensure the people within the limit of its economic capacity and development (a) Employment, (b) education, and (c) public assistance in case of unemployment, old age, sickness and disablement and in other cases of undeserved want.
45. Article 47 imposes duty upon the State to raise the level of nutrition and the standard of living of its people and the improvement of public health. In particular, the State should bring about prohibition of the consumption except for medicinal purposes of intoxicating drinks and of drug which are injurious to health.

The Supreme Court not only cast an obligation on the State to protest the life of the citizens but also lays down an obligation on the health profession to protect the life of accident victims through its landmark judgment in *Pt. Parmanand Katara* v. *Union of India & Ors.*,[46] ruled that every doctor whether at a Government hospital or otherwise has the professional obligation to extend his services with due expertise for protecting life. No law or State action can intervene to avoid/delay, the discharge of the paramount obligation cast upon members of the medical profession. The Court also laid down the following guidelines for doctors, when an injured person approaches them: Firstly, whenever, a man of the medical profession is approached by an injured person, and, if he finds that whatever assistance he could give is not really sufficient to save the life of the person, but some better assistance is necessary, it is the duty of the man in the medical profession so approached to render all the help which he could, and also see that the person reaches the proper expert as early as possible.[47] Secondly, a doctor does not contravene the law of the land by proceeding to treat an injured victim on his appearance before him, either by himself or with others. Zonal regulations and classifications cannot operate as fetters in the discharge of the obligation, even if the victim is sent elsewhere under local rules, and regardless of the involvement of police.[48] Thirdly, there is no legal impediment for a medical professional, when he is called upon or requested to attend an injured person needing his medical assistance immediately. The effort to save the person should be the top priority, not only of the medical professional, but even of the police or any other citizen who happens to be connected with the matter, or who happens to notice such an incident or a situation.[49]

In *A.S. Mittal & Ors.* v. *State of Uttar Pradesh & Ors.*,[50] the Supreme Court, while dealing with a public interest litigation under Article 32 of the Constitution, alleging negligence on the part of the doctors in providing services at an eye camp organized by the Lions Club, observed that the whole programme at Khurja, however laudable the intentions with which it might have been launched, proved a disastrous, medical misadventure for the patients. The operated eyes of the patients were irreversibly damaged owing to a post-operative infection of the intraocular cavities. It is now undisputed that this

46. AIR 1989 SC 2039.
47. *Ibid.*
48. *Ibid.*, the 1985 decision of the Standing Committee on Forensic Medicine is the Effective Guideline.
49. *Ibid.*
50. AIR 1989 SC 1571.

terrible medical mishap was due to a common contaminating source. The suggestion in the report of the enquiries that ensued, is that in all probability, the sources of the infection was the 'normal saline' used on the eyes at the time of surgery. It was further observed that despite every care taken by the answering respondent and his associates and assistants, a large number of patients could not regain their vision in the Khurja Camp. It is extremely unfortunate that some 84 patient's vision could not be restored, despite every care bestowed by the answering respondent. The Court held that a mistake by a medical practitioner, which no reasonably competent and careful practitioner would have committed, is a negligent one. The Indian Medical Council constituted a Sub-Committee after the above proceedings, and submitted its recommendations before the Court. The Court gave suggestions to the Ministry to incorporate the following guidelines under the revised guidelines:

Staff: The operation in the camps should only be performed by qualified, experienced Ophthalmic Surgeons registered with Medical Council of India or any State Medical Council. The camp should not be entrusted to post-graduate students. There should be a pathologist to examine urine, blood sugar, etc. It is preferable to have a dentist to check the teeth for repairs and a physician for general medical check-up.

Medication: All medicines to be used should be of standard quality duly verified by the doctor in charge of the camp.

The Court further held that maintenance of the highest standards of aseptic and sterile conditions at places where ophthalmic surgery—or any surgery—is conducted cannot be over-emphasized. It is not merely on the formulation of the theoretical standards, but the professional commitment with which the prescriptions are implemented that the ultimate result rests. The government, the states and the Union, incur enormous expenditure of public money on health care. However, the standards of cleanliness and hygiene in public hospitals leave much to be desired. Maintenance of sterile aseptic conditions in hospitals, to prevent cross-infections should be a routine hospital activity. Purity of drugs intended for human use should be ensured by prior tests and inspection. But owing to a general air of cynical irreverence and complaisance, with the continuing deterioration of standards, the very concept of standards and the imperatives of their observance tend to be impaired. The remedy lies in a ruthless adherence to the virtue of method, and laying down practical procedures in minute detail and by exacting—not merely expecting—strict adherence to these procedures.

In view of the facts of the case, the Court observed that indeed, the factual foundations requisite for establishing the proximate causal connection for the injury, has yet to be established conclusively. The Court held that the State Government should afford the victims some monetary relief, in addition to the sum of Rs. 5000 already paid by way of interim relief. The State government was directed to pay a further sum of Rs. 1,25,000 to each of the victims.

Right to life is guaranteed under Article 21 of the Constitution of India. This right has been couched in the negative form and when read literally, it empowers the state to interfere with the enjoyment of life and liberty according to procedure established by law. A new facet was given in *Maneka Gandhi* v. *Union of India*,[51] when, by its interpretation, the Supreme Court changed the scenario from one that calls for procedural rights to one that provides for substantial rights. While constitutionalizing these substantive rights with the aid of Article 21, the Supreme Court has drawn support from the International Convention on Human Rights. Now the State is mandated to provide to a person all rights essential for the enjoyment of the right to life in its various perspectives. Of late, the right to health and access to medical treatment has been included in the plethora of rights brought under the ambit of Article 21.

Though the Constitution of India does not confer an enforceable fundamental right to medical assistance to have better health on its citizens but under Part IV, Article 47 imposes a primary duty upon the State to raise the level of nutrition and the standard of living and to improve public health. The mode of improving public health has also not been explicitly mentioned in the Constitution, the Court by the harmonious construction of fundamental rights and the Directive Principles has prescribed the modality of access to medical treatment.[52]

The Supreme Court, while examining the issue of the Constitutional right to health care under Articles 21, 41 and 47 of the Constitution of India in *State of Punjab* v. *Ram Lubhaya Bagga*,[53] observed that the right of one person correlates to a duty upon another, individual, employer, government or authority. Hence, the right of a citizen to live under Article 21 casts an obligation on the State. This obligation is further reinforced under Article 47, it is for the state to secure health to its citizens as its primary duty. No doubt, the government is rendering this obligation by opening government hospitals and health centres, but to be meaningful, they must be within the reach of its people, and of

51. AIR 1978 SC 597.
52. C. Manickam and S. Sajith, "Right to Health and Access to Medical Treatment under the Indian Constitution", AIR (1997), Journal Section, p. 104.
53. (1998) 4 SCC 117.

sufficient quality. Since it is one of the most sacrosanct and valuable rights of a citizen, and an equally sacrosanct and valuable rights of a citizen, and an equally sacrosanct and sacred obligation of the state, every citizen of this welfare state looks towards the state to perform this obligation with top priority, including by way of allocation of sufficient funds. This in turn will not only secure the rights of its citizens to their satisfaction, but will benefit the State in achieving its social, political and economic goals.

The Court held that the State can neither urge nor say that it has no obligation to provide medical facilities. If that were so, it would be *ex facie* in violation of Article 21 under a policy where medical services continue to be given, though an employee may be given a free choice to get treatment in any private hospital in India, the amount of reimbursement may be limited. Without fixing any specific rate, such a policy does not leave this limitation to the will of the director, but it is done by a committee of technical experts. The Court further held that no state or country can have unlimited resources to spend on any of its projects. That is why it only approves projects that appear feasible. The same holds true for providing medical facilities to its citizens. Provision of facilities can not be unlimited. It has to be to the extent that finances permit. If no scale or rate is fixed then in case private clinics or hospitals increase their rate to exorbitant scales, the state would be bound to reimburse the same. The principle of fixing of rate and scale under such a policy is justified, and cannot be held to violative of Article 21 or Article 47 of the Constitution.[54]

In *Vincent Panikur Longara* v. *Union of India*,[55] a public interest litigation, the petitioner challenged the drug policy of the Government. The respondents contended that the matter of public health is incorporated only in directive principles and so they are not enforceable before the Court of law. The Court rejected their argument on the basis of its earlier decision in *ABSK Sang* v. *Union of India*,[56] wherein it made the following observations:

> "…notwithstanding their great importance, the Directive Principles cannot in the very nature of things be enforced in a court of law…it does not mean that Directive Principles are less important than Fundamental Rights or that they are not binding on the various organs of the State"[57] and held that a healthy body is the very foundation for all human activities. That is why the

54. *Ibid.*
55. AIR 1987 SC 990.
56. AIR 1981 SC 298.
57. *Id.* at 335.

adage, "*Sariramadyam Khalau Dharma Sadhanam*" and so in a welfare state, it is the obligation of the State to ensure the creation and the sustaining of conditions congenial to good health. The Supreme Court asserted the significance of public health as follows:

"In a series of pronouncements during recent years this Court has culled out from the provision of Part IV of the Constitution these several obligations of the State and called upon it to effectuate them in order that the resultant pictured by the Constitution Fathers may become a reality. As pointed out by us, maintenance and improvement of public health have to rank high as these are indispensable to the very physical existence of the community and on the betterment of these depends the building of the society of which the Constitution-makers envisaged. Attending to public health in our opinion, therefore, is of high priority-perhaps the one at the top."[58]

The importance of health promotion at the work place is increasingly recognized particularly in larger workplace health promotion reduces absenteeism and can lead to gain productivity. The Supreme Court thus has recognized the rights of the workers and their right to basic health facilities under the Constitution, as well as under the International Conventions to which India is a party. In its path-breaking judgment in *Bandhua Mukti Morcha* v. *Union of India*,[59] the Court delineated the scope of Article 21 of the Constitution, and held that it is the fundamental right of every one in this country assured under the interpretation given to Article 21 by this Court in *Francis Mullin's Case*[60] to live with human dignity enshrined in Article 21 derives its life breath from the Directive Principles of State Policy and particularly clauses (e) and (f) of Article 39 and Articles 41 and 42. It must include protection of: the health and strength of workers, men and women; and children of tender age against abuse; opportunities and facilities for children to develop in a healthy manner and in conditions of freedom and dignity; educational facilities; just and humane conditions of work and maternity relief. These are the minimum requirements, which must exist in order to enable a person to live with human dignity. No state, neither the central government nor any state government has the right to take any action which will deprive a person of the enjoyment of these basic essentials.

In *CESE Ltd.* v. *Subhash Chandra Bose*,[61] the Supreme Court

58. *Id.* at 339.
59. AIR 1984 SC 804.
60. AIR 1980 SC 849.
61. (1992) 1 SCC 461.

surveyed various functions of the State to protect safety and health of the workmen and emphasized the need to provide medical care to the workmen to prevent disease and to improve general standards of health consistent with human dignity and right to personality. It was held that medical care and health facilities not only protect against sickness but also ensure stable manpower for economic development facilities of health and medical care generate devotion and dedication among the workers to give their best physically as well as mentally, in productivity. It was held that the medical facilities are, therefore, part of social security and like gift-edged security, it would yield immediate returns to the employer in the form of increased production and would reduce absenteeism. Just and favourable conditions of work imply ensuring safe and healthy working conditions to the workmen. The periodic medical treatment invigorates the health of workmen and harnesses their energy resources. Prevention of occupational disabilities enthuses them to render efficient service which is a valuable asset for greater productivity to the employer and national production to the State. Medical facilities, therefore, is a fundamental and human right to protect his health. It was held that health insurance, while in service or after retirement was fundamental right and even private industries are enjoined to provide health insurance to workmen.[62]

The expression 'life' as held by the Supreme Court does not connote mere animal existence or continued drudgery through life but has a much wider meaning which includes right to livelihood, better standard of life, hygienic conditions in work place and leisure.[63]

A three judge bench of the Supreme Court in *Consumer Education and Research Centre & Ors.* v. *Union of India*[64] also ruled that:

> "...Right to health to a worker is an integral facet of meaningful right to life to have not only a meaningful existence but also robust health and vigour without which worker would lead life of misery. Lack of health denudes his livelihood. Compelling economic necessity to work in an industry exposed to health hazards due to indigence to bread-winning for himself and his dependants, should not be at the cost of the health and vigor of the workman. Facilities and opportunities, as enjoined in Article 38 should be provided to protect the health of the workman. Provision for medical test and treatment invigorates the health of the worker for higher production or efficient service continued

62. *Id.*, at 462, para 30.
63. Agther, "Right to Life includes Right to Health and Medical Care", (1997), *Labour and Industrial Cases,* 30: August, pp.119-22.
64. (1995) 3 SCC 922.

treatment. While in service or after retirement is a moral, legal and constitutional concomitant duty of the employer and the State. Therefore, it must be held that the right to health and medical care is a fundamental right under Article 21 read with Articles 39(c), 41 and 43 of the Constitution and make the life of the workman meaningful and purposeful with dignity of person. Right to life includes protection of the health and strength of the worker and is a minimum requirement to enable a person to live with human dignity. The State, be it the union or the State Government or an industry, public or private is enjoined to take all such actions which will promote health, strength and vigour of the workman, during the period of employment and leisure and health and happiness. The health and strength of the worker is an integral facet of right to life. Denial thereof denudes the workman of the finer facets to life violating Article 21. The right to human dignity, development of personality, social protection, right to rest and leisure are fundamental human rights of a workman assured by the Charter of Human Rights in the Preamble and Articles 38 and 39 of the Constitution. Facilities for medical care and health against sickness to the worker, ensure stable manpower for economic development and would generate devotion to duty and dedication to give, best physically as well as mentally in production of goods or services. Health of the worker enables him to enjoy the fruit of his labour, keeping him physically fit and mentally alert for leading a successful life, economically, socially and culturally. Medical facilities to protect the health of the workers are, therefore, the fundamental and human rights to workman".

Finally, the Court ruled that "...linked with the right of self-preservation, is the anxiety of a person to see that he or his dependants do not suffer on account of inadequate treatment. Such anxiety is normal human beaviour and if a person has taken his parent to a nearby place where better facilities are available, no obnoxious notification should stand on the way. The pre-independence notification was issued at a time when right to life was not recognized to be sacrosanct, sacred as it is today".

Yet in another case relating to reimbursement of medical expenses the Rajasthan High Court examined the issue in *Shyam Singh* v. *State of Rajasthan*,[65] where an Assistant Accounts Officer, while on leave, fell ill by suffering from 'Extra Sock (Shock) wave Lithotripsy and got

65. 1996 Lab 1C 1377 (Raj.).

admitted in Mulji Bhai Patel Urology Hospital, Naidad. There he was operated and received medical treatment. Incidentally the Government of Rajasthan has not recognized the above said Hospital, based on which the reimbursement claim was rejected by the Government of Rajasthan. While dwelling on the subject of reimbursement of medical treatment, the Court identified the pivotal point of the case saying that, "...the only question in these circumstances which is required to be answered, is as to whether in such a situation, an employee of the State of Rajasthan, who falls sick at a place, where the required treatment is not available in the Government Hospital, and where no hospital having the treatment has been recognized by the State Government should remain untreated and if he gets treatment, can be deprived of the benefit of being treated at the cost of the State Government". The Court very firmly further held that, "...Health is the prime consideration of every one and on falling ill one has to take the medical aid, at such a place, where it is available".

It is apt to reiterate here, the view expressed by the Supreme Court in *Kirloskar Brothers Ltd.* v. *Employee's State Insurance Corporation*,[66] where it firmly laid its approach when it is said that "..... health is thus a state of complete physical, mental and social well-being and right to health therefore is a fundamental and human right to workmen. The maintenance of health is the most important constitutional goal whose realization requires interaction of many social and economic factors. Just and favourable conditions of work imply to ensure safe and healthy working conditions to the workmen. The periodical medical treatment invigorates the health of the workmen and harnesses their human resources. Prevention of occupational disabilities generates devotion and dedication to duty the enthuses the workmen to render efficient service which is valuable asset for greater productivity to the employer and national production to the State.

The Constitution of India enunciates certain fundamental rights of the individual. The fundamentals of the Indian Constitution which are laid down in the 'Preamble' aims at securing to its citizens, justice, social, economic and political, liberty of thought, expression, belief, equality of status and opportunity, promoting fraternity amongst them; and assuring the dignity of the individual and the unity of the nation.[67] Article 14 of the Constitution of India ensures that," the State shall not deny to any person equality before the law or the equal protection of the laws within the territory of India." This right to equality can be used for the protection of the human rights of the UN/AIDS patient for the

66. AIR 1996 SC 3261.
67. *Shukla, V.N.*, Constitution of India, 10th Edn., 2003 at p.A-43.

reason that Bhagwati, J. once stated: "Equality is a dynamic concept with many aspects and dimensions and it cannot be 'cribbed, cabined and confined' within traditional and doctrinaire limits. From a positivistic point of view, equality is antithetic to arbitrariness where an act is arbitrary, it is implicit in it that it is unequal both according to political logic and constitutional law and is therefore violative of Article 14."[68]

Article 21 of the Constitution of India guarantees a higher level of right to every person wherein we can conveniently bring the HIV/AIDS patient under it to claim right to life and personal liberty. The Supreme Court in *Francis Carolie* v. *Union Territory of Delhi*,[69] held that "the right to life with human dignity", and all that goes along with it, namely, the bare necessities of life such as, adequate nutrition, clothing and shelter and facilities for reading, writing and expressing ourselves in diverse forms, freely moving about and mixing and commingling with fellow human being. When we interpret this decision of the Hon'ble Supreme Court, Article 21 rightfully guarantees a life of human dignity even to the HIV/AIDS patients. Article 21 further provides for another imperative right, i.e. right to health and medical assistance. With reference to right to privacy Jeevan Reddy, J. in *R. Rajagopal and R.R. Gopal* v. *State of Tamil Nadu*[70] the right of privacy *vis-à-vis* the right of the press under Article 19 of the Constitution were considered and in the research-oriented judgment, it was laid down, *inter alia*, as under:

> "The right to privacy is implicit in the right to life and liberty guaranteed to the citizens of this country by Article 21. It is a "right to be let alone". A citizen has a right to safeguard the privacy of his own, his family, marriage, procreation, motherhood, child bearing and education among other matters without his consent, whether truthful or otherwise and whether laudatory or critical. If he does so, he would be violating the right to privacy of the person concerned and would be liable in an action for damages. Position may, however, be different, if a person voluntarily thrusts himself into controversy or voluntarily invites or raises a controversy."

Article 21 of the Constitution of India in consonance with Article 25(1) of the Universal Declaration of Human Rights, 1948 that reads:

> "Everyone has the right to a standard of living adequate for the health and well-being of himself and his family including food,

68. *Ibid*.
69. AIR 1978 SC 597.
70. (1994) 6 SCC 632: (1994 AIR SCW 4420).

clothing, housing and medial care and necessary social services, and the right to security in the event of unemployment, sickness, disability, widowhood, old age or other lack of livelihood in circumstances beyond his control."[71]

Thus, Article 21 of the Constitution provides a *sine quo non* protection in respect of human rights of the HIV/AIDS patient. Part IV of the Constitution of India under the Directive Principles of the State Policy has set out the aims and objectives to be taken up by the States in the governance of the country. It imposes certain obligations on the State to take positive action in certain obligations on the state to take positive action in certain directions in order to promote the welfare of the people and achieve economic democracy.[72] Under Article 39(e) the State has to direct its policy towards protecting the health and strength of workers, men and women and to see that the tender age children are not abused and that citizens are not forced by economic necessity to enter avocations unsuited to their age or strength. Taking this into consideration the Andhra Pradesh High Court in *M. Vijaya* v. *Chairman and M.D. Singareni Collieries Co. Ltd., Hyd. & Others*[73] directed the Government to provide anti-AIDS drug free of cost like in anti-TB and anti-leprosy programmes and family welfare programmes and also to conduct awareness programmes amongst the masses to take preventive measures against AIDS. Further, for the protection of the human rights of the AIDS/HIV patients, Article 47 which imposes duty upon the State to raise the level of nutrition and the standard of living of its people and the improvement of public health. This implies that the state is obligated to improve the public health and raise the standard of living of all people. Hence, with respect to the disease of AIDS, the state has to take appropriate means and to provide medical facilities to the patients who are suffering from HIV/AIDS. Apart from the Constitution of India, there are certain minor enactments which can be used to counter the violations of the AIDS/HIV patients as well as to counter the spread of the disease. They are:

(a) The carriage of passengers suffering from Infections/ Contagious Diseases Rules, 1990;
(b) The Drugs and Cosmetics [First Amendment) Rules, 1993; and
(c) The Delhi Artificial Insemination Human Act, 1995.

All these enactments provide certain rules to counter infectious and contagious diseases like that of AIDS/HIV in India, an abrogated

71. *Ibid.*
72. Pandey, J.N., Constitutional Law of India, 298, 1996.
73. (2001) 5 ALD 522.

attempt was made to pass the AIDS/HIV in India, an abrogated attempt was made to pass the AIDS Prevention Bill, 1989 that provided for the prevention and control of the spread of HIV/AIDS infection and to provide for specialized, medical treatment and such support and rehabilitation of persons suffering from HIV/AIDS and for matters connected therewith and incidental thereto.

The Andhra Pradesh High Court in *M. Vijaya* v. *Chairman and M.D. Singareni Collieries Co. Ltd., Hyd. & Others*[74] took serious note of the negligence of blood transfusion on the part of the authorities of the Singareni maternity and family welfare hospital, wherein due to negligence of the authorities the petitioner contracted the HIV/AIDS disease. The Hon'ble High Court laid down certain directions to the State Government and also to the hospitals in handling of the AIDS/HIV situation. Some of the suggestions and directions are as follows:

(a) Sufficient AIDS/HIV positive test kits/equipment to all hospitals and institutions should be provided. The Government blood banks as well as licensed blood banks should be compelled to buy proof HIV positive/aids test equipments.

(b) Bio-medical waste collected from hospitals and nursing homes should be properly destroyed or disposed of.

(c) There should be more awareness programmes undertaken by the Government in respect of AIDS/HIV.

(d) There should be proper schemes for rehabilitation of patients who are diagnosed as HIV positive as there is 'social ostracizing' is attached to HIV/AIDS infected person.

(e) There should be compensatory mechanism to deal with the AIDS in case of negligence on the part of the blood banks/hospitals by way of free facilities and free access to state funded health institutions.

(f) Indent of patients who came for treatment of HIV/AIDS should not be disclosed so that other patients will also come forward for taking treatment.

The Supreme Court of India in *Common Cause v. Union of India*[75] noticed and made comment on the system of blood transfusion and also showed anxiety as follows:

> "It is a mandatory requirement to conduct tests on blood which is to be administered to a patient or to be issued to hospitals for transfusion. The blood so issued has to be free from AIDS, viral hepatitis, malaria, veneral diseases, etc. It is reported; that

74. *Ibid.*
75. AIR 1996 SCW 333.

mandatory tests which are required to be done are rarely conducted. Most of the AIDS surveillance centres are not functioning efficiently and upto 85 percent of blood collected in the country is not screened for AIDS. Under an action plan to screen blood for AIDS 37 bloods testing centres were to be set-up in 29 cites, but only 11 testing centres were functioning by July, 1990, and training of technicians for these centres was lagging".

In *Vincest Parikulangara* v. *Union of India*,[76] the Supreme Court held that "duty of the state is to ensure the practices and polices to create conditions in which people can be healthy. State health care institutions are obliged to provide medical treatment to all persons in emergency and non-emergency situations. They can not discriminate on the basis of HIV status".

The Supreme Court of India held in *Mr. X* v. *Hospital Z*[77] wherein the appellant contended that right to privacy was infringed by the respondents by disclosing the appellant as HIV positive. They were, therefore, liable for damages. The Court observed that the right to privacy has been culled out of the provisions of Article 21 and other provisions of the Constitution relating to fundamental rights read with Directive Principles of State Policy. The Supreme Court, in several judgments, has made attempts to trace the origin of 'right to privacy' and a number of American decisions including *Munn* v. *Illinois*,[78] *Wolf* v. *Colorado*,[79] and various articles were considered and it was ultimately laid down as under:

> "Depending on the character and antecedents of the person subjected to surveillance as also the objects and the limitation under which surveillance is made, it cannot be said surveillance by domiciliary visits would always be unreasonable restriction upon the rights of privacy. Assuming that the fundamental rights explicitly guaranteed to the citizen have penumbral zones and that the right to privacy is itself a fundamental right, that fundamental right must be subject to restriction on the basis of compelling public interest."

The Court observed that as one of the human rights, the right to privacy is not treated as absolute, and is subject to such action as may be lawfully taken for the prevention of crime or disorder or protection of health, or morals, or protections of rights and freedoms of others. The

76. AIR 1987 SC 990.
77. (1998) 8 SCC 296.
78. (1877) 94 US 113.
79. (1949) 338 US 25.

right to privacy may arise out of a particular specific relationship, which may be commercial, matrimonial, or even political. As already discussed above, the doctor-patient relationship, though basically commercial, is professionally a matter of confidence and, therefore, doctors are morally and ethically bound to maintain confidentiality. In such a situation, public disclosure of even true private facts may amount to an invasion of the rights of privacy which may sometimes lead to the clash of one person's right to be alone with another's right to be informed. The Court held that disclosure of even true private facts, have the tendency to disturb a person, and ruled that the right to privacy is an essential component of the right to life envisaged by Article 21. The right, however, is not absolute and may be lawfully restricted for the prevention of crime, disorder, or protection of health, or morals, or protection of rights and freedoms of others. The Court further ruled that having regard to the fact that the appellant was found to be HIV positive, its disclosure would not be in violation of either the rule of confidentiality of the appellant's right to privacy as Ms. W with whom the appellant was likely to be married, was saved in time by such disclosure. She would have been infected with the dreadful disease, had the marriage taken place and been consummated.

III. LAW OF TORTS VERSUS HEALTH

The history of the development of tort[80] litigation with regard to health care cases, is of recent origin in India. It is derived from English Common law[81] of *ubi remedium ibi jus* (where there is a remedy there is a right) to *ubi jus ibi remedium* (where there is a right there is a remedy). Its transplantation in India by Courts, to exercise their power to administer law according to 'justice, equity and good conscience' indicate that torts are primarily those wrongs for which either statutory remedies are not available or, if available, are inadequate or inappropriate. But with changes in social, political and economic conditions, there are inevitable changes in the nature and extent of the protected interest.

80. John Salmond defined 'tort' as 'a civil wrong for which the remedy is an action for damages, and which is not exclusively the breach of a contract or breach of a trust or other merely equitable obligation'.

81. With the passage of time and to meet the emerging situations and demands the legislature in UK has resorted to enactment of legislations such as the Fatal Accidents Act, 1846, 1959, 1976; the Workmen's Compensation Act, 1897; Law Reform (Miscellaneous Provisions) Acts, 1934 and 1971; Law Reform (Contributory Negligence) Act, 1945; Crown Proceedings Act, 1947; Defamation Act, 1952; Law Reform (Husband and Wife) Act, 1962, etc.

Now the scope and dimension of the liability of the health professional for the acts of medical negligence is very wide and includes the government hospitals and dispensaries. Any person or his/her family members (including dependents) can file a case claiming damages in the Courts specified herein. As per the procedure generally followed a case in which the amount claimed is less than one lakh, will fall under the jurisdiction of Civil Judge or Munsif, whichever exists and if the value is more than one lakh but doesn't exceed five lakhs will fall under the jurisdiction of the District Judge. If the value exceeds five lakhs it may be filed in the High Court of the concerned State.[82] An appeal, may also be filed in the Supreme Court. Besides appealing, a petition can also be filed in the High Court or the Supreme Court for the violation of fundamental rights, especially the right to life guaranteed under the Constitution of India.[83] In order to protect the interest of weaker sections of the society, the Legal Services Authorities Act, 1987 was enacted to set-up the legal aid and advice boards in all the Courts in districts and to provide free legal aid and advice to the various categories of people.[84]

(i) Duties of a Doctor Towards the Patient

The Supreme Court, while clarifying the duties of a doctor towards the patient in *Laxman Balkrishna Joshi* v. *Dr. Trimbak Bapu Godbole*,[85] ruled that a person who holds himself ready to give medical advice and treatment undertakes that he is possessed of skill, and knowledge for the purpose. A doctor when consulted by a patient owes certain duties viz:

(a) a duty of care in deciding whether to undertake the case;
(b) a duty of care in deciding what treatment to give; or
(c) a duty of care in the administration of that treatment.

A breach of any of the aforesaid duties gives a right of action for negligence to the patient.

(ii) Liability of Doctors for Negligence

The Supreme Court, while clarifying the position as early as in 1906 in *Domingo M. Parreira* v. *Gabriel F. Gonsalves*,[86] held that: "It is a good defence in an action by a surgeon or an apothecary that he treated the patient ignorantly or improperly".

---

82. Section 12; The Legal Services Authorities Act, 1987.
83. *Ibid.*
84. Section 12, The Legal Services Authorities Act, 1987; various categories includes SC/ST, person with disabilities industrial workmen and other economically weaker sections.
85. AIR 1969 SC 128.
86. (1906) 8 Bom. LR 93.

Lord Kenyon added:

> "In a case where a demand is compounded of skill and things administered, if the skill, which is a principal part, is wanting, the action fails, because the defendant has received no benefit".

The Supreme Court in *A.S. Mittal* v. *State of Uttar Pradesh*,[87] ruled that the law recognizes the dangers, which are inherent in surgical operations. The Court added that mistakes may occur despite the exercise of reasonable, skill and care. Where the operation is a race against time, the Court will greater allowance for mistakes on the part of the surgeon or his assistants, taking into account the 'risk-benefit' test. However, a mistake by a medical practitioner which no reasonably competent and a careful practitioner would have committed is a negligent one.

The Privy Council in *John Oni Akerele* v. *The King*[88] ruled that the degree of negligence required to hold a doctor liable is that:

(i) it should be gross;
(ii) neither a jury nor a Court can transform negligence of a lesser degree into gross negligence merely by giving it that application; and
(iii) negligence to be imputed depends upon the probable, not the actual result.

The law requires that the practitioner must bring to his task a reasonable degree of skill and knowledge and must exercise a reasonable degree of care. Neither the very highest nor a very low degree of care and competence judged in the light of the particular circumstances of each case is what the law requires.[89]

In *Balbir Singh Makol* v. *Chairman, M/s. Sir Ganga Ram Hospital & Ors.*,[90] the National Commission dealt with the most contentious issue of liability of legal representatives of the doctor for the negligent acts of the doctor after his death. The Commission while dismissing the complaint, relied on the maxim (*actio personalis moritur-cum-persona*)[91] which as a general rule is applicable to actions in torts and, therefore, the cause of action against the party against whom an action in torts is brought is extinguished on his death. It held the legal

87. (1998) 3 SCC 223.
88. AIR 1943 PC 72.
89. See Halsbury's Laws of England, 3rd Edn., Vol. 26 at p.17. See also *Laxman* v. *Trimbak*, AIR 1969 SC 128.
90. (2001) 1 CPR 49.
91. Means a personal right of action dies with the person. In other words, death destroys the right of action.

representatives of the deceased doctor not liable to pay compensation. While arriving at the above conclusion the Commission relied upon the decision of the Supreme Court in *G. Jayaprakash* v. *State of Andhra Pradesh*,[92] where in it was held that the death of the doctor extinguished his liability for damages and the suit against him stood abated. The maxim, *actio personalis moritur-cum-persona* applied to the case.

The Courts and Consumer Forums have adopted an approach of extreme caution in determining medical malfeasance. In *Dr. N.I. Subrahmanyam* v. *Dr. Krishna Rao*,[93] the National Consumer Disputes Redressal Commission held the doctor guilty of negligence merely because in a matter of opinion made an error of judgment.

The Supreme Court in *Laxman* v. *Trimbak*,[94] ruled that the doctor has discretion in choosing treatment, which he proposes to give to the patient and such discretion is relatively greater in case of emergency. In *Dr. Ravindra Gupta & Ors.* v. *Ganga Devi & Ors*,[95] it was held that a mistaken diagnosis is not necessarily a negligent diagnosis.

The Supreme Court in *Ram Bihari Lal* v. *J.N. Shrivastava*[96] observed that it may not be questioned that the defendant possessed the necessary skill and knowledge to undertake the operation, but his over-confidence and hurry failed him. He paid no heed to the advice of his superior, that since the patient had stabilized herself, it was not an emergency case. He should have been catheterized. The defendant failed in his duty of care in undertaking the operation, and in doing the operation, without taking necessary precautions. His act of removing the gall-bladder was highly dangerous which resulted in the death of the patient. So the defendant was liable to pay damages for his wrongful acts.

Not only this, 'quacks'[97] are also liable for their wrong deeds. In *Poonam Verma* v. *Ashwin Patel*,[98] a person was registered as a medical practitioner for homoeopathic practice only. He treated Pramod Verma for a ailment 'prevalent' at that time without getting the pathological test conducted. The Maharashtra State Commission did not provide relief to the complainant, the wife of the deceased. The Supreme Court of India, while fixing the responsibility of doctors entering into other

92. AIR 1977 AP 20.
93. (1996) 11 CPJ 233.
94. AIR 1969 SC 128.
95. (1993) 3 CPR 255.
96. AIR 1985 MP 150.
97. 'Quack' is a person who does not have knowledge of a particular system of medicine but practices in that system and is a mere pretender to medical knowledge or skill or to put it differently a 'charlatan'. They are guilty of negligence. (see *Avtar Singh Bhatora* v. *Dr. Swaran Singh Prakash*) (2001) ICR 44.
98. (1996) 4 SCC 332.

streams of medicine observed that since the law, under which respondent 1 was registered as a medical practitioner, required him to practice in homoeopathy only, he was under a statutory duty not to enter the field of any other system of medicine as he was not qualified in the other system, and particularly allopathy. The Court added that he trespassed into a prohibited field and was liable to be prosecuted under Section 15 sub-section (3) of the Indian Medical Council Act, 1956. A person who does not have knowledge of a particular system of medicine but practices in that system is a quack and a mere pretender to medical knowledge or skill, or to put it differently, a charlatan. The Court in its various judgments held that the person having practiced allopathy without being qualified in that system was guilty of negligence and the appeal against him had to be allowed in consonance with the maxim *sic utere tuo ut alienum non laedas* (a person is held liable at law for the consequences of his negligence). For this it is the duty of Health Departments and District Magistrates to initiate the action against 'Quacks'. But they did not take any effective step to stop this menance. The Supreme Court of India in its landmark judgment in *D.K. Joshi* v. *State of Uttar Pradesh & Ors.*,[99] remarked that:

> "It is distressing to note that in spite of the directions of the State Government, the District Magistrates and the Chief Medical Officers did not take effective steps to stop this menace which is hazardous to human life."

Now the question arises what standard of care should be taken by the doctors? In the answer of this the Supreme Court in *Achutrao H. Khodwa* v. *State of Maharashtra*,[100] pointed out that the skill of medical practitioners varies from doctor to doctor. The very nature of the profession is such that there may be more than one course of treatment, which may be advisable for treating a patient. Courts would indeed be slow in attributing negligence on the part of a doctor if he has performed his duties to the best of his ability, and with regard to the course of action to be taken by a doctor treating a patient, but as long as doctor acts in a manner which is acceptable to the medical profession, and the court finds that he has attended on the patient with due care, skill and diligence, and if the patient still does not survive of suffers a permanent ailment, it would be difficult to hold the doctor guilty of negligence.

99. (2002) 5 SCC 80; See also *Avtar Singh Bhatora* v. *Dr. Swaran Prakash Garg* (2001), 1 CPR 44.
100. AIR 1996 SC 2383; also see *Ram Bihari Lal* v. *J.N. Shrivastava*, AIR 1985 MP 150; *Philips India Ltd.* v. *Kunju Punnu & Anr.*, AIR 1975, Bom. 306.

(iii) Liability of Hospitals and Nursing Homes

The Supreme Court in *Achutrao H. Khodwa* v. *State of Maharashtra*,[101] while overruling the judgment of the High Court, made it clear that the government cannot be held liable in tort for acts committed in a hospital that was not maintained, because the High Court considered that maintaining and running a hospital was an exercise of the state's sovereign function. Disapproving this line of thinking, the Supreme Court held that running a hospital is a welfare activity undertaken by the government, but is not an exclusive function or activity of the government so as to be classified as one which could be regarded as being in exercise of its sovereign power. The Court referred to its earlier decision in *Kasturilal's case*,[102] wherein it was noticed that in pursuit of the welfare ideal, the government may enter into many commercial and other activities which have no relation to the traditional concept of governmental activity in exercise of its sovereign function, similarly, the running of a hospital, where the members of the general public can come for treatment, cannot be regarded as being an activity having a sovereign character. Applying this principle, the Court held that the State would be vicariously liable for the damages which may become payable on account of negligence of its doctors or other employees.

Further, the Supreme Court in *Joseph alias Pappachan & Ors.* v. *Dr. George Moonjely & Anr.*,[103] ruled that regarding the vicarious liability of those who run hospitals for the negligent acts of the doctors employed by them, the question is no longer *res integra*. Persons who run a hospital are in law under the self-same duty as the humblest doctor. Whenever they accept a patient for treatment, they must use reasonable care and skill to cure him of his ailment. The hospital authorities can not, of course, do it by themselves; they have no ears to listen through the stethoscope, and no hands to hold the surgeon's scalpel. They must do it by the staff, they employ, and if their staff is negligent in giving the treatment, they are just as liable for that negligence as is anyone else who employs others to do his duties for him. Therefore, the first defendant being the owner of the hospital, is vicariously liable for the negligent conduct of the first defendant.

(iv) Role of Consent in Fixing Liability

It is also the duty of the medical authority to take consent of the patient, preferably in writing in all cases where a treatment consists of

101. AIR 1996 SC 2383.
102. AIR 1965 SC 1039.
103. AIR 1994 Ker. 289.

certain dangerous instruments.[104]

The Supreme Court in *T.T. Thomas* v. *Elisa*[105] ruled that:

(a) Failure to perform emergency operation and the death of the patient on account of such failure amounts to negligence on part of surgeon.

(b) The burden is on the surgeon to prove that the non-performance of the surgery or the non-administration of the treatment was on account of the refusal of the patient to give consent thereto. A surgeon, who fails to perform an emergency operation, must prove with satisfactory evidence that the patient to give consent thereto. A surgeon, who fails to perform an emergency operation, must prove with satisfactory evidence that the patient refused to undergo the operation, not only at the initial stage but even after he was informed of the dangerous consequences of not undergoing the operation. This is especially so in a case where the patient is not alive to give evidence.

(c) Consent is implicit in the case of a patient who submits to a doctor, and the absence of consent must be made out by the person alleging it.

IV. LAW OF CONTRACT VERSUS HEALTH

Unlike the Constitutional Law, Law of Crimes, Consumer Law and Law of Torts, the Law of Contract[106] is based on the principles of 'agreement[107] between the parties for consideration'. The scope and dimension of the liability of the health professional for the acts of breach of contractual obligation is very narrow when compared to other legal options. Any person or his/her family members including dependants can file a case claiming damages in the Courts.

The law of contract is based on the principles of agreement between the parties for consideration. A detailed review and examination of the provisions related to the relationship between doctor and the patient under the Indian Contract Act, 1872 reveals that inspite of its direct bearing on the services being provided by doctors and hospitals has very limited application to medical negligence.

104. *Arunachala Vadivel & Ors.* v. *Dr. N. Gopal Krishnan* (1992) 2 CPR 548.

105. AIR 1987 Ker. 52.

106. Contract: According to Section 2(h) of Indian Contract Act, 1872, An Agreement enforceable by law i.e., for the formation of a contract there must be (1) an agreement; and (2) the agreement should be enforceable by law.

107. Agreement: According to Section 2(e) of Indian Contract Act, 1872, every promise and every set of promises forming the consideration for each other.

Though the relation between the doctor and the patient clearly falls under the ambit of the Law of Contract, these provisions have been invoked in very rare circumstances. A bare reading of the provisions reveal that even an implied contract between a doctor and a patient fall under the ambit of the Act. But after the enactment of the Consumer Protection Act, the litigation has been diverted from the Civil Courts to the Consumer Fora.[108]

(i) Duties of a Doctor Towards the Patient

The Supreme Court, in *Joseph alias Pappachan & Ors.* v. *Dr. George Moonjely & Anr.*,[109] while dealing with the matter of death of a 24 years old woman due to the negligence and breach of legal duty under Section 73 of the Contract Act observed that the vicarious liability of those who run hospitals for the negligent acts of the doctors employed by them, the question is no longer *res integra*. It added that persons who run a hospital are by law under the self-same duty as the humblest doctor. Whenever they accept a patient for treatment, they must use reasonable care and skill to cure him of his ailment. The hospital authorities cannot, of course, do it by themselves; they have no ears to listen through the stethoscope and no hands to hold the surgeon's scalpel. They must do it by the staff, which they employ; and if their staff is negligent in giving the treatment, they are just as liable for that negligence as is anyone else who employs others to do his duties for him. While awarding damages to the tune of Rs. 1,60,000, the Court ruled that the doctor has legal duty to take all reasonable care. It further held that the first defendant is primarily liable for his negligent act, and the second defendant being the owner of the hospital is vicariously liable for the negligent conduct of the first defendant.

(ii) Liability of Doctors for Negligence

In *Indian Medical Association* v. *V.P. Shantha*,[110] the Supreme Court ruled that professional men should possess a certain minimum degree of competence and that they should exercise reasonable care in the discharge of their duties. In general, a professional man owes to his client a duty in tort as well as in contract to exercise reasonable care in giving advice or performing services. Certain professions on the grounds of public interest enjoyed immunity from suit. The trend now is the narrowing of such immunity. Medical practitioners do not enjoy any immunity, and can be sued in contract or tort on the ground that they

108. S.K. Verma, Legal Framework for Health Care in India, 154, 2002.
109. AIR 1994 Ker. 289.
110. (1995) 6 SCC 651.

have failed to exercise reasonable skill and care. Thus, medical practitioners, though belonging to the medical profession, are not immune from a claim for damages on the ground of negligence.

(iii) Liability of Hospitals

The Supreme Court in *Syed Abdul Khader* v. *Rami Reddy*,[111] ruled that the relation of agency arises whenever one person called the agent has authority to act on behalf of another called the principal and consents so to act. The relationship has its genesis in a contract.

V. LAW OF CRIMES VERSUS HEALTH

(i) Duties of a Doctor Towards a Patient

Before looking into the aspect of criminal liability of health providers it is necessary to see the liabilities of medical practitioners for negligence and the duties they owe to patients. In Halsbury's Law of England,[112] it is mentioned that a person who holds himself out as ready to give medical advice or treatment implies that he is possessed of skill and knowledge for the purpose. Medical practitioner owes certain duties towards patient namely, a duty of care in deciding whether to undertake the case; a duty of care in deciding whether to undertake the case; a duty of care in his administration of that treatment and; a duty of care in answering a question put to him by a patient in circumstances in which he knows that the patient, intends to rely on his answer. A breach of any of these duties will support an action for negligence by the patient. The practitioner must bring to his task a reasonable degree of skill and knowledge, and must exercise a reasonable degree of care. Neither the very highest nor a very low degree of care and competence judged in the light of the particular circumstances of each case, is what the law requires. A person is not liable in negligence because someone else of greater skill and knowledge would have prescribed a different treatment or operated in a different way, nor is he guilty of negligence if he has acted in accordance with practice accepted as proper by a responsible body of medical men skilled in that particular art, even though a body of adverse opinion also existed among the medical men. Deviation from normal practice is not necessary evidence of negligence. To establish liability on that basis it must be shown that: (a) there is a usual and normal practice; (b) the defendant has not adopted it; and (c) the course in fact adopted is one which no professional man of ordinary skill would have taken had he been acting with ordinary care. It is a defence to a

111. (1979) 2 SCC 601.

112. Halsbury's Laws of England, 4th Edn., Vol. 30 in paras 34 and 35.

practitioner that he acted on the specific instructions of a consultant who had taken over responsibility for the case. Failure to use due skill in diagnosis with the result that wrong treatment is given is negligence.[113]

(ii) Liability of Doctors for Negligence

The Supreme Court, in its landmark judgment *Pt. Paramanand Katara* v. *Union of India & Ors.*[114] ruled that Article 21 of Constitution casts an obligation on the State to preserve life. The patient whether he be an innocent person or a criminal. Every doctor whether at a government hospital or otherwise, has the professional obligation to extend his services with due expertise for protecting life. The obligation being total, absolute and paramount. Law of Procedure whether in statutes or otherwise, which would interfere with the discharge of this obligation cannot be sustained and must therefore give way. The matter is extremely urgent and brooks no delay to remind every doctor of his total obligation, and assure him of the position that he does not contravene the law of the land, by proceeding to treat the injured victim on his appearance before him, either himself or by others. The Court further ruled that all government hospitals, should be asked to provide immediate medical aid to all the cases irrespective of the fact whether they are medico-legal cases or otherwise.

Where a practitioner is utterly ignorant of the science of medicine or practice of surgery, then a favourable view of his conduct in giving any treatment prescribed in that science cannot be taken and his ignorance alone would make his act of giving treatment rash and negligent. The question is whether a *hakim* had any knowledge of penicillin treatment of the precautions to be taken before giving a penicillin injection and of the methods of counter-acting any adverse reaction of the injection. As a *hakim* he clearly has no occasion to make a study of penicillin injection or for the matter of that of any injection of the methods of counter-acting any adverse reaction of the injection given in allopathic treatment. It was further observed that their Lordships in another case did not accept the view that criminal negligence was proved merely because a number of persons were made gravely ill after receiving an injection of sobita from the appellant, coupled with a finding that a high degree of care was not exercised.[115]

A person is guilty of gross negligence when he gives medical treatment for which he is unqualified. It was observed in Dr. Khushal

113. *Laxman* v. *Trimbak*, AIR 1969 SC 128; *Ram Bihari Lal* v. *J.N. Shrivastava*, AIR 1985 MP 158.
114. AIR 1989 SC 2039.
115. *John Oni Akerele* v. *The King*, AIR 1943 PC 72.

Das's case:

> "Where a practitioner is utterly ignorant of the science of medicine or practice of surgery, then a favourable view of his conduct in giving any treatment prescribed in that science cannot be taken. His ignorance alone would make his act of giving treatment rash and negligent.[116]

In *Juggankhan* v. *State of MP*,[117] a registered Homeopath administered 24 drops of stramonium and a leaf of *dhatura* without studying their probable effect to the patient suffering from guinea worm. On these facts the Supreme Court observed that according to the evidence on record, in no system of medicine except perhaps in the ayurvedic system, the *dhatura* leaf is given as cure for guinea worms. It seems that appellant prescribed the medicine without thoroughly studying what the effect of giving 24 drops of stramonium and a leaf of *dhatura* would be. The Court added that it is a rash and negligent act to prescribe poisonous medicines without studying their probable effect. Section 299, IPC does not apply in the present case. It cannot be held that the appellant administered the stramonium drops and the *dhatura* leaf with the knowledge that he was likely to cause death by such an act. The Court further held that it is true, that care should be taken before imputing criminal negligence to a professional man acting in the course of his profession, but even taking this there is no doubt that the appellant was guilty of rash and negligent act. The Court also held that the two elements, of consent on the part of the patient, and of good faith on the part of the medical practitioner, are inter-dependent and nobody can claim the benefit of his exception without good faith. Thus, the appellant is not entitled to the exception given in Section 88. He was therefore, rightly convicted under Section 302 of IPC. The act was undoubtedly a very callous one because the treatment was repeated in spite of his recent experience in the case of Hiralal. However, the Session Judge awarded the lesser penalty, and there was nothing more to be said in that regard. In view of the above, the Court upheld the conviction and sentence and dismissed the appeal accordingly.

(iii) Liability of Quacks for Negligence

In *Ram Niwas* v. *State of Uttar Pradesh*,[118] a person (not a qualified doctor carried on the profession of a doctor) administered a full dose of an injection without giving the test dose and the subsequent reaction,

116. AIR 1960 MP 50.
117. AIR 1965 SC 831.
118. (1968) Cri. LJ 635 (All.).

resulted in death. The Allahabad High Court observed that the evidence shows that the accused did not give any test dose to the deceased before administering the full dose of the injection. He did not claim that the injection was such that in all probability it could not have caused the allergic reaction and so the giving of a test does of the injection was not necessary. The accused denied the very giving of injection which was proved beyond a shadow of doubt by the prosecution case. The Court further ruled that accused not being a qualified doctor, an injection given without the test dose and the immediate and subsequent death of the person so injected shows not only that the death was the direct consequence of administering the injection, but also that he acted with rashness, recklessness, negligence and indifference to the consequences. It amounted to taking a hazard of such degree, that the injury was likely to be occasioned thereby. So it was amply established that the accused, caused the death of the deceased by doing the said rash and negligent act, which did not amount to culpable homicide. The accused was convicted by the trial court under Section 304A, IPC to undergo a sentence of one year's rigorous imprisonment (RI). The High Court observed that the appellant had been on bail and there being no allegation of any misuse of bail by him, the Court gave him the benefit of probation under Section 4 of the UP (Uttar Pradesh) First Offenders Probation Act, 1938 on furnishing an amount of Rs. 4,000 with two securities in the like amount.

In *Sukaroo Kobiraj* v. *The Empress*[119] herein a Kobiraj with no regular education in medicine, operated upon a patient by cutting out his internal piles, but did not stop the consequent bleeding, which resulted in death of the patient. The Court observed that the prisoner was uneducated in matters of surgery, and had no regular education in matters of medicine. He acted, as he thought, for the benefit of the patient. But the prisoner is not entitled to the benefit of Section 88 (Indian Penal Code).[120] A patient can hardly be said to accept a risk of which he is not aware. It was for the defence pleading the exception, to show that the patient in the present case did accept the risk, and that consequently he was aware of it. But no attempt was made to show that the patient did know the risk he was undertaking. The evidence is only to the extent that he consented to the operation with great unwillingness, and that the only information communicated to him on the subject by

119. (1877) ILR 14 Cal. 566.
120. Section 88 of Indian Penal Code, 1860 says that nothing which is not intended to cause death, is an offence by reason of any harm which it may cause, or be intended by the doer to cause, or be known by the doer to be likely to cause, to any person for whose benefit it is done in good faith and who has given a consent, whether express or implied, to suffer that harm, or to take the risk of that harm.

the prisoner was that if he submitted to the operation he would be cured. Upon that understanding, did he submit and consequently died. It seems, therefore, quite impossible to say that he accepted the risk of the prisoner's act. The Court ruled that he caused the death of the deceased by his act. In England, he would have been indicted for manslaughter. In this country, the provisions of Section 304A seem to apply to cases where there is no intention to cause death, and no knowledge that the act done in all probability would cause death. The Court ruled that it was impossible to acquit him of the offence of which he has been convicted, so the conviction was confirmed. But it is not necessary for the ends of justice to sustain the severe sentence passed upon the prisoner. The Court further held that the sentence of one years imprisonment would, therefore, be set aside, and a fine of a Rs. 100 imposed upon the prisoner. In default of payment, he must suffer three months' rigorous imprisonment.

In another case of *Dr. Khusaldas Pammandas* v. *State of Madhya Pradesh*,[121] a *hakim* registered under the Madhya Bharat Indian Medicine Act, 1952, advised and administered a procaine penicillin injection to the patient without the knowledge or study of penicillin treatment, resulting in the death of the patient. The Court while dealing with the issue held that it matters not whether he was a registered or unregistered *hakim* registered under the Madhya Bharat Indian Medicine Act, 1952, advised and administered a procaine penicillin injection to the patient without the knowledge or study of penicillin treatment, resulting in the death of the patient. The Court while dealing with the issue held that it matters not whether he was a registered or unregistered *hakim*. The question is whether he had any knowledge of penicillin treatment, the precautions to be taken before giving such an injection and the remedies that should be applied for combating any adverse reaction to the injection. It is the petitioner's ignorance of the knowledge that makes his act rash and negligent. The Court, while confirming the conviction of the petitioner, observed that no doubt *hakims* and *vaidyas* are legitimately entitled to exercise their profession for which they have been trained. But at the same time it is necessary that they should not dabble in medicines and treatments of which they have no knowledge whatsoever. It is very essential that the public, and especially the poorer part of the public, who very often rely upon such practitioners as *hakims* and *vaidyas*, should be protected from ignorant experiments of dangerous character.

121. AIR 1960 MP 50.

(iv) Role of Consent in Fixing Liability

In Criminal Law, consent and *actus reus (mens rea)* play an important role in deciding the cases of criminal liability of a person. The real question often raised in the criminal liability of health professionals is why should a doctor insist on a consent from his patient for the course of treatment to be adopted by him? Consent from the patient is for the protection of the physician or the surgeon.[122] Every surgery, whether minor or major is fraught with some degree of hazard of risk, which varies in accordance with the seriousness of the disease. If a patient collapses during the course of a surgery or during the course of a treatment, law gives protection to the medical man, provided, he establishes that the risky step was adopted with the consent, express or implied from the patient. In fact, the consent factor is important only in selective operations because in emergency operations, where a doctor cannot wait for the consent of his patient have to perform the operation without consent. In this context, it would be relevant to refer to a passage from 'Law and Medical Ethics'.[123]

As a general rule, medical treatment, even of a minor nature, should not proceed unless the doctor has first obtained the patient's consent. This consent may be expressed or it may be implied, as it is when the patient presents himself to the doctor for examination and acquiesces in the suggested routine. The principle of requiring consent applies in the overwhelming majority of cases, but therefore certain circumstances in which a doctor may be implied, as it is when the patient presents himself to the doctor for examination and acquiesces in the suggested routine. The principle of requiring consent applies in the overwhelming majority of cases, but there are certain circumstances in which a doctor may be entitled to proceed without this consent—firstly, when the patient's balance of mind is disturbed; secondly, when the patient is incapable of giving consent by reason of unconsciousness; and, finally, when the patient is a minor.

Very often poor and illiterate patients and sometimes even the educated members of the society are adverse to surgery, but most of them would agree to it when they are told about the grave consequences otherwise. When a surgeon or a medical man advances a plea that the patient did not give his consent for the surgery or for the course of treatment advised by him, the burden is on him to prove that the non-

122. Section 88 of Indian Penal Code, 1860 says that nothing, which is not intended to cause death, is an offence by reason of any harm which it may cause, or be intended by the doer to cause, or be known by the doer to be likely to cause, to any person for whose benefit it is done in good faith, and who has given a consent, whether express or implied, to suffer that harm, or to take the risk of that harm.

123. Mason and M.C. Call Smith, 1983 edn., p.113.

performance of the surgery or the non-administration of the treatment was on account of the refusal of the patient to give consent thereto. This is especially so in a case where the patient is not alive to give evidence. Consent is implicit in the case of a patient who submits to the doctor, and the absence of consent must be made out by the person alleging it.—In most instances, the consent of a patient is implied.[124]

A surgeon who failed to perform an emergency operation must prove with satisfactory evidence, that the patient refused to undergo the operation, not only at the initial stage, but even after he was informed of the dangerous consequences of not undergoing the operation.[125]

Nathan, in his book on 'Medical Negligence' has stated that,[126] "The intentional interference with person of another without legal justification amounts to an actionable assault and battery for which damages may be recoverable by the injured person. Such damages will of course include compensation for actual injuries suffered as the result of the assault. In addition, a judge or jury is at liberty, to award the plaintiff exemplary damages in respect of an assault or battery as a means of punishing the defendant for reprehensible conduct in invading the plaintiff's personal rights without justification. Bodily interference which would otherwise amount to an assault and battery may, however, be justified by showing that the patient voluntarily submitted to the conduct in question. No action lies, therefore, against a medical man who interferes with the person of a patient if the patient's consent to the interference has been obtained. But for a medical man to administer treatment to or perform an operation upon a patient without the latter's consent amounts, subject to some exceptions which will be noticed in due course, to an actionable assault."

Glanville Williams in his text book on Criminal Law,[127] while examining the relevance and scope of consent stated as under:

> "Although English authority is lacking the operation is clearly lawful. This was stated by an eminent member of the United States Supreme Court, Cardozo, J. every human being of adult years and sound mind has a right to determine what shall be done with his own body.... This is true except in the case of an emergency where the patient is unconscious and where it is necessary to operate before consent can be obtained."

It appears that there is a kind of hybrid between the defences of

124. S. Swaminathan, Mayre's Criminal Law of India, 198, (4th Edn.).
125. *T.T. Thomas* v. *Elisa*, AIR 1987 Ker. 54.
126. Nathan, *Medical Negligence*, 156 (1957).
127. Glanville Williams, *Criminal Law*, 568, (78th Edn.).

necessity and consent. It is not an ordinary case of consent, because, consent is not in fact given; so from that point of view, the justification must be one of necessity. On the other hand, the justification could clearly not be avoided of if the surgeon ascertained, before the patient fell unconscious, that the patient withheld his consent. So, it is not a case where social necessity overrides a refusal of consent. American writers have called the defence, with more punch than accuracy, 'future consent'. The Surgeon is entitled in the circumstances to suppose that what he does will be ratified by a grateful patient, having nothing to cause him to suppose the contrary, and he will be protected in law even though the patient turns out to be ungrateful. His defence must be grounded on necessity. The only distinctive feature is that the defence is curtailed when it conflicts with the patient's express exercise of his right of self-determination.

Sometimes, in the course of an operation, a surgeon sees a need for some other operation. He is generally protected in performing this by the consent from signed by the patient, which authorizes such further or alternative operative measures as may be found to be necessary. But sometimes, a consent form has not been offered to the patient, as when a maternity patient is under anesthesia and it is discovered that delivery by caesarean section is necessary. In such circumstances, the Medical Defence Union encourages its members to do what is required, the justification being either implied consent or necessity. The surgeon would of course be ill-advised to perform an expected operation having serious consequences if there is no great urgency for it.[128]

VI. SUM UP

The Judiciary, in its activist role, has played an effective part in extending protection to various human rights. Courts have widened the scope of Article 21 greatly to include a number of rights. The courts have time and again reiterated that the health is an integral part of the right to life under Article 21. They have also, at times, called upon the State to give effect to the provisions of the Directive Principles, which are not as such, enforceable.[129]

Our Constitution contains no provision conferring right to wholesome right to health within ambit of fundamental right. But the attempt of the Court should be to expand the reach and ambit of the fundamental right. But the attempt of the Court should be to expand the

128. *Ram Bihari Lal* v. *J.N. Shrivastava*, AIR 1985 MP 165.
129. Mallika Ramachandran, *The Right to Health and the Indian Constitution*, 1 *DLR* (S) (2004).

reach and ambit of the fundamental rights rather than to attenuate their meanings and content by process of judicial Constitution,[130] Principle of Interpretation requires that constitutional provision must be construed, not in narrow and constricted sense, but in a wide and liberal manner so as to anticipate and take account of changing conditions and purposes so that the Constitutional provision does not get atrophied or fossilized but remain flexible to meet with newly challenges.[131]

Moreover, most legislation in India makes no distinction between health and female in the area of health.[132] Thus, in order to ensure adequate protection to all aspects of the health of persons, it is necessary to provide health care facilities as well as ensure the maintenance of conditions essential for good health. However, it has to be noted that provision of these facilities alone would not be sufficient to ensure protection of the health of persons. What has to be ensured is that all people can access these facilities equally, without discrimination of any kind.

130. *Ganesh Chandra Bhat* v. *Distt. Magistrate, Almora*, AIR 1993, All. 291, 298.
131. Rakesh Kumar, Environment Protection *vis-à-vis*, Right to Health: Judicial Approach, *Chetnanagar Law Journal*, Vol. 1, No. 1, 2008-09.
132. K.P.S. Mahalwar, Indian Constitution and Weaker Sections, 109, (2007).

CHAPTER 7

Right to Health as a Right to Life: A Case Study

I. INTRODUCTION

The right to health is a fundamental right of every human being and not merely the absence of disease or infirmity. It is a fundamental right of every human being irrespective of area, regions, state, country or continent.[1]

Articles 55 and 56 of United Nations Charter and also Article 25 of Universal Declaration of Human Rights provide that everyone has the right to standard of living adequate for the health and well-being of himself and of his/her family including food, clothing, housing, medical care, etc. Article 1(2) of International Covenant on Civil and Political Rights provides that people shall not be deprived of means of subsistence.[2]

Delivery of proper health care to people is a basic task before the nation. The situation in respect of many diseases affecting the health of the people has been deteriorating. India had accepted the responsibility of ensuring "Health for all by 2000" A.D. But this could not achieved at the current rate of expansion of health services. Besides health delivery system in rural areas are inadequate and defective. The burden on health programmes has become more enormous with environmental degradation and its impact on the physical life of the people.[3] So this

1. International Conference on Global Health Law, 1997 (Dec.), p. 1.
2. *Ibid.*
3. Ninth Five Year Plan (1997-2002) and Annual Plan (1997-98) by Planning Department, Govt. of Himachal Pradesh, Shimla–171002, p. 315.

chapter opens with a brief summary of health planning in Himachal Pradesh, and analyses of various issues, such as trends in outlays and expenditure during the different five year plans, availability of infrastructure facilities and other health services in Himachal Pradesh, morbidity and treatment pattern, health-seeking behaviour and utilization pattern of available health care facilities and services including cost of treatment and a vision of the State of health of the people of Himachal Pradesh and work out some operational strategies to achieve the same.

At the time of the formation of Himachal Pradesh on 15th April 1948, medical and health care facilities were virtually primitive. Since the First Five Year Plan, the government of Himachal Pradesh has been making continuing efforts to provide medical care of a reasonable standard. During the initial years of planning, it attempted to provide access to health care services to the people by increasing the number of health care institutions and diagnostic facilities. The programme to control venereal diseases, implementation of the national programmes, providing quality education, and training programmes were assigned top priority. Later, measures were taken to strengthen rural health care and reduce the existing regional disparities in this area.[4] The previous three plans had laid emphasis on strengthening the existing infrastructure, dental health care, food and drug laboratory, audit planning and legal cell besides implementation of different national health programmes. The Tenth Plan, for the first time, aims at improving the quality of the health services.[5]

II. PROMOTION OF HEALTH SERVICES IN HIMACHAL PRADESH

In recent years, the state government has focused more on the development of the Indian System of Medicines and Homeopathy (ISM&H), particularly Ayurveda, involving members of the Panchayati Raj Institutions (PRIs), and ensuring greater community participation through hospital welfare societies, etc. However, providing tertiary health care services in the form of super specialized hospitals, both in the public and private sectors, establishing a strong Health Management Information System (HMIS), proper referral linkages, management of lifestyle diseases, and involvement of the voluntary sector in different

4. Himachal Pradesh Development Report; Planning Commission, Government of India, New Delhi, p. 157.
5. *Ibid.*

health programmes are some areas which are still lagging behind in the state.[6]

It is well known that Himachal Pradesh, like most other States, has made significant progress in decreasing the Crude Death Rate (CDR), Infant Mortality Rate (IMR), and in raising the living standard and expectancy of life at birth. Moreover, successful attempts are also made to control different communicable and non-communicable diseases, such as diphtheria, poliomyelitis, tetanus (both neonatal and others) whooping cough measles, leprosy, malaria, goitre, blindness, etc. Although the State has made remarkable achievements in controlling the spread of veneral diseases through family health awareness campaigns, tuberculosis remains the major killer in the State.[7]

In Himachal Pradesh, health services (Preventive, Promotive and Curative) are provided through the Department of Health and Family Welfare and the Department of Indian System of Medicines and Homeopathy (ISM&H). Since primary health care is the first and the nearest contact between the individual and the health care services, the State has made sufficient provisions for primary health care services through a network of Sub-Centres (SC), Primary Health Centres (PHCs) and Community Health Centres. Further, tertiary level health care has been catered for through specialized hospitals and those attached to the State Medical Colleges and manpower development for the health services of the State.

In recent years, the State has been attaching greater importance to Ayurvedic Institutions and Indian System of Medicines and Homeopathy (ISM&H). The number of Health Institutions as on 31.03.2003 are shown in Table 1.

The Table 1 shows that the State also has a number of specialized institutions for treating tuberculosis, leprosy, and sexually Transmitted Diseases (STDs). Besides these, there are adequate facilities of dental clinics, X-ray clinics, ENT clinics, and Maternal and Child Welfare (MCW) centres.[8] Further, the State receives World Bank Assistance to the Reproductive and Child Health (RCH) sub-project in Kinnaur district, UNICEF (United Nations International Children Emergency Fund) assistance for Kangra and Chamba districts and World Bank assistance for Prevention of Gastrointestinal diseases and AIDS (Acquired Immuno Deficiency Virus). The rural population covered is 2,738 per sub-centre, 12,832 per PHC and 85,745 per CHC against the

6. *Ibid.*
7. Himachal Pradesh Development Report; Planning Commission, Government of India, New Delhi, (2002), p.158.
8. ENT.

stipulated norms of 3,000 per sub-centre, 20,000 per primary health care and 80,000 per community health centre in the hilly and tribal areas.[9] For the tribal areas, comprising Kinnaur, Lahaul and Spiti, Pangi and Bharmour, there are three Hospitals, nine Community Health Centres (CHCs), 36 Primary Health Centres (PHCs), 100 Sub-centres, 84 Ayurvedic Dispensaries and two State Special Hospitals. There are 422 allopathic and 58 ayurvedic beds in the region.[10]

Table 1: Number of Health Institutions as on (31.3.2003)

S.No.	*Type of Hospital*	*Rural*	*Urban*	*Total*	*Remarks/Observations*
1.	General Hospitals (GHs)	17	33	50	No GH in rural areas in Bilaspur and Kullu district
2	Community Health Centres (CHCs)	56	10	-66	No primary health care facilities to be set-up in urban areas. The Institutions shown in urban were earlier in rural areas
3.	Primary Health Centres (PHCs)	437	4	441	
4.	Civil Dispensaries (CDs)	3	18	21	Available in rural areas of Solan, Sirmaur & Kangra district. No urban CD in Chamba, Hamirpur, Kullu, Mandi and Una districts. Maximum 8 Urban CDs in Shimla district.
5.	Sub-centres	2067	-	2067	
Tuberculosis Institutions					
1.	Hospitals	2	0	2	One in Kangra and another in Solan
2.	District TB Clinics/Centres	2	10	12	
3.	TB Sub-clinics	4	3	7	Two each in rural areas of Chamba & Kinnaur. All three urban sub-clinics in Shimla
Leprosy Institutions					
1.	Hospitals/ wards	4	2	6	Chamba, Kangra, Kullu and Solan in rural areas. Mandi and Sirmaur in urban areas.
2.	District nucleus	2	10	12	One at each district
3.	State Survey Assessment Units (SSAU)	-	1	1	At Shimla.

9. *Ibid.*, also see Department of Health and Family Welfare, Government of Himachal Pradesh, Health at a Glance (2002), Pamphlet.
10. *Ibid.*

S.No.	*Type of Hospital*	*Rural*	*Urban*	*Total*	*Remarks/Observations*
4.	Leprosy Training Centres	2	4	6	Rural areas of Solan and Kangra districts, urban areas of Shimla, Sirmaur, Kullu and Chamba districts.
STD Institutions					
1.	Clinics/Sub-clinics	11	15	26	No STD clinic in rural areas of Bilaspur, Hamirpur, Kangra, Kullu and Una districts.
2.	Units	34	11	45	No STD unit in rural areas of Hamirpur, Kangra and Una districts. No STD unit in urban areas of Chamba, Hamirpur, Kangra, Solan and Una districts.
Indian System of Medicines and Homeopathy (ISM&H)					
1.	Ayurvedic College	1	0	1	Kangra district
2.	Ayurvedic hospitals	10	13	23	No rural ayurvedic hospital in Mandi, Shimla, Sirmaur and Solan districts. No urban ayurvedic hospital in Kullu.
3.	X-ray clinics	38	44	115	None in rural areas
4.	Eye-ENT clinics	0	11	11	None in rural areas of Hamirpur, Kullu and Una districts.
5.	Maternal and Child Welfare (M&CW) centres	19	27	46	None in urban areas of Hamirpur district.

Source: Information provided by the Department of Health and Family Welfare and Department of ISM&H, Government of Himachal Pradesh.

Note: There is no urban area in Kinnaur and Lahaul and Spiti districts. All SHGs were converted into PHCs in the year 1986-87.

As on 31 March 2003, the total number of beds available under the modern system of medicine were 8,872. Of these, 5,558 beds were in general hospitals, 1,202 in Community Health Centres (CHCs) and 990 in Primary Health Centres (PHC), and 35 beds were reserved for cancer, 751 for tuberculosis, 232 for leprosy, four for sexually transmitted diseases.[11] A separate department of Indian System of Medicines and Homeopathy (ISM&H) was also created on 7th of November, 1984. There has been a tremendous increase in the number of institutions and the amount of budget for Indian systems of medicines and homeopathy since then. In addition, there are 22 district level/sub-divisional ayurvedic hospitals. The department also started a Nature Cure Unit at Oel in Una district. It intends to upgrade the existing Nature Cure

11. *Ibid.*

Hospital to 10-50 bedded hospital besides establishing college of Naturopathy and Yoga to provide five and half year degree in Naturopathy and Yoga.[12]

To conserve and enlarge the valuable herbal wealth of the State and to provide a sustainable supply of raw material to the pharmaceutical industry, the State has launched a programme for promotion and conservation of the herbal wealth by setting up herbal gardens in the different agro-climatic zones.

Herbal gardens have already been established in Jogindernagar (district Mandi), Neri (district Hamirpur). Dhumrehra (Rohru district Shimla) and Jungal-Jhalera (district Bilaspur). In addition, proposals are to set-up herbal gardens at Rakcham/Chitkul (district Kinnaur) and Paprola (district Kangra). Besides a Herbarium has been established at Jogindernagar to keep the specimens of medicinal plants systematically and scientifically, separate counters are maintained for root drugs, bark drugs, flower drugs, fruit/seed drugs, leaf drugs and whole plant drugs, etc. During the year 2002-03, the department also organized 33 farmers training camps and three department exhibitions in different districts to create awareness among the farmers/participants with respect to identification, conservation, propogation, cultivation and utilization of the medicinal flora existing in the State of Himachal Pradesh. A total of 960 farmers were trained/participated. Tenth Plan (2002-07) proposed to strengthen the health care facilities of the ayurvedic system by strengthening the infrastructure and introducing specialized services like *Panchkarama* and *Kshar Sutra*. The Plan also laid stress on the conservation, development, cultivation and utilization of medicinal plants to improve the quality of raw herbs, material for herbal medicines, and to develop Himachal Pradesh into a herbal State of India. It also recognized the need for modern facilities for drug testing, research, and development of drugs. It contemplated the introduction of modern technology and management techniques to improve the quality and competitiveness of medicines produced in government and private pharmacies of State. The plan also proposed to expand the Ayurveda tourism activities in close collaboration with public and private sector hostel industry/health institutions in all parts of the State. Two such centres (one in Joginder Nagar and another at Kullu) has already been started.[13]

Regarding the homeopathic systems of medicines, the State opened 12 Homeopathic Dispensaries (one at each district headquarters) in 1995-96. During the Tenth Five Year Plan, provisions were made for

12. *Ibid.*
13. *Ibid.*, 160.

opening 10 more Homeopathic Centres (two each year). There are only three Unani Dispensaries in the State functioning since very long. No Unani institution was opened after bifurcation of the Department since the Department feels absence of public demand for this system of medicine from other parts of the State.[14]

Himachal Health vision 2020 lists some problems related to the infrastructure. Some of these are uneven distribution of primary health care facilities (400 panchayats are still without primary health care facilities, whereas a number of them have two primary health care institutions including ayurvedic health centres) and uneven distribution of health manpower (better staffing in comfortable areas than those in rural and remote areas). Further, the lack of well-defined service norms and standards (absence of hospital manual), poor referral system resulting in underutilization of health services and overburdening of the secondary and tertiary health care centres to make a negative contribution. Buildings are poorly maintained and there is absence of residential accommodation, Information, Education and Communication (IEC) and Health Management Information System (HMIS) are lacking in many respects and are still at a rudimentary stage.[15]

Himachal Pradesh is the only State in this region to have started a community financial management programme. It has set-up hospital welfare societies at zonal/district hospitals to collect user charges and utilize these for fulfilling the needs of these hospitals. Earlier these societies were known as *Rogi Kalyan Samitis* (Patient Welfare Committees). These Committees were autonomous in nature and were capable of improving the hospitals by collecting finances from the community and levying user charges. By 2001-02, these were set-up in all the 12 zonal/district hospitals and 21 sub-divisional hospitals. Since, these Committees were fixing user charges for domestic and other services differently in different parts of the State, there was resentment among the population. As a result, the State government recently changed the name of these Committees to Hospital Welfare Societies and rationalized the user charges. Now uniform user charges (as prevailing before 1998) would be applicable throughout the State in all hospitals for diagnostic and other services.[16]

Himachal Pradesh has also set-up Health and Family Welfare Advisory Committees known as *Parivar Kalyan Salahkar Samiti*

---

14. *Ibid.*
15. *Ibid.*, also see Department of Health and Family Welfare, Himachal Pradesh, Himachal Health Vision, 2002, pp. 21-23.
16. *Id.*, p. 162.

(PARIKAS) at the Panchayat, Block and District level[17] for the involvement of the PRIs (Panchayati Raj Institutions). The functions of the Panchayat *Parivar Kalyan Salahkar Samiti* (PARIKAS) include supervision and monitoring; implementation of national health programmes; ensuring cleanliness of the villages; checking pollution of water, air and noise; making people aware of dog and snake bites and their first aid treatment, cleaning and using bleaching powder, etc. for traditional water sources; disseminating information about Reproductive and Child Health (RCH) Care checking regular opening of sub-centres and ensuring that immunization and other necessary facilities are being provided to the new born by the health functionaries, helping in updating the records of births deaths and marriages, and preparing health plans every year.

The Directorate of Health and Family Welfare, Government of Himachal Pradesh, entrusted a special study to the Department of Community, Medicine, Post-graduate Institute of Medical Education and Research (PGIMER), Chandigarh, to assess the burden of diseases in Himachal Pradesh. The findings of the draft estimation report are shown in Table 2. It shows the top ten causes of the burden of diseases (DALYs) in Himachal Pradesh classified by age and sex. According to it, the disease pattern with age and sex in Himachal Pradesh. Lower respiratory infections and diarrhareal diseases are the most frequent causes of the disease burden among children aged 0-4 years irrespective of sex. While iron-deficiency anemia is the most frequent among the children in the age group of 5-14, diarrhareal diseases, asthma and other unintentional injuries are also widely prevalent in this age group. Whereas road accidents and other unintentional injuries are most common among males in the age group of 15-44, it is iron-deficiency anemia and other maternal conditions that account for most of the burden of diseases among females in this age group. From the age 45 and above, chronic obstructive pulmonary disease constitute the largest burden of disease among both sexes. Further, tuberculosis, ischemic heart disease, other unintentional injuries and asthma are widely prevalent among the males aged 45 and above, while other maternal conditions, asthma, iron-deficiency anemia and ischemic heart diseases are prevalent among the females of the same age group.[18]

17. *Ibid.*, also see vide Notification No. HFW-B(F)7-2/2001 dated 10.12.2001 of Department of Medical Education, Department of Health and Family Welfare, Government of Himachal Pradesh and orders of Commissioner-*cum*-Secretary (Health) to the Government of Himachal Pradesh.
18. *Id.*, at 165.

Table 2: Top 10 Causes of Burden of Diseases (DALYs) in Himachal Pradesh Classified by Age and Sex

Rank	Males					Females				
	0-4	*5-14*	*15-44*	*45-59*	*60+*	*0-4*	*5-14*	*15-44*	*45-59*	*60+*
1	Lower respiratory infections	Iron-deficiency anemia	Road accidents	Chronic obstructive Pulmonary disease	Chronic obstructive Pulmonary disease	Lower respiratory infections	Iron-deficiency anaemia	Iron-deficiency anaemia	Chronic Obstructive Pulmonary disease	Chronic obstructive Pulmonary disease
2	Diarrhoreal diseases	Asthma	Other uninten-tional injuries	Tuberculosis	Ischaemic heart disease	Diarrhoreal diseases	Diarrhoreal diseases	Other maternal conditions	Other maternal conditions	Asthma
3	Other maternal conditions	Other uninten-tional injuries	Iron-deficiency Anaemia	Other uninten-tional injuries	Asthma	Other infectious diseases	Other uninten-tional injuries	Other uninten-tional injuries	Iron-deficency anaemia	Ischaemic heart disease
4	Perinatal conditions	Diarrhoeal diseases	Chronic obstructive pulmonary disease	Ischaemic heart disease	Tuber-culosis	Other maternal conditions	Otitis Media	Maternal haemorr-hage	Other uninten-tional injuries	Other infectious diseases
5	Other	Otitis media infectious diseases	Self-inflicted injury	Iron deficiency anemia	Other uninten-tional injuries	Perinatal conditions	Asthma	Chronic obstructive pulmonary disease	Tuber-culosis	Tuber-culosis
6	Road accidents	Dental caries	Ischaemic heart disease	Asthma	Other infectious diseases	Birth asphyxia and birth trauma	Dental Caries	Asthma	Dental Caries	Cataracts

(Contd.)

Table 2 (Contd.)

Rank	*Males*					*Females*				
	0-4	*5-14*	*15-44*	*45-59*	*60+*	*0-4*	*5-14*	*15-44*	*45-59*	*60+*
7	Iron deficiency anaemia	Lower respiratory infections	Asthma	Dental caries	Iron-deficency anaemia	Iron deficiency anaemia	Lower respiratory infections	Road accidents	Ischaemic heart diseases	Iron-deficiency anaemia
8	Birth asphyxia and birth trauma	Upper respiratory infections	Upper respiratory infections	Road accidents	Diarrhoeal diseases	Measles	Upper respiratory infections	Dental caries	Other cardiac diseases	Diarrhoeal diseases
9	Dental caries	Other infectious diseases	Dental caries	Pepti-culcer	Cataracts	Falls	Falls	Upper respiratory infections	Diarrhoeal diseases	Other uninten-tional injuries
10	Falls	Falls	Diarrhoreal diseases	Cataracts	Dental caries	Low birth weight	Other infectious diseases	Abortion	Other infectious diseases	Dental caries

Source: Department of Community Medicine, Post-Graduate Institute of Medical Education and Research, (2003), Himachal Burden of Disease Study Draft Estimation Report, 2003.

Table 3 gives us picture of the role of the public and the private sectors in providing contraceptives, preventive and curative services in Himachal Pradesh, as pointed out by NFHS-I. The table shows that the public sector plays a crucial role in all spheres of health including preventive, contraceptive, immunization, and curative services in the State. The public sector caters more to the rural population than to the urban. The table shows that 98 per cent of all children received vaccination from the public sector. Ninety-four per cent of the contraceptive users in rural areas and 68 per cent in urban areas obtain contraceptives from the public medical sector. The survey has revealed that the share of the private health sector in immunization has a direct relationship with urbanization, mother's education (at least high school), and households with a high standard of living.

Table 3: Share of Public and Private Sector in Contraceptive, Preventive, Curative Services

Type of Service	*Share of Public Sector*			*Share of Private Sector including shops*		
	Rural	*Urban*	*Total*	*Rural*	*Urban*	*Total*
All Modern Contraception	94.2	68.4	91.7	4.8	29.3	7.1
Male Sterilization	100.0	(100.0)	100.0	0.0	0.0	0.0
Female Sterilization	99.2	97.8	99.1	0.7	1.8	0.8
IUD	(85.3)	56.0	77.2	14.7	44.0	22.8
Oral Pills	(59.3)	*	(53.1)	(37.0)	*	(42.6)
Condoms	36.1	14.8	29.2	48.2	78.3	57.9
Childhood Vaccination	98.3	94.9	98.0	1.0	4.6	1.3
Percent share in institutional delivery	20.6	55.6	23.2	4.8	16.4	5.7
Usual source of health care	58.6	60.5	58.8	41.3	39.5	41.1

Source: National Family Health, Survey (NFHS)-II, Himachal Pradesh, India, 1998-99.
Note: The totals will not add up to 100 due to the presence of other categories such as missing and source unknown.

( ) based on 25-49 unweighted cases.

* Percentage not shown: based on fewer than 25 unweighted cases

As for the curative services, the table shows that 59 per cent of the households in Himachal Pradesh normally visit the public medical sector. In fact, the utilization of public health services is much higher in Himachal Pradesh than in the country as a whole (29%). Overall, three types of health providers are generally the households. Thirty percent of the household prefer treatment from private doctors, 55 per cent from the government (Municipal Hospital, Government Dispensary),

Community Health Centres (CHC), Primary Health Centres (PHC) and 10 percent from private hospitals. Moreover, the pattern of service utilization is almost similar in rural and urban areas. As for institutional deliveries, more people visit public health institutions than private nursing homes (23.2% as against 5.7% of the total deliveries).[19]

Thus, Health-seeking behaviour or utilization of health care services is influenced largely by access to health facilities, individual and family beliefs and attitudes related to illness and the system of medicine, cost of treatment and individual capacity to pay.

Table 4: Administrative Set-up of Himachal Pradesh and India, 2001

Items	*HP*	*India*
No. of Districts	12	609
No. of Blocks	75	5428
No. of Towns	57	5161
No. of Tehsils/Sub-tehsils	109	5470
No. of Villages	20118	638588
No. of Inhabited Villages	17495	587226
No. of Un-inhabited Villages	2623	51352
No. of Gram Panchayats	3243	227905
No. of ICDS Projects	76	4348
No. of Anganwaris	18248	500000

Source: Health and Family Welfare Department, Himachal Pradesh: Health at a Glance, 2006 (Director of Health Services, Himachal Pradesh).

Table 4 shows the administrative structure of Himachal Pradesh as well as of India. Since 1st September, 1972, there have been no changes in the administrative structure of Himachal Pradesh except carving out of new sub-divisions, sub-tehsils, raising of sub-tehsils to the level of tehsils within the district boundaries. Presently, there are 12 districts, 52 sub-divisions, 109 tehsils and sub-tehsils in Himachal Pradesh. From development point of view, the Himachal Pradesh is divided into 75 development blocks, the smallest unit for development-*cum*-administration is panchayat and their number is 3243. The State has a three-tier Panchayati Raj structure comprising of 12 Zila Parishads, 75 panchayat samitis and 3243 Gram Panchayats on the rural side; and 1 Municipal Corporation, 20 Municipal Councils and 28 Nagar Panchayats on the urban side besides Cantonment Boards.

According to Table 5 the total population of Himachal Pradesh is 60,77,900, which gives density of population as 109. There are wide variations in area and population of the districts. Out of the total

19. *Id.*, at 168.

population the number of males and females is 30,87,940 and 29,89,960 respectively, which means that the number of females per 1000 males is 968. The total percentage of rural population is 90.20 per cent of the total population residing in 17,495 inhabited villages, Himachal Pradesh has the highest percentage of rural population among all the States of the country. The scheduled castes population in the State is 15,02,170 persons which is 24.72 per cent of the total population as per 2001 census. About 60 per cent of the State's tribal population falls under the tribal sub-plan area. According to 2001 census, the overall literacy percentage of Himachal Pradesh was 76.5 per cent (85.30% for males and 67.40% for females). Comparatively, it is much higher than the All-India literacy rate which is 65.38 per cent. The literacy rate in Himachal Pradesh has been improving faster than the all India figures. Himachal Pradesh characterized by a very strong correlation between sex ratio (females per thousand males) and literacy. The districts with higher density of female population *vis-à-vis* male have high literacy rates.

Table 5: Domestic Indicators of HP and India, 2001

Items	*HP*	*India*
Area (Sq.Kms.)	55673	3287263
Population (2001 Census) Total	6070900	1028737436
Males	3087940	532223090
Females	2989960	496514346
Rural	5482319	742617747
Urban	595581	286119689
%age of Rural Population	90.20	72.19
SC Population	1502170	166635700
ST Population	244587	84326240
Sex Ratio	968	933
Decennial Growth Rate (%)	+17.54	+21.34
Density (Per Sq.Km)	109	325
Literacy Rate (%)	76.5	64.9
Per Capita Income (2004-05)	Rs. 27486/-	Rs. 23,222/-

Source: Health and Family Welfare Department, Himachal Pradesh: Health at a Glance, 2006 (Director of Health Services, Himachal Pradesh).

Table 6 shows the district-wise demographic profile of Himachal Pradesh of 2001 census. According to Surveyor General of India, the total area of Himachal Pradesh is 55,673 square kilometers. Area-wise Hamirpur is the smallest district of the Pradesh which covers an area of 1,118 sq. kilometers (2.01%) and Lahaul & Spiti has the largest area of

13,835 sq. kilometers (24.85%). The total population of Himachal Pradesh, according to 2001 census was 60,77,900 which gives a density of population of 109 persons. There are wide variations in area and population of 109 persons. There are wide variations in area and population of the districts and the district-wise density varies from 2 persons per sq. kilometer in Lahaul and Spiti to 369 persons in Hamirpur district. Out of the total population the number of females per 1000 males is 968. The overall literacy percentage of Himachal Pradesh was 76.5 percent (85.30% for males and 67.40% for females). Comparatively, it is much higher than the all-India literacy rates which is 65.38 percent. Himachal Pradesh is characterized correlation between sex ratio and literacy. Districts with higher density of female population *vis-à-vis* male population have high literacy rate.

Table 6: District-wise Demographic Scenario (Census 2001)

Districts	*Area Sq.km.*	*Pop. 2001 Census*	*Dec. Growth Rate*	*Sex-Ratio*	*Lit. Rate %*	*Sex Ratio at Birth 2004*	*Mid-Year Est. Pop. 2006*
Bilaspur	1167	340885	+15.40	990	77.8	850	369123
Chamba	6528	460887	+17.19	959	62.9	864	503143
Hamirpur	1118	412700	+11.80	1099	82.5	814	439268
Kangra	5739	1339030	+14.05	1025	80.1	835	1439268
Kinnaur	6401	78334	+09.91	857	75.2	948	82475
Kallu	5503	381571	+26.17	927	72.9	918	435174
L. & Spiti	13835	33224	+06.17	802	73.1	934	34317
Mandi	3950	901344	+16.10	1013	75.2	894	978871
Shimla	5131	722502	+17.02	896	79.1	920	790143
Sirmaur	2825	458593	+20.78	901	70.4	886	509460
Solan	1936	500557	+30.94	852	76.6	903	594207
Una	1540	448273	+18.51	997	80.4	876	492543
HP	55673	6077900	+17.54	968	76.5	872	6668292

Source: Health and Family Welfare Department, Himachal Pradesh: Health at a Glance 2006 (Director of Health Services, Himachal Pradesh).

Table 7 shows that as on 31st March, 2006 the Himachal Pradesh is divided into 75 development blocks, 3243 gram panchayats, 17,495 villages, 50 hospitals and 8824 beds in hospitals which are now increased in number.

The growth of Health Institutions in Himachal Pradesh from 1971 onwards is depicted in Table 8.

Table 7: Number of CD Blocks, GP, Villages & Number of Medical Institutions (as on 31.3.2006)

Districts	*Blocks*	*GPs*	*Villages*	*Hosps.*	*CHCs*	*PHCs*	*CDs*	*SCs*	*Bed(s)*
Bilaspur	3	151	965	2	5	27	2	117	385
Chamba	7	283	1118	4	7	40	0	169	611
Hamirpur	6	229	1635	2	5	24	0	152	434
Kangra	14	760	3619	8	13	78	2	434	1462
Kinnaur	3	65	234	2	3	17	0	33	226
Kallu	5	204	172	2	5	17	0	100	392
L. & Spiti	2	41	287	1	3	14	0	35	136
Mandi	10	473	2833	6	9	59	0	311	1110
Shimla	9	363	2520	11	6	77	9	261	2174
Sirmaur	6	228	966	5	3	34	3	148	604
Solan	5	211	2388	5	3	32	5	178	921
Una	5	235	758	2	4	20	1	131	369
HP	75	3243	17495	50	66	439	22	2069	8824

Source: Health and Family Welfare Department, Himachal Pradesh: Health at a Glance, 2006 (Director of Health Services, Himachal Pradesh).

Table 8: Health Institutions in Himachal Pradesh as on 31st March of Each Year

Sr.No.	Items	1971	1980	1985	1990	1995	1997	2002	2003	2004	2005	2006	2007	2008	2009
1	2	3	4	5	6	7	8	9	10	11	12	13	14	15	16
1.	Allopathic Hospitals*	39	58	73	73	72	74	89	89	89	89	89	92	93	93
2.	Ayurvedic Hospitals	Included in Sr. No. 1 above						23	24	25	25	25	25	25	27
3.	PHC/CHC/RH/ SHCs^	72	77	145	225$	275	310	369	507	504	505	505	514	522	522
4.	Allopathic Dispensares#	119	186	214	197	165	167	155	21	22	22	22	22	41	41
5.	Ayurvedic Colleges	-	1	1	1	1	1	1	1	1	1	1	1	1	1
6.	Ayurvedic Dispensaies***	363	404	431	458	611	981	1133	1139	1139	1139	1126	1126	1126	1126
7.	HSCs	256	856	1299	1851	1907	1980	2068	2067	2067	2068	2069	2071	2071	2071
8.	Dental College	0	0	0	0	1	1	1	1	1	1	1	1	1	1
9.	Nursing	0	0	0	3	4	4	6	6	6	6	6	6	6	6
	Total	849	1582	2163	2808	3036	3618	3845	3856	3854	3856	3844	3858	3886	3888

Note: PHC = Primary Health Centre, CHC = Community Health Centre, RH = Rural Hospital, SHC = Subsidiary Health Centre & HSC = Health Sub-Centre.

* Including Government, State Special, Cantonment Board, Private Ayurvedic Hospitals (upto 1997).

$ Subsidiary Health Centres were converted into PHCs during the year 1986-87.

^ Rural Hospitals were converted into Community Health Centres during the years 1993-94 to 1997-98.

*** Includes Unani, Amchi, Nature Care Unit and Homeopathic Dispensaries.

Allopathic Dispensaries functioning in Rural areas were classified as Primary Health Centres during the year 2002-03 and these also included Dispensaries of Cantonment Board, Universities, Police, Railways, GOI and Private, etc.

Table 8 shows the growth of medical institutions in the State has resulted in better medical care to the people. This is also reflected in considerably lowering down in crude birth and death rates and significant improvement in the infant mortality rate. The comparative data on vital statistics for Himachal Pradesh and All-India is as under:

Table 9 shows that health indicators of Himachal Pradesh are better than the national average. The birth rate of the State is 17.7 per 1000 against 22.8 of the country; crude death rate is 7.4 against 7.5 at national level and infant mortality rate is 44 against the national figure of 53. Total fertility rate of the State is 1.9 against all India figure of 2.7. So in birth and death registration the coverage of Himachal Pradesh is one of the best performing states with nearly 100 per cent registration of birth.

The birth rate and death rate of H.P. is depicted in the Table 10.

Table 9: Comparative Data on Vital Statistics

Sr.No.	*Parameter*	*All India*	*Himachal Pradesh*
1	*2*	*3*	*4*
1.	Birth/Thousand (SRS 2008)	22.8	17.7
2.	Death/Thousand (SRS 2008)	7.4	7.4
3.	Infant Mortality/Thousand (SRS 2008)	53	44
4.	Couple Protection Rate:		
5.	(i) As on 31.3.2000	46.2	51.57
6.	(ii) As on 31.3.2009	NA	43.59
7.	Life Expectancy at Birth (2002-06)		
8.	Male	62.6	66.5
9.	Female	64.2	67.3

Source: Draft Annual Plan 2009-10: Planning Department, Government of Himachal Pradesh.

Table 10 shows the population of the State registered a decadal growth of 17.7 percent and death rate of 7.4 with difference of 10.3 percent as against 21.34 percent at All India level during the decade 1991-2008. This has been possible through a three-pronged strategy of intensive health cover, improvement in literacy rates, specially among the women and making family planning a people's movement alongwith a positive thrust of incentives.

Table 11 shows that Infant Mortality Rate (IMR) has fallen from 118 in 1971 to 62 in 1999 which is almost half. Some sources also provide sex-wise data on the IMR for a relatively recent period which brings out a welcome trend of the IMR having fallen from 54 in 2001 to 44 in 2008. It is, however, difficult to say how far the sample registration system, the source of this data has brought out these trends reliably.

Table 10: Data on Birth Rate and Death Rate in H.P. (SRS Rates)

(Per thousand)

Year	*Birth Rate*	*Death Rate*	*Differential*
1	2	*3*	*4*
1971	37.3	15.6	21.7
1981	31.5	11.1	20.4
1991	28.5	8.9	19.6
1999	23.8	7.3	16.5
2000	22.1	7.2	14.9
2001	21.2	7.1	14.1
2002	20.7	7.5	13.2
2003	20.6	7.1	13.5
2004	19.2	6.8	12.4
2005	20.0	6.9	13.1
2006	18.8	6.8	12.0
2007	17.4	7.1	10.3
2008	17.7	7.4	10.3

Source: Draft Annual Plan 2008-09: Planning Department, Government of Himachal Pradesh.

Table 11: Comparative Data on Infant Mortality Rate

(Per thousand)

Year	*Persons*	*%age Decadal Variation*
1	2	*3*
1971	118	129
1981	71	110
1991	75	80
1999	62	70
2000	60	68
2001	54	66
2002	52	63
2003	49	60
2004	51	58
2005	49	58
2006	50	57
2007	47	55
2008	44	53

Source: Draft Annual Plan, 2008-09: Planning Department, Government of Himachal Pradesh.

The decadal variation in the population since 1901 has been reported as under:

Table 12: Decadal Variation in Population

Year	*Persons*	*%age Decadal Variation*
1	2	*3*
1901	19,20,294	-
1911	18,96,944	(-) 1.22
1921	19,28,206	(+) 1.65
1931	20,29,113	(+) 5.23
1941	22,63,245	(+) 11.54
1951	23,85,981	(+) 5.42
1961	28,12,463	(+) 17.87
1971	34,60,434	(+) 23.04
1981	42,80,818	(+) 23.71
1991	51,70,877	(+) 20.79
2001	60,77,900	(+) 17.54

Source: Draft Annual Plan 2009-10: Planning Department, Government of Himachal Pradesh.

Table 12 shows that life expectancy data since 1981 is available for overlapping periods. These estimates do not seem to be very reliable and credible since different sources provide contradictory figures even for the same period. According to these estimates, life expectancy at birth rose quite sharply between the 1970s and the 1980s, but there was hardly a change during the period between 1981 and 1991.

As would reveal from Table 13, Himachal Pradesh has created motorable road infrastructure measuring length of 25,968 km. by the end of 31st March, 2006. As per National policy, all villages in hill areas are to be connected with all weather motorable roads but considering topography and location of isolated village upon high slopes of hill ranges, it may be not feasible to provide motorable roads to connect all villages. In accordance with an assessment made some time back only 12,347 villages excluding isolated villages fall in the range of connectivity. Hence, motorable road length to connect all these villages works out to about 30,500 kms. Thus, Himachal Pradesh has almost achieved 81.71 percent of its ultimate goal. In so far as the connectivity to feasible villages 12,347 excluding isolated villages is concerned, the state has achieved 66.06 percent of the targets.

Table 13: Position of Rural Infrastructure at the End of 31st March, 2006

Sr.No.	*Item*	*Unit*	*Position as on 31.3.2006*
1	2	*3*	*4*
1.	Road Length (Motorable)	Kms.	25968
2.	Village connected with Roads	Nos.	8344
3.	Bridges	Nos.	1416
4.	Primary Schools	Nos.	10652
5.	Middle Schools	Nos.	2186
6.	High Schools	Nos.	953
7.	Senior Secondary Schools	Nos.	708
8.	Veterinary Hospitals	Nos.	303
9.	Veterinary Dispensaries	Nos.	1796
10.	PHC/CHC/RH/SHCs	Nos.	505
11.	Health Sub-centres	Nos.	2069
12	Civil Dispensaries	Nos.	22
13.	Ayurvedic Dispensaries	Nos.	1122
14.	CCA Created	Lakh Hect.	2.07

Source: Draft Eleventh Five Year Plan (2007-12), Planning Department, Government of Himachal Pradesh, Shimla-171002.

To universalize the primary education, the state government embarked upon an expansion programme to identify unserved areas so that primary schools could be opened in order to provide access to all eligible children in the age group of 6-11 years. As a result of these efforts larger number of primary schools were opened all over the state which aggregated to 10,652 as on 31.3.2006 as against 808 opened by the end of First Five Year Plan (1951-56).

In order to universalize the coverage of eligible children in the age group of 11-14 years, significant expansion of middle school infrastructure was the need of the hour. Keeping in view the topographical situation of the state, Himachal Pradesh would require about 3500 middle schools, against which 2186 schools stood opened by 31st March, 2006.

With a view to provide basic health facilities to the rural masses, large number of PHCs/CHCs/RH/SHCs, civil dispensaries have been opened. Category-wise number of these institutions as existed on 31st March, 2006 has been given in the table mentioned above.

(i) Review of Tenth Plan (2002-07)

The Tenth Plan (2002-07) envisaged an indicative target of 8.9 per cent average GDP growth for the State. The economy of Himachal Pradesh posted an impressive average annual growth rate of 6.4 per cent per annum during the Ninth Five-Year Plan and was poised to achieve this target. The growth performance for the Ninth Plan showed some recession at the national level as the rate of economic growth came down to 5.6 per cent per annum. On an average the State economy grew by 6.4 per cent per annum despite the fact that devastating floods occurred during 2000-01 and farm output reduced especially on the horticultural front. Even then pace of growth witnessed a significant upward trend with that of National Economy.

The size of the State's Tenth Five Year Plan, 2002-07 was originally approved at Rs. 10,300 crore and was agreed to be financed by total Central Support of Rs. 5440 crore. The share of center's plan was anticipated to be 52.8 per cent.

The size of the State's Tenth Five Year Plan, 2002-07 was originally approved Rs. 10,300 crore and was agreed to be financed by total Central Support of Rs. 5440 crore. The share of center's plan was anticipated to be 52.8 per cent.

(A) Objectives

(i) Hydel capacity addition of 6100 MW by 2010.

(ii) The state's free power share was aimed at 800 MW by 2010 thereby envisaging generation of annual revenue of about Rs. 700-800 crore.

(iii) To enhance the productivity in the agriculture/ horticulture and quality of crops by way of low productive varieties of crops with high yielding varieties.

(iv) Vegetable production target of 10 lakh tones by 2007.

(v) Diversification towards high valued crops and projectisation approach for the same.

(vi) Emphasis on increasing of area under irrigation by tapping all smaller sources of water including rain water harvesting structures through people's participation.

(vii) Upgradation of air, rail and road access and improvement of power, water, communication and other basic facilities.

(viii) Universal rural connectivity to open up the economy.

(ix) Providing drinking water to all the PC/NC habitations.

(x) Attracting large-scale private investment in IT&BT sectors, besides a quantum jump in the industrial investment at large in pursuance of the new package of incentives announced by the

Government of India.

(xi) To increase private sector participation in tourism both as means of generating employment and building sound infrastructure.

(i) Consolidate the gains made in the social sectors.

(B) Physical Targets and Achievements

The physical performance of some selected items for the overall Tenth Plan period is given in the Table 14.

Table 14: Physical Performance of Selected Items

Sl. No.	*Item*	*Unit*	*Tenth Five Year Plan (2002-07)*		
			Target	*Annual Antici-pated Achievement*	*Perfor-mance Percent-age*
1	*2*	*3*	*4*	*5*	*6*
1.	Foodgrain Production	000 M.T.	1875.00	1668.85	89
2.	Vegetable Production	000 M.T.	1000.00	1000.00	100
3.	Fertilizer Consumption	'000' Tonnes	46.00	46.00	100
4.	Fruit Production	000 M.T.	657.67	695.52	106
5.	Mushroom Production	M.T.	15000.00	4986.00	33
6.	Hops Production	M.T.	200.00	42.60	21
7.	Olive Fruit Production	Qtls.	200.00	NA	0
8.	Honey Production	M.T.	1000.00	1605.00	160
9.	Milk Production	000 M.T.	840.00	870.00	104
10.	Wool Production	Lakh Kgs.	16.50	16.50	100
11.	Fish Production	Tonnes	15000	8100	54
12.	Afforestation	Hectares	11595	6934	60
13.	IRDP Family Assisted (i) SGSY	Disburse-ment of credit (Rs. in lakhs)	10000.00	9960.31	100
14.	Additional CCA Created	Hect.	10000	8287	83
15.	Road Length Added	Kms.	3750	2714	72
16.	Installed capacity added	M.W.	645.833	471.830	73
17.	Power Generated	M.U.	8695.000	7224.420	83
18.	Opening of Ayurvedic Dispensaries	Nos.	125	22	18
19.	RWS (left out habitation covered)	Nos.	8000	10196	127
20.	Construction of Housing Units	Nos.	10000	8216	82
21.	Hand pumps installed	Nos.	5000	1779	36

Source: Draft Eleventh Five Year Plan, 2007-12 and Annual Plan (2007-08), Planning Department, HP.

From the perusal of the above table, it is observed that targets set for the production of vegetable, fruit, honey, milk and wool will be achieved comfortably by the end of Tenth Five Year Plan. For the shortfall in other key areas, reasons in brief are explained in the succeeding paragraph.

The year 2002-03, agriculturally, remained a lean year and the production of foodgrains was recorded as 11.11 lakh MTs as against 15.99 lakh MTs during 2001-02. During 2003-04 and 2004-05 the production was 13.98 lakh MTs and 16.36 lakh MTs respectively. It is expected that the likely achievement will be around 16.69 MTs against the target of 18.75 lakh MTs of food grains production by the end of the Tenth Plan.

Against additional irrigation potential of 10,000 hectares, under major, medium and minor projects/schemes during the Tenth Plan, the achievable potential will be around 82.87 hectares.

(C) Implementation of Special Programmes

(a) Pradhan Mantri Gramodya Yojana (PMGY)

During 2000-01, Government of India had initiated a new programme viz. PMGY (Pradhan Mantri Gramodya Yojana). This new programme was replaced the ongoing Basic Minimum Services (BMS). The programme envisaged earmarked provisions for five components of the BMS (excluding PDS). As the major focus remained on Human Development which has shifted the basic approach of Development Planning from mere material attainment in general, and growth of per capita income in particular to Planning for development of human well-being. The results can be evidenced in indicators of health, longevity, literacy, environmental sustainability, etc. The financing of the programme titled PMGY trough ACA was discontinued w.e.f. 1.4.05 but the ongoing activities will continue as such.

Further to meet the inadequacies in rural and urban infrastructure both in social and economic terms, special infrastructure development and employment generation programmes like Bharat Nirman Yojana, National Rural Health Mission, National Rural Employment Guarantee Act and Sarv Shiksha Abhiyan were launched by the Central Government during the Tenth Plan period. The focus is to build a strong base for the development of productive sector basic facilities such as health, education, clean drinking water and sanitation, to the large pockets of population will not only benefit those who live below the poverty line and remained deprived of such amenities so far, but act as catalyst for accelerating the growth process. A brief account of these programmes is given as under:

(b) Bharat Nirman

Bharat Nirman will be a time bound plan for the five years (2005-09) for the development of basic rural infrastructure-wise status of the implementation of Bharat Nirman Yojana is as under:

Road Connectivity: All the habitations in the state with a population more than 500 will be connected with all weather roads by the end of year 2009. The funding is available from the GOI under PMGSY (Pradhan Mantri Gram Sadak Yojana)/ Bharat Nirman/World Bank funded rural roads. The GOI has sanctioned rural roads worth Rs. 425 crore during 2005-06 under Bharat Nirman. During 2006-07 rural roads with an estimated cost of Rs. 164.81 crore have been sanctioned under PMGSY and roads with a financial implication of Rs. 103.46 crore are lying pending with the NRRDA for sanction under PMGSY. An amount of Rs. 88.00 lakh has been released under the World Bank aided rural roads projects during 2006-07.

Irrigation: Himachal Pradesh envisaged bringing about 90,000 hectares of land under irrigation by 2009 with the funds made available under Bharat Nirman with the following details:

Project/Scheme	*Area to be covered (Hectares)*	*Estimated cost (Rs. Crore)*
Major/Medium Irrigation Projects	22,161	369.37
Minor Irrigation Projects	57,722	214.40
Underground WD Schemes	8,307	99.86

The above proposal has been submitted to the Government of India vide letter dated 3/3/2006 for approval and sanction is awaited.

Rural Water Supply: The Government of Himachal Pradesh has envisaged the target of covering 6000 PC habitations under Bharat Nirman by 2007 but the Government of India has indicated that the funds flow is possible with the objective of meeting the target by 2009 only. An expenditure of Rs. 23.65 has been incurred up to 30/9/2006.

Housing: The Ministry of Rural Development run Indira Awas Yojana has been included in Bharat Nirman to provide houses to the houseless rural poor. During the year 2006-07 an amount of Rs. 839.94 crore will be spend for construction of 3054 rural houses.

Rural Electrification: Rajeev Gandhi Grameen Vidyutikaran Scheme has been included under Bharat Nirman. The target of universal electrification in a period of four years has been fixed. Plans for all the twelve districts of Himachal Pradesh with an estimated cost of Rs. 459.60 crore have been submitted to the M/S REC. So far one scheme for Chamba district has been approved.

Rural Telephone Connectivity: This is not a scheme under the State Plan but has been included in the Bharat Nirman. Such villages, which do not have Public Telephone Booths in Himachal Pradesh, are proposed to be provided this facility under Bharat Nirman. As per the provisions of an agreement with the BSNL, 1002 such villages are to be provided this facility by November, 2007. As on 30.06.2006, VPTs have been provided in 630 villages. Out of the remaining, 372 villages, 27 VPTs have been provided up to September, 2006 and the rest will be provided by 9.11.2007.

(D) National Urban Renewal Mission (NURM)

Shimla is one of the 63 cities elected for developing basic infrastructure in urban areas of India under the Jawahar Lal Nehru National Urban Renewal Mission launched in December, 2005. The funding for developing infrastructure in Shimla will be contributed in the ratio of 80:10:10 by the Government of India, Government of Himachal Pradesh and Municipal Corporation, Shimla. There is a budgetary provision of Rs. 349.00 lakh during 2006-07 for implementation of various works under the City Development Plan for Shimla under NURM.

The Himachal Pradesh Housing and Urban Development Authority (HIMUDA) has been designated as the nodal agency for implementation of the CDP for Shimla. The State Level Steering Committee approved the City Development Plan (CDP) for Shimla as prepared by the IL & FS Infrastructure Corporation on 14th November, 2006. Other formalities are being completed to ensure early start of implementation of the CDP.

The Municipal Corporation, Shimla has already started the process of introducing reforms. The reform components under e-governance and double entry accounting have already been initiated.

(E) Mahatma Gandhi National Rural Employment Guarantee Act (MNREGA)

Became operational in Chamba and Sirmaur districts of Himachal Pradesh w.e.f. 2nd February, 2006. The Act ensures the livelihood security of the household in the rural areas by guaranteeing 100 days of assured employment in every financial year to every household whose adult members volunteer to do unskilled manual work. If the applicant doesn't get employment within 15 days of applying, he/she is entitled to get unemployment allowance @25 percent of the daily wage for the first 30 days and @50 percent of the daily wage on the subsequent days. The scheme is shared between the Government of India and the Government of Himachal Pradesh on the 90:10 sharing basis. However, expenditure on the unemployment allowance is to be met by the State Government.

(ii) An Approach to 11th Plan (2007-12)

Himachal Pradesh entered the planning era with a weak economic and institutional base. Due to severe topographical and climatically constraints, it required a different approach for its economic development. Since the time of independence, the State has made tremendous progress on the socio-economic fronts. At the time of its formation in 1948, there were just 288 kilometre motorable roads. In 1950-51, surface road length of 8.5 Kilometre per lakh population was the lowest in India. The per-capita consumption of electricity in 1948 was 0.99 kwh against the national average of 17.8 kwh. There were only 261 Primary schools and literacy percentage was just 7, according to 1951 census, against the national average of 16.6 percent.

During the last 56 years of development planning, Himachal Pradesh has witnessed an era of tremendous development. Today, it is regarded the model for developing economies of Hill States.

In terms of economic growth, the State Economy grew at an annual rate of 1.6 percent during the First Five Year Plan as against the national average of 3.6 per cent. In the Third Five Year Plan, the growth rate was 3.0 which was slightly higher than the national level.

In the post-1971 period upto the Sixth Plan (1980-85), the State economy grew at a slower pace than the national average. In the Sixth Plan, the rate of growth was almost half the national average. During the Seventh Plan, the State Economy achieved all time high growth rate of 8.8 per cent which was 2.8 per cent higher than the national level. During the Ninth Plan, the State's economy grew at an annual rate of 6.4 percent as against 5.4 percent at the national level.

During the Tenth Five-Year Plan, the growth rate further accelerated. During the year 2004-05, growth rate of 7.5 percent was recorded in Himachal Pradesh. This is attributed to the progressive policies of the State Government on economic and social fronts. By the end of 10th Plan, an average growth rate of around 8 per cent is expected to be achieved.

The National Development Council, in its meeting held on 9th December, 2006 unanimously resolved to adopt the vision of 'Faster' and 'More Inclusive Growth' spelt out in the Approach Paper to the 11th Five Year Plan. At the national level, the 11th Plan will aim at putting the economy on a sustainable growth trajectory with a growth rate of approximately 10 percent by the end of 11th Plan period. The Planning Commission has set a 9.5 percent average annual growth rate target for Himachal Pradesh to be achieved by the end of the 11th Plan. The State will endeavour to achieve double digit growth rate by the end of the plan period.

The major plan objectives would include the provision of essential public services, increasing farm incomes, developing better infrastructure, nurturing human capital, protecting the environment and improving governance. The focus would remain on reduction of poverty, enhancing equity among various sections of the society and a balanced regional development.

The other important areas which need to be addressed include:

(i) Accelerate the pace to harness the huge hydro-power potential in the State.

(ii) To reverse deceleration in agriculture growth and improve the productivity in Agriculture and Horticulture.

(iii) Capitalize natural advantages in tourism, bio-diversity, medicinal and aromatic herbs, organic cultivation, etc. for diversifying the economy and raising income of the masses.

(iv) Accelerate the process of industrialization especially for employment generation.

(v) Consolidation and qualitative improvement of social services.

(vi) Improving the quality of infrastructure especially in the areas of Transport, Power, Rural, Water Supply and Sanitation.

(vii) Opening up the economy for private sector investment in a manner that sub-serves the interests of the locals.

(viii) Creation of productive employment at a faster pace.

Thus, it is analyzed that the State Government is committed to provide basic health care facilities to the people of the State. So health is a priority area for spending by the State Government. Despite various constraints, the State Government has endeavoured to increase the allocation for health sector from time to time.

National Rural Health Mission focuses on decentralized implementation of the activities and funneling of funds, it sets the stage for district management of health and active community participation in the implementation of health programmes. The programme also focuses on convergence with IPH, Rural Development, Panchayati Raj, Ayurveda and Social Justice and Empowerment Departments.

The medical check-ups of the school children is a very important to timely check the diseases in the children but this programme has been suffering for want of adequate funds. The department requires funds under this programme for printing of health cards and logistic arrangements for the visit of medical teams and training of teachers.

(A) Strategy for 11th Five Year Plan

- Provision of health care services both in public and private sector.
- More scientific and technology advanced health care system.
- Adequate monitoring and supervision of health institutions.
- To effectively achieve the national goals and objectives.
- To work on a state health policy with a proper time schedule for different activities.
- To clearly spell out the future health care requirement.
- Adequate research through primary survey.
- Higher level of efficient functioning.
- Special emphasis on preventive measures.
- Strengthening the existing public health services and widening their network.
- To develop appropriate strategy to regulate the private sector.
- Viable health insurance policy.
- To open more trauma wards.
- Introduction of telemedicines for appropriate consultations for the treatment of illness.
- To assess the health needs of the State.
- Proper computerized health management information system at different levels.
- Development of skilled manpower in health sector.

(B) Issues to be addressed during the Eleventh Five Year Plan

(a) Efforts to Improve the Sex Ratio

The sex ratio in the State is reported to be 968 females per thousand males in the year 2001. But, the child sex ratio which was 951 in 1991 has declined to 896 in 2001. It was a matter of great concern and the State initiated measures to stop this decline which has improved to 901 during 2003-05 period. The State has already formulated an incentive strategy for the improvement in sex ratio under PNDT Act, the details of which are given as under:

- To mobilize the community and make it partner in tackling the problem of sex selective abortions and dwindling sex ratio in certain packets of the state. The department has decided to initiate following activities/schemes in the state:
- The Panchayat which will have the best sex ratio will be awarded the cash prize of rupees five lakh for the developmental activities.
- Female will be given Rs. 25,000, 20,000 respectively if she goes for family planning method (Permanent) after first girl child and second girl child respectively. The informer who shall inform the department about the sex selection activities will be awarded a cash prize of Rs. 10000.
- There will be regular inter state meeting and inter-district meeting at the border areas to implement the PNDT Act effectively.

(b) Provisions of Residential Accommodation at Primary Health Centre (PHC) Level

Himachal Pradesh is a hilly State and the Primary Health Centres are located at remote localities where good residential accommodation for the essential health care staff is not easily available. In order to improve the primary health care facilities in the rural areas and to encourage the health staff to live in the health institution premises we need to construct residential accommodation for the doctors, nurses and other supporting staff in the Primary Health Centres (PHCs). This will not only encourage the willingness of health staff to serve in the rural and remote areas but will also improve the health facilities and help in increasing the institutional deliveries reducing the Infant Mortality Rate (IMR) and Maternal Mortality Rate (MMR) considerably. The State would require additional plan allocations for the construction of residential accommodation at Primary Health Centre (PHC) and CHC level.

(c) Improvement in Trauma Services

This hilly state is prone to recurrent traffic and other accidents. Therefore, there is an urgent need to improve the trauma care services. The State Government plans to strengthen the trauma services at R.H. Solan, R.H. Kullu, R.H. Una, R.H. Chamba and MGMSC Khaneri at Rampur. The Government of India has already sanctioned Rs. 1.5 crores for the establishment of trauma centre at Kullu. The services also need to be extended in Kangra District (Nurpur). The cases for establishment of other places have also been taken up with the Govt. of India. In order to run the trauma centres effectively, the additional trained staff would also be required at each place for which additional plan support in the Eleventh Five Year Plan would be required.

(d) Disposal of Bio-Medical Waste

The disposal of bio-medical and hospital waste has now become an important health issue and the health institutions need to be equipped for the proper disposal of bio-medical and other hospital wastes. The provisions for equipments and disposal procedures need to be supported by the plan.

(e) Problems Faced by the State Government for Smooth Development in Health Sectors

- Emergence of lifestyle diseases—the overall burden of communicable diseases like leprosy, malaria has reduced and is not a public health problem. The other communicable diseases like tuberculosis, water borne diseases have also shown a declining trend. The occurrence of cutaneous Leishmaniasis particularly in Kinnaur district is a new problem of the State. The lifestyle diseases like Hypertension, Coronary Artery Diseases, Diabetes is posing a new threat to the people of the State.
- Irrational distribution of health institutions/ Manpower—There are few areas where there is no fair distribution of health institutions and manpower. However, Himachal Pradesh is doing well in terms of health indicators as compared to the nation as a whole.
- Shortage of specialists—The State is facing shortage of specialists at Sub-divisional and Community Health Center level especially in the field of Anaesthesia, Gyanecology, Surgery and Paediatrics.
- Deficiencies of infrastructure (building and residences)—Some Health Institutions are functioning in rented buildings. Lack of residences lead to non-attendance of patients some times.
- Lack of causality services at district level—The causality services at district level is still lacking. This is an area of concern.

(f) Improvement in the Health Infrastructure

- DOH&FW, covered one health institution in each constituency of Himachal Pradesh by granting financial assistance to improve service quality so that these centers become more patient and public-friendly especially adaptive to women and children needs.

- Total of 64 institutions have been covered under the facility improvement plan to upgrade the facilities and provide better services to the people under the model OPD scheme.

(g) National Rural Health Mission

Recognizing the importance of health in the process of economic and social development and improving the quality of life of our citizens, the National Rural Health Mission (NRHM) was launched on 12th April, 2005 with the objectives of universal access to public health services, prevention and control for communicable and non-communicable diseases, access to integrated comprehensive primary health care, revitalizing local health traditions and promotion of health lifestyle. Under National Rural Health Mission (NRHM), following goals have been targeted for 2005-12:

- Reduction in Infant Mortality Rate (IMR) to 30/1000 live births.
- Maternal Mortality Rate (MMR) to be reduced to 100/1,00,000 live births.
- Reduction in Total Fertility Rate (TFR) to 2.1 by 2012.
- Reduction in Malaria Mortality Rate to 50 percent upto 2010, additional 10 per cent reduction by 2012.
- Cataract operations increasing to 300 contract operators per lakh of population per year by 2012.
- To maintain existing 85 per cent cure rate through TB, DOTS services for the entire mission period.
- Kala Azar Mortality Reduction Rate 100 per cent by 2010 and sustaining elimination until 2012.
- Filaria Micro Filaria Reduction 70 per cent by 2010, 80 per cent by 2012 and elimination by 2015.
- Dengue Mortality Reduction Rate 50 per cent by 2010 and sustaining that until 2012.
- Leprosy prevalence rate reduce for 1.8 per 10,000 in 2005 to less than 1 per 10,000.

Sustained efforts are being made to meet above goals in the fixed time frame. Schemes being implemented under National Rural Health Mission in Himachal Pradesh:

- Mission Flexipool activities.
- Re-productive and Child Health RHC Flexipool activities.
- Universal Immunization Programme (UIP).
- Disease Control Programme. (The plans and budget of the vertical programmes have been integrated in the State NRHM-PIP (w.e.f. 2008-09).
- Convergence activities with Panchayati Raj, Rural Development, Irrigation and Public Health, Social Justice and Empowerment and AYUSH (Ayurveda Department).

Description of Programmes/Schemes

National Vector Borne Disease Control Programme: Under this programme during year 2009 (upto Oct., 2009) 863 fever treatment depots, 3994 drug distribution centres and 228 malaria clinics were functioning the State. During the year 2009 (upto Oct., 2009) 3,32,051 blood slides were collected and 3,31,698 blood slides were examined out of which 171 slides were found positive. During this period 166 positive cases were given radical treatment and no death has occurred due to malaria.

National Leprosy Eradication Programme: Under National Leprosy Eradication Programme the prevalence rate which was 26 per thousand in 1955, has been reduced to 0.26 per ten thousand as on October, 2009. The National Leprosy Control Programme was converted to Leprosy Eradication Programme in 1994-95 by the Government of India and with the assistance of World Bank, Leprosy societies were formulated in the districts. During 2009-10 (upto October, 2009), 102 new cases of Leprosy have been detected, 96 cases were deleted and 181 cases of leprosy are under treatment. They are getting MDT from different health institutions free of cost.

National TB Control Programme: Under this programme, 1 Tuberculosis Sanatorium, 12 District Tuberculosis Centres/clinics, 41 Tuberculosis Units and 168 microscopic centers having a provision of 463 beds were functioning in the State. During the year 2009 (upto Sept., 2009) 49,785 suspects were examined and 11,026 patients were given treatment and total case detection rate remained 227/per lakh population. Himachal Pradesh is one of the State where all the districts have been covered under this project.

National Family Welfare Programme: This programme is being carried out in the State as a part of Reproductive and Child Health Programme, on the basis of community needs assessment approach. Under this approach grass-root level workers like multipurpose health workers (both male and females give an estimate of the various Family Welfare activities required in the area/population covered by them.

The RCH programme includes the components of Universal Immunization, RTI and STI programmes. It also includes adolescent health education. Under the programme RCH society has been set-up in the State. The funds are provided by the Government of India for implementation of the programme through RCH Society. In addition to this, there is also provision of funds in the general budget of the State for 24 hours delivery services scheme which is being implemented in all the district of the State.

(h) Hospital Autonomy and Rogi Kalyan Samitis

Rogi Kalyan Samitis (Hospital Welfare Societies) were created in the secondary and tertiary health systems in Himachal Pradesh to provide more autonomy to the Hospitals in the State. The RKS (Rogi Kalyan Samitis) which are broad-based in nature are responsible for day-to-day operations of the hospitals, provide strategic direction, improve the functioning of hospitals with focus on patient satisfaction and improved service deliveries. RKSs are functional in all the Civil District, Zonal Hospitals and PHCs/CHCs.

- RKS are responsible and accountable to improve the service quality, system efficiency and patient satisfaction.
- Societies have autonomy to carry out the activities pertaining to the welfare of Hospitals and initiate measures that result in better and improved services delivery to patients.
- RKS are authorized to use the user charges accrued to spend on the welfare of Hospitals and patients on the basis of approval.
- RKS societies, through user charges have been instrumental in collection of funds and creating an action plan for the expenditure. There are 12 RKS societies functional at Regional and Zonal Hospital levels, 35 RKS are operating at 35 Hospital levels and 444 RKS are operating at 444 PHCs in the State.

(i) Public-Private Partnership in Health Sector in Himachal Pradesh

Government of Himachal Pradesh (GOHP), has decided to implement PPP initiatives on pilot basis in the following areas:

- PPP in Diagnostic Services.
- PPP in Ambulances (Emergency Transport).
- PPP in Managing Selected Sub-Centres and Primary Health Centres.

Department of Health & Family Welfare has developed broad operational guidelines for the identified areas of Public-Private Partnership (PPP).

- Finally it will strengthen primary health care in the state, making services available to the people in the places where they need it.
- Directorate of Health services will fix user charges and ensure that interests of people are protected and will lead to better regulation of private sector than at present.

(j) Capital Outlay

The capital outlay approved in Health Sector is being utilized for the construction of 169 PHCs, 25 CHCs, 12 CH, and 81 HSCs. For the year 2009-10 there is a provision of Rs. 4445.00 lakh and proposed outlay for the year 2010-11 is Rs. 1667.00 lakh. With this outlay, it is proposed to construct the above health institutions to give better infrastructure for service delivery.

The department of Indian Systems of Medicine and Homeopathy also plays a vital role in the health care delivery system of the State. With the passage of time, these systems are becoming more popular amongst the rural as well as in urban population of the State for the treatment of seasonal and chronic diseases. The Department is providing health care facilities to the general public through the following ISM&H Institutions.

Table 15: Expansion of Health Institutions

Sl. No.	*Institutions*	*Nos.*
1.	Regional Ayurvedic Hospitals (100/50-bedded each)	02
2.	Ayurvedic Hospitals (20 bedded 04, 10 bedded-18)	22
3.	Ayurvedic Health Centres	1122
4.	Homeopathic Health Centres	14
5.	Unani Health Centre	03
6.	Nature Cure Hospital	01
7.	Amchi Clinics	04
	Total	1168

Source: Annual Plan Draft 2010-11: Planning Department, Government of Himachal Pradesh.

Table 15 shows that the State Government has laid special emphasis on the expansion of Indian Systems of Medicine and Homeopathy (ISM&H) institution by opening of Ayurvedic Health Centres (AHCs),

Upgradation of Ayurvedic Health Centres into 10/20 bedded hospitals. Besides, the department has three pharmacies which are manufacturing medicines that are supplied to the Ayurvedic institutions of the department and drug testing laboratory for keeping the quality control of medicines being manufactured by departmental/private pharmacies. These institutions are being strengthened from the funds provided by the Government of India.

Besides above, the department has laid special emphasis for the opening of herbal gardens in different agro-climatic zones of the State for the promotion, cultivation and propagation of varied medicinal plants. Presently, we have established three herbal gardens.

Similarly, for the same purposes, one Vanaspati Van Society and State medicinal plant board have been established under which activities at Kullu and Chamba are being undertaken and under medicinal plant board, we are educating the farmers, Non-Governmental Organizations (NGOs), Governmental Organizations (GOs) to provide know-how about the value of medicinal plants by organizing camps at different places, so that they are able to generate extra income by cultivating medicinal plants in their private land. Recently, about 150 projects have been recommended under promotional/contractual farming to National Medicinal Plant Board of Govt. of India.

Presently, there are 50 number of seats for BAMS degree courses. The course of study for BAMS degree is five and half year which includes one year compulsory rotary internship and is governed by the rules & regulations of H.P. University to which this institution is affiliated. The post-graduate courses in the faculty of Kavya-Chikitsa, Shalya, Shalkya Tantra, Prasuti Tantra, Samhita Sidhant and Ras Shashtra is available in the College to provide educational inputs to the students and make them professionally competent as teacher, researcher and specialist in their respective fields. The post graduate course is of three year duration having intake capacity of 24 students. The Government of India has provided financial assistance not only to strengthen the College but also for DTL/Pharmacies.

To improve the services being offered by the Ayurveda hospitals, the department intends to introduce specialized services like Panchkarma/Kshar sutra/Yoga and Naturopathy in selected district hospitals where there is a space to accommodate this facility. During 11th Plan period, the department proposes to start these facilities in five district hospitals, i.e. one each in annual plan period. To equip these hospitals, the department needs at least Rs. 22.00 lakh per Unit, i.e. Rs. 110.00 lakh during the 11th Plan period for purchase of equipments, medicines, salary of staff and other miscellaneous expenditure, etc.

To improve the standard of para-medical staff, the department intends to impart training by organizing refresher courses for pre-service and in-service para-medical staff, so that the general public could avail the specialized facility at their door step.

To improve the skill of in-service AMOs the department intends to organize interaction with outside experts by organizing workshops, refresher courses, conferences, etc. to have knowledge in all the fields, so that public could avail better health facilities.

During 11th Plan period the department proposes to upgrade Ayurvedic Health Centres (AHCs) to 10-bedded hospitals by rationalizing of institutions where the turn out the patients are high and deserve upgradation and also opening of new institutions in such area/panchayats where there exist no health facilities. The department proposes to upgrade at least 5 AHCs to 10-bedded hospitals and opening of 25 AHCs (five in each plan) in needy areas.

The department has already submitted project proposals amounting to Rs. 382.13 lakh to Government of India for allocating funds for starting Post-graduation (PG) in additional specialties of Bal Rog, Rog Nidan and Swasthvritta but the State Government has to keep budgetary provision to meet out the requirement of salary and stipened to PG students for future in respect of specialty already in existence in the College.

To improve the quality and competitiveness of Ayurvedic medicines manufactured in Government and private pharmacies by providing modern facilities for drug testing and research and development of drugs and introduction of modern technology and management techniques, the department needs at least Rs. 2.00 crore during 11th Plan period.

The department intends to set-up herbal gardens in the left out pockets of the agro-climatic zones, i.e. Kinnaur, Lahaul & Spiti, Pangi & Bharmour for which the department needs at least 25.00 lakh during 11th Plan period to create all infrastructural amenities.

During 11th Plan period, the department intends to expand Ayurvedic tourism in collaboration with Public and Private partnership and in all famous religious places and hotel industry by providing rejuvenation packages. Also start such Units in District Ayurvedic hospitals where there is sufficient space Regional Ayurvedic Hospital, Shimla, District hospital, Chamba, Una and Rohroo in Shimla district where sufficient accommodation is available.

To complete the on going construction works and clearing the pending liabilities of the executing agencies, the department needs at least Rs. 19.19 crore during 11th Plan period. Besides this to reside all

AHCs in Government building the department needs funds amounting to Rs. 34-35 crore approximately.

A token provision of Rs. 150.00 lakh as State share has been proposed in the Annaul Plan, 2010-11 for this scheme named as Ayush.

III. VISION AND STRATEGIES OF HIMACHAL PRADESH FOR THE FUTURE

Himachal Pradesh provides health services of a reasonable standard in the public sector, with an adequate choice of allopathic and ayurvedic treatment. The vision of the State of Himachal Pradesh for the immediate future includes the provision of primary, secondary and tertiary health care services, both in the public and private sectors on par with the neighboring states of Punjab and Haryana. Such a vision looks forward to a picture of a generally healthy population, free from communicable and non-communicable diseases, and a client-friendly manpower in the health and family welfare centres. Besides the continuation of the usual preventive health care measures, the State must ensure the availability of quality health care services (including secondary and tertiary health care services) to everyone. The health care system of the future should be more scientific and technologically advanced. Better health care services in the future are envisaged, with the introduction of selected health sector reforms, such as integration of the public and private sector, framing of rules to regulate the private sector, introduction of sustainable approaches towards treatment and cure of communicable diseases, particularly HIV/AIDS and a viable health insurance policy. We also look forward to immediate State interventions, such as setting up special clinics for the vulnerable sections (children, adolescents, women, and the elderly) and also bringing about an attitudinal and behavioural change in the removal of existing socio-cultural practices, particularly related to the reproductive health care institutions through reforms in governance with greater involvement of the Panchayati Raj Institutions), and provision of additional funding on a self-sustainable basis (levying of user charges in consultation with the PRIs) would help the State come out of the administrative problems and resource crunch. The researcher also foresee greater inter-sectoral and inter-departmental co-ordination, which would not only ensure effective and optimal utilization of the existing and future health care programmes, but also result in increased public awareness towards healthy practices. Periodic assessment of health problems and needs of the State is an essential prerequisite for assessing the future requirements. To achieve the above, the following policy interventions are suggested:

1. For efficient and smooth functioning of health institutions, adequate monitoring and supervision is necessary. The performance of various health indicators would improve to a large extent if there is regular monitoring and supervision. All officials of the Directorate, Chief Medical Officers (CMOs) and Block Medical Officers (BMOs) must make periodic field visits to different health institutions under their jurisdiction. Adequate POL (Petrol, Oil and Lubricants) expenses should be provided for regular monitoring and supervision work. Induction training and regular refresher courses are necessary for updating the knowledge of healthcare providers.
2. During the last few annual and five year plans, the Government of Himachal Pradesh has advocated rapid expansion of Indian System of Medicines and Homeopathy. It is time to integrate its functioning with the Department of Health and Family Welfare. To effectively achieve the national goals and objectives of health, both modern and Indian systems of medicine must work as harmonious units rather than in two separate compartments. Though some work has already been started in this direction and the necessary notification has been issued by the State Government to implement various National Health Programmes jointly by the two departments, much needs to be done. Further, inter-departmental co-ordination between the Department of Health and Family Welfare and the Departments of Education, Public Health, Women and Social Welfare, Public Relations, etc. is needed for effective health intervention programmes.
3. That State has a Health Vision 2020 document. Besides, some policy objectives have been highlighted in the Tenth Plan document. Considering the fact that, with the changing composition of the population, changing life-styles, urbanization and industrialization, Himachal Pradesh would have newer morbidity challenges in the future, it should work on a State Health Policy with a proper time schedule for the different activities. The policy should clearly spell out the future health care requirements of the State in the field of preventive, promotive, curative and rehabilitative health care. Adequate research through primary surveys should be conducted before fixing the goals and advocating policy prescriptions.

4. The primary health care facilities in the rural areas and the existing number of medical institutions in the State are sufficient to meet the needs of the people, but they have to be brought to a higher level of efficient functioning, shortcomings, such as inadequate para-medical staff, buildings and equipment, must be overcome. The inconsistency in the distribution of primary health care facilities and health manpower (more staffing in comfortable areas than in the rural and remote areas) must be rectified immediately. The buildings of health institutions have to be maintained properly with adequate residential accommodation for the staff. Separate wings have to be established in each hospital in the urban areas for proper implementation of primary health care such as updating of records, undertaking survey work, etc. Further, implementation of service norms and standards (through hospital manual), and a proper referral system would contribute to reducing the burden of the secondary and tertiary health care services. The same applies to institutions under the Indian System of Medicines and Homeopathy wherein an institution require restructuring for delivering proper health care services and very often these institutions are lacking in proper infrastructure amenities. Sufficient funds are required to provide specialized treatments at these centres.
5. Special emphasis needs to be given to prevent the measures, such as vaccination against communicable diseases and identification of high risk pregnancies to detect deformities and disabilities. Special clinics should also be established in each district to deal with problems related to infertility, reproductive health and menopause.
6. Focused attention needs to be given to curative aspects of health care, particularly in hilly State like Himachal Pradesh where the share of the private sector in the number of illness episodes treated is almost negligible. Strengthening the existing public health services and widening their network through the involvement of private practitioners, voluntary non-government organizations and research institutions will improve the health care services in the State.
7. It is important that professional medical bodies and the Government of Himachal Pradesh rules and regulations and develop appropriate strategies to regulate the private sector. It is important to have directives on the manufacture, sale and prescription of pharmaceutical drugs on the one hand, and

medical and clinical practices, including licence to practice, basic code of conduct, negligence and consumer complaints on the other. The rating of private clinics, nursing homes and hospitals based on physical facilities, manpower, equipment and technology will be useful.

8. Rising medical costs raises the question of available financing options. Hospitalized treatment in both the public and private sectors is very expensive and leads to loss of lifetime's savings, leaving no money for future social security. It is suggested that the State Government should work out the modalities for a viable health insurance policy to meet the rising health costs in both public and private sectors. It is also an essential ingredient or social security measures.
9. Urbanization brings with it mental stresses and strains. Efficient strategies need to be evolved to combat such stresses leading to accidents and other eventualities. More trauma wards need to be established to handle such cases.
10. In tune with the objectives of National Health Policy, 2002, convergence of all national programmes of health, such as malaria, tuberculosis, HIV/AIDS, RCH and universal immunization programme, under the management of autonomous bodies for overall implementation, is desirable. Effective implementation by such bodies would not only reduce the incidence of communicable and non-communicable diseases in the State but also reduce the burden of the State Government, enabling it to plan and implement alternative strategies for health care.
11. Special strategies need to be planned for HIV positive cases in the State. The present Voluntary Counseling and Testing Centres (VCTC) for HIV/AIDS testing in Indira Gandhi Medical College, Shimla, is grossly inadequate. Such testing facilities should be made available at all zonal/district hospitals.
12. Although the Panchayati Raj Institutions have been involved through the formation of Health and Family Welfare Advisory Committees known as PARIKAS at the Panchayat, Block and District levels, yet effective decentralization of powers, according to the 73rd Amendment of the Constitution is still to take place. Its implementation will help PRIs to identify their area-specific priorities, develop programmes and mobilize resources. Sensitization and training of the elected PRI representatives on different health issues is important.

13. Introduction of telemedicine for appropriate consultation for the treatment of illness in the far-flung areas of the State through connection with the State Headquarters would be useful in reducing people's hardship and the number of patients in specialized health institutions.
14. A number of primary studies should also be undertaken through autonomous research institutions, to assess the health needs of the State.
15. Last but not least, a proper computerized health-management information system should be developed from the block level to provide immediate access to information on health and other indicators. An effective Health Management Information System will help in planning area specific and need-based policies and programmes in the future.

A future concerns which are outside the domain of this chapter, but constitute an integral part of the healthy growth of the human minds and body are environment and occupational health, adequate availability of drinking water, hygienic living conditions, nutritious food, removal of drug addiction and other health hazards. Excessive use of alcohol is a deterrent to growth. The State has to design the future of the generation by ensuring minimization of alcoholism and drug addiction. The researcher visualize the need for extending the scope of interconnectivity and interdependence of the State within the region to ensure a disease-free, and an environmentally clean society.

(i) Himachal Health Vision

A task force has been set-up for the Pradesh. The task force envisions the scenario of health services, its impact on the people, looks into modernization and improvement of quality of services *vis-à-vis* better utilization of services provided by the health infrastructure. A glimpse of the vision reveals that all the residents in the State will be ensured quality physical and mental health. The small families will be the norm. It would be the endeavour to provide comprehensive health care services which will include spiritual element also. Ultimate objective is that health care will be a major power house of growth and economic development in the State.

Based on this, the task force has worked out health indicators which are likely to be achieved by the year 2020. To give some insight in the vision statement, we aim to eradicate diseases like malaria, leprosy, polio, water borne disease, nutritional deficiency disorders like goitre, etc. reduce the burden of other diseases such as tuberculosis, diabetes mellitus and to gear up to meet the challenges we are likely to face in the two decades such as increased incidence of health diseases and trauma and accidents.

(ii) New Health Policy of the State Government

The State government has formulated a new health policy. The main features of the new health policy are as under:

(i) The State government has set before it stiff targets for the coming two decades in a bid to provide health services to the masses, specially those living far-flung regions with the most in hospitable terrain.

(ii) The immediate focus would be on pregnant women, children, the elderly and the adolescent.

(iii) For pregnant women, the objective include identifying high risk pregnancy, attaining a level of institutional deliveries upto 80 percent ensuring all deliveries are by trained personal and controlling.

(iv) For children they include eradicating vaccine-preventable diseases, reducing malnutrition, increasing the level of exclusive breast-feeding to 100 percent and bringing down the incidence of anaemia to less than 10 percent.

(v) For the elderly it includes ensuring geriatric care of reasonable degree for 50 percent of the geriatric population, and for the adolescents, to establish adolescent counseling centres upto block level so as to cover 100 percent of the age group on problems of premarital sex, unwed mothers, alcoholism, narcotic and drug addition and HIV, AIDS and STD.

(vi) Alongside these, there will be efforts to eradicate leprosy, reduce water borne disease, reduce incidence of STD to less than 2 percent in the adult population besides containing the prevalence of HIV and AIDS at the present level.

(vii) On the non-communicable diseases front efforts will be on reducing the prevalence of blindness to less than 0.3 percent and to reduce incidence of heart diseases, preventable mortality due to trauma and also cancer to 10 percent of the current level and thereby reduce these diseases to 25 percent of the current level.

(viii) As far fertility control, efforts will include to bring down the annual growth rate to 1 percent, increase the contraceptive usage rate to more than 70 percent and to reduce the total fertility to 1.5 percent.

(ix) On the health management side 100 percent families would be covered under the health insurance scheme and primary health care facilities will be made available and accessible to 90 percent population through the public sector and 10 percent of the population through voluntary and private sectors.

The strategy to reach these objectives is by empowering families and communities with knowledge for adopting responsible health care practices and seeking medical attention as and when needed, and making graded health cares available through the referral system in primary, secondary and territory institutions.

For this the strategy/vision statement will focus on efforts to consolidate and rationalize health infrastructure, decentralize the planning and management process, develop partnerships with NGOs (Non-Governmental Organizations) make a functional integration of the health services with Indian systems of medicine and to make greater utilization of information technology.

Himachal Pradesh which started its development journey in 1971 has not only emerged as a benchmark in the development of hill areas in the country but has also shown the way to big states by becoming a pioneer in various fields. Today, it is reckoned as the best state in the country, a fact which has been under scored in various surveys conducted by prestigious agencies from time to time. A comparison between the figures for various indicators of development in 1971 and today, bears out the speedy progress the State has made during all these years. The per capita income has gone up from Rs. 615 in 1971 to Rs. 44,803 in 2008 and is likely to cross Rs. 46,000 in the coming years. The Gross Domestic Product (GDP) at current prices has shotup from Rs. 223 crore to Rs. 36,940 crore. The Annual Plan expenditure which was only Rs. 211 crores in 1971, went upto Rs. 2,700 crore in 2009-10 and has been pegged at Rs. 3,000 crore for 2010-11. Himachal Pradesh today has road length of more than 31,000 kms against only 7.740 kms. in 1971. All census villages in the State enjoy the facility of electricity and water. Having attained the status of apple state of the country, Himachal Pradesh is now being recognized as fruit state and is poised to become the power state of the country. The credit for whatever the State has achieved goes to the hardworking, honest and sincere people of Himachal Pradesh who have exploded the myth that hills are destined to be poor. Not only this, but the specialized and better health care facilities are also being ensured at the doorsteps of the people. The *Mahila Gram Panchayat, Swasthya Sahayika Yojna* has been started to strengthen health care services at the panchayat level. The existing health institutions and medical colleges are being strengthened with latest equipment and specialized services. The government plans to open medical colleges in Mandi, Hamirpur and Una districts in the public-private-participation mode. To accelerate the pace of development we have been ensuring effective implementation of the plan and other schemes by taking up frequent review at various levels. Annual plan of Rs.3000 crore has been proposed for the year 2010-11 as against annual plan of Rs. 2700 crores approved for 2009-10.[20]

IV. EMPIRICAL ANALYSIS OF RIGHT TO HEALTH AS A RIGHT TO LIFE

A purely theoretical study of "Right to Life as a Right to Health Standards of Right in Himachal Pradesh" and analysis of legislative provisions related to health cannot prove beneficial unless an empirical study is performed in order to identify the functional and technical deficiencies in health system awareness of health related laws in the community. Thus, the study was conducted of existing laws, and to have insight into people's perception about health-related knowledge. For this purpose the universe of the study was restricted to Shimla town of Himachal Pradesh. Shimla being the capital of Himachal Pradesh wherein different shades of persons reside and were served questionnaires to know their responses about the health right and laws. Questionnaires were designed for different categories of respondents keeping in view the objectives of the survey and informational needs in mind. Questions were common for general public and medical officers. In addition, the researcher has collected information with the help of extensive interviews. The questionnaire prepared by the researcher in association with the experienced teachers having skill and accumenship in this field are quite comprehensive which envelope within their ambit almost every aspect of functional and technical deficiencies in health system, awareness of health-related laws in the community.

In order to know the real picture of existing laws and people's perception about health laws, the multi-pronged approach and endeavoured has used to collect as much relevant information as possible through different sources. The author has mainly relied on the available record and literature in various libraries of the State including Reports of the government, New-letters, newspapers and the data available with the Directorate of Health, Shimla. In addition to these sources, the researcher has also collected information with the help of

20. Himachal on the path of progress and prosperity, *The Tribune*, Monday, January 25, 2010, at p. 17.

extensive interviews and the questionnaires. With a view to gather information with regard to the standards of health rights, the researcher has constructed questionnaires to elicit the views of the Medical Officers (doctors) and general public.

Accordingly, the study has been extended to the whole Shimla town. The author has put earnest efforts to construct a systematic design of the study to find answers to the hypothesis raised in the study. The emphasis has been laid on five aspects of the functioning and regulations of health laws with a view to find correct answers to the hypotheses which are:

(1) Right to Health is an emerging right and had an existence.
(2) It is obligatory upon the State to provide adequate medical services and clean environment to preserve human life under the Constitution.
(3) The provisions of the Medical Council of India have the ample powers to award compensation for the negligent acts of medical professionals.
(4) The role of legislative and administrative authorities in protecting health care rights needs more improvement.
(5) The judiciary has contributed a lot in protecting the interest of patients and defining the responsibilities of health providers.

Every effort has been made by the author to give an opportunity to express their views and for this purpose the views of a total number of 50 Medical Officers (doctors) and 120 people of different walks of life have been obtained through the questionnaires.

Since the objective of the questionnaires has been to conduct an in-depth study of the Health Rights in India, sample surveys of 120 respondents were carried out for General Public and 50 respondents were carried out for Medical Officers. The responses were analyzed and elucidated in the charts and presented in the study. Filled questionnaires[21] were collected and data was processed. Following questions posed to medical officers and general public were common.

- Are you aware of the health laws that exist in India?
- Do you agree that yoga be made compulsory right from primary level?
- Do you agree that sex education should be made part of school education as a measure to improve all round health of teenage children?

21. See Questionaires in Appendix.

- Today drug abuse amongst children youth is an rampant. Do you think that society has a responsibility to educate and raise awareness amongst children regarding ill-effects of drug addiction?
- Do you agree that the standard of health services provided in the health institutions are adequate?
- Which type of problems do you face in the health institutions?
  - Non-availability of beds in the hospitals.
  - Insufficient and/or untrained para-medical staff.
  - Non-availability of medicines.
  - Inadequacy of good quality of machines.
  - Any other problem.
  - None.
- Do you agree that health insurance is beneficial for every individual?
- Are you satisfied with the legislative provisions made for the protection of health?
- Do you agree that there is an urgent need to strengthen the implementation of all the existing nutrition intervention programmes?
- Do you think budget allocation on health system by government is sufficient to provide quality health care to the public?
- Do you agree the National Rural Health Mission (NRHM) is going to make changes in health status of rural population?

Relevant data has been prepared for various parameters in geographical form and is given below:

(i) Responses to Questionnaire for General Public

The author has served questionnaire on 120 respondents belonging to the general public of Shimla town. The researcher has endeavoured to have responses from Government servants viz., Teachers, Lecturers, Engineers, Architects, Nurses, Revenue department officials; social activists; students studying in different standards; women with partially having urban and partially rural background; persons in private employments; and political leaders, both from ruling as well as opposite parties. The researcher served questionnaires on the above mentioned persons except politicians. However, the politicians were interviewed in person to ascertain their actions and reactions with regard to health services in the State in general and Shimla town in particular. The researcher has endeavoured to have responses from 10 with rural background, 15 from urban background, 25 government servants, 25 students studying in different standards, 20 women with partially having urban and partially rural background, 5 scheduled castes and 30 politicians, both from ruling as well as opposite parties. The politicians were interviewed in person to ascertain their actions and reactions with regard to health services in the State.

1. Are you aware of the Health Laws?

Response	*Total*	*Percentage*
Yes	100	83
No	12	10
Can't Say	8	7
Total	120	100

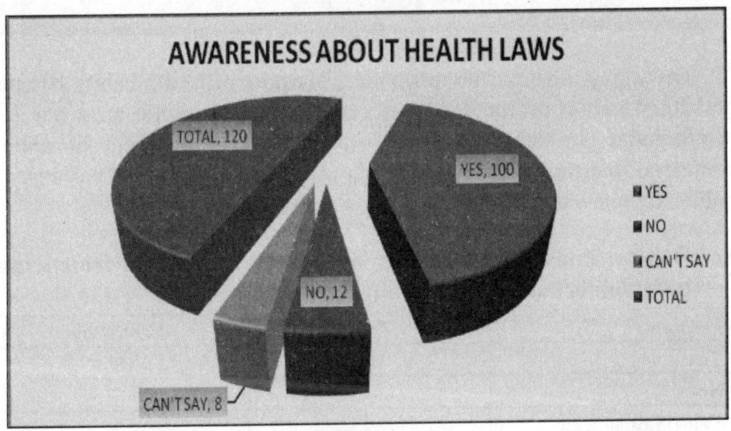

The very first question in the questionnaire regarding with the awareness about health legislation amongst different classes of people suggested that maximum number of people are aware about health laws. 83 per cent of general public are aware about health laws. 10 per cent have stated clearly that they do not have any knowledge about health laws. While 7 per cent of respondents were not able to give response.

2. Are you aware of Health Habits?

Response	*Total*	*Percentage*
Yes	101	84
No	8	7
Can't Say	11	9
Total	120	100

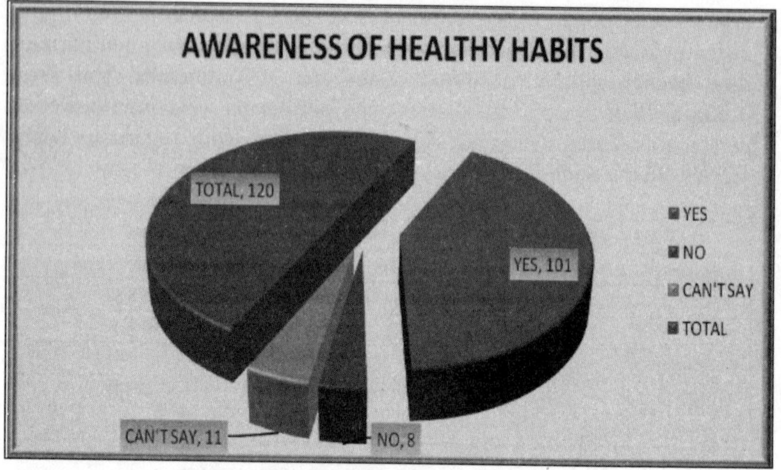

On asking whether the respondent is aware of health habits 101 out of 120; which constituted 84 per cent of general public are aware of health habits in their day to day life. While 7 per cent of public confessed that they are not aware about health habits and 9 per cent of public are unaware about the healthy habits.

3. Do you know that smoking and other type of environmental pollution is harmful for health?

Response	*Total*	*Percentage*
Yes	103	85
No	8	7
Can't Say	9	8
Total	120	100

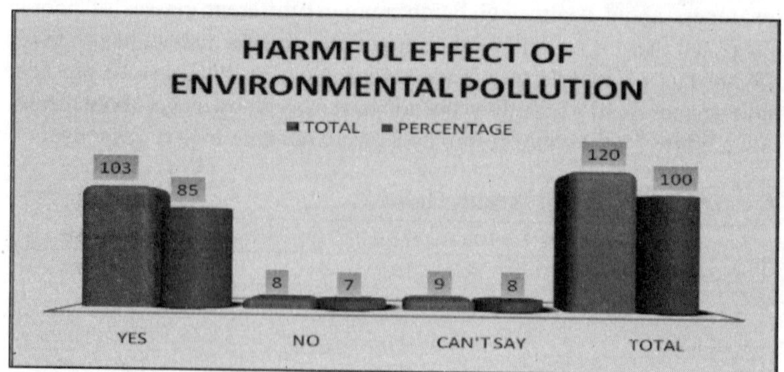

On asking whether the respondent know that smoking and other type of environmental pollution is harmful for health, 85 per cent respondents answered the question in affirmative and they don't have it. But on the other side 7 per cent of people stated clearly that they do not have any knowledge that smoking and other type of environmental pollution is harmful for health and 8 per cent of people are not able to give response.

4. From which source do you get the information about health laws?

Response	*Total*	*Percentage*
Radio	10	8
Television	40	33
Newspaper	12	10
All	42	35
Any Other Source	16	14
Total	120	100

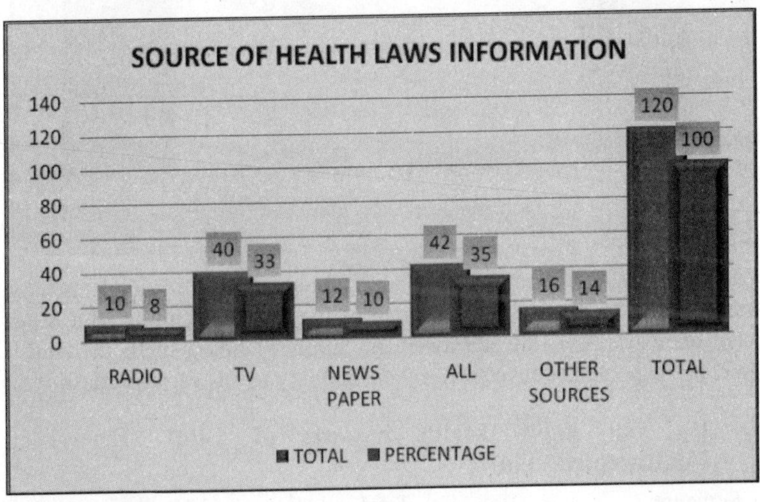

On asking the source of information about health laws, 8 per cent (10 respondents) receive information from radio whereas 33 per cent of public get the information from television and 10 per cent of public get this information from newspaper and while 35 per cent of public have stated that they get the information about health laws from all the above said sources and rest 14 percent of public get the information from their friends, relatives, nebious, through seminars, workshop, health practitioners (MBBS-Doctor, Teachers), etc. as well.

5. Do you know about family planning methods?

Response	*Total*	*Percentage*
Yes	100	83
No	9	8
Can't Say	11	9
Total	120	100

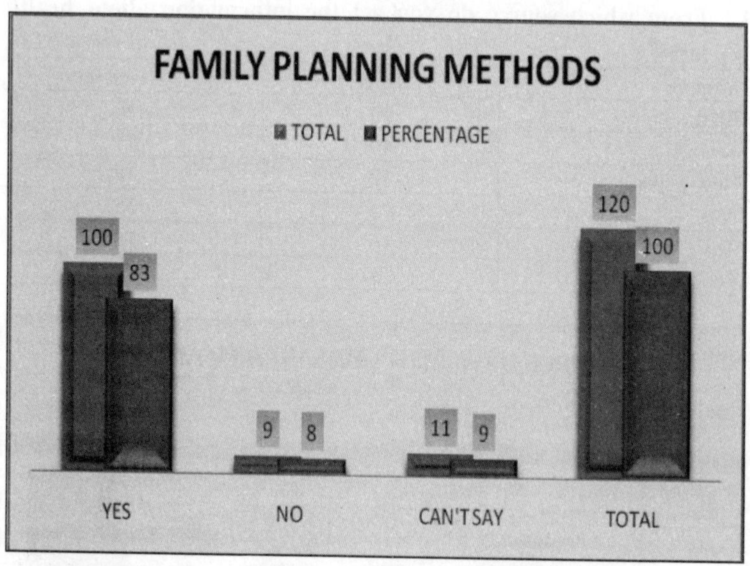

While asking about family planning methods, 100 respondents have stated that they have the knowledge of the family planning. But 8 per cent of respondents are not aware of family planning methods. And 9 percent respondents have shown their inability to answer this question.

6. **Do you know health hazards of I-Pill (Emergency Contraceptives Pill)?**

Response	*Total*	*Percentage*
Yes	51	42
No	33	28
Can't Say	36	30
Total	120	100

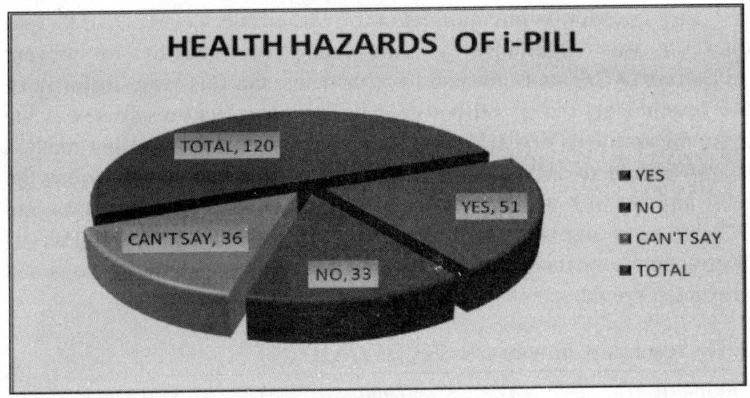

The next question whether the general public has the knowledge of health hazards of emergency contraceptive I-Pill. Regarding this question 42 per cent of public admitted to have knowledge of the side effects of emergency contraceptive pills. And 28 per cent of public were found to be unaware so far as the knowledge of health hazards of I-Pills are concerned. While 30 per cent did not gave any response.

7. Are you aware of contraceptive methods like condom, contraceptive Pill, etc. to prevent sexually transmitted diseases (AIDS) and unwanted pregnancies?

Response	*Total*	*Percentage*
Yes	97	80
No	9	8
Can't Say	14	12
Total	120	100

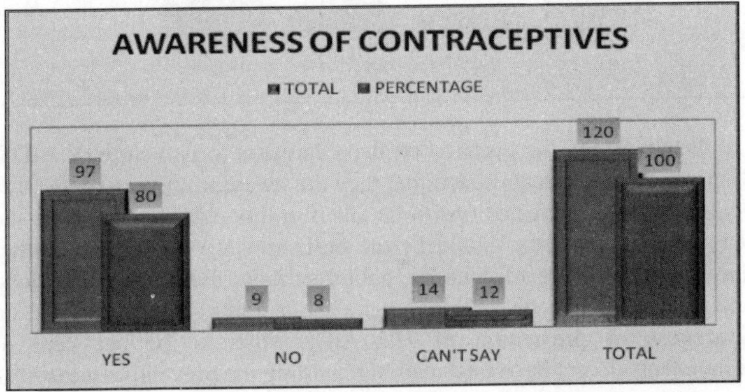

This question is in continuation of earlier one, i.e. HIV/AIDS, and question was regarding the knowledge of methods to prevent STDs/HIV/AIDS and unwanted pregnancies. On this issue majority of the respondents that is 80 per cent have shown that unsafe sex is the main reason of HIV/AIDS. They have the awareness regarding method of prevention of HIV/STD's and unwanted pregnancies. Whereas the least number of 8 per cent respondents have shown their ignorance and 12 per cent did not gave any response about the awareness of contraceptive methods which prevent sexually transmitted diseases and unwanted pregnancies.

8. Do you know how to prevent HIV/AID?

Response	*Total*	*Percentage*
Yes	100	83
No	8	7
Can't Say	12	10
Total	120	100

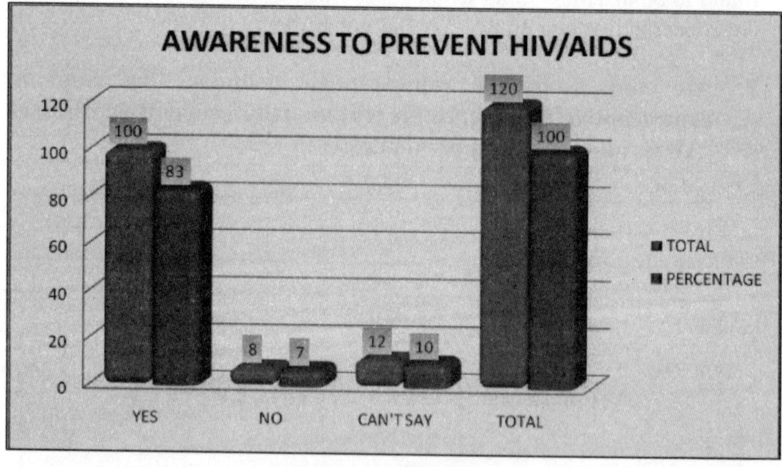

While asking the question on the awareness to prevent HIV/AIDS, 83 per cent respondents stated that they are aware as to how HIV/AIDS be prevented and precautions to be taken in this regard. They have the opinion that safer sex should be the best preventive measure. Further they focused on use of condom, boiled syringe, use of checked blood and use of new blade. While 7 per cent of public found to have no awareness of prevention of HIV/AIDS whereas 10 per cent of respondents do not have information regarding the preventive measures.

9. Do you agree that yoga and meditation be made compulsory right from primary level?

Response	*Total*	*Percentage*
Compulsory	86	71
Not compulsory	22	19
Can't Say	12	10
Total	120	100

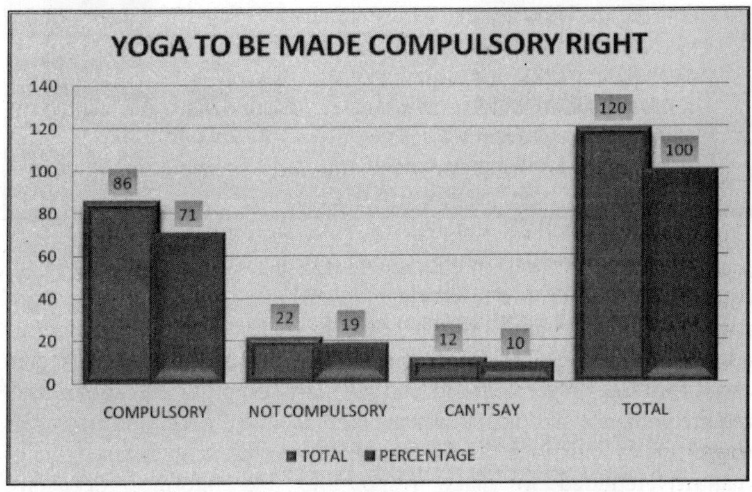

In order to improve the health of public at large, yoga and meditation proved to be a boon in the State of Himachal in general and Shimla town in particular. While asking the question that yoga and meditation be made compulsory right from primary level, 71 per cent of the respondents answered in affirmative. However, the minority view (19 per cent) of the respondents in this regard appears in negative. 10 per cent of the respondents have shown their ignorance about compulsory right from primary level.

10. Do you agree that sex education should be made part of school education as a measure to improve all round health of teenage children?

Response	*Total*	*Percentage*
Agree	68	56
Disagree	29	25
Can't Say	23	19
Total	120	100

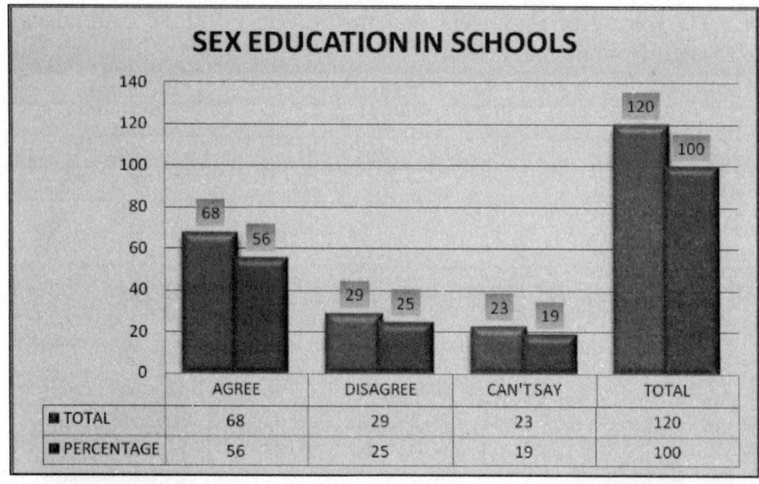

Next question was in relation to sex education. Majority in all categories 56 per cent of respondents agreed that sex education be made part of school education as a measure to improve all round health of adolescents teenage children while 25 per cent respondents disagree about this and 19 per cent did not gave any response. The adolescents require guidance and independence simultaneously, education as well as opportunities to explore life for themselves in order to attain the level of maturity required to make responsible and informed decisions. Therefore, an urgent need make sex education part of school education.

Today drug abuse amongst children and youths is on rampant. Do you think that society has a responsibility to educate and raise awareness amongst children regarding ill-effects of drug addiction. But 8 percent of public gave negative response to this question.

11. Are you Satisfied with the Quality of Services Provided in the Health Institutions ?

Response	*Total*	*Percentage*
Satisfied	28	23
Not Satisfied	72	61
Can't Say	20	16
Total	120	100

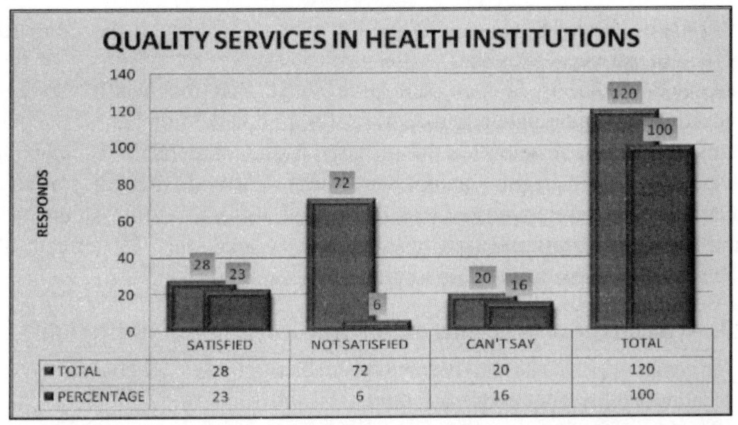

Delivery of proper health care services are the basic task before the nation. India has accepted the responsibility of ensuring health for all. It is revealed from the responses of the respondents that the current rate of expansion of health delivery system is inadequate and defective. On the quality of services provided in the health institutions 23 per cent of public admitted that they are satisfied whereas 61 per cent have shown their dissatisfaction as they face many problems due to bad quality of services. 16 per cent of public were not able to give their opinion.

12. Do you agree that the standard of health services provided in the Health Institutions are adequate ?

Response	*Total*	*Percentage*
Adequate	21	18
Not Adequate	69	57
Can't Say	30	25
Total	120	100

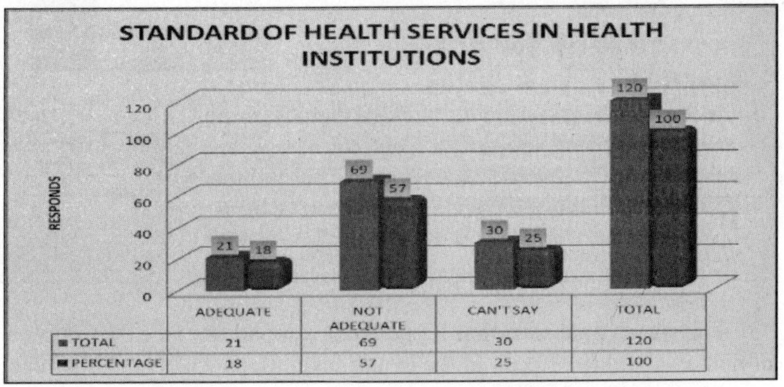

Again about 18 per cent of public were satisfied with the standard of health services provided in the health institutions. Majority of the respondents that is 57 per cent have stated that the health services provided are inadequate and defective. They quoted a number of reasons namely, uneven distribution of primary health care facilities, uneven distribution of health manpower, poor referral system, poorly maintained buildings, absence of residential accommodation to doctors and supporting staff and lack of infrastructure amenities. 25 per cent of the respondents were not able to give their opinion.

13. Which type of problems do you face in the health institutions?

Response	*Total*	*Percentage*
Non-availability of beds in the hospital	26	22
Insufficient and/or untrained para-medical staff	22	19
Non-availability of medicines	15	13
Any Other Problem	15	12
All	31	26
None	10	08
Total	120	100 %

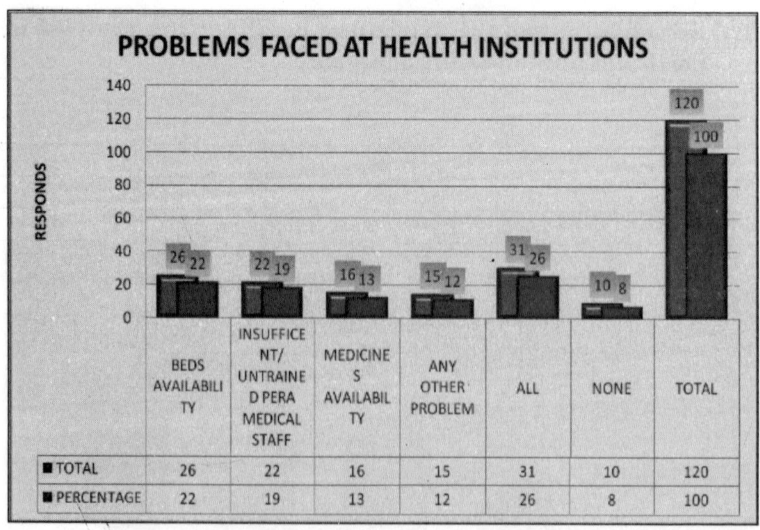

The survey indicates that 22 per cent respondents face the problem of non-availability of beds in the health institutions whereas 19 per cent respondents expressed dissatisfaction that there is insufficient and/or untrained paramedical staff. 13 per cent respondents have stated that medicines are not available in hospitals while 26 per cent respondents expressed their opinion that there are all type of above mentioned problems in the hospitals. 12 per cent respondents face any other problem such as charging of high fee, bad quality of machines, approach, vacant posts, lack of infrastructure, not proper-preventive, promotive-rehabilitative measures, etc.

14. Do you agree that health insurance is beneficial for every individual?

Response	*Total*	*Percentage*
Agree	70	58
Disagree	17	14
Can't Say	33	28
Total	120	100

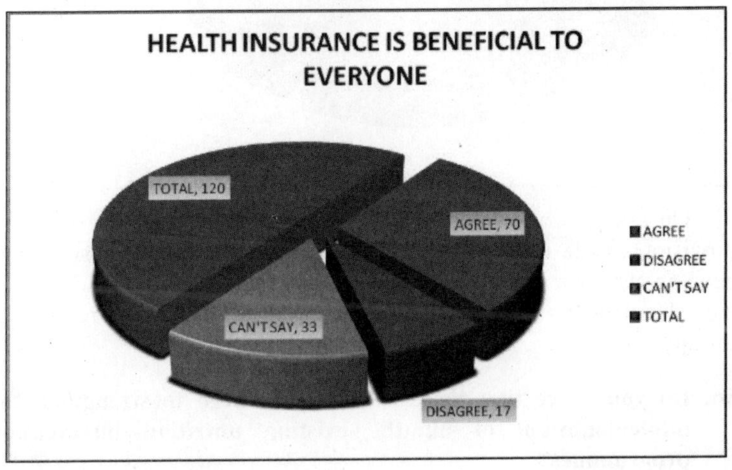

On asking whether health insurance is beneficial to every individual, 70 respondents (58 per cent) have admitted that health insurance serve much purpose and is beneficial. 14 percent respondents have shown their denial and moreover, they have admitted that the health insurance is not beneficial for every individual and 28 per cent respondents were unable to respond to this question.

15. Are you satisfied with the Legislative Provisions made for the Protection of Health?

Response	*Total*	*Percentage*
Satisfied	31	26
Not Satisfied	60	50
Can't Say	29	24
Total	120	100

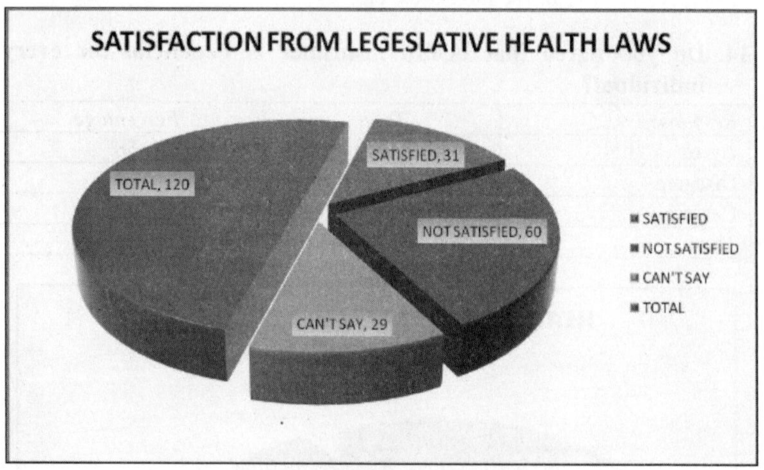

On asking whether the respondent is satisfied with the legislative provisions made for the protection of health, 26 per cent respondents have shown their satisfaction whereas 50 per cent have clearly stated their dissatisfaction. 24 per cent respondents were unable to respond to this question.

16. Do you agree that there is an urgent need to strengthen the implementation of all the existing nutrition intervention programmes?

Response	*Total*	*Percentage*
Agree	80	66
Disagree	14	12
Can't Say	26	22
Total	120	100

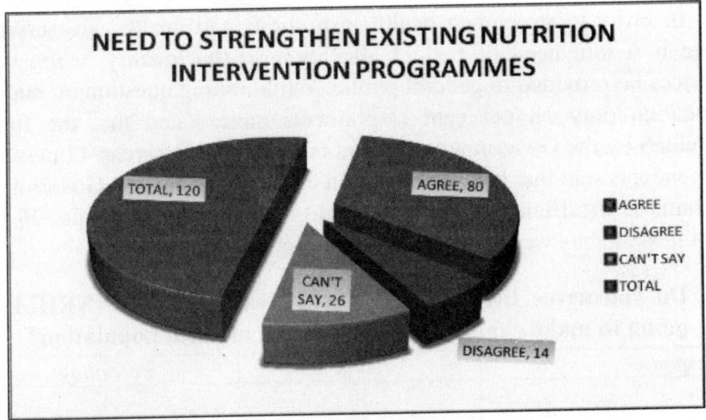

In response to this question, majority of the respondents (66 per cent) expressed urgent need to strengthen the implementation of all the existing nutrition intervention programmes whereas 12 % have shown dissent and 22 per cent did not gave any reply.

17. Do you think budget allocation on health system by government is sufficient to provide quality health care to the public?

Response	*Total*	*Percentage*
Sufficient	22	18
Not Sufficient	51	43
Can't Say	47	39
Total	120	100

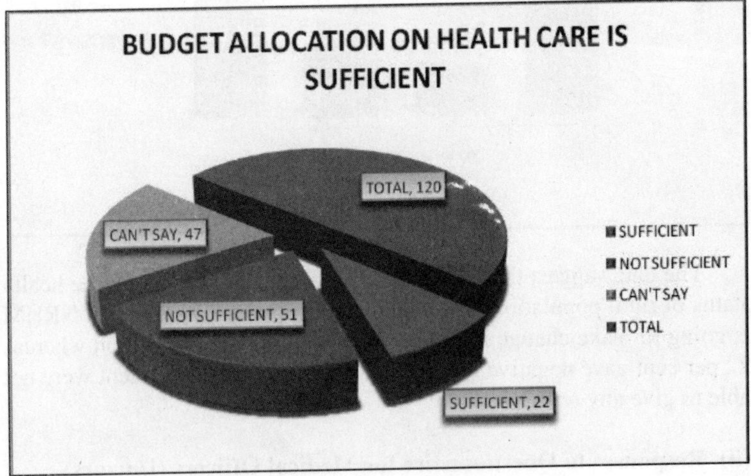

In order to strengthen health institutions and health care services there is a dire need of budget allocation so that quality health care services be provided to general public. While asking question on budget allocation only 18 per cent respondents have stated that the funds provided by the Government of India is sufficient. Whereas 43 per cent respondents said that budget allocation on health system by Government of India is insufficient to provide quality health care to public. 39 per cent respondents were unable to respond to this question.

18. Do you agree the National Rural Health Mission (NRHM) is going to make changes in health status of rural population?

Response	*Total*	*Percentage*
Yes	56	47
No	27	22
Can't Say	37	31
Total	120	100

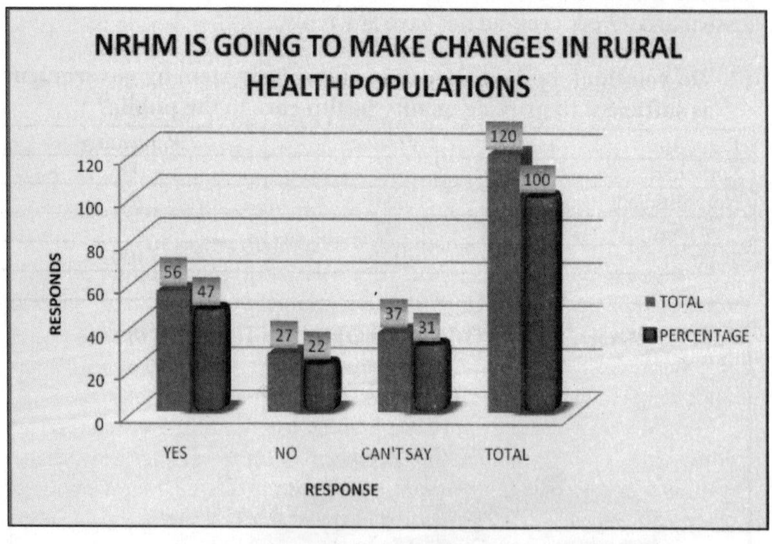

The data suggest that NHRM has created some impact on the health status of rural population. 47 per cent of respondents agreed that NRHM is going to make change in the health status of rural population whereas 22 per cent gave negative reply to this question and 31 per cent were not able to give any reply.

(ii) Responses to Questionnaire for Medical Officers (Doctors)

The author served questionnaires on 50 doctors with a purpose to have their views on the different aspects of health care standards in the hospitals situated in Shimla town. The author has framed 20 questions dealing with the different aspects of health standards and awareness of health regulations and policies.

The author have collected responses from 50 medical officers. The research has endeavoured to have responses from 15 doctors of Indira Gandhi Medical College, Shimla; 10 doctors of Kamala Nehru Hospital; 10 doctors of Deen Dayal Upadhaya Hospital; 5 doctors of Sri Ram Hospital, New Shimla; 2 doctors of Sanitarium Hospital; 2 doctors of Indus Hospital, Sanjauli; 2 doctors of Tara Hospital; 2 doctors of Astha Hospital, Panthaghati; and 2 Homeopathic doctors of Homeopathic Hospital, Chhota Shimla.

1. Are you aware about the health legislations that exists in India?

Response	*Total*	*Percentage*
Yes	33	66
No	8	16
Can't Say	9	18
Total	50	100

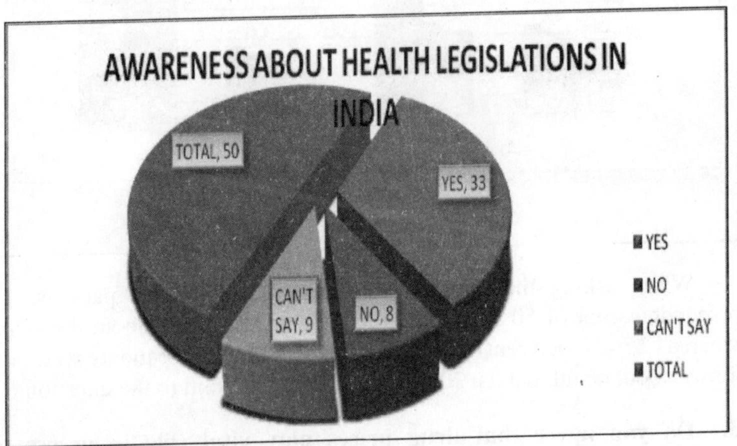

In the very first question asked from the doctors about their awareness on the health legislations that exists in India. Out of 50 doctors 33 (66 percent) know the health legislations that exist in India and 8, i.e. 16 per cent did not knew about the same and 9 (18%) gave no response to this question.

2. Do you think that patients come to you are aware about health habits?

Response	*Total*	*Percentage*
Aware	13	26
Not Aware	27	54
Can't Say	10	20
Total	50	100

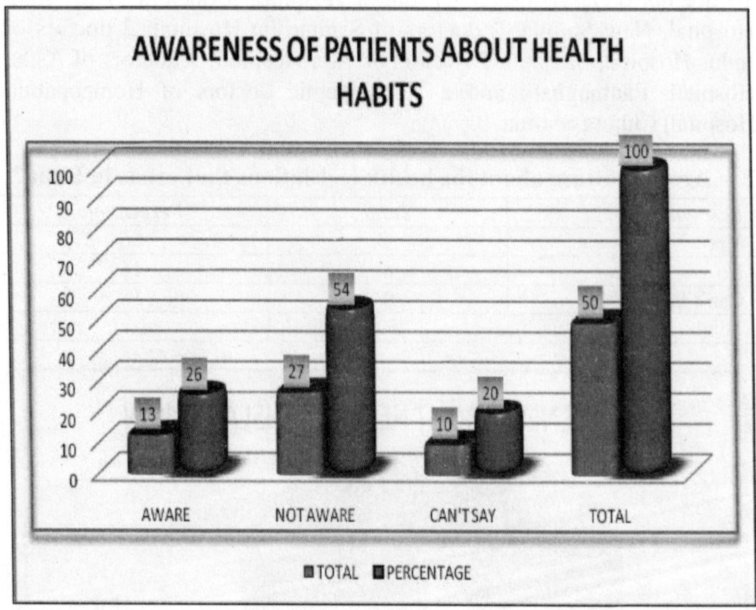

While asking the question on health habits of the patients, 13 respondents out of 50 stated that the patients are aware about the same whereas 27 (54 per cent) gave negative response that patients were not aware about health habits. 20 per cent did not respond to the question.

3. Do you agree that drug prices play vital role in access to essential medicines?

Response	*Total*	*Percentage*
Agree	39	78
Disagree	07	14
Can't Say	04	08
Total	50	100

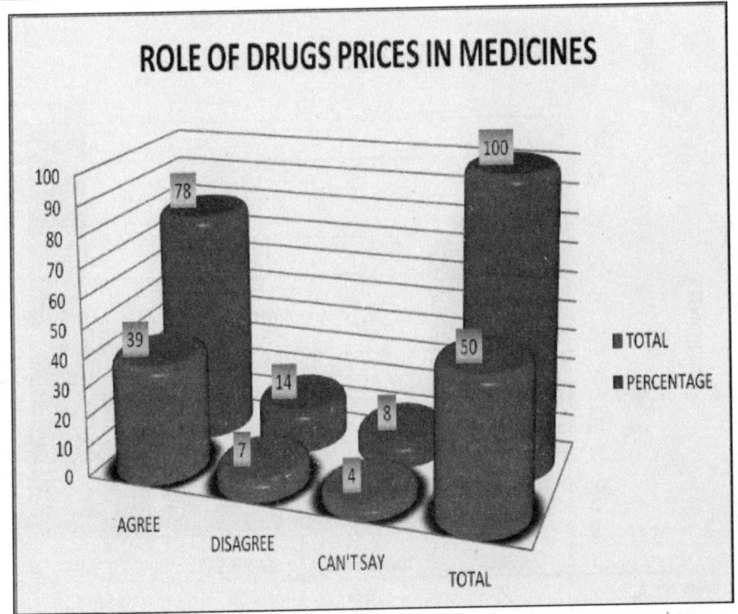

The question whether the doctors have the knowledge that the drug prices play important role in access to essential medicines is responded by them differently. The survey indicated that about 78 per cent of doctors agreed that drug prices play vital role in access to essential medicines and 14 per cent of doctors gave different opinion. According to them drug prices does not play vital role in access to essential medicines. Only 4 respondents were unable to answer this question.

4. Do you agree that price control of drug is necessary particularly for providing affordable health care to the disadvantaged sections of the society whose disposable income is extremely low and who do not have easy access to institutional health care?

Response	*Total*	*Percentage*
Agree	35	70
Disagree	06	12
Can't Say	09	18
Total	50	100

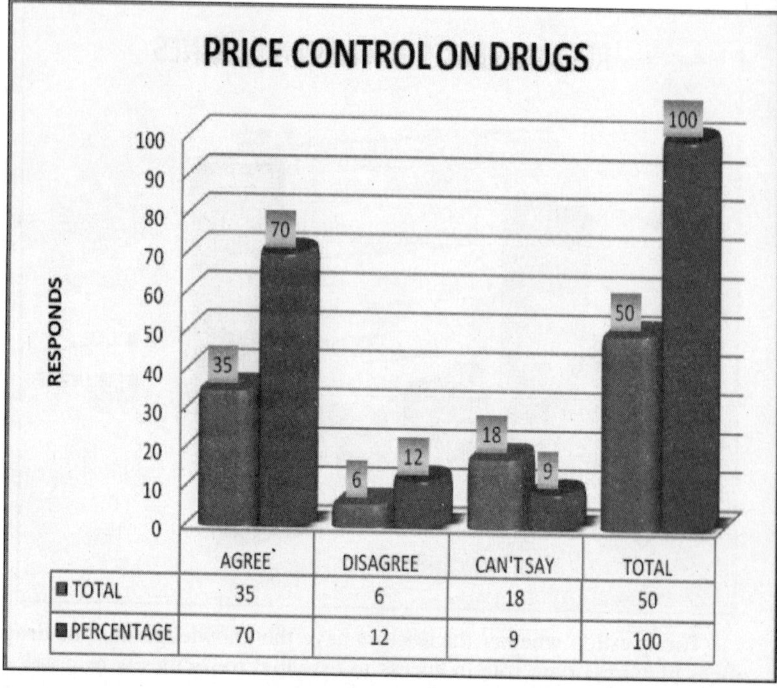

Next question was again on the control of prices of drugs so that disadvantageous sections of the society whose disposable income is extremely low and who do not have easy access to institutional health care. In answer to this 70 per cent of doctors agreed that prices of drugs should be controlled and 12 per cent of doctors have shown their dissatisfaction. According to them price control of drugs did not pay any role for providing affordable health care to the disadvantaged sections of the society and 18 percent of doctors were silent on this question.

5. Are there any gender differentiation between male and female children health care?

Response	*Total*	*Percentage*
Yes	17	34
No	25	50
Can't Say	08	16
Total	50	100

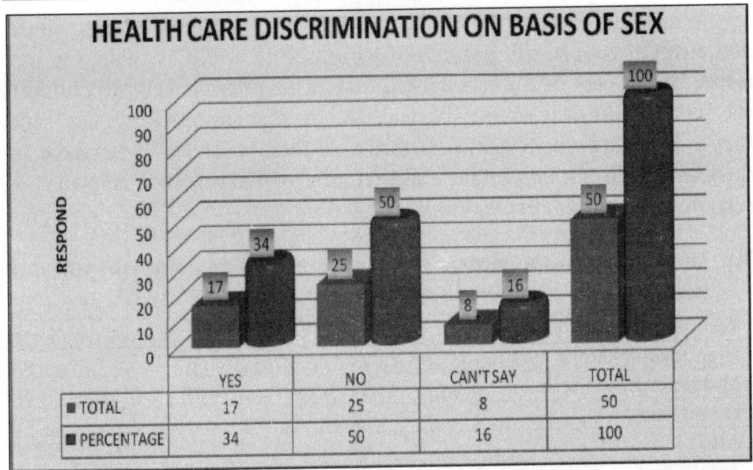

The next question asked on gender differentiation between male and female children's health care, 34 per cent of doctors agreed that there is gender differentiation between male and female children's health care in the community while 50 per cent of doctors disagreed to this fact and 16 per cent could not give their response.

6. In the present scenario children are involved in drug abuse (like cough syrup abuse, smoking, etc.) are they aware of health hazards of various drug abuse?

Response	*Total*	*Percentage*
Aware	13	26
Not Aware	29	58
Can't Say	08	16
Total	50	100

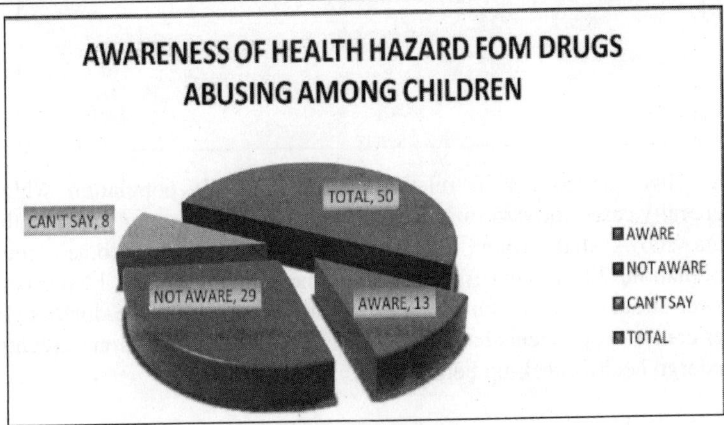

While asking question to the indulgence of children in drug abuse and awareness of health hazards of various drug abuse by them. On this issue, 26 per cent of doctors agreed that in the present scenario children are involved in drug abuse (like cough syrup abuse smoking, etc.) and they are not aware of health hazards of drug, whereas 58 per cent of doctors are do not agree that children are involved in such activities. 8 respondents did not respond to this question.

7. In your opinion which kind of population come to you for health check-up?

Response	*Total*	*Percentage*
High Income Group	25	22
Middle Income Group	11	50
Lower Strata	06	12
All	08	16
Total	50	100

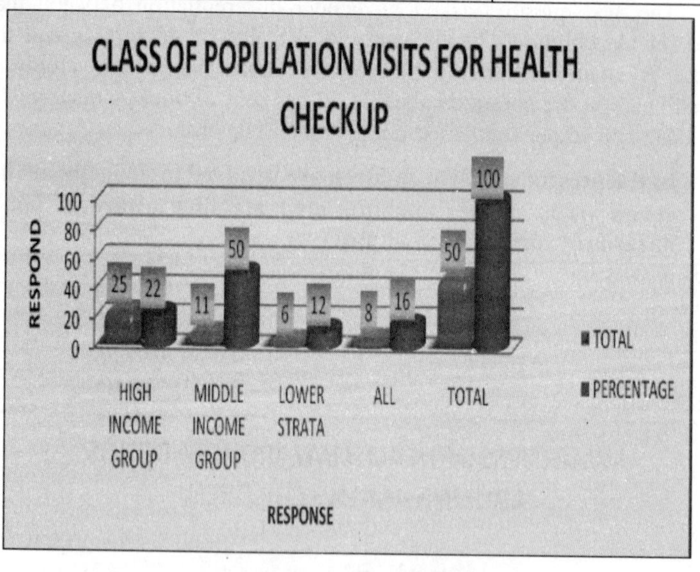

This question is in relation to the kind of population which generally came forward to undergo health check-up. In reply to this, the data shows that around 50 per cent from middle income group population, 22 per cent from high income group and only 12 per cent lower strata come forward to their health check-up before doctors. 16 per cent of respondents have stated that all kinds of population (patients) undergo health check-up before them.

8. Do you agree that health education should be made compulsory in school?

Response	*Total*	*Percentage*
Made Compulsory	50	100
Not Compulsory	0	0
Can't Say	0	0
Total	50	100

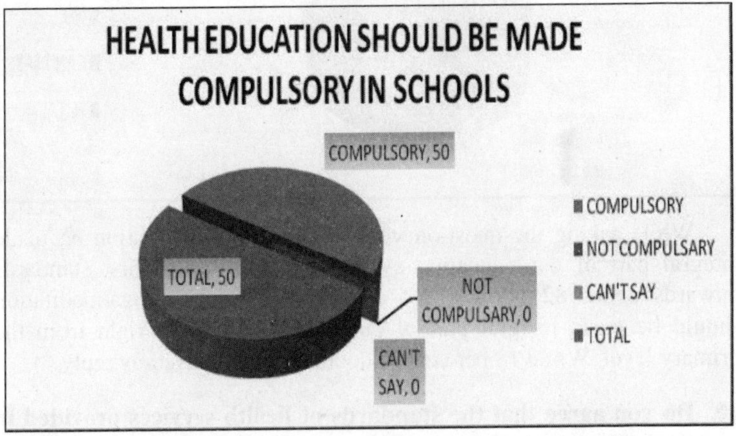

Right to health is a fundamental right of every human being irrespective of area, regions, state, country or continent, sex or age, etc. It is, therefore, the immediate focus should be made to make health education compulsory at school level. On this issue all the respondents gave positive reply. 100 per cent of respondents expressed their opinion that health education be made compulsory in schools so that the child may grow physically and mentally.

9. Do you agree yoga/meditation be made integral part of our education system right from the primary level?

Response	*Total*	*Percentage*
Yes	41	82
No	0	0
Can't Say	09	18
Total	50	100

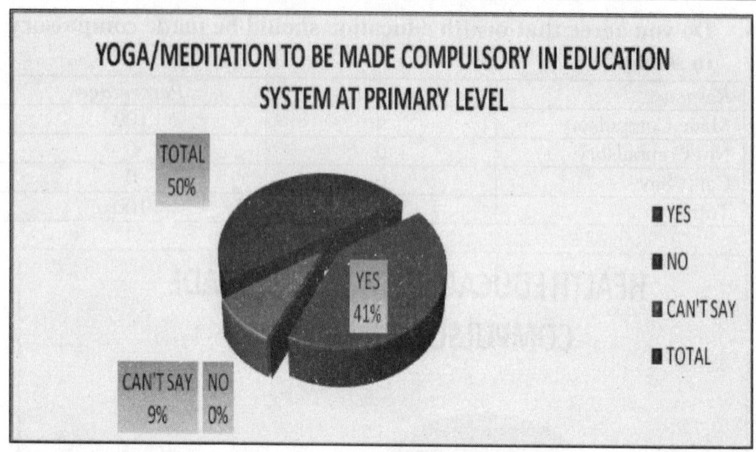

While asking the question whether yoga and meditation be made integral part of our education system that right from first standards onwards about 82 per cent of doctors agreed that yoga/meditation should be made integral part of our education system right from the primary level. While 18 per cent of doctors did not gave any reply.

10. Do you agree that the standards of health services provided in the health institutions are adequate ?

Response	*Total*	*Percentage*
Adequate	10	20
Not Adequate	32	64
Can't Say	08	16
Total	50	100

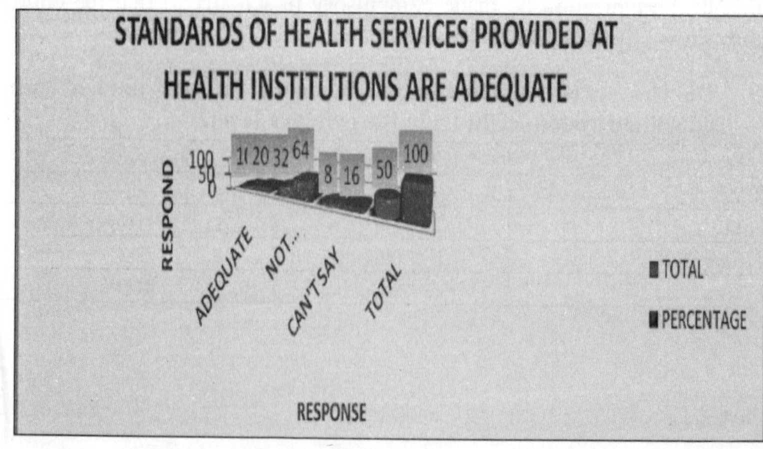

On the standards of health services provided in the health institution, 20 per cent of the respondents expressed their view that the standards of health services provided in the health institutions are adequate. While 64 per cent respondents feel that the standard of health services provided in the health institutions are not adequate and it should be improved for better service. 16 per cent of doctors were not able to gave their opinion.

11. Are you satisfied with the quality of services provided in the Health Institutions ?

Response	*Total*	*Percentage*
Satisfied	13	26
Not Satisfied	28	56
Can't Say	09	18
Total	50	100

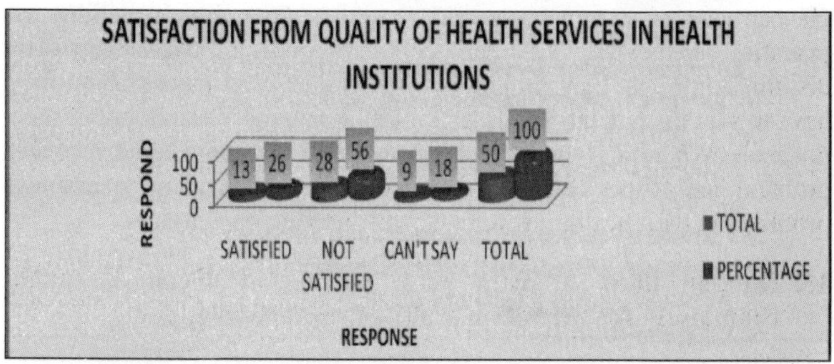

Again about 26 per cent of respondents were satisfied with the quality of services provided in the health institutions. But 56 per cent of respondents were not satisfied with the quality of services provided in the health institutions and 18 per cent did not gave any reply to this question.

12. Which type of problem do you face while providing health services to patients?

Response	*Total*	*Percentage*
Insufficient and/or untrained paramedical staff	13	26
Non-availability of essential medicines	10	20
Inadequacy of good machines	09	18
None	08	16
All	10	20
Total	50	100

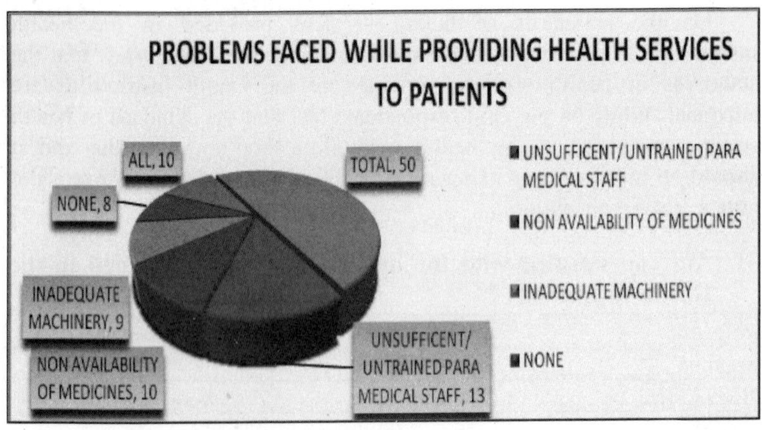

In reply to this question 26 per cent of respondents have stated that they face the problem of insufficient and/or untrained paramedical staff. 20 per cent of respondents said that they face non-availability of essential medicines. 18 per cent respondents expressed their dissatisfaction that they do not have good quality of machine and they have to sent the patients for essential test to any other places out of their hospitals. Whereas 16 per cent of doctors said that they do not face any problem and 10 per cent of respondents face all the above mentioned problems in their health institutions while serving patients.

13. Do you think 2 years rural posting of doctor be made compulsory for the better health of rural population?

Response	*Total*	*Percentage*
Compulsory	22	44
Not Compulsory	20	40
Can't Say	08	16
Total	50	100

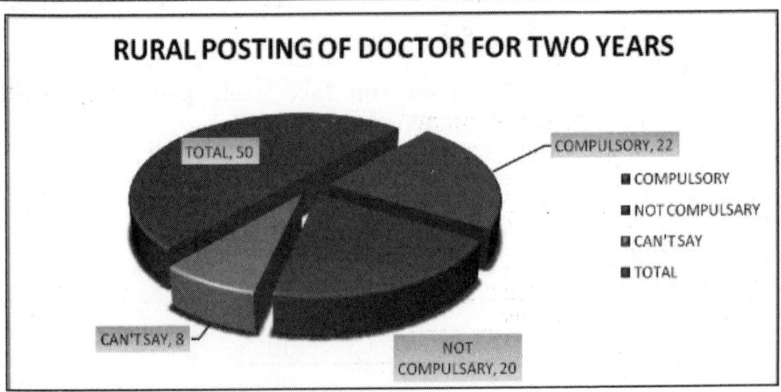

To the question regarding two year rural posting of doctors be made compulsory for the better care of rural population, 44 per cent of doctors admitted that it is going to prove beneficial, but 40 per cent of doctors responded that is not compulsory. They expressed their opinion that only compulsory rural posting may not be the solution unless a sensitivity is inculcated amongst the young breed of doctors towards the rural health problems. Thus, without any awareness sensitivity to the problem rural posting may be a futile endeavour. 16 per cent doctors did not respond to this question.

14. Do you think the budget allocation on health system by government is sufficient to provide quality health care to public?

Response	*Total*	*Percentage*
Sufficient	13	26
Not sufficient	28	56
Can't Say	09	18
Total	50	100

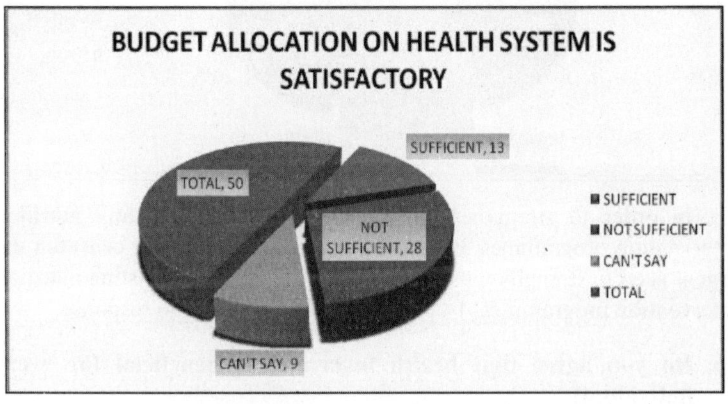

In reply to the question on sufficiency of budget allocation on health system by government to provide quality health care to public 26 per cent respondents admitted that the allocation of budget is sufficient whereas 56 per cent answered in negative, that is the budget allocation on health system by government is not sufficient to provide quality health care to public. 18 per cent of doctors were not able to respond to this question.

15. Do you agree that there is an urgent need to strengthen the implementation of all the existing nutrition intervention programmes?

Response	*Total*	*Percentage*
Yes	39	78
No	04	08
Can't Say	07	14
Total	50	100

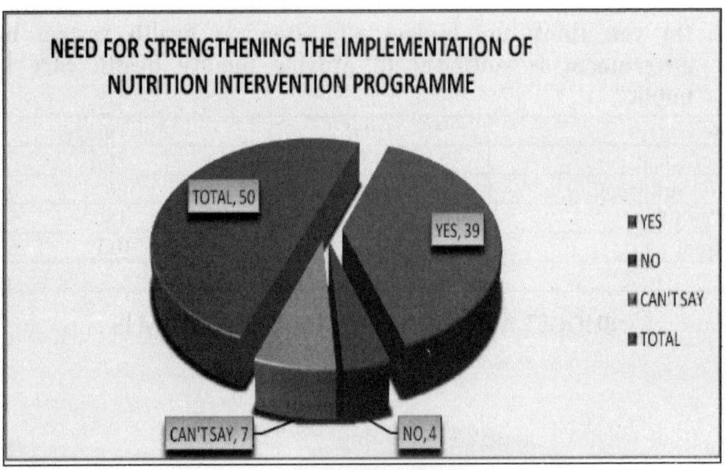

In order to strengthen the implementation of existing nutrition intervention programmes 39 out of 50 respondents (78 per cent) felt the urgent need to strengthen the implementation of all the existing nutrition intervention programmes. 14 per cent of doctors gave no response.

16. Do you agree that health insurance is beneficial for every individual?

Response	*Total*	*Percentage*
Yes	37	74
No	06	12
Can't Say	07	14
Total	50	100

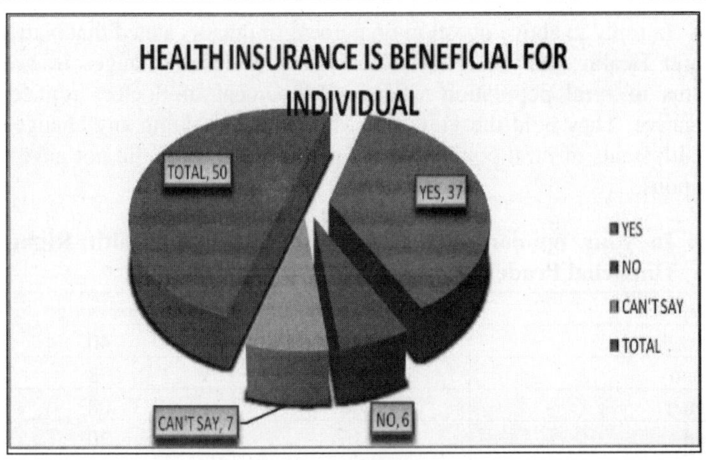

74 per cent of respondents hold the view that health insurance is beneficial for every individual and 12 per cent feel that health insurance is not beneficial for every individual. Whereas 14 per cent respondents did not gave any reply.

17. Do you agree that National Rural Health Mission (NRHM) is going to make changes in health status of rural population?

Response	*Total*	*Percentage*
Yes	33	66
No	06	12
Can't Say	11	22
Total	50	100

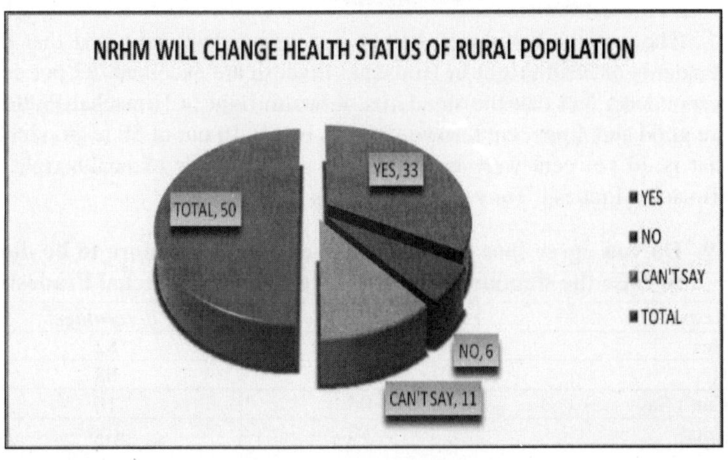

In reply to above question 66 percent of doctors stated that National Rural Health Mission (NRHM) is going to make changes in health status of rural population whereas 12 percent of doctors replied in negative. They hold the view that MRHM is not doing any changes in health status of rural population. 22 percent of doctors did not gave any response.

18. In your opinion what is the standard of Health Right in Himachal Pradesh ?

Response	*Total*	*Percentage*
Excellent	20	40
Good	16	32
Better	04	08
Bad	10	20
Total	50	100

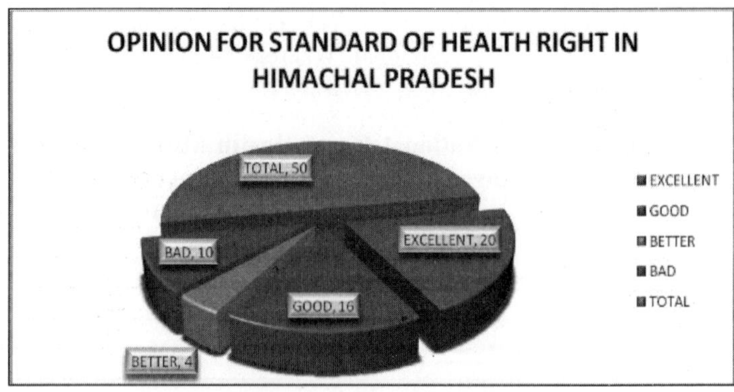

The survey shows that 40 per cent respondents admitted that the standards of health right in Himachal Pradesh are excellent. 32 per cent respondents feel that the standards of health right in Himachal Pradesh are good and 4 per cent termed these as better. 10 out of 50 respondents, that is 20 per cent were critical about the standards of health right in Himachal Pradesh. They termed them as bad.

19. Do you agree that there should be some thing more to be done to raise the standard of health care right in Himachal Pradesh?

Response	*Total*	*Percentage*
Yes	41	82
No	04	08
Can't Say	05	10
Total	50	100

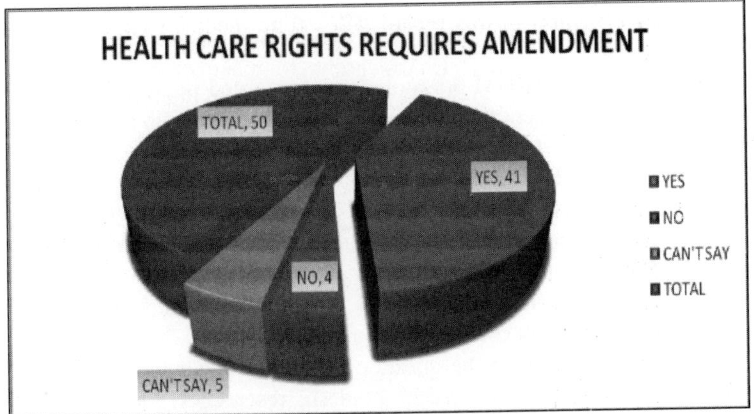

82 per cent respondents stated that there should be something more to be done to raise the standards of health care rights in the Himachal Pradesh and 8 per cent respondents have negative reply whereas 10 per cent respondents were unable to respond.

(iii) Research Findings

A deep examination of the responses obtained from respondents stated above, the interviews held with the politicians of different shades, data collected with regard to standards of health care rights enable us to come to the following findings:

- The responses to the fundamental question relating to the awareness of the health laws that exists in India, it was found that majority have the knowledge of such laws. They get the information about health laws through all sources, e.g. television, radio, newspaper, friends and relatives, etc.
- On the issues of I-Pill (Emergency Contraceptives Pill), health hazards smoking and other type of environmental pollution, it is clear from the views of the majority that they have the awareness of such hazards.
- On the issue of making yoga/meditation as part of education system majority of doctors as well as general public agreed that these should be made integral part of our education system right from primary level, that is from first standards onwards.
- As far as sex education should be made part of school curriculum is concerned, though majority agreed on this, yet some parents have expressed their opinion that it should not be made part of the school education as they apprehend that prior

information in this regard will excite them for experimenting the sex.

- As far as NRHM programme is concerned majority of doctors as well as general public agreed that it is going to make change in health status of rural population. But few were of opinion that NRHM is a laudable mission but it has not been implemented forcefully. The scheme is falling flat on the bed rock of bureaucratic indifference. A large amount of budget of NRHM lapsed due to poor implementation on this scheme. If it is implemented in a judicious manner, the health scenario in the rural area can change drastically.
- The response to the question relating to the standard of health care rights in Himachal Pradesh, researcher got the various opinions from the general public as well as doctors. These are as under:
  - More health workers be appointed and there is a need to open more health centres.
  - Rural areas may be sensitized by frequent campaigning by the trained personnels about health care services.
  - There is a need to provide health-related education at the village level.
  - Strict rules relating to health care laws should be implemented.
  - There is a dire need to give wide publicity in order to promote Health Laws and prevention of health through phone calls, print media and messages, banners, playcards and use of other modes of communication, etc.
  - There is a need to provide quality education to the students.
  - Awareness, if neglected somewhere concentration should be provided to those areas.
  - Raise Living Standards and Health Standard will also raise itself.
  - The Government should organize extensive health camps especially in rural areas reinforced with expert team of doctors rather than merely completing a formality.
  - There is a immediate need to provide health facilities in rural areas through panchayat level.
  - Proper Check on the doctors and paramedical staff. Strict action is required to be taken against erring medical staff.
  - Government should provide free medical check-up through their medical mobile services in every panchayat.

- Government should provide sufficient budget to health department so that National Rural Health Mission (NRHM) can achieve their goal from ground level because most of the people in rural area cannot avail the facility because they are living below poverty line.
- Awareness through education and strict laws/policies in villages where till today accessibility is major problem.
- There is need of information to villages and backward areas through education, medical presentations and even some compulsory laws.
- Particularly in Govt. Hospitals where common/poor people go for treatment have to wait for a long times by standing in queues whereas those who have a good position in society are given special treatment. This practice should be stopped.
- Just like urban areas the facilities of health should also be provided in rural areas.
- Something innovative and easy, economically to accept in the field of health system should be done.
- Door to door survey should be organized from time to time.
- Monthly or weekly free check-up camps should be organized.
- It all depend on the individual that how to secure ourself from the health diseases. Health laws are only for show off not for implement. As written on the Cigarette packet that smoking is injurious to health and not for minors even then it is sold and purchased.
- By providing rebates on medicines to the people of rural area.
- Medicines should be provided at low price or fair price or at reasonable rates for poor people.
- To provide free campaign for the below poverty line and provide them all the facilities related to health care with free of cost and provide every facilities related to health for grown up children of BPL (Below Poverty Line) peoples. If government seriously think to raise the standard of health.
- Promotion of more advertisements and promotional activities for better health and good healthy habits, etc.
- Standards of health care rights can't be raised by only promotional methods. What we exactly need is

motivational methods. It can only be done by proper demonstration system.

- Standard of health care rights in Himachal Pradesh should be raised by improving the health system at the village level. Also by developing the infrastructure in the village and block level and fill the vacant posts of doctors.
- The government should provide sufficient doctors and other supporting staff to avoid rush/crowd in the hospitals situated in the town. This will also raise the standard of health care rights in Himachal Pradesh.
- More facilities of every type of like good food, medicines, free check-up, etc. to poor people (BPL).
- Medicines should be provided properly to the people reserved under various categories like BPL (Below Poverty Line), etc.
- There is huge gap in the health care infrastructure specially in rural areas. So give more attention to the rural areas.
- All the health policies of the Government should be implemented in full with proper utilization of man-power to the involvement of community people.
- Promotion of advance technologies like MRI and more better health facilities.
- A lot can be done in Himachal Pradesh especially in the field of Yoga so that people can prevent a lot of diseases from occurrence. Prevention is better than cure.
- For this researchers should carry out survey in rural and urban population to check that better health facilities are being provided or not.
- To aware general public regarding health programmes like health camps, routine check-up, Balanced diet vaccination, personal hygiene, safety measurement regarding drinking water, etc.
- This can be done by improving the standard of medicine providing good medical instruments and proper education to the students. More information about diseases through media.
- Government should encourage research work and should control prices of drugs.

V. SUM UP

The above study reveals that majority of population in Himachal Pradesh lives in rural areas. The improvement of health status is the prime focus area of the State Government policies. According to data collected from the Planning Department, Government of Himachal Pradesh, Shimla-171002, the Himachal Pradesh has indeed for better health indicators than the country averages. State as lowered its birth rate to 22.5 against the goal of 21, brought down the crude death rate to 7.7 against the goal of 9.[22] Infant Mortality Rate (IMR) is at 64 per 1000 live birth against the goal of 60. The State has established a network of health institutions in far flung areas. Currently, there are more than 2600 health institutions providing curative, preventive and promotive services. Two Medical Colleges with attached hospitals of 1000 bed capacity, two dental colleges, 10 Zonal Hospitals (50 beds to 300 beds) located at sub-divisional to zonal level. 65 community health centres, 302 primary health centres, 155 civil dispensaries and 2069 health sub-centres in rural areas with a total bed capacity of 8.747 provide curative, preventive, promotive and rehabilitative services to the 60.77 lakh population. Presently, one Primary Health Centre (PHC) caters to approximately 17,600 persons against the norm of 3,000 and one Community Health Centre (CHC) caters to approximately 99,000 persons against the norm of 1 lakh population. Although normatively population coverage has been achieved, the State Government will continue to expand the health care network so that the aspirations and needs of the people are met fully.[23] This reflects the commitment of the State Government and sincerity and dedication of health services provider which has resulted in achieving the above mentioned indicators. The State is considered to be a front runner in north India and is on way to become a mode of health development for Hill States in India,[24] but the survey conducted by the researcher shows that there is lot of difference between data collected from the Government department and the problems faced by the General public as well as of doctors. Although Government of Himachal Pradesh has opened so many Health Institutions, Health Care Centres, etc. to provide better health care.

But it faced the shortage of workers and doctors especially at village level so there is a need to provide health-related education at village level. For this government should organize extensive health camps especially in rural areas reinforced with expert team of doctors and provide free medical check-up through generally public faced the

22. Tenth Five Year Plan (2002-07) and Annual Planning Department, Government of Himachal Pradesh, Shimla-171002, p. 217.
23. *Ibid.*, also see Health at a Glance, 2006, Health & Family Welfare Department, Himachal Pradesh.
24. *Ibid.*

shortage of beds, medicines, paramedical staff and improper condition of medicines. For this government should provide rebate on medicines at reasonable rates and should provide sufficient doctors and other supporting staff to avoid rush/crowd in the hospitals.

In Educational Institutions also there is a need to provide health-related education and quality education to the students. The Government has framed so many policies, programmes, plans, health law, etc. for the betterment of the public but public is not aware of these all. So there is a dire need to give publicity in order to promote these policies, programmes, policies, etc. and prevention of health through phone calls, print media, messages, banners, play cards and use of other modes of communication, etc.

So inspite of various efforts done by the Government of Himachal Pradesh by opening of many health institutions, education institutions at urban to the rural level to raise the standards of health care but it faced many drawbacks. Although normatively population coverage has been achieved. Now the aim would be to bring the improvement in the quality of services after having achieved the quantity.

CHAPTER 8

Conclusion and Suggestions

Health has been declared as a fundamental human right. This implies that the State has a responsibility for the health of its people. National governments all over the world are striving to expand and improve their health care services. Health care system of any State must have certain institutional characteristics to realize the right to health. This includes the availability, accessibility, acceptability and quality of needed health care services and facilities. "Availability" means that the State party has sufficient facilities and services for the population given the country's State of development. Services include those that affect the underlying determinants of health, such as safe and potable drinking water. "Accessibility" to health care facilities and services include the four dimensions: non-discrimination, physical accessibility, economic accessibility and information accessibility. "Acceptability" means that services and facilities must be respectful of medical ethics and culturally appropriate as well as being designed to respect confidentiality and improve the health status of those served. "Quality" means that services must also be scientifically and medically appropriate and of good quality.[1]

Thus, by including these rights the Indian Supreme Court has not only taken the right to life to new horizons but transform negative duties of the State into positive and affirmative obligations.

Justice Ramaswami has made unique and valuable contribution to

1. The Right to the Highest Attainable Standard of Health. General Comment 14. Official Record of the Economic & Social Council of the United Nation (ECOSOC OR, CESR) Report, 22nd Session, Agenda Item 3, Para 12 (E/C. 12/2000/4 of 11 August, 2000).

declare the right to health as a human right and fundamental right under the Constitution. He took assistance from the provisions of the Universal Declaration of Human Rights, International Covenant on Economic, Social and Cultural Rights and Constitution of India. Justice Bhagwati and Justice Krishna Iyer are called champions to recognize Civil and Political Rights in Part III of the Constitution. Justice Ramaswami may be called as champion to recognize economic, social and cultural rights as human right and fundamental right under the Constitution. He stated that the right to health is the most important aspect of social justice. It is obligation of the State to improve public health. The contribution of the learned Judge was recognized by the Government and other bodies. The National Human Rights Commission (NHRC) has made important recommendations regarding human right to health in its Annual Reports. In its Annual Report, 2001-02, the Commission has stated that intrinsic to the dignity and worth of human person is the enjoyment of the right to health. The right to health is a fundamental right under Article 21 of the Constitution. The Commission has made important recommendations regarding access to health care, tobacco control and nutrition and HIV/AIDS. The Government of India, the National Human Rights Commission (NHRC) and Non-Government Organizations initiate a movement to enrich and strengthen the human right to health and prevent the dangers affecting public health. For the proper and effective implementation of the human right to health, it should be made a compulsory subject in competitive examinations. The Union Public Service Commission (UPSC) should recognize health as a compulsory subject in its examinations. In modern times, physical education and health has been recognized as a subject of teaching in Universities and higher education. Several states have recognized physical education as a subject in secondary education. To build a strong and powerful nation, the human right to health should be recognized and implemented properly and effectively and health education must be made compulsory.[2]

In India the vastness of the land area, huge population and shortage of resources constitute immense drawbacks in making available a quality health care service for all. Even the basic health care is denied to a large population for reasons of their poverty and illiteracy. Lack of infrastructure and lack of initiative are the major stumbling blocks in the way of putting in place quality health care services thereby depriving a large population in general and the rural masses in particular of a reasonable health care. In India sixty-seven million children under the

2. Jai Singh, "The Human Right to Health and Social Justice: A Survey", *Maya Deep*, 2008, Vol. IX, Issue 4 at p. 46.

age of five years (over 53% children in India in that age) live without basic health care facilities. This means that India alone accounts for about one-third of all children in the world aged below five who don't have basic health care.[3] According to the latest global report, which examined 55 countries that together account for 59 per cent of the world's under-five population and 83 per cent of the deaths among these children, India ranks 27th along with Ghana Eritrea when it comes to providing basic health care to its children, which includes life-saving interventions like prenatal care, skilled child birth, immunization and treatment for diarrhea and pneumonia. The report—'state of the World's Mothers'—brought out by global humanitarian organization 'Save the Children', says that India is seeing alarming inequalities with respect to health services reaching the poorest child and the wealthiest. The report says that while 66 per cent of the poorest children in India receive no or minimal healthcare, the number stands at 31 per cent of well-off children, who are not covered.[4]

Huge amounts of money are spent on defense sector compared to social service sector. In the 2007-08 budget Rs. 96,000 crore (US$ 22 million) was allocated for defense while only Rs. 9,321 crore (about US$ 2 billion) was allocated for social services (which includes education, health care and broadcasting out of the allocation of about US$ 2 billion for social services health care receives an insignificant amount. The sharp rise in the defense budget and the relatively low allocation for social services in India is evident from the budgetary allocation for the two sectors for the past few years as shown in the table. India is the world's No. 2 arms importer after China, shelling out more than $ 10 billion on arms imports between 2002 and 2006.[5]

Budgetary Defence Allocation in India (Rs. in Crores)

Year	*2001-02*	*2002-03*	*2003-04*	*2004-05*	*2005-06*	*2006-07*	*2007-08*
Welfare Defense	57,000	67,000	59,200	77,000	83,000	89,000	96,000
Social Service	6,341	6,724	7,063	8,488	7,522	9,494	9,321

Source: Indian Budget for the Relevant Years.

3. Mohammad Ali Matta, "Management of Health Care Services", *Kashmir University Law Review*, 2008, Vol. XV at p. 10.
4. Cf Samachar.com. 08 May 2008, quoting, *The Time of India*.
5. www.foreignpolicy.com/story/cms.php, 16 May, 2008.

In a recent report the Federation of Indian Chambers of Commerce and Industry (FICCI) has viewed that access to quality health care in India is gradually diminishing. In order to arrest the trend and solve the crisis the sector would need an investment of about $202.75 billion. India's health care situation requires much faster growth rate as it would require 2.2 million beds. FICCI has suggested PPP (Public-Private Partnership) model to bridge this huge deficit. At present, there is lack of regular framework and the sector attracts substandard private health care providers and quacks. There is slow implementation of the accreditation process that impacts the quality of health care. The larger population does not have health insurance. There is shortage of adequately trained health care professionals leading to poor quality of service delivery. Absence of infrastructure status and appropriate incentive restrict private sector entry to rural and semi-urban area where 72.2 per cent of Indian population lives. The urban areas attract better professionals and larger investment. These areas have 60 per cent of the hospitals, 80 per cent of the doctors and 755 dispensaries, which leave little for the rural areas making it nearly impossible for the rural people especially poor to avail a quality health care service. FICCI has suggested ways to attract private investment in health sector including Foreign Direct Investment (FDI), following PPP route and expanding medical education and training. It has suggested for the government to grant industrial status to the sector, government to grant industrial status to the sector, making provision for soft loans from public sector banks and reducing custom duty on medical equipments. It has also suggested bilateral initiative like Joint Economic Trade Committee (JETCO) between Britain and India, business to business facilitation for British and Indian companies for medical equipment.[6]

The innovative judicial strategy is most needed in the field of health care. In India it is a national imperative to transform the non-justiciable state's duty to improve public health into a statutorily enforceable basic human right or need.[7]

Although process has been made in the provision of better health care services for the people, much remains to be desired. Even in new millennium there are countries where proper and affordable health care remains a distant dream for the people. Many governments, even in developed countries, have failed to pay an adequate, effective and responsible role in the management of health care services in public

6. Sifty News http://www.samachar com., 22-07-2007.
7. B. Errabbi, "The Right to Health Care: Need for Its Conversion Into a Statutorily Enforceable Basic Human Need—An Indian Perspective", *Delhi Law Review*, 1998, Vol. XX at p. 50. Also see Rakesh Bhatnagar, 'Right to Life', includes 'Right to Health' (1997), *The Times of India*, New Delhi, January 28.

sector which is not in good order. The infrastructure, the facilities, the medical and the supportive manpower are inadequate and the equipment is either worn out or in sufficient to cater to actual needs, the insufficient funds that are made available for the health care sector in most countries render it ineffective and inequitable. The private sector health care facilities are certainly better but unaffordable for the poor. The political prerogative gives the governments an absolute direction discretion in fixing the priorities for various sectors of national development. In the process of prioritization the health care services have suffered especially in the developing and the underdeveloped countries. The targets fixed by international and regional institutions for investment in the health care sector have not been met. Corruption is eating up much of the resources that are supposed to be used for various developmental and welfare activities including health care. Surely, this is not a satisfactory situation. Health care deserves high priority, as good health is necessary for a good mind, which produces good thinking and good thinking in turn generates better policies and planning. Denial of proper and reasonable health care may tantamount to a denial of human right. In the premise 'law' cannot afford to remain a silent spectator. Rather than being responsive, it has to play a more proactive role. Judicial activism may serve a good cause in helping humanity. Let it be made mandatory for the governments to allocate a minimum of 20 per cent of their budget for social services, 50 per cent of which should be reserved for the health care. That would help improve medical services and put doctors in a better position to observe their duty to care to their patients.

The judgment of *State of Punjab* v. *Lubhaya Bagga*[8] shows a clear change in the policy of the Court with regard to the right to health. In this case the Court observed that the right of one person correlates to a duty upon another, individual, employer, government or authority. Hence, the right of a citizen to live under Article 21 casts an obligation on the State. This obligation is further reinforced under Article 47; it is for the State to secure health to its citizens as its primary duty. No doubt, the government is rendering this obligation by opening governmental hospitals and health centres, but to be meaningful, they must be within the reach of its people and of sufficient liquid quality. This bitter reality has been experienced by the legal systems of many developing nations. For example, in the case of Vietnam, the Constitution of 1980, included the right to health care and the State guaranteed free medical examination and treatment but upon the country facing an economic crunch, this right was deleted and a narrower right

8. Maria, L., Vietnam, Human Rights in Developing Countries Year Book, 1997, Kluwer Law International Nordic Human Rights Publication.

which provides that "the citizen is entitled to a regime of health population" was accorded. The tragic choice of resources seems to be a reality, which may be seriously contemplated while according the right to health. This is not only the case with developing nations like India but is also true for developed and resource laden countries like the U.K. and the U.S.[9] The choice that has to be made is between having a narrow, resource based, right to health accorded to the citizens or to having a wide and idealistic right of health which has no connection with the amount of resources available. The argument in favour of having the former is that only through such a system can be accorded rights, which can realistically availed. One can avoid a situation where there is "loss of faith" in the judiciary and the legal system as a whole. This would bring a great amount of certainty in the rights available to the citizens and would make them more concrete while in favour of the latter, it can argue that only when a wide right of health is granted, can the bounds of the rights that can be realistically be availed be increased when one would consider the resources before considering the extent of rights available, one would not be able to increase the resources made available for such purposes.[10]

The other major argument in support of this is that the real problem is not one of "lack of resources" but of "improper allocation of resources". Corruption, undersized budgets allocated to the health sector, are some of the examples of such improper allocation. In the face of such a situation a resource-based system of rights would not be correct solution. Keeping in view the situation in India, where the courts have not followed a resource based system of rights for the last decade or so, it is submitted that the best solution would be to try out this system of rights (as the courts have already started doing), while trying to tackle the problem of "improper allocation of resources" through other channels.

The goal of extending the benefits of sustainable health over an expanding life span to all members of the human family is the cardinal tenet of public health and medicine. Prevention of disease and good health, instead of cure of illness alone, has to be the emphasis. Considerable progress in that direction has been made and yet the goal remains a distant dream in the developing nations. While the average life expectancy in India has risen to 62.9 years (1998), the threat posed by the rise in incidence in India has risen of diseases like cancer, cardio-vascular disease and HIV/AIDS, etc. pose greater threat to more people.

9. R.V. Secretary of State for Social Services ex P. Hinks (1992), BMLR 93; R.V. Cambridge—Shiri HA EX PB (A Minor) 1995) 23 B MLK 1.
10. As Michael Freedman puts it, "The existence of the right to a good ensures that some of it will be available to any right bearer, M., Rights, Buckingham Open up, p. 192.

The need, therefore, is to prevent the higher incidence of these diseases and ensure availability of life saving drugs at affordable price to those afflicted inspite of the impact of the TRIPS regime. The role of research in medical sciences hardly needs any emphasis. Population explosion in the country needs urgent attention. The figure of 1.02 billion has already been crossed. It is another area of concern. Steps which are affective in controlling the population growth by means which are acceptable to the people need to be devised, developed and popularized. Here again, the medical men have a significant role to play. Lack of health care and malnutrition in addition to illiteracy are identified by Dr. Amartya Sen as the continuing unfreedoms in our country even after half a century of political freedom. True freedom envisages freedom from want of any kind and a healthy body and mind for all. That remains to be achieved. These areas are your serious concerns.[11]

The Universal Declaration of Human Rights upholds the 'right to life' as an inalienable entitlement of all human beings and this is a special guarantee in Article 21 of the Constitution of India. Right to life has been construed by the Supreme Court of India as 'right to life with dignity' which includes a healthy body and mind. Human development index is now an acknowledged indicator of a nation's ranking and progress. There is a definite linkage between human rights and human development. Protection of health being, 'Right to Development' is a basic right of every child. Protection of health is integral to the mandate of human rights. The Directive Principles in Article 47 of the Constitution of India mandates the State to raise the level of nutrition and the standard of living and to improve public health.

There has thus to be shared vision and shared mission to pave the way for natural alliance between the advocates of public health and the defenders of human rights. Purposeful partnership between the two groups, catalyzed by a conjoint consultation, would be very productive in improving public health.

One of the fundamental duties of every citizen in Article 51A of the Constitution is to develop the scientific temper, humanism and the spirit of inquiry and reform. Every citizen is, therefore, duty-bound to join in this effort so that the optimum results are achieved and the State is enabled to perform its duty as required by Article 47 of the Constitution. These are broad parameters to indicate the need for a conjoint exercise by institutions like the National Academy of Medical Sciences and all instruments of governance as well as every citizen.

It is because of this perception in the National Human Rights Commission that we have accorded a pivotal position to the promotion

11. *Ibid.*

of public health in our plan of action. A core group on public health to assist the Commission with technical advice on matters related to health has been constituted a year back. The National Human Rights Commission in collaboration with the Ministry of Health and UN agencies has already organized two national workshops on Maternal Anemia and HIV/AIDS to consider issues related to their control. It is to hold another similar exercise to consider issues related to access to health care and nutritional deficiencies. The recent debate relating to Iodized Salt needs an informed expert opinion about its need to allay the uncertainty in public mind. The NHRC would welcome the benefit of expert advice from the National Academy of Medical Sciences in the performance of its task of sharing in the State's effort to improve public health. To reiterate, this is an Herculeam task which must be the concern of every citizen and every institution who must join hands so that the desired results be achieved. Eili Wilsel, the Noble Peace Prize Laureate, has said, "one cannot, one must not approach public health today without looking for its human rights component."

The late Jonathan Mann, a crusader in the fight against HIV/AIDS believed that health and human rights movement has a collective responsibility to move forward the work of earlier giants in health and human rights as 'equal partners in the work of earlier giants in the belief that can change'. Protecting and promoting health requires and concrete efforts to promote and protect human rights and dignity and greater fulfilment of human rights necessitates sound attention to health and its social determination. The goal of linking health and human rights is to contribute to advancing human well-being beyond what could be achieved though an isolated health – or human rights-based approach. The need and efficacy of joint venture is beyond controversy.

The Supreme Court of India in *Pt. Parmanand Katara* v. *Union of India*[12] held that "preservation of human life is of paramount importance. That is soon account of the fact that once life is lost, the *status quo ante* cannot be restored as resurrection is beyond the capacity of men. The patient whether he be an innocent person or be a criminal liable to treatment under the laws of the society. It is the obligation of those who are inchrage of the health of the community to preserve life..." Thus, the Court ruled that it is the obligation of the State to preserve life by virtue of Article 21 of the Constitution and indicated that it is the duty by the medical professional to help an injured person and to do all that is within its power to save life. This is equally true for every doctor, whether in public service or private practice. This obligation arises merely from the fact of being a medical professional.

12. AIR 1989 SC 2039.

The high ethical component places medicine on the highest pedestal amongst all professions.

One of the greatest humanists Albert Schweitzer, was a medical man whose contribution to human welfare is too well known. It is the path shown by such noble men which is the true inspiration for research in medical sciences to help alleviate suffering of the humanity. The distinguished members of the National Academy of Medical Sciences deserve acclaim and gratitude of the people for the zeal with which they are engaged in the performance of their task. There is no dearth of medical men who have spurned lucrative assignments at considerable personal cost and inconvenience and continue to retain the inherent professionalism to serve the humanity. The people of this country are grateful to all for their services to the humanity. It is necessary that the medical education includes ethics as essential component to arrest the trend of growing commercialization of Medicare and to retain professionalism of the medical man. In a country where the common man suffers from want in many ways, provision for health care for everyone must be a reality.

The disturbing trend of mushroom growth of medical institutions indulging in commercialization of medical education must be arrested. The moot question is that how far the decision of the Supreme Court of India in *J.P. Unikrishnan* v. *State of Andhra Pradesh*[13] has helped to control this trend in medical education. If it has not, to the desired extent, should be one of the areas of concern so that one can highlight the loopholes and suggest the required modification to prevent commercialization of medical education. The quality of medical education imparted in the medical colleges will determine the quality of medical professionals of the future. Advancement in the medical sciences in the future will depend on their caliber and ethical values.

Medical research in our country must also focus attention on alternate systems of medicine such as the indigenous systems like *Ayurveda*, *Unani* and *Homeopathy*, etc. Recent experience has shown the efficacy of these systems in certain areas of medical and public health. The lack of greater public confidence to these systems is attributable to the want of an authentic machinery to control its practice and research. The need is to combine modern scientific methods with the practical experience of the utility of the alternative systems. India is a rich source of medicinal herbs, the utility of which is being realized in the west. Dean Orhish's research in the field of reversing heart disease through methods of Indian origin has received worldwide recognition.

13. AIR 1993 SC 2173.

We must make the best possible use of our natural sources. Properly focused and well directed search in this sphere is needed.

Mental health is an area of considerable neglect inspite of the Mental Health Act, 1987. Even how mentally ill persons are kept in prisons inspite of National Human Rights Commission's direction to the States that this practice must be stopped without any delay. The emphasis need be on treatment of mentally ill while the approach continues to be on custodial care rather than therapeutic. Multi-dimensional actions are required to deal with mental health problems. Most of the mental hospitals are not even maintained properly and the conditions therein are deplorable. Research should be conducted on the prevalence, pattern, course, treatment and response of different interventions. There is an urgent need to understand the impact of social change and development on the mental health of the people, especially the vulnerable sections of society like children, women and elderly persons. This continues to be a neglected area and results in greater deprivation of the already deprived.

The World Health Day in 2001 proclaims the theme of Mental health and gives the slogan: Stop Exclusion, Dare to Care. Message of UN Secretary General, Kofi Annan on this day was as under:

> "Mental illness ravages the hippen landscape of the human mind, after with no outword physical signs to betray its debilitating effects. In turn, many who suffer from such disorders suffer in silence, trapped by the shame for stigma of their often very treatable disease. To draw global attention to this problem, the World Health Organization (WHO) has dedicated this years World Health Day to addressing the medical research, care police and ethical issues related to mental health. The Day's Slogan Stop exclusion, Dare to Care, captures the need for the world community to address mental health concerns the openly and honestly. And let there be no doubt concerns are urgent."
>
> "Yet despite the enormous social and economic conditions posed by mental health problems, more than 40 per cent of the World's countries have no articulated mental health policy and over 30 per cent have no mental health programmes. A global crisis is needed one which will incorporate both prevention and care... "It is time for governments to allocate resource and establish public policy to meet mental health needs. It is time for us individually to face our fears and overcome our misconception about mental disorders. Through honesty and understanding, we can break down the walls of social stigma that surrounded mental illness. On this World Health Day let us commit ourselves to these tasks

to ensure that those who suffer from mental illness no longer suffer in silence."

Another matter which requires your urgent attention is the rights of the persons with disability to have equal opportunity for development including that in medical education.

Disability is defined in Section 2(1) of the Act and it also includes blindness. The right of a person suffering from disability to medical education has come up for consideration in some High Courts. The High Courts have helped that the provision applies even to medical colleges which are required to comply with the statute.

The linkages between medicine, public health, ethics and human rights are evolving rapidly. This is also because of the shock of worldwide pandemic of HIV/AIDS, Women's health, etc. Common strategies must be developed to move from thought to action and the focus must be on the partners who need to join in the common strategies, the points of entry and resources that can be marshaled. The points of entry are: policy-making process, service delivery area, research agenda and education, etc. The National Academy of Medical Sciences must be an important partners in the development of common strategies and the means for its implementation.

Delivery of proper health care to people is basic task before the nation. In a country like India where three-fourth of the population still live in the villages, providing universal access for health care has become even more difficult. The empirical study by the researcher has been carried out to make an assessment of the ground reality amongst different categories of people in the Shimla town. The objective of the study was to make an evaluation of the perception, awareness and standards of right to health as right to health. Though the field study was limited to Shimla town yet it is representative of a fair cross-section of people in general. The empirical research reveals that majority of population in Himachal Pradesh lives in rural areas and there is a need to open more health centres; to provide health-related education; to give wide publicity in order to promote health laws; to provide sufficient budget to health department so that National Rural Health Mission can achieve the goal. The study reveals that a large amount of budget of NHRM lapsed due to poor implementation on this scheme. It is also revealed that the scheme is falling flat on the bed rock of bureaucratic indifference. The people have suggested that there is a need to provide sufficient doctors and other supporting staff to avoid rush in the hospitals situated in the town. The government has framed so many policies, programmes, plans, health laws, etc. for the betterment of public and the need of the hour is to organize more and more awareness camps amongst the ignorant people of the State.

In view of this, it is suggested that the legislature should take immediate and necessary steps to incorporate the obligations imposed upon the State and accordingly amend the relevant statutes.[14]

1. It is suggested that in order to make judicial intervention in the field of health care more effective, it is necessary to elevate the right to health to the position of a fundamental right. Right to Health Care should be made fundamental right by suitable constitutional amendment so that it becomes easier for the Supreme Court to compel the State to transform the right to health care into basic human needs and to promote a viable health development strategy in the country. Public Health Law should act as an umbrella legislation to regulate, implement, monitor various health legislation. 'Right to Health' should be given the status of fundamental right in the chapter of fundamental rights through amendment in the Constitution.
2. Despite the Supreme Court's directives that the denial of medical assistance to emergency patients by the State hospitals on the ground of non-availability of beds amounts to a violation of the right to life under Article 21 of the Constitution, cases of refusal to admit the patients are still common. There are number of cases where patients were discharged against their wishes even when they require further medical attention in the hospital. This is unfortunate in a country like ours where a good number of people are below poverty line and cannot afford the assistance of paid hospitals. To overcome this, there is a need that not only state hospitals but even private hospitals and nursing homes should be directed to provide medical assistance to an emergency patient by implementing the Supreme Court's directive.[15]
3. An increasing tendency among nursing homes and hospitals these days is to withhold important medical records, including results of various tests, from the patient. As far as the hospitals are concerned, this prevents patients from seeking a second opinion or going to another doctor, but more importantly, it makes it difficult for the patient or the relatives to seek legal remedy when things go wrong. That is why it is obligatory for the doctor to supply free of cost to the patient a copy of his medical record on or before the conclusion of his visit,

14. Butterworths, Legal Framework for Health Care in India, 160, (2002).
15. *Id.*, at 160.

treatment or discharge so that gradually each patient would be in possession of a medical record which would facilitate further treatment as and when necessary.[16]

4. It has generally been noticed that HIV/AIDS (Human Immuno Deficiency Virus/Acquired Immuno Deficiency Syndrome) patients are denied treatment and the health providers adopt a discriminatory attitude towards them. The researcher, therefore, suggest that it should be obligatory on the part of the health provider to provide medical treatment to HIV/AIDS patients. The necessary directions in this regard should be issued by the Union Ministry of Health and State governments. Further, there is a need to sensitize the doctors.[17]
5. In India, particularly in villages, a good number of patients take recourse to an alternate system of medicine and often consult '*quacks*' who earn huge sum of money. Apart from the aforesaid recognized categories of health providers in our country there are private practitioners not having any formal qualifications such as *herbalists*, *tantricks*, *hakims*, *vaidyas* and others. They are very popular in rural sectors and among the poor and illiterate class of people. There is a need to deal with them with a heavy hand. This is all the more so, due to lack of education and general awareness among the people in villages, and particularly due to non-availability of adequate medical services. Unless the government provide medical services it is doubtful that malpractice can be eradicated. It is, therefore, suggested that the law should be amended to prescribe deterrent punishment for violators. The Indian Penal Code and the Medical Council Act be accordingly amended.[18]

   Steps should be taken to implement the judgment of the Apex Court in *D.K. Joshi* v. *State of UP & Ors.*[19] wherein, the Court directed the District Magistrates, and Chief Medical Officers of

16. Pushpa Girimaji, 'Hospital Can't Withhold Medical Records, *Business Times*, New Delhi, Saturday, November 1, 1997,p. 1.
17. Kalpana Jain, Government Watch on Salons to Chech HIV Spread, *The Times of India*, New Delhi, Thursday, October 14, 1997; *Express News Line*, AIDS, TB trap many in vicious circle, November 12, 1997, p. 3; Bombay High Court asks PSU to Compensate AIDS Patients, *Indian Express*, New Delhi, April 4, 1997; Shivanath Jha, One death and Chochi is branded 'AIDS Village', *Indian Express*, New Delhi, July 14, 1997; AIDS Telephone hotline launched, *The Hindu*, New Delhi, Thursday, October 23, 1997; Rajesh Kumar, 'Reuse of Syringes Aiding HIV Spread', *Indian Express News Lines*, New Delhi, August 28, 1997.
18. HT (Hindustan Times) Correspondent, Quackery Prohibition Bill on the Anvil, *The Hindustan Times*, New Delhi, July 15, 1997.
19. (2000) 5 SCC 80.

all the districts in Uttar Pradesh to identify and take appropriate action against all the persons practicing medicine without recognized qualifications. The Medical Council of India may give wide publicity to the judgment so that the States may also follow the procedure for preventing the entry of '*quacks*' in protecting the life and health of individuals.

6. A survey of decided cases reveals that the complainants find it difficult to prove medical negligence before the consumer fora and courts. So it is suggested that too much emphasis should not be laid on technicalities and the Indian Evidence Act, 1872 may not be strictly followed. Further, the rules and procedure in dealing with medical negligence cases should be simplified.[20]
7. Strongly felt that the Union and State Governments besides formulating a health policy should enact a comprehensive health legislation on the lines of the Patients, Bill of Rights in USA (United States of America) and Patients Charter in UK (United Kingdom) keeping in view the contextual and socio-economic scenario of our country. The proposed legislation should incorporate the guidelines suggested by the Supreme Court on the rights and obligations of the doctors, nurses, hospitals, nursing homes and health centres. Further, there is a need to have special provisions for health provider services in villages where more than 75 per cent of the population of the country resides. Besides, it is also necessary to formulate health insurance schemes at nominal rates within the reach of all sections of society. It is hoped that the proposed legislation will go a long way and will mitigate the hardships caused to the patients' particularly those who are poor and below the poverty line and are unable to meet the health expenses. This would bridge to a great extent the gulf between the rich and the poor and bring accountability. It will also be a step towards achieving the Universal slogan 'Health for All'.[21]
8. Poverty is the worst enemy of the development of health and other economic, social and cultural rights. Poverty cannot be eradicated as long as the economics of developing countries are crippled by external dept. Debt forgiveness for countries, crippled by external debt, makes sense economically and for

---

20. Staff Reporter, Hospital Ordered to Pay 17.5 lakh Compensation, *The Hindu*, Delhi, September 4, 1997.
21. Butterworths, *op. cit.*, at p. 172.

serving human needs. This way the global economy must serve human needs.[22]

9. Priorities and approaches to health solutions must be individualized and must be contextualize within in local realities. Since health right has little meaning without availability of health care infrastructure in adequate quantity as per the need and location of the population, at least the basic requirements to maintain a reasonable standard of health must be provided. Furthermore, if infrastructure is in place it may not necessarily mean that it is accessible to the people, especially the poor. Thus, differences based on location (rural-urban and distance), purchasing power (pricing), ethnicity, race and caste, gender, etc. must also be eliminated so that access is not hampered due to any form of discrimination or conditionality.[23]
10. It is the time to realize that health is a global issue. It should be considered as an essential component of the continuing globalization process that is reshaping interaction between countries in terms of world trade, services, foreign investment and capital markets. A wonderful opportunity now exists to build a new international partnership for health based on social justice, equality and solidarity, which the world community, all governments, the political parties, the organizations of various section of the people, the NGO's (Non-Government Organizations) and the medical professionals should unite to achieve 'Health for All' without any discrimination, during the first quarter of the 21st century, i.e. by the year 2025.[24]
11. Laws will have to be ready to accept the development of new technologies in the area of medical sciences. If laws are to lag behind then it can lead to grave violation of right to health. So what can be suggested is that State should play an active role in appreciating the practical problems and thinking of possible measure to solve it. This will help law to go hand in hand with the development of medical technology and consequently improve the doctor-patient relationship.
12. The overview of the Plans and policy reports not only throws light on the gap between the rhetoric and reality but also, the framework within which the policies have been formulated.

22. Avanish Kumar, Human Right to Health, 198 (2007).
23. *Ibid.*
24. *Id.*, at 201; also see Parduman Singh, Health Protection in India in the year 2000, (New Delhi: Friedrich Ebert Stiftung/Social Security Association of India, 34-35 (2000).

There has been an excessive preoccupation with single purpose driven programmes. Above all, the spirit of primary health care has been reduced to just primary level care. The health reports and plans mostly concentrated on building the health services infrastructure and even this lacked a sense of integration. Most of the policy reports miss out on the importance of a strong referral system. Instead, there has been more emphasis on building the primary level care and even that has lacked proper implementation. The Bhore Committee Report and later, the primary health care declaration discussed the operational aspects of integrating the other sectors of development related to health. The Multi-sectoral approach that is much needed and the inter-sectoral linkages that are essential for a vibrant health system have not been well thought out, and there has been no plan drawn out for it later. The outline of plan documents and their implementation have been incremental rather than being holistic. It is important to question whether it is only the low investment in health that is the main reason for the present status of the health system or is it also to do with the framework, design and approach within the policies have been planned.[25]

13. In order to ensure adequate protection to all aspects of the health of persons, it is necessary to provide health care facilities as well as ensure the maintenance of conditions essential for good health. However, it has to be noted that provision of these facilities alone would not be sufficient to ensure protection of the health of persons. What has to be ensured is that all people can access these facilities equally, without discrimination of any kind.[26]

14. Polices must balance the efficacy of a proposed intervention with its impact on human rights. Human Rights principles are binding on the State legally, morally, politically and internationally. A policy interfering with human rights must be adopted only as a compelling public health measure. Even then the burden should be minimal and least restrictive. Non-coercive public health strategies must be considered as the first alternative. These are education, counseling, voluntary testing and support services. Mandatory measures should be the last option only if the non-coercive measures are found inadequate

25. http://www.the Sunday Indian.com/16-22 Oct./Special-Report/Special-report.htm/.
26. Mallika Ramachandran, The Right to Health and the Indian Constitution, 1, *DLR* (S) (2004).

to meet the challenge. Public pressures for adopting coercive measures in the first instance must be resisted in formulation of the policy. Procedural safeguards such as 'due process' or 'natural justice' are necessary, if coercive strategies need to be adopted. This decision then should be by an impartial tribunal, with no institutional bias and the restriction imposed ought to be the minimum needed to achieve the objective.[27]

15. The judiciary has played a vital role to recognizing the right to live in healthy environment as a fundamental right under Article 21 of the Constitution in which right to life includes the right to live in health environment.[28] The enactment of Employment of Manual Scavengers (EMS) and Construction of Dry Latrines (CDL) Act, 1993 is also one aspect to remove the pollution of human excretion in order to make the right to live in healthy environment. The E.M.S. and C.D.L. Act provides the right to live with dignity and enjoy healthy environment to the scavengers as well as to the public in general. However, this right has been violated in most of the states in which the EMS and CDL Act has not been adopted. The urban area is worst hit by the human excretion in comparison to rural localities. The migrant workers are denied right to live in healthy environment due to the human excretion scattered around their place of living. The poverty may be one of the reasons that compels people to construct and maintain dry latrine or to go in open to ease themselves. Hence, the following submissions are made to ensure the quick realization of right to live in healthy environment. (a) E.M.S. and C.D.L. Act must also be made applicable to all the remaining states; (b) the public must be made aware of dangerous implications of the environmental pollution through mass media; (c) sufficient number of water-seal latrines must be constructed near the jhuggi clusters to prevent the environmental pollution by the human excreta; (d) the open space used by the public to ease themselves may also be included in the definition of dry latrine under Section 2(c) of E.M.S. and C.D.L. Act; and (e) the effluents from the water-seal latrines must be properly

27. J.S. Verma, *The New Universe of Human Rights*, 231 (2004).
28. *Law Society of India* v. *Fertilizers and Chemicals, Travancore Ltd.*, AIR 1994 Ker. 308; *Kholamuhana Primary A Sherman Co-operative* v. *State of Orissa*, AIR 1994 Ori. 191; *T. Damodhar Rao* v. *Municipal Corporation, Hyderabad* (1987) (Cri. LJ) SC 171; *Chetriya Pradushan Mukti Sangharsh Samiti* v. *State of U.P.*, AIR 1990 SC 2060.

drained out under the cover.[29]

16. The Constitution of India contains no provision conferring right to wholesome environment right to health within ambit of fundamental right. But the attempt of the Court should be expanded the reach and ambit of the fundamental rights rather than to attenuate their meanings and content by process of judicial Constitution. Principle of interpretation required that Constitutional provision must be construed, not in narrow and constricted sense, but in a wide and liberal manner so as to anticipate and take account of changing conditions and purposes so that the Constitutional provision does not get atrophied or fossilized but remain flexible enough to meet the newly emerging problems and challenges, applied with greater force in relation to a fundamental right enacted by the Constitution.[30]
17. The Indian government should pull up its sleeves to come to grips with the goal of achieving health care for all by the year 2020. The Indian Government will have to take more effective legislative and administrative measures to make the Primary Health Program Work a success. This is essential to combat and control the spread of AIDS and other infectious diseases in the country. There is need to have a comprehensive health care law enacted to deal with all aspects of health care in the country. This process is necessary as one can not expect the Supreme Court to ignore the constitutional scheme court to ignore the constitutional scheme of fundamental rights and directive principles of state policy in order to transform the fundamental rights into basic needs.[31]
18. There is wide discrimination against the people living with HIV/AIDS. Unfortunately the society treats people with HIV/AIDS with hatred and dislike. It is a pity that when such people should be given love, care, sympathy and support, they are ill-treated and isolated. Many times discrimination arises out of ignorance and fears of infection. So there is a need to address the fears and ignorance of the medical staff and society. HIV/AIDS is a problem which raises many social, economic and cultural issues, which relate to human rights, ethics and

29. B.P. Singh Sehgal, Human Rights in India, Problems & Perspectives, at 380-81.
30. Rajesh Kumar, Environment Protection *vis-a-vis* Right to Health: Judicial Approach, Vol. 1, 2008-09, at p. 132.
31. B. Erabbi, The Right to Health Care: Need for Its Conversion into a Statutorily Enforceable Basic Human Need—An Indian Perspective, *Delhi Law Review*, at p. 64.

law. But in reality all have the right to enjoy basic human rights and fundamental rights under the law. These rights also shall not be deprived to a person who is infected with HIV/AIDS. Making aware of the human rights to the HIV/AIDS patients would not solve the problem of ostracizing but we have to secure the full sensitivity from the people and should be made aware that even the HIV/AIDS patients are to be treated equally at par with them. Spreading of the human rights awareness and education among the masses will strengthen not only the spirit of humanism but also the natural foundations of the human rights of the HIV/AIDS patients.[32]

19. Non-recognition of health as a citizen's social right only under scores the law priority it has had in the shaping of public policy. With few exceptions, most legislation in India makes no distinction between health and female in the area of health. Some legislation, taking note of the specific features of our society, is, however, protectionist in nature. The protectionist kind of legislation would include Maternity Benefit Act, Medical Termination of Pregnancy Act, etc. The extra ordinary and rapid advance of biological and genetic technology is going to give rise to new and complicated legal issues in the future that is still unknown. We already have been the misuse of technology in pre-natal diagnostic techniques to determine the sex of the child foetus and then its selective abortion. Amniocentesis is carried on in parts of the country despite legislation in certain states to regulate the tests. The status of children born by artificial insemination, the legal status of surrogate mothers, is some of the issues that might come to the Courts in the future. There are certain issues related to women's health and have laws but, there is scope for changes in various areas. Legislation in itself cannot, curb deep-rooted prejudices and traditional custom that there are detrimental to women's well-being.[33]

20. The ASHAs are a new ray of hope for public health. Village Health and Sanitation Committees are seeking convergence in initiatives for water, health, sanitation, education, nutrition and women's empowerment. Good health is not only about hospitals, it is much more about clean drinking water, good hygiene practices, sanitation and a pursuit of equity and entitlement for all. NRHM is fighting public health challenges

32. N.S. Sreenivasulu, Human Rights Many Sides to a Coin, (2008), pp. 127-28.
33. Naresh Kumar, Indian Constitution and the Weaker Sections, 108-09 (2007).

not only water and sanitation as well. The challenge before NRHM today is to improve motivation wherever there is a lack of it, and seek service guarantees from public systems at each level. NRHM is not about inputs; it is about concrete service guarantees as per the Indian Public Health standards. So it should do more in taking the public health challenge to every household through a network of community health workers.[34]

21. The Government recognizes that considerable time has elapsed since the last revision of the Drug Price Control Order (DPCO) in 1995. The meanwhile around 29 drugs out of the 74 that are under price control are not being produced in the country. Also, in 2003 the Ministry of Health notified 354 drugs including those used for the treatment of cancer and other ailments as essential medicines and there have been demands from the public at large to bring them under price control especially those that are very expensive. At the same time the pharmaceutical industry wants that there should be minimum price control and also there should be tangible encouragement for research leading to the development of new drugs. The Government wishes to balance these conflicting interests so that while protecting the larger public interest, encouragement can be provided to the Indian Pharmaceutical industry to continue to grow at a fast pace. It may be mentioned here that since 1947, when the production value was only Rs. 10 crore, the Indian Pharmaceutical industry has taken great strides and today with a total production of around Rs. 75,000 crore and providing employment to around 3 million people, it is a force to reckon within the world. The industry is growing at a rate of more than 11 per cent per annum for the domestic market with the growth in exports being higher at roughly 20 per cent per annum. The Indian pharmaceutical industry is today the 4th largest in terms of production volume after USA, Japan and China and 14th in terms of value. The Government has, therefore, initiated the process for formulating a new pharmaceutical policy, which seeks to compressively address the various issues in the pharmaceuticals sector including the ambit of price control and the form of the DPCO.[35]
22. There is an urgent need to strengthen the implementation of all the existing nutrition intervention programmes and improve

34. Tarun Seem, "National Rural Health Mission", *Yojana*, October 2009 at p. 14.
35. Banerjee, A.K., "The Pricing of Drugs in India, *Yojana*, October 2009 at p. 15, also see (e-mail: banerjeeanjan @gmail.com.).

infant and young child feeding practices among lactating women through IEC. Scope of micronutrient fortification of food supplements under ICDS Programme should be explored. Fortification of staple foods such as wheat flour, rice and other foods like milk, bread, etc. also should be considered. There is also a need to strengthen indirect intervention programmes such as environmental sanitation, supply safe drinking water, household nutrition security, income generating activities, and initiation of timely interventions in emergencies such as droughts, earthquakes, floods, etc. Simultaneously, there is a need to sensitize the community regarding the causes and consequences of obesity, hypertension and diabetes and also educate them to adopt appropriate lifestyles and dietary habits.[36]

23. It has been found that the doctor practicing, *ayurvedic* or *unani* system of medicine also practices allopathy. This has serious repercussions. The Courts have also taken a serious note of this and ruled that if a person practices medicine without possessing the requisite qualifications or enrolment under the medical council qualifications or enrolment under the Medical Council Act, he becomes liable to be punished with imprisonment and fine. The Court added that, since the law requires him to practice in a particular system of medicine, he is under a statutory duty not to enter in the field of other systems. According to the Supreme Court, a person who does not have knowledge of a particular system of medicine but practices in that system is a '*quack*'. In India, particularly, in villages, a good number of patients take recourse to an alternate system of medicine and often consult '*quacks*' who earn huge sum of money. Apart from the aforesaid recognized categories of health providers in our country there are private practitioners not having any formal qualifications such as *herbalists, tantriks, hakims, vaidyas* and others. They are very popular in rural sectors and among the poor and illiterate class of people. It is now time to deal with them with a heavy hand. This is all the more so, due to lack of education and general awareness among the people in villages, and particularly due to non-availability of adequate medical services. Unless the government provides medical services it is doubtful that malpractice can be eradicated. It is, therefore, recommended

36. Laxmaiah, A., "Nutritional Status of Rural Population in India; *Yojana*, Oct., 2009, at p. 27.

that the law should be amended to prescribe deterrent punishment for violators. The Indian Penal Code and the Medical Council Act be accordingly amended. Steps should be taken to implement the judgment of the apex Court in *D.K. Joshi* v. *State of UP & Ors.*[37] Wherein, the Court directed the District Magistrates, and Chief Medical Officers of all the districts in Uttar Pradesh to identify and take appropriate action against all the persons practicing medicine without recognized qualifications. The Medical Council of India may give wide publicity to the judgment so that the states may also follow the procedure for preventing the entry of '*quacks*' in protecting the life and health of individuals.

24. For achieving the constitutional goals and also the objective of 'Health Care for All' there is a lot of need on the part of the Government to mobilize Non-Governmental Organizations (NGOs) and the general public towards their participation for monitoring and implementation of health care facilities. To this end the Government should formulate legislations and health policies facilitating the participation of the public in health care.
25. We need regulatory measures to ensure that human organ transplant are kept within the realm of legitimate surgical procedure and do not degenerate into criminal butchery. The medical profession should co-operate with administrative and legal efforts to tackle problems like organ trade, spurious drugs sale and quackery.
26. The government should adopt, implement and review health polices, strategies and plans of action, on the basis of epidemiological, sociological and environmental evidence, addressing the health concern of the whole population. It should include methods such as right to health indicators and bench marks, by which progress can be closely mentioned, and evaluate them on the basis of outputs.

37. (2002) 5 SCC 80.

Annexure I

Dear Recipient,

Through this questionnaire the researcher wishes to draw your kind attention towards the emerging issue of health rights. The main focus of this research is to check the standards of health rights in the State of Himachal Pradesh by testing the level of health awareness amongst the public.

There is no denying the fact that the health standards of Himachal Pradesh have improved significantly. State has lowered its birth rate to 22.5 against the goal of 21, also brought down the crude death rate to 7.7 against the goal of 9. Another important health indicator, Infant Mortality Rate (IMR) is at 64 per 1000 live births against the goal of 60.

Yet, these achievements notwithstanding, the fact remains that we are nowhere near world standards in public health—infact, we compare poorly even with many of the developing and similarly placed countries with 16.5 percent of the global population, we bear the burden of one-fifth of the world's share of diseases, one-third of diarrheal and respiratory conditions, one-fourth of maternal conditions and one-fifth of nutritional disorders. An estimated 2-3. 1 million people in the country are living with HIV/AIDS, even within the country there are huge regional disparities in the health standards both in term of access to care as well as health outcomes, with most northern states lagging way behind the south. Difference in socio-economic conditions levels of education and access to information also tends to accentuate these disparities. There are huge gaps in the health care infrastructure, especially in rural areas. Adding to the problems is the rapidly increasing burden of life system. Out laurels in the health arena are therefore totally eclipsed by the enormity of what still remains to be done.

So you are requested to fill up the questionnaire. The information given by you will only used for research purposes and it will not used to taking any legal action neither it will make public.

(Sunita Kashyap)

QUESTIONNAIRE FOR GENERAL PUBLIC

1. Are you aware of the health Laws ?

   ❑ Yes ❑ No ❑ Can't Say

2. Are you aware of healthy habits ?

   ❑ Yes ❑ No ❑ Can't Say

3. Do you know that smoking and other type of environmental pollution is harmful for health ?

   ❑ Yes ❑ No ❑ Can't Say

4. From which source do you get the information about health laws?

   ❑ Radio ❑ Television ❑ News Paper

   ❑ All ❑ Any other source

5. Do you know about family planning methods ?

   ❑ Yes ❑ No ❑ Can't Say

6. Do you know health hazards of I-pill (Emergency contraceptives pill) ?

   ❑ Yes ❑ No ❑ Can't Say

7. Are you aware of contraceptive methods like condom, contraceptive pills, etc. to prevent sexually transmitted diseases (AIDS) and unwanted pregnancies?

   ❑ Yes ❑ No ❑ Can't Say

8. Do you know how to prevent HIV/AIDS ?

   ❑ Yes ❑ No ❑ Can't Say

9. Do you agree that yoga be made compulsory right from primary level?

   ❑ Compulsory ❑ Not compulsory ❑ Can't Say

10. Do you agree that sex education should be made part of school education as a measure to improve all round health of teen age children?

    ❑ Agree ❑ Disagree ❑ Can't Say

11. Today drug abuse amongst children youth is an rampant. Do you think that society has a responsibility to educate and raise awareness amongst— children regarding ill-effects of drug addiction?

    ❑ Yes ❑ No ❑ Can't Say

12. Are you satisfied with the quality of services provided in the health institutions ?

    ❑ Satisfied ❑ Not satisfied ❑ Can't Say

13. Do you agree that the standard of health services provided in the health institutions are adequate ?

    ❑ Adequate ❑ Not adequate ❑ Can't Say

14. Which type of problems do you face in the health institutions?

    ❑ Non-availability of beds in the hospitals
    ❑ Insufficient and/or untrained para medical staff
    ❑ Non-availability of medicines
    ❑ Any Other Problem
    ❑ All
    ❑ None

15. Do you agree that health insurance is beneficial for every individual?

    ❑ Agree ❑ Disagree ❑ Can't Say

16. Are you satisfied with the legislative provisions made for the protection of health?

    ❑ Satisfied ❑ Not satisfied ❑ Can't Say

17. Do you agree that there is an urgent need to strengthen the implementation of all the existing nutrition intervention programmes?

    Agree ❑ Disagree ❑ Can't Say

18. Do you think budget allocation on health system by government is sufficient to provide quantity health care to the public.

    ❑ Sufficient ❑ Not sufficient ❑ Can't Say

19. Do you agree the national rural health mission (NRHM) is going to make changes in health status of rural population.

    ❑ Yes ❑ No ❑ Can't Say

20. Is there any additional information to raise the standard of health care rights in Himachal Pradesh you think researcher should know then comment: ____________________

    ____

    ____

Name ____________________

Occupation ____________________

Address ____________________

____

____

Annexure II

Dear Recipient,

Through this questionnaire the researcher wishes to draw your kind attention towards the emerging issue of health rights. The main focus of this research is to check the standards of health rights in the State of Himachal Pradesh by testing the level of health awareness amongst the public.

There is no denying the fact that the health standards of Himachal Pradesh have improved significantly. State has lowered its birth rate to 22.5 against the goal of 21, also brought down the crude death rate to 7.7 against the goal of 9. Another important health indicator, Infant Mortality Rate (IMR) is at 64 per 1000 live births against the goal of 60.

Yet, these achievements notwithstanding, the fact remains that we are nowhere near world standards in public health—infact, we compare poorly even with many of the developing and similarly placed countries with 16.5 percent of the global population, we bear the burden of one-fifth of the world's share of diseases, one-third of diarrheal and respiratory conditions, one-fourth of maternal conditions and one-fifth of nutritional disorders. An estimated 2-3. 1 million people in the country are living with HIV/AIDS, even within the country there are huge regional disparities in the health standards both in term of access to care as well as health outcomes, with most northern states lagging way behind the south. Difference in socio-economic conditions, levels of education and access to information also tends to accentuate these disparities. There are huge gaps in the health care infrastructure, especially in rural areas. Adding to the problems is the rapidly increasing burden of life system. Out laurels in the health arena are therefore totally eclipsed by the enormity of what still remains to be done.

So you are requested to fill up the questionnaire. The information given by you will only used for research purposes and it will not used to taking any legal action neither it will make public.

(Sunita Kashyap)

QUESTIONNAIRE FOR GENERAL PUBLIC

1. Are you aware about the health legislations that exists in India?
   ❑ Yes ❑ No ❑ Can't Say
2. Do you think that patients come to you are aware about health habits ?
   ❑ Aware ❑ Not aware ❑ Can't Say
3. Do you agree that drug prices play vital role in access to essential medicines ?
   ❑ Agree ❑ Disagree ❑ Can't Say
4. Do you agree that price control of drug is necessary particularly for providing affordable health care to the disadvantaged sections of the society whose disposable income is extremely low and who do not have easy accesses to institutional health care?
   ❑ Agree ❑ Disagree ❑ Can't Say
5. Are there any gender differentiation between male and female children health care?
   ❑ Yes ❑ No ❑ Can't Say
6. In the present scenario children are involved in drug abuse (like cough syrup abuse, smoking, etc.), are they aware of health hazards of various drug abuse ?
   ❑ Aware ❑ Not aware ❑ Can't Say
7. In your opinion which kind of population come to you for health check-up?
   ❑ High income group ❑ Middle income group ❑ Lower strata
8. Do you agree health education should be made compulsory in school?
   ❑ Made compulsory ❑ Not compulsory ❑ Can't Say
9. Do you agree yoga/meditation be made integral part of our education system right from the primary level?
   ❑ Yes ❑ No ❑ Can't Say
10. Do you agree that the standards of health services provided in the health institutions are adequate?
    ❑ Adequate ❑ Not adequate ❑ Can't Say
11. Are you satisfied with the quality of services provided in the health institutions?
    ❑ Satisfied ❑ Not satisfied ❑ Can't Say
12. Which type of problems do you face while providing health services to patients?
    ❑ Insufficient and/or untrained paramedical staff
    ❑ Non-availability of essential medicines
    ❑ Inadequacy of good quality of medicines

❑ None
❑ Any other problems

13. Do you think 2 years rural posting of doctor be made compulsory for the better health of rural population?
❑ Compulsory ❑ Not compulsory ❑ Can't Say

14. Do you think the budget allocation on health system by government is sufficient to provide quality health care to public?
❑ Sufficient ❑ Not sufficient ❑ Can't Say

15. Do you agree that there is an urgent need to strengthen the implementation of all the existing nutrition intervention programmes?
❑ Yes ❑ No ❑ Can't Say

16. Do you agree that health insurance is beneficial for every individual?
❑ Yes ❑ No ❑ Can't Say

17. Do you agree that national rural health mission (NRHM) is going to make changes in health status of rural population?
❑ Yes ❑ No ❑ Can't Say

18. In your opinion what is the standard of health right in Himachal Pradesh
❑ Excellent ❑ Good ❑ Better
❑ Bad ❑ Can't Say

19. Do you agree that there should be some thing more to be done to raise the standard of health care right in Himachal Pradesh?
❑ Yes ❑ No ❑ Can't Say

20. Is there any additional information to raise the standard of health care rights in Himachal Pradesh you think researcher should know then comment ______________________________
____
____

Name ______________________
Address ______________________
____

Signature/Stamp
____

Table of Cases

Bibliography

(a) Books

Arjun Dev, *Social Science—Part-I*, (2005), NCERT, Sri Aurobindo Marg, New Delhi-110016.

Avanish Kumar, *Human Right to Health*, Satyam Ansari Road, Darya Ganj, New Delhi-110002.

B.P. Singh Sehgal, *Human Rights in India: Problems and Perspectives*, New Delhi, Deep & Deep Publications Pvt. Ltd., 2008

Bajpai, Asha, '*Child Rights in India—Law Policy and Practice*', Oxford University Press, New Delhi, 2003.

Bangia, R.K., '*Law of Torts*', Allahabad Law Agency, Faridabad, Haryana, 2006.

Basu, Durga Das, '*Commentary on the Constitution of India*', Lexis Nexis Butterworths Wadhva Nagpur, New Delhi, 2008.

Batra Manjula, '*Woman and Law and Law Relating to Children in India*', Allahabad Law Agency, Faridabad, Haryana, 2003.

Bhagwan Dash, *Fundamentals of Ayurvedic Medicine*, (1978), Konark Publishers Pvt. Ltd., A-149, Main Vikas Marg, Delhi-110092.

Bhagwan Dash, *Acarya Manfred M. Junius: A Hand Book of Ayurveda*, (1988), Naurang Rai, Concept Publishing Company, New Delhi.

Brugha, Ruairi and Anthony Zwi (1998), "*Improving the Quality of Private Sector Delivery of Public Health Services: Challenges and Strategies*", Health Policy and Planning, 13 (2), 107-20.

Caldwell, *et al.*, "*What We Know About Health Transition, the Cultural, Social and Behavioural Determinants of Health*", Human Transition Series, Vol. 1 and 2. The Australian National University Printing Service for the Health Transition Centre, National Centre for Epidemiology and Population Health, The Australian National University, Canberra, Australia.

Chandrashekhar, S., *Indian Health Economy and Policy*. Allahabad, Chugh Pub., 1989.

Chatterjee, Meera, *Implementing Health Policy*, New Delhi, Centre for Policy Research, 1988.

Chief Justice Anand, A.S., '*Justice for Women*', Universal Law Publishing Co. Pvt. Ltd., Delhi, 2003.

Craven, Mathew, *The International Covenant on Economic Social and Cultural Rights: A Perspective on It's Development*, Oxford, Clarendon Press, 1998.

Davar V. Bhargavi, '*Mental Health from a Gender Perspective*', Sage Publications India Pvt. Ltd., New Delhi, 2001.

Dheer, S., Basu, Mitra and Kamal, Radhika, *Introduction to Health Education*, Delhi, Friends Pub., 1991.

Dhillon, H.S. and Philip, Lois, *Health Promotion and Community Action for Health in Developing Countries*, Geneva, WHO, 1994.

Domink Wujastyk, *The Roots of Ayurveda*, Penguim Books India (P) Ltd., 1998.

Doyal Lesley, '*What makes women Sick-Gender and the Political Economy of Health*', Macmillan Press Ltd., London, 1995.

Dutta, D.C., "*Text Book of Obstetrics*", New Central Book Agency P. Ltd., Kolkatta, 2004.

Dworkin, Ronald, *Taking Rights Seriously*, Delhi, Universal Law Pub. Co., 1999.

Fidler, David P., *International Law and Infectious Diseases*, Oxford, Clarendon Press, 1999.

Fulop, T.F. and Roemer, M.I., *International Development of Health Manpower Policy, Geneva*, WHO, 1982.

Gaur, K.D., '*A Textbook on the Indian Penal Code*', University Law Publishing Co. Pvt. Ltd., New Delhi, 2004.

Goyal, M.R., *Anatomy of Medical Education*, Central Subscription Agency Pvt. Ltd., New Delhi, 1986.

H.M. Seervai, "*Constitutional Law of India*", Universal Publishing Co., 4th Edition.

H.O. Aggarwal, '*Human Rights*', Central Law Publication, Allahabad, 2003.

Halsbury's Laws of England, 3rd Edn., Vol. 26.

Jain, K. Ashok, '*Socio-Legal Off Shoots, The Saga of Female Foeticide in India*', Ascent Publications, Delhi, 2006.

Jain, M.P., "*Indian Constitutional Law*", Wadhwa & Company, Nagpur, Nehru Place, New Delhi, 2003.

Jais, S. Singh, "*The Human Right to Health and Social Justice: A Survey,*

Maya Deep Publication, 2008, Vol. IX, Issue 4.

Jaswal, P.S., '*Environmental Law*', Pioneer Publications, 2003.

Jayanti Sengupta, *The Trail*, (2005), Manzar Khan Oxford University Press, YMCA Library Building, Jai Singh Road, New Delhi-110001.

K. Park, *Preventive and Social Medicine (2000)*, M/s. Banarsidas Bhanot, 1167, Prem Nagar, Jabalpur, 482001.

Kangle, R.P., *The Kautilya Arthashastra*, Part-II, University of Bombay, 1972.

Kishore, J., '*National Health Programs of India*', Century Publications, New Delhi, 2006.

Kishwar, Madhu, '*Off the beaten track rethinking gender justice for Indian Women*', Oxford University Press, New Delhi, 1999.

Knight, Bernard, *Legal Aspects of Medical Practice*, New York, Churchill Livingstone, 1987.

Kulkarni, Suresh, *Health for Peace*, New Delhi, Institute of Peace Research and Action, 1992.

Kumar, Narender, "*Constitutional Law of India*", Pioneer Books, Delhi, 2005.

Lalonde, M., *A New Perspective on the Health and Canadians: A Working Document*, Ottawa, Govt. of Canada, 1974.

M.C. Gupta, *Health and Law*, Kanishka Publishers, Distributors, New Delhi-110002.

Mahalwar, K.P.S., "*Indian Constitution and the Weaker Sections*", British Law House, 105, Vadhman City-2 Plaza, Asaf Ali Road, New Delhi, 2007.

Mann, Jonathan, *Health and Human Rights: A Reader*, New York, Routledge, 1999.

Manoj Kumar Sinha, *Right to Health in the Context of HIV/AIDS in India & Africa*, Manak Pub. Pvt. Ltd., B-7, Saraswati Complex, Subhash Chowk, Laxmi Nagar, New Delhi.

Misra Preeti, '*Domestic Violence Against Women, Legal Control and Judicial Response*', Deep & Deep Publications Pvt. Ltd., Rajouri Garden, New Delhi, 2007.

Nomani, Zafar Mahfooz, *Right to Health: A Socio-Legal Perception*, New Delhi, Uppal Publishing House.

Parmanand Desai, *Law of Disability—Medical & Non-medical* (Dwivedi & Company Law Publishers & Booksellers, Adarsh Nagar, Bhawapur, Allahabad, 2004.

Patel Tulsi, '*Sex-Selective Abortion in India, Gender, Society and New Reproductive Technologies*', Sage Publications India Pvt. Ltd., New Delhi, 2007.

Rajesh Kumar, "*Environment Protection vis-à-vis Right to Health: Judicial Approach*", *Chotanagpur Law Journal*, Vol. I, No. 1, 2008-09.

Ramachandran Mallika, "*The Right to Health and the Indian Constitution*", IDLR (S) (2004).

Ramchandran, L. and Dharmalingam, T., *Health Education: A New Approach*, New Delhi, Vikas Pub., 1990.

Rangarajan, L.N., *Kautilya*: *The Arthashastra*, Penguin Books, New Delhi, 1992.

Rao, B. Shiva, "*The Framing of India's Constitution*", Universal Law Publishing Co. Pvt. Ltd., Vol. 2, Delhi, 1967.

Rao, Mamta, '*Law Relating to Women & Children*', Eastern Book Company, Lucknow, 2005.

Rao, Yetukuri Venkateswara, '*Law Relating to Medical Negligence*', Asia Law House, Hyderabad, 2006.

S.R. Bakshi, *Advanced History of Medieval India*, published by J.L. Kumar of Anmol Publication Pvt. Ltd., New Delhi, 1995.

S.V. Joga Rao, *Criminal Justice and Medical Law*, Eastern Law House, 54, Ganesh Chander Avenue, Calcutta, 700013.

SARIQ, '*Landmark Judgments on Violence against Women and Children from South Asia*', South Asia Regional Initiative/Equity Support Program, Vasant Vihar, New Delhi.

Sharma, Ashok Kumar, '*Legal Boundaries of Nature Cure*', Dr. Sharmas Legal Consultancy, Pune, Maharashtra, India, 2004.

Shukla, C.K., Ali, S., '*Child Labour and the Law*', Sarup & Sons, New Delhi, 2006.

Singh, Indira Jai, '*Law of Domestic Violence*', Universal Law Publishing Co. Pvt. Ltd., 2007.

Singh, Jagdish, Bhushan, Vishwa, '*Medical Negligence & Compensation*', Bharat Law Publications, Jaipur, 2004.

Singh, Parduman, *Health Protection in India in the Year 2000*, New Delhi, Friedrich Ebert Stiftung, 2000.

Sreenivasulu, N.S., "*Human Rights Many Side to a Coin* – (2008), Regal Publications, New Delhi-110027.

Srivastava, S.C., Verma, S.K., '*Legal Framework for Health Care in India*', Lexis Nexis Butterworth, The Indian Law Institute, New Delhi, 2002.

Stephen P. Marks, "*The Right to Development: A Primer 2004*, published by Sage Publications, New Delhi.

Swarup Jagdish, '*Constitution of India*', Modern Law Publications, Allahabad, Vol. 1, 2006.

Tones, Keith, *et al*, *Health Education: Effectiveness and Efficiency*, London, Chapman and Hall, 1990.

Tripathi, S.C., Arora, Vibha, '*Law Relating to Women & Children*, Central Law Publications, Allahabad, 2006.

Urmila Thatee, S. Sharadini Dahanukar, *Ayurveda Unravelled* (1998), National Book Trust, India, A-5, Park, New Delhi.

Verma, J.S., *The New Universe of Human Rights, 2004*, Published by Universal Law Publishing Co. Pvt. Ltd., C-FF-IA, Ansal's Dilkhush Industrial Estate, G.T. Karnal Road, Delhi.

Verma, S.K., *Legal Framework for Health Care in India,* Nu Tech Photolithographers, C-74, Okhla Industrial Area, Phase-I, New Delhi.

Verma, S.K., *Legal Framework for Health Care in India, New Delhi*, Lexis Nexis Butterworths, ILI, 2002.

(b) Articles and Journals

Amrith Sunil, "Political Culture of Health in India: A Historical Perspective", *Economic and Political Weekly*, January 13, 2007, p.114.

Anand Grover & Priti Patel, "Legal Aspects in the Relationship Between Doctors, Patients and HIV/AIDS" in the Lawyers, September, 1995.

Anand, K. and Baridalyne, N. *et al.*, "Ethical Issues in Public Health Policy", *National Medical Journal of India*, Vol. 15, 2002, p. 97.

Andorno, Roberto, "Biomedicine and International Human Rights Law: In Search of a Global Consensus", *Bulletin of the WHO*, Vol. 80, 2002, p. 959.

B.V. Sandhyavani, "Health Problems of Rural Women", *Kurukshetra*, Oct., 2008, p. 28.

Badruddin, Ahmad Anis, "Intellectual Property Law and Right to Health in India: A Human Right Perspective", *Vidhigya—The Journal of Legal Awareness*, Vol. 3, 2008, p. 34.

Basoglu, Metin, "Prevention of Torture and Care of Survivors: An Integrated Approach", *Journal of American Medical Association*, Vol. 270, 1993, p. 606.

Benerji Debabar, "Politics of Rural Health in India, *Economic and Political Weekly*, July 23, 2005, p. 3253.

Cassels, Jamie, "Judicial Activism and Public Interest Litigation in India: Attempting the Impossible", *American Journal of Comparative Law*, Vol. 37, 1989, p. 495.

CDC: "Acquired Immuno Deficiency Syndrome (AIDS) Precautions for Clinical and Laboratory Staff", *Morbid Mortal Weekly*, Rep. (1982).

Chakravarthi, Indira, "Role of thė World Health Organization", *Economic and Political Weekly*, November 22, 2008, p. 41.

Chandra Subhash, "Reproductive Rights as Human Rights: Issues and

Challenges", *Indian Socio-legal Journal*, Vol. XXXI, Nos. 1 & 2, 2005, p. 59.

Chauhan, Sushila, "Female Foeticide and the Law in India", *Panjab University Law Review*, Vol. 48, 2007, p. 235.

Chawla Archana, "Female Foeticide in Punjab", *M.D.U. Law Journal*, Vol. XII, Part II, 2007, p. 189.

Das, Kamleshwar, "United Nations Institutions and Procedures Founded on Convention on Human Rights and Fundamental Freedom", in: Vasaka, Karel (ed.), *The International Dimension of Human Rights*, Vol. I, *Westport*, Greenwood Press, 1982, p.303.

Duggal, Ravi, "Health Care as a Human Right", *Radical Journal of Health*, Vol. 3, 1998, p. 141.

Fluss, S.S., "The Role of WHO in Health Legislation: Some Historical Perspectives", *International Digest of Health Legislation*, Vol. 49, 1998, p. 113.

Friedman, Emily, "Money Isn't Everything: Non-financial Barriers to Access", *Journal of American Medical Association*, Vol. 271, 1994, p. 1535.

Friesen, Tasnara, "The Right to Health Care", *Health Law Journal*, Vol. 9, 2001, p. 205.

Gautam, Harender Raj, "Concerted Efforts Vital to Provide Safe Drinking Water in Rural Areas", *Kurukshetra*, March 2009, p. 3.

Ghosal, B.C., "Health Education", *Swasth Hind*, Vol. 25, 1982, p. 29.

Giri, H.N., "Constitutional Base for Public Health Law", *Supreme Court Journal*, Vol. 1, 1979, p. 22.

Goldfield, Anne E. *et al.*, "The Physical and Psychological Sequelae of Torture: Symptomatology and Diagnosis", *Journal of American Medical Association*, Vol. 259, 1988, p. 2725.

Gonsalves Colin, "Lowering Depths, Growing Pangs", *Combat Law*, Vol. 5, Issue 3, June-July, 2006, p. 7.

Grad, Frank P., "Public Health Law: It's Form, Function, Future and Ethical Parameters", *International Digest of Health Legislation*, Vol. 49, 1998, p. 19.

Gruskin Sofia, Dickens Bernard, "Human Rights and Ethics in Public Health", *American Journal of Public Health*, Vol. 96, No. 11, November 2006, p. 1903.

Gruskin, Sofia and Tarantola, Daniel, "Health and Human Rights", in: Detels, R. *et al* (ed.), Oxford Textbook of Public Health: The Scope of Public Health. Volume 1, Oxford: Oxford University Press, 2002, p. 311.

Gupta Arun, "Infant and Young Child Feeding", *Economic and Political*

Tripathi, Purnima S., "Depressing Scene", *Frontline*, April 10, 2009, p. 113.

Venogopal, B.S., "Informed Consent to Medical Treatment", *Journal of Indian Law Institute*, Vol. 46:3, (2004), p. 393.

Voluntary Health Association (1992), "Health for the Millions," *Specialty Issue on Consumer Action*, Vol. 18, No. 6, December.

Vouri, H., "The Medical Model and the Objectives of Health Education", *International Journal of Health Education*, Vol. 23, 1980, p. 12.

Vyas, Girija, "Remedy for Social Elevation", *Yojana*, October, 2008, p. 16.

Wani, M. Afjal, "State Responsibility for Health: An Onerous Facing of the Tempest", *Cochin University Law Review*, Vol. 22, 198, p. 45.

(c) **Reports**

Community Based Education of Health Personnel, WHO Technical Report Series No. 746, Geneva, WHO, 1987.

Control of Hereditory Diseases, WHO Technical Report Series No. 865, Geneva, WHO, 1996.

Global Strategy for Health For All By the Year 2000, Geneva, WHO, 1981.

Guidelines For Good Clinical Practice for Trials on Pharmaceutical Products, WHO Technical Report Series No. 850, Geneva, WHO, 1995.

Health Education of the Public. WHO Technical Report Series No. 89, Geneva, WHO, 1954.

Health For All: An Alternative Strategy, Report of Joint Study Group of Health Survey and Development Committee (Bhore Committee) Report, Delhi, Govt. of India, 1946.

Implementation of Global Strategy for Health for All By the Year 2000: Second Evaluation – 8th Report on the World Health Situation, Volume I, Global Review, Geneva, WHO, 1993.

Manual on Human Rights Reporting, Geneva, UN Center for Human Rights, 1996.

Mental Health Care Law: Ten Basic Principles, Geneva, WHO, 1996.

National Report on 'A World Fit for Children', Ministry of Women and Child Development, Government of India, 2007.

New Approaches to Health Education in Primary Health Care, WHO Technical Report Series No. 690, Geneva, WHO, 1983.

NRHM (DRAFT) National Rural Health Mission, Ministry of Health & Family Welfare, Government of India.

Reducing Health Inequalities: An Action Report, London, HMSO/UK, Department of Health, 1999.

The National Family Health Survey-3, 2005-06.

The National Population Policy, 2000.

The Role of the Health Sector in Food and Nutrition, WHO Technical Report Series No. 667, Geneva, WHO, 1981.

The World Health Report, 1995 : Bridging the Gaps, Geneva, WHO, 1995.

The World Health Report, 1996: Fighting Diseases, Fostering Development, Geneva, WHO, 1996.

The World Health Report, 1997: Conquering Suffering, Enriching Humanity, Geneva, WHO, 1997.

The World Health Report, 1998: Life in the 21st Century – A Vision for All, Geneva, WHO, 1998.

The World Health Report, 1999: Making a Difference. Geneva, WHO, 1999.

The World Health Report, 2002. Oxford, Oxford University Press, 2002.

The World Health Report, 2005.

The World Health Report, 2007: Global Public Health Security in the 21st Century, WHO, 2007.

The World Health Report, 2008: Primary Health Care, Now More than Ever, Geneva, WHO, 2008.

World Development Report, 1993: Investing in Health. New York, Oxford University Press, 1993.

World Development Report, 2000/2001, Washington D.C., World Bank, 2001.

Statutes

Air (Prevention and Control of Pollution) Act, 1981 amended in 1988.

Consumer Protection Act, 1986.

Environment (Protection) Act, 1986, Eighth Amendment Rules, 2008.

Food Safety and Standards Act of 2006.

Hazardous Wastes (Management and Handling) Rules, 1989; Hazardous Wastes (Management Handling and Transboundary Movement) Rules, 2008.

Health and Safety at Work Act, 1947.

Immoral Traffic (Prevention) Act, 1956.

Indian Medical Council Act, 1956.

Medical Termination of Pregnancy Act, 1971.

Mental Health Act, 1987.

The Child Labour (Prohibition and Regulation) Act, 1986.

The Cigarettes and Other Tobacco Products (Prohibition of Advertisement and Regulation of Trade and Commerce, Production Supply and Distribution) Act, 2003.

The Commissions for the Protection of Child Rights Act, 2005.
The Consumer Protection Act, 1986.
The Dangerous Machines (Regulation) Act, 1983.
The Delhi Artificial Insemination (Human) Act, 1995.
The Delhi Prohibition of Smoking and Non-smokers Health Protection Act, 1996 (Delhi Act No. 1 of 1997).
The Dock Workers (Safety, Welfare and Health) Act, 1986.
The Drugs (Control) Act, 1950.
The Drugs and Cosmetics Act, 1940, Rules, 2008.
The Drugs and Magic Remedies (Objectionable Advertisements) Act, 1954.
The Employees State Insurance Act, 1948.
The Epidemic Diseases Act, 1897.
The Factories Act, 1948 (as amended in 1987).
The Factories Act, 1948.
The Fatal Accidents Act, 1855.
The Infant Milk Substitutes, Feeding Bottles and Infant Foods (Regulation of Production, Supply and Distribution) Act, 1992.
The Mental Health Act, 1987.
The National Trust for Welfare of Persons with Autism, Cerebral Palsy, Mental Retardation and Multiple Disabilities Act, 1999.
The Pre-natal Diagnostic Techniques (Regulation and Prevention of Misuse) Act, 1994.
Transplantation of Human Organs Act, 1994.
Water (Prevention and Control of Pollution) Act, 1974, amended in 1988.

Documents

Additional Protocol to the American Convention on Human Rights in the Area of Economic, Social and Cultural Rights – "Protocol of San Salvador", 1988.
Convention on the Elimination of All Forms of Discrimination Against Women 1979.
Convention on the Rights of Child, 1989.
Council of Europe Official Records.
Declaration of Alma Ata, 1978.
Declaration on the Role of Medical Ethics and A Women's Right to Health, Including Sexual and Reproductive Health, 1997.
Jakarta Declaration on Health Promotion into 21st Century, 1997.
Ottawa Charter on Health Promotion, 1986.
UN Principles for the Protection of People with Mental Illness and the Improvement of Mental Health Care, 1991.

Universal Declaration of Human Rights, 1948.
Universal Declaration on the Human Genome and Human Rights, 1997.
WHO Guidelines for the Promotion of the Rights of Persons with Mental Disorders, 1995.
World Health Declaration, 1998.

Websites

http://www.ilo.org/public/english/dialogue/sector/techmeet/jmnso2/jmhs-res.pdf
http://www.who.int/director-general/speeches/2001/english/20010210_healthpoliciessanderstolen.en.html.
http://www.hsph.harvard.edu/fxbcenter/VIN1gostin.htm
http://www.phmovement.org/charter/pch-english.html
http://www.healthydocuments.info./rights/doc4.html
http://www.healthydocments.info/rights/doc5.html
www.who.int/archives/hfa/ear7.pdf
http://www.unhchr.ch/pdf/chr59/58 AV.pdf
http://www.phrusa.org/healthrights/link.html
http://www.islamset.com/healnews/aged/rights.html
http://www.afronets.org/files/health-human-rights-readers.pdf
http://www.un.org/geninfo/bp/enviro.html
http://www.mentalhealth.asn.au/resources/rights.htm.
http://www.aids.gov.br/pdf/resolucao_comissao_dh.pdf
http://www.wma.net/e/policy/C4-htm
http://www.virtual-institute.de/en/hp/embryo/global/VURJ57BF.pdf
http://www.un.org/overview/rigts.html
http://www.icmr.nic.in/ethical.pdf.
http://www2.law.uu.nl/english/sim/instr/limbsur.asp
http://www.Idb.org/v1/top/wha51.html
http://indylaw.indiana.edu/programs/CLH/kinneyihrh.pdf.
http://www.cehat.or/rthc/policy.brief2.pdf
http://en.wikipedia.org/wiki/kurdaitcha.
http://www.unani.com/comparison.htm
http://www.medterms.com/script/main/art.asp?articlekey=3817
http://www.iep.utm.edu/g/galen.htm
http://www.books.google.co.in/books?Isbn=04152&.jpg17938
http://www.cybermedic.org/avicenna.htm
www.altMedworld.org
http://www.pioneerthinking.com
http://indianmedicine.nic.in//html/nature/nature.htm

http://indianmedicine.nic.in/html/yoga/yoga.htm
http://www.Jstor.org/PSS/2943361
http://www.women-fitness.org
http://www.un.org/en/documents/udhr/
http://www2.ohchr.org/English/Law/ccpr.htm
http://www.who.int/archieves/hfa/ear7.pdf
http://conventions.coe.int/treaty/en/treaties/html/164.htm
http://www.who.int/whr/1995/en/index.html
http://www.who.int/whr/1996/en/index.html
http://www.who.int/whr/1997/en/index.html
http://WHO2006.wwwWho.int/reproductive-health/
http://www.cirp.irg/library/ethics/UN-convention/
http://www.wwda.org.au/dechung1.pdf.
http://www.achpr.Org/english/_info/charter-en.html
http://en.wikipedia.org/wiki/food-and-agriculture-organization
http://en.wikipedia.org/wiki/oxfam
http://www.soros.org/about/overview
http://www.indiakanoon.org/doc/59148.
http://www.medindia.net/buy
http://fcamin.nic.in/EC_Act2006.pdf
http://en.wikipedia.org/wiki/Bhore-Committee.
http://meansanamonographs.Tripod.com/id77.html
http://www.ncbi.n/m.nih.gov/Pumbed/15276945.
Http://www.ebc-india.com/lawyer/articles/847.htm
http://www.nalbari.nic.in/disables-chool.htm
www.fctc.org
http://icmr.nic.in/ijmr/2006/may/0501.pdf
http://www.mohfw.nic.in/np2002.htm
http://www.mohfw.nic.in
www.census.gov/ipc/prod/wid-9803.pdf
http://www.indiatogether.org/2006/sep/ksh.habbies.htm
http://www.tribuneindia.com/2005/20050411/edit.htm#6
http://www.avert.org/indiaids.htm.
http://wcd.nic.in/wdvact.pdf.
http://www.india.gov.in/allimpfrms/allacts/1873.pdf
http://www.unicef.org/India/child-protction-2053.htm
http://web.worldbank.org/wbsite/external/topics
http://www.mohfw.nic.in/NRHM/RCH/index.htm
http://www.iipsindia.orgor
http://www.mohfw.nic.in
http://wcd.nic.in

www.mohfw.nic.in/nfhs3/cd.htm
http://www.unicef.org/pon00/
www.mohfw.nic.in/nfhs3/cd.htm
www.commonlii.org/in/legis/num-actva1880121/
http://www.unicef.org/crc/index-30204.html
http://www.thehindu.com/2006/03/28/stories.
http://www.wcd.nic.in/The%20Gazettee%20India.pdf.
http://mohfw.nic.in/AIMC/html
http://www.ijme.in/072or052.htm
http://en.wikipedia.org/wiki/universal_health_care
http://www.stanford.edu/group/womenscourage/surrogacy/index.html.
http://enwiki.org/wiki/surrogate-mother
http://www.fas.org/spp/civil/crs/rl31015.pdf.
http://www.ncsl.org/programs/health/genetics/rt-shcl.htm
http://www.aljazeerah.info/news/2009/march/9%2on/obama%20lifts%20limits%20on%20embryonic20stem%20cell%20research%20scientists%20hail.htm
http://www.answers.com/topic/organ_transplant?Cat=healh
http://www.gemun.it/studyguides/shr2.doc
http://www.wma.net/e/policy/wma.htm
http://www.ntc.org.sd/download/mobile%20%hazard.pdf
http://medind.nic/jaa/to2/3jaat0213p69.pdf.
http://www.alternet.org/environment/61607.
http://littleecofriends.org/polybag.htm.
Http://www.monsanto.corn
http://www.epha.org/a/3404.
http://www.gene.ch/genet/2005/dec/msg0040.html.
http://www.fssai.gov.in/EOI/Fresh-EO%20for%20consult/FSSAI.doc.
http://www.indiagminfo.org.
http://www.nlm.nih.gov/medlineplus
http://www.udaan.org/botulinum/botulin.html
www.polioeradication.org.

Newspapers

The Tribune
The Times of India
Hindustan Times
Indian Express
The Hindu

Journals and Magazines

All India Reporter
Journal of Indian Law Institute
Journal of Institute of Human Rights
Legal News and Views
UN News Letter
Law Teller
Lawyers Collective
Frontline
Woman's Era
Yojana
Judgment Today
Journal of Constitutional and Parliamentary Studies
Supreme Court Law Journal
Supreme Court Cases
Combat Law
NRHM News Letter
Economic and Political Weekly
Kare Law Journal
Kashmir University Law Review
Delhi Law Review
Bangalore Law Journal
Panjab University Law Review
Criminal Law Journal
Supreme Court Weekly
Chronicle
Competition Wizard

INDEX